BERTOLT BRECHT

Collected Plays: Two

Man equals Man
translated by Gerhard Nellhaus

The Elephant Calf
translated by John Willett

The Threepenny Opera
translated by Ralph Manheim and John Willett

**The Rise and Fall of
the City of Mahagonny**
translated by W.H. Auden and Chester Kallman

**The Seven Deadly Sins
of the Petty Bourgeoisie**
translated by W.H. Auden and Chester Kallman

*Edited and introduced by
John Willett and Ralph Manheim*

Methuen Drama

METHUEN WORLD CLASSICS

5 7 9 10 8 6 4

This edition first published in 1994
Reissued with a new cover in 1998
by Methuen Drama
215 Vauxhall Bridge Road, London SW1V 1EJ
by arrangement with Suhrkamp Verlag, Frankfurt am Main

Methuen Publishing Limited Reg. No. 3543167

CAUTION
These plays are fully protected by copyright. All enquiries concerning the rights for professional stage
production of *Man equals Man* should be directed to the International Copyright Bureau Ltd, 22a Aubrey
House, Maida Avenue, London W2 1TQ and those for amateur stage production to Samuel French Ltd, 52
Fitzroy Street, London W1P 6JR. All enquiries concerning rights for both professional and amateur stage
productions of *The Threepenny Opera* and *The Rise and Fall of the City of Mahagonny* should be directed to
Universal Edition, 48 Great Marlborough Street, London W1V 2BN; and for *The Seven Deadly Sins* to
Schott & Co., 48 Great Marlborough Street, London W1V 2BN. In the United States and Canada
enquiries concerning all the plays should be directed to Jerold L. Couture, Fitelson, Lasky, Aslan & Couture,
551 Fifth Avenue, New York, NY 10176–0078.

Enquiries about use of any material other than in performance
should be directed to the publishers.

Contents

Introduction

By Brecht's own account, he 'rewrote *Man equals Man* ten times'. Nearly all his plays were copiously revised, while there are two or three great unfinished works which he tussled with for years, leaving a mountain of paper for his interpreters to sort out as best they can. But of the completed plays only *Galileo* and *The Good Person of Szechwan* preoccupied him to anything like the same extent as this quite early piece. He wrote it over a period during which he was evolving rapidly, as was the whole German theatre of the time and (for better or worse) the Weimar Republic under which that theatre so flourished. And so, for all its surface flippancies, it may well be of lasting importance for the understanding of Brecht and his age. It is at once a vital piece of theatre and something like an archaeological site.

He started planning it when he was still a twenty-year-old student oscillating between Augsburg and Munich around the time of the end of the First World War. Two years later his early diaries show that he was writing the odd scene, very much in the spirit of his Augsburg poems:

> Galgei was a solid citizen
> His head was rather thick.
> Some villains told him that he was
> The butter merchant Pick.
>
> They were such wicked people
> To play this dirty trick.
> Reluctantly he in the end
> Became the wicked Pick.
>
> How could he prove he wasn't?
> God left him high and dry.
> His catechism hadn't told
> Him he was named Galgei.

> The name might come in church lists
> Or on his tomb perhaps?
> The name Galgei however
> Could be some other chap's.
>
> Citizen Joseph Galgei
> Born April '83
> Devout and neat and honest
> As God likes men to be.

So his original concept of a worthy Augsburg citizen persuaded to lose his own identity in favour of that of a missing butter merchant had something of the quality of his one-act farces at that time: of *Lux in Tenebris* and the other Bavarian sketches which he is thought to have written under the impact of the great Munich clown Karl Valentin. But before he had got very far with it *Drums in the Night* took priority, followed by *In the Jungle of Cities* which he started in the autumn of 1921, around the time of his first long visit to Berlin.

The Augsburg *Galgei* play, then, went into cold storage throughout the period of his first Munich successes. This was a time during which the German Expressionist theatre was expiring, along with the Expressionist element in Brecht's own writing. When finally he moved to Berlin for good in the late summer of 1924 his work already had a much more urban, industrialised flavour to it – the transitional poem 'Of Poor BB' being crucial here – but *Galgei* was still high on the list of the tasks he had set himself. So too were a 'Mahagonny opera' and a vast plan for an urban trilogy of which *In the Jungle* would be the first section. The trilogy ran into difficulties, partly because the second play proved unexpectedly hard to write, but partly too, no doubt, because the production of *In the Jungle* with which the Deutsches Theater, Berlin, introduced its new dramaturg that October was not a success. At the same time his publisher was pressing him to complete his first book of poems, the *Devotions*, which he had promised them at least two years earlier, and to that end supplied him with an assistant called Elisabeth Hauptmann. It seems to have been her arrival, combined with the lack of any serious work to do at the Deutsches Theater, that decided the way in which he now set about *Galgei*, renaming it *Galy Gay oder Mann = Mann*.

In its second stage, then, *Man equals Man*, as we have called it, emerged not only as the first real product of Brecht's Berlin period but also as the first work of what became known as the 'Brecht collective' – that shifting group of friends and collaborators on whom he henceforward depended. As such it mirrored the artistic climate of the middle

1920s, with their attitude of 'Neue Sachlichkeit' (or New Matter-of-Factness), their stressing of the collectivity and downplaying of the individual, and their new cult of Anglo-Saxon imagery and sport. Together the 'collective' would go to fights, not only absorbing their terminology and ethos (which permeates much of *Man equals Man*) but also drawing those conclusions for the theatre as a whole which Brecht set down in his theoretical essay 'Emphasis on Sport' and tried to realise by means of the harsh lighting, the boxing-ring stage and other anti-illusionistic devices that henceforward appeared in his own productions. Nothing could be less like the passionate, intensely egocentric gloom of so many Expressionist plays.

But there was another, perhaps even more important new element involved in Brecht's changed approach to the *Galgei* project. This lay most obviously in the shedding of the original Bavarian background and the shifting of the basic theme of human identity to a new setting in British India, something that German audiences even today must find utterly exotic. The precedent here was of course the Chicago background adopted for *In the Jungle*; and the inspiration quite clearly came from Kipling, who had already played a rather more marginal part in the mishmash of literary influences that went to make up the earlier play. Thus the three soldiers who transform Galy Gay into their fourth man recall the classic 'soldiers three'; the temple episode seems to echo the short story 'Krishna Mulvaney'; the song 'Johnny' is the old Boer War song 'Pack your kit and trek' which Kipling cites in 'Song of the Banjo'. And Brecht's own songs too – both the Man equals Man song of the early versions and the Widow Begbick song – are redolent of Kipling (as our translation tries to bring out). This affinity was already there before Brecht's move to Berlin, though at that point he had read Kipling only in German translation. But Hauptmann had studied English and acquired a real feeling for the language, and with her arrival the Kipling ties became more authentic. Nothing perhaps is more amazing to the English reader today than the quality of the soldiers' language. And it is instructive to see how it accords with the echoes from Hašek's novel, *The Good Soldier Schweik*, whose German translation had just appeared.

. . .

At the end of 1925 Brecht had the finished typescript bound up in red leather and gave it to 'Bess Hauptmann'. 'It was a troublesome play,' said his covering note,

and even piecing together the manuscript from 20 lb of paper was heavy work; it took me 2 days, ½ bottle of brandy, 4 bottles of soda water, 8–10 cigars and a lot of patience, and it was the only part I did on my own.

Up to that moment it seems that there had been no definite prospect of a production, and the result was an enormously unwieldy play, in which the whole of *The Elephant Calf*, virtually as we now have it, formed the penultimate scene. Then in the course of 1926 two provincial theatres decided to stage it, and in the spring Brecht and Hauptmann reworked it yet again ('for the seventh time, I think,' said her diary for 30 April, 'and some scenes even more than that'). This, as far as can be seen, is the text actually performed at the double première, which took place at Darmstadt and Düsseldorf on 25 September 1926. By then Brecht had been without regular employment for a year, while Hauptmann had gone on working for him for nothing after the previous publisher's commission had run out.

The Düsseldorf production fell flat, but Darmstadt (which is only some seventeen miles from Frankfurt) was another matter. Here the director of the former court theatre was Ernst Legal, a man who like his successor Carl Ebert was soon to move to a key position in Berlin; and he brought in two of Brecht's associates – the director Jacob Geis and the designer Caspar Neher – to take charge of the production, himself acting the part of Galy Gay. Visually it was most original: paper-thin, elegant, brilliantly lit with whites and khakis predominating; this was also the first time that Brecht's characteristic half-height curtain was used. Jazz music was played by Widow Begbick's three (subsequently eliminated) daughters. The Widow spoke her new Interlude speech with its key line 'Tonight you are going to see a man reassembled like a car.' Geis himself wrote in the Berlin theatre magazine *Die Szene* of his guiding aim

> to show the play's underlying sense by making the surface meaning as clear as possible. In other words, no implications, secrets, ambiguities, half-light; but facts, brilliant illumination, light into every corner, absence of feeling, no humour-with-a-catch-in-the-throat. The theatre considered as craft rather than art; avoidance of private affairs. These should make a secondary appearance, emerge as self-evident.

Though Geis advised them to get hold of this play the Berlin theatres were slow to take up the challenge. However, Alfred Braun's still quite new drama department at Radio Berlin was more enterprising, and in March 1927 it broadcast a radio adaptation specially made by Brecht. Introduced by a critical notice in *Der deutsche Rundfunk* (roughly equivalent to *The Listener*) which presented the play 'as the most powerful and original stage play of our time', this was linked by anonymous announcements which, again according to the same critic, were not merely

> a rehash of the stage directions in the book, but short sentences foretelling how the plot will develop, and reflecting something of the fairground barker's technique or the film titles of earlier times. Being written by a poet, these announcements give the whole evening a new form and one congenial to the radio medium.

The critic was Kurt Weill, whose first contact with Brecht and his work this seems to have been. The Galy Gay was again Legal, the Begbick Helen Weigel, taking her first step on the road that led to her Mother Courage some twenty years later. The music was by Edmund Meisel, Piscator's regular composer. The speech which Brecht wrote to introduce the broadcast (see pp. 263–4) reappeared almost unchanged as his contribution to the first programme of Piscator's 1927–28 season, for which he was now acting as one of a 'collective' of dramaturgs. It shows him reconsidering the play in a new context of rapid technological advance, which seemed to demand just that malleability and relativity of human identity that its protagonist – for entirely different reasons – displays.

   The published text of the play, which appeared the same year, reads like a shortened and somewhat subdued version of the 1924–25 script, with *The Elephant Calf* separated off as an appendix with the very Pirandellesque subtitle *or the Demonstrability of Any Conceivable Assertion*. The direction saying that this should be performed in the foyer only came later, nor does it ever seem to have been followed in Brecht's lifetime. This version also gives a melody and a piano accompaniment for the Man equals Man song (derived allegedly by Brecht and Hauptmann from *Madame Butterfly*), which subsequently disappeared from the play. Though it might have been expected that Piscator, who frequently complained about the dearth of plays for his new company, would give it its Berlin première, there is no sign that he even considered this; nor did he ever himself direct a Brecht work before 1945. On the contrary, it was Piscator's rivals and former employers at the Volksbühne who next staged it, in January 1928, using Neher once again as the designer, directed by another kindred spirit, Erich Engel. Heinrich George was the Galy Gay, with Weigel as a shingled, raucous-voiced Begbick in riding breeches and boots. It looks as though the text this time was severely shortened, cutting out scenes 5 and 7 and rolling 4, 6 and 8 together to make one long canteen scene; the play ended with scene 9.

The aim seems to have been to make this production more sharply anti-militarist, but it clearly did not satisfy Brecht. At the beginning of 1930, however, Leopold Jessner resigned as director of the Berlin Staatstheater – partly on account of the failure of a boxing play by Brecht's American friend Reyher, which Hauptmann had translated – and was succeeded by Legal, who must have had good memories of *Man equals Man* since he was quite willing to see it staged again. The surprising thing now was that in this time of economic cuts and incipient cultural conservatism he let it be directed by Brecht himself, whose long-standing ambition to direct his own plays had generally been thwarted so far. The result was that generally unpopular but highly original production of February 1931 which was seen by the visiting Soviet playwright Sergei Tretiakoff and 'produced a tremendous impression on him', second only (he said) to that made by Meyerhold's 1922 production of *Le Cocu magnifique*.

> Giant soldiers armed to the teeth and wearing jackets caked with lime, blood and excrement stalk about the stage, holding on to wires to keep from falling off the stilts inside their trouser legs.

As indeed we see from the many surviving photographs, though in fact only two of the three monsters were on stilts (the other being grotesquely padded out) while the wires appear to be those of the half-curtain in what was perhaps the lightest and subtlest of all Caspar Neher's sets. Dwarfed by the soldiery, who already seem a long way from Kipling, are the small figures of Weigel, as a rather more mature and less masculine Begbick, and the round-eyed Peter Lorre, the relatively obscure but greatly gifted young actor who played Galy Gay. Brecht made him an 'Irishman', and evidently did not follow Neher's drawings, where he has a red-brown skin.

So far as the text went two things distinguished Brecht's interpretation at this time. First of all, he made Lorre deliver his speeches in a broken, jerky manner, so as to emphasise the fact that they were a stringing-together of contradictory passages, each with its own specific attitude or 'gest'. (His answer to the critics who took exception to this will be found on pp. 268–71.) Secondly he yet again rewrote the play, this time with the advice of Dudow and Bernhard Reich, basing himself on the stage script of 1930 and greatly reducing its more frivolous aspects. Thus Begbick's daughters went out, as did the Man equals Man and Drinking Truck songs with their Kipling echoes; Bloody Five too became Germanised as the much less farcical-sounding Blutiger Fünfer. For the production (though not for the version subsequently published) Begbick's Interlude speech was shifted to make a prologue. Her 'Song of the Flow of Things' made its first appearance, closely recalling the 'Reader for Those Who Live in Cities' poems which Brecht had written in 1926–27; so too did most of the passages of spoken verse. This time Kurt Weill wrote the music, which included a 'Nachtmusik' and a 'Schlacht-' (or Battle-) 'musik'. Unfortunately it disappeared after Hitler's advent to power two years later, and has never since been found.

In 1938 the play was again published as part of the exiled Malik-Verlag's edition of Brecht's work, using a text evidently close to that of Brecht's production. It was never staged during the Nazi era, though there is an English version of scene 1 in Brecht's handwriting dating from his years in California which suggests that he may have thought of doing something with it there (this has been used, almost unamended, in our version since it sounds so like his authentic voice). Nor was it one of the plays which Brecht worked on with the Berliner Ensemble, so that it is difficult to tell how his final version might have turned out. What we now have in his German Collected Works (the basis for our edition) is the 1938 version as rather hurriedly amended when his German publishers began republishing the plays in the 1950s not long after his return to East Berlin. To this he once again appended *The Elephant Calf*, which had not been published at all in 1938. But none of this was tried out by him in the theatre, as he always wished before accepting a text as final.

·   ·   ·   ·

The whole tangled story is of course grist to the slow mills of what some term *Brechtforschung* and others, less flatteringly, 'the Brecht industry'; for students and scholars can spend happy hours trying to decide what Brecht really meant and at what point he meant it. The reader too can get considerable enjoyment from simply taking the end product as it comes, appendix and all; and if this is not enough there is some fairly amazing material in the notes. But for anybody wishing actually to perform the play the problem is not so easy. Here the interpreters have differed widely, perhaps because so few have distinguished between the different layers making up the text as we now have it; thus it is not uncommon to find passages added in 1931 being taken virtually as the starting-point of the whole affair. Roughly speaking there seem to be three main approaches. One is to treat the play as the first true example of the 'epic theatre' advocated in Brecht's theoretical writings of the 1920s, and therefore as a significant piece formal theatrical innovation. Another is to regard it as something of a confession: a denial of the importance of individual personality and specifically of Brecht's own, culminating in the episode where the sergeant castrates himself in a bloody parody of Lenz's *The Tutor*, an eighteenth-century play which Brecht was to adapt and stage much later. Finally there is the devoutly Marxist–Leninist view, according to which Galy Gay is a symbolic victim of capitalism, whom the British can turn into cannon-fodder because his job has infected him with petty-bourgeois values. He ends by being caught up in what Ernst Schumacher calls

> a piece of grisly colonial reality. The atrocities committed by colonial armies in Vietnam, Korea and other oppressed lands are still awaiting portrayal; or are they too great for any writer's imagination?

Far be it from us to tell potential directors which of the possible lines they should choose. For the play has not really got one; it is more a tangle of threads, each starting at a different point in the playwright's own evolution and each leading in a different direction. But there are certain things which should not be ignored. To start with, this is a play which is easily taken too solemnly (which is not the same thing as seriously), though the temptation is perhaps less in this country, where the irony and humour involved in Kipling's approach to British India are not always overlooked. Nor is there anything very new about its structure compared with the episodic form of Brecht's own earlier plays, or the use of acrobatic and music-hall methods by Eisenstein and others around 1922–23. The nature of its concern with 'personality' too can be misunderstood, for on the one hand the 1920s were a time of collective undertakings, even in the arts, where the ego had necessarily to make concessions, while on the other Brecht's specific *bête noire* – the notion of the *Charakterkopf* whose very features single him out as 'a personality' – probably goes back to some youthful irritation. Certainly it long antedated his first reading of Karl Marx, though the notion of the man who doesn't live but 'is lived' does indeed stem from his private, quasi-dialectical vision of the world as continually in flux. Why should identity itself not be part of that flux too?

* * *

Although the opera *Mahagonny* (to give it its short title) is often placed after *The Threepenny Opera* in chronological arrangements of Brecht's works, in fact it was started almost a year before Brecht began work on the latter, and his general conception of it goes back earlier still. It was *Mahagonny* that inaugurated the collaboration with Kurt Weill, and unlike *The Threepenny Opera*, where Weill was brought in at a relatively advanced stage to set the songs, it was from the first a co-operative venture. *Mahagonny* was *durchkomponiert*, or set to music right through. Not only the song texts but the whole structure was jointly established in such a way as to offer prospects of a more radical kind of work, an 'epic opera' whose form, content and ethos would reflect the considerable area of agreement between two highly original minds.

Like Strauss and Hofmannsthal or Gilbert and Sullivan, Brecht and Weill were in their own way peculiarly fitted for the common task. When they met for the first time in March 1927 the poet was just twenty-nine, and his experience of performing his own songs, often to home-made tunes, had accustomed him to writing for singing; moreover he had been married to an opera singer, Marianne Zoff, for whom he thought of writing a libretto. Two years younger, the composer had since 1925 been a most productive writer, contributing regular articles to the new radio journal *Der deutsche Rundfunk* on music and a variety of other cultural topics. In 1924 he had met Georg Kaiser, the one Expressionist playwright respected by Brecht, and had thereafter collaborated with him on two operas; while around the same time he also worked with the poet Iwan Goll who had first proclaimed the death of that school. His marriage too had been to an actress: the youthful Lotte Lenya whose voice was to give its very timbre to so many of their songs.

Right away, according to Weill, his conversation with Brecht turned to 'opera's possibilities' and the notion of 'a paradise city' as a theme echoing (as we can now see) certain ideas which Brecht had had in his head for some time. For even before moving to Berlin in the autumn of 1924 he was using the private codename 'Mahagonny' for some of the crazier aspects of Bavaria (then in the aftermath of Hitler's failed coup), and following this he had written the first three 'Mahagonny Songs' with their vaguely Wild West imagery of *Poker-drinksalons* and the like; a 'Mahagonny opera' indeed was part of his mental luggage for the move. Though he did nothing to develop th further during the subsequent two and a half years, his new collab ator Elisabeth Hauptmann had studied English and she wrote him two English-language 'Mahagonny Songs' which have ever figured among his poems. With her he had started working related projects: an opera to be called *Sodom und Gomorrah* or *From Manhattan*, and a radio play called *Die Sintflut* (*The F*

The opera project which the two men instantly began to discuss aimed accordingly to deal with the biblical theme of the Cities of the Plain; but in terms of the *Amerikanismus* prevalent in Germany after the stabilisation of 1923/24. Under the impact of the latter *The Flood* had already become known as *Collapse of Miami, the Paradise City*, for which Hauptmann had made a collection of newspaper cuttings dealing with hurricanes, and which clearly underlay the new scheme from the start. Though nothing is known of Weill's contribution at this initial stage it is already evident that if the outward trappings of the opera were to be modish and up-to-the-minute its message would be a Jeremiah-like warning derived from both men's knowledge of the Old Testament. A solemn moral was to be wrapped in an enjoyably flippant package.

Almost at once there was an interruption. Weill was already an established contributor to the new music festivals at Donaueschingen and Baden-Baden, and in the spring of 1927 he was commissioned to provide one of a batch of very short operas to be performed at the latter that summer. This struck him as a perfect pretext for what he termed 'a stylistic exercise' for the new project, so before either partner got down to work on the opera proper the so-called *Songspiel* or *Little Mahagonny* was prepared and performed. This consisted of the five 'Mahagonny Songs' from Brecht's first book of poems (including Hauptmann's Alabama and Benares Songs) followed by the unpublished 'Poem on a Dead Man' as a finale; and with Brecht's participation it was staged in a boxing ring in front of projections by his friend Caspar Neher. Lenya was one of the singers. The milieu was mock-American, the characters bearing such names as Jessie, Bessie, Charlie, Billy and so forth; and this was matched by Weill's use of the jazz idiom, which took one or two of Brecht's own tunes as a jumping-off point. The other works presented at the same time were by Milhaud, Hindemith and Ernst Toch, Hindemith being the festival's principal moving spirit. His contribution *Hin und Zurück*, in which music and action alike run backwards from a midway point, was based on a Berlin revue sketch.

The Little Mahagonny was a success, even though there seems to have been no question of performing it elsewhere. After the show, in ...enya's words,

...uddenly I felt a slap on the back, accompanied by a booming laugh: ...here no telephone?' It was Otto Klemperer. With that, the whole ...n was singing the Benares Song, and I knew that the battle was

...e at a moment when the 'New Objectivity' of the painters

(formally launched in the *Neue Suchlichkeit* exhibition of 1925) seemed to be merging in a wider movement of a down-to-earth, deliberately impersonal yet socially critical kind, of which *Amerikanismus* with its cult of jazz and sport formed part. Novel as their contribution was, Weill and Brecht were by no means alone in this, for Ernst Křenek's jazz opera *Jonny spielt auf* had already been performed at Leipzig at the beginning of 1927, and a whole new wave of *Zeitopern* or 'operas of the times' was to follow. Soon the critic Herbert Ihering was writing of Brecht as part of a modern musical-theatrical complex stretching from Chaplin and Piscator to the experiments of Klemperer, Hindemith and Weill: 'All that has hitherto been running along parallel or divergent paths is now joining up. . . . The age of isolation is over.'

After the summer holidays the three collaborators – for from now on Neher was a vital part of the team – got down to serious work on the opera libretto, which seems to have taken nearly a year. Their aim was to create an 'epic opera' of a new kind, in which a sequence of self-contained musical units would correspond to a 'step by step juxtaposition of situations' on the model (evidently) of *Man equals Man*. Projections like those used at Baden-Baden would add the third dimension to this scheme, which was based on Brecht's idea of an alternative to the integrated Wagnerian *Gesamtkunstwerk*: the new principle which he termed 'the separation of the elements'. What this amounted to in practice was a variety of montage, the major structural principle of the decade, and so far as Brecht's share was concerned he used his previous writings as the main source of raw material for it. On to the nucleus of 'Mahagonny Songs' used in the *Songspiel* therefore were grafted early poems like 'Tahiti' and 'Lucifer's Evening Song' dating from his youth in Augsburg as well as city poems dating from 1926–27 which reflect his first appalled reactions to Berlin. The hurricane advancing on Pensacola came, complete with its thousand victims and its diagrammatic arrow, from a report in the *Chicago Daily News* of 22 September 1926 which was among the *Collapse of Miami, the Paradise City* material. Leokadia (or Ladybird) Begbick is a self-evident importation from *Man equals Man*, Trinity Moses a quasi-Biblical guide through the wilderness to the Promised Land. Such was the mixture used to provide the required musical 'numbers'.

This work had to be fitted in between a succession of more or less demanding distractions. First of all came Brecht's new role as one of the team of dramaturgs for Piscator's Communist-inspired company at the Theater am Nollendorfplatz, which staged four epoch-making

productions in the 1927–28 season. Here he found a highly original
approach to the use of film, slide projections and other new technical
devices, his work on the *Schweik* production in particular making a
lifelong impression on him. Weill too wrote incidental music for one
of the productions.

The particular plays which he was trying to write – notably *Joe P.
Fleischhacker*, based on Frank Norris's novel *The Pit* about the Chicago
wheat market, and *Decline of the Egoist Johann Fatzer* about soldiers
deserting in the First World War – were neither performed there nor
even completed. Indeed from *Man equals Man* in 1926 to *Saint Joan of
the Stockyards* in 1931 he remained unable to finish the large-scale
plays that preoccupied him most.

●   ●   ●

The critical interruption came in March–April 1928, when Piscator
had taken on a second theatre and was fast heading for bankruptcy.
Some three months earlier a new management had been set up in
Berlin, headed by a young actor called Ernst-Josef Aufricht, once a
member of Berthold Viertel's much respected company 'Die Truppe'.
Around Christmas he had been given 100,000 marks by his father
with which to open his own Berlin theatre, and he used this to rent the
medium-sized late nineteenth-century Theater am Schiffbauerdamm
not far from Reinhardt's Deutsches Theater. He booked Erich Engel,
then busy with Brecht's *Man equals Man* at the Volksbühne, to direct
the opening production, if possible to coincide with his own twenty-
eighth birthday on 31 August. All that remained was to find a play.
This was not quite so simple, even after he had brought in a young
friend of Karl Kraus's called Heinrich Fischer to help him and act as his
deputy. Kraus, Wedekind, Toller, Feuchtwanger, Kaiser, even the
much older Sudermann were in turn considered or actually
approached, but to no effect. Then one of those happy accidents
occurred which go to make theatre history: Fischer ran into Brecht in a
café, introduced him to Aufricht and asked if he had anything that
would answer their needs. Brecht's own work in progress – presumably
Fleischhacker – would not do; it was already promised – presumably to
Piscator – and Aufricht appears to have been bored by his account of
it. But Brecht also mentioned a translation of John Gay's *The Beggar's
Opera* which his collaborator Elisabeth Hauptmann had begun making
the previous November. This eighteenth-century satire had been an
immense success in Nigel Playfair's revival at the Lyric, Hammersmith
some five or six years earlier, and to the two entrepreneurs the idea
'smelt of theatre'. They read all that had so far been written, under the

provisional title *Gesindel*, or *Scum*, and decided that this was the play with which to open.

Just how much Brecht had had to do with the script at this exploratory stage is uncertain, but he now took the lead and proposed that Weill should be brought in to write modern settings for the songs. Aufricht, by his own account, thereupon went privately to hear two of Weill's Kaiser operas, was appalled by their atonality and told his musical director Theo Mackeben to get hold of the traditional Pepusch arrangements in case Weill came up with something impossibly rebarbative. In mid-May the whole team were packed off to Le Lavandou in the south of France to complete the work: the Brechts, the Weills, Hauptmann, Engel. Here, and subsequently on the Ammersee in Bavaria, Brecht seems to have written some brand-new scenes (the stable wedding for instance, which bears no relation to Gay's original), and started adding his own songs, four of them piratically derived from a German version of Villon. On 1 August rehearsals started, with a duplicated script which, as our notes show, still contained a good deal of the original work, as well as songs by Gay himself and Rudyard Kipling which later disappeared. A succession of accidents, catastrophes and stopgaps then occurred. Carola Neher, who was to play Polly, arrived a fortnight late from her husband Klabund's deathbed, and abandoned her part; Roma Bahn was recruited and learned it in four days. Feuchtwanger suggested the new title; Karl Kraus added the second verse to the Jealousy Duet. Helene Weigel, cast as Mrs Coaxer the brothel Madame, developed appendicitis and the part was cut. The cabaret singer Rosa Valetti objected to the 'Song of Sexual Obsession' which she had to sing as Mrs Peachum, so this too went; Käte Kühl as Lucy could not manage the florid solo which Weill had written for another actress in scene 8, so this was eliminated and later the scene itself was cut; Weill's young wife Lotte Lenya was accidentally left off the printed programme; the play was found to be three-quarters of an hour too long, leading to massive cuts in Peachum's part and the dropping of the 'Solomon Song'; the finale was only written during the rehearsals; and late on the 'Ballad of Mac the Knife' was added as an inspired afterthought.

All accounts agree that the production's prospects seemed extremely bad, with only Weill's music and Caspar Neher's sets remaining unaffected by the mounting chaos. Even the costumes were simply those available, so Brecht was to say later (p. 323), while the Victorian setting was decided less by the needs of the story than by the shortage of time. The dress rehearsal must have been disastrous, the reactions of the first-night audience a confirmation of this, lasting right into the second scene, even after the singing of 'Pirate Jenny' in the stable. But with the 'Cannon Song' the applause suddenly burst loose. Quite unexpectedly, inspiredly, improvisedly, management and collaborators found themselves with the greatest German hit of the 1920s on their hands.

• • •

It struck Berlin during an interregnum, as it were: at a moment when Piscator had temporarily disappeared as an active force in the left-wing theatre and the various collective groups which succeeded him had not yet got off the ground. For Brecht and Weill there was now the composition of *Mahagonny* to be resumed – as well as a small Berlin Requiem which Weill had agreed to write for Radio Frankfurt on texts by Brecht, and which they sketched out in November and December 1928. Both men probably also had some involvement in the production of Feuchtwanger's second 'Anglo-Saxon Play' *Die Petroleuminseln* at the Staatstheater in the former month, for which Weill wrote the music and Neher once more provided sets. But the immediate effect of *The Threepenny Opera*'s success was to establish the Theater am Schiffbauerdamm as the leading left-wing theatre of the moment in Berlin. Retrospectively Brecht came to speak of it as 'his' theatre, and indeed to a great extent he does seem to have dominated its entire opening season. For with *The Threepenny Opera* temporarily transferred to another theatre (and Carola Neher at some point assuming her original role as Polly), he took over the direction of Marieluise Fleisser's anti-militarist Bavarian farce *Die Pioniere von Ingolstadt*, a sequel to the play which he had recommended to the Junge Bühne three years earlier. This opened on 31 March 1929 and featured an unknown actor whom Brecht had advised Aufricht to engage on a three-year contract – Peter Lorre – along with Kurt Gerron and Lenya, the Brown and Jenny from his own play. The farce itself was too outspoken for the police and the military, and had to be bowdlerised, but it none the less ran for two months and broke even; Aufricht later judged it the best of all the productions which he sponsored. Then *The Threepenny Opera* returned for the rest of the season, and the problem of the next play had to be faced.

Rather than concern himself with the *Mahagonny* project, Aufricht wanted another Brecht–Weill work on the same lines as before. It was scheduled once more for 31 August; Engel and Neher were again booked, and a number of the same actors already under contract. But the moment had passed, the first symptoms of the imminent economic crisis were beginning to make themselves felt, the veneer of political tolerance was wearing thin. Brecht had a seismographic feeling for such changes, and he was already heading towards a much more didactic kind of theatre, in which he briefly also managed to involve Weill. As a result *Happy End*, the Chicago comedy which was supposed to follow up *The Threepenny Opera*'s success, never really stirred his interest or drew the same inspired ideas from him as had Gay's inherently much superior original. Superficially the prospects might have seemed the same as before, with Elisabeth Hauptmann providing the basic dialogue and Brecht writing a number of characteristic songs, some of them eliciting first-rate settings from Weill. But whereas in 1928 Brecht was willing to make many radical changes in the former, so that his stamp on the final play is unmistakable, only a year later this was no longer the case. At some point during the spring of 1929 he began writing his first *Lehrstücke* or didactic plays under the twofold influence of the Japanese Noh drama and Hindemith's concept of *Gemeinschaftsmusik* – the educational implications of making music in common. Two works for that summer's Baden-Baden festival resulted. Almost at the same time his hitherto uncommitted left-wing opinions crystallised as a consequence, it seems, of the Berlin May Day demonstration at which the police killed thirty-one people. From then on he was aligned with the German Communist Party, and in the autumn both *Happy End* and Piscator's theatre alike failed.

. . .

Meantime, the full *Mahagonny* libretto had been completed by the middle of 1928, and the understanding between the two men, though never intimate, continued to be good. Brecht still assumed, as he had written in the Baden-Baden programme, that Weill's work was

> moving in the same direction as those artists in every field who foresee the collapse of 'society' art . . . It is already addressing an audience which goes to the theatre naïvely and for fun.

– while Weill for his part told the music magazine *Melos* that

> there is no ground whatsoever for the frequently voiced fear that any collaboration with literary figures of real stature must make the relationship between music and text into one of dependence subordination or at best parity. The more powerful the writer, th greater his ability to adjust himself to the music . . .

The libretto once finished, Weill composed the music durin run of *The Threepenny Opera*, sending off both script and score

Viennese publishers Universal-Edition in April 1929. The latter had already warned him that the new work looked like being both controversial and financially hazardous to stage, and now they became even more alarmed at the sight of Brecht's text for the brothel scene (the original text, that is, as given on pp. 369–70). On being told by their director Alfred Hertzka that any established opera house would certainly reject it, Weill agreed after some argument to drop the most outrageous passage; marked the whole 'Mandalay' section, with its depiction of the Men queueing up, as an optional cut; and got Brecht to provide him with the poem of the cranes and the cloud, which he set in 3/8 time as a love duet. Shortly afterwards the two collaborators, who may well by now have come to feel that *Amerikanismus* had become rather hackneyed, agreed as far as possible to eliminate the exaggeratedly 'American' names and allusions in the text, and thereby to make it clear that 'the amusement town [or fun city] of Mahagonny . . . is international in the widest sense' and the satire applicable a good deal nearer home. The Weill–Neher 'prompt-book' accordingly carries a warning (p. 353) against creating any kind of 'Wild West and cowboy romanticism', while there is a prefatory note in the full score suggesting the use of German names for the original lumberjack quartet of Jim, Fatty, Billy and Jack or Jake. (This was not, however, in time to affect the piano score, whose first edition retains the American names.)

•   •   •

In the cultural life of the Weimar Republic 1929 was a crucial year: and much of the subsequent history of this opera – and perhaps even of the whole Brecht–Weill collaboration – would have been different if the work had been completed twelve months sooner. For the whole climate in which it had been originally conceived now changed, further stages in the process being the death of Stresemann (whose foreign policy ever since 1923 had made quite amazingly few concessions to German nationalism) and the Wall Street crash of October which initiated the world economic crisis. Nationalsim now once more asserted itself, to the great advantage of the Nazis; the Communist left went over to a policy of aggressive confrontation, largely directed against the Socialists; while a period of economic retrenchment began which affected every aspect of life. So far as *Mahagonny* was concerned the effects were threefold. First of all the opera houses, compelled to economise, started to cut back on modern works, while Klemperer's Kroll-Oper on the Platz der Republik was finally closed down. Secondly there was a considerable wave of feeling against 'decadent' modern art and music, which the crazier Nazis like Alfred Rosenberg interpreted racially as part negroid (rhe jazz influence) and partly a destructive operation by the Jews. Finally Brecht's own attitude to politics and the theatre changed radically as he aligned himself with the Communist Party and began developing the new didactic form.

With Brecht apparently losing interest once the opera had gone off to the publishers, it was left to Weill to arrange its production. This might possibly have been undertaken by Piscator, who in March had listed it among the forty works under consideration by his company; but that company died in October. Aufricht too, the impresario of *The Threepenny Opera*, was so angry with Brecht over *Happy End* that it was two years before he would consider another work by him. Thus the choice would probably have been limited to the opera houses even if Universal-Edition had not in any case seen them as the natural and preferred outlet. Here the obvious candidate would of course have been the Kroll-Oper with its truly remarkable record of modern productions, for Klemperer knew both collaborators and had a high regard for Weill's music. But such negotiations as took place with the Kroll must have been prior to the opera's completion. For in July the Prussian government's public accounts committee proposed to abolish the Kroll-Oper altogether, and from that point the latter was doomed.

In the end the choice fell on the Leipzig Opera, where two previous Weill premières had been staged (likewise Křenek's *Jonny spielt auf*), with a second production to follow at Kassel a few days later. These took place in March 1930, by which time the cultural reaction was well under way, with a Nazi, Wilhelm Frick, actually heading the responsible ministry in nearby Thuringia. Though the Kassel production went calmly enough (after some modifications in the last scene to make its slogans seem less 'communistic') the première proper was interrupted by demonstrators, and from then on the opera became a prime target for such people. Accordingly (to quote David Drew), 'the few music-directors who wished to stage it were anxious to do so only with "closed performances" '.

Fortunately Berlin was different, and right up to the Nazi takeover in 1933 left-wing plays and productions continued to be staged; thus Brecht's own extremely radical re-staging of *Man equals Man* could be seen at the Prussian State Theatre in February 1931 (though it only ran for a few performances). It was Aufricht, then, who came to the rescue of *Mahagonny* by deciding to put it on at the specially rented Theater am Kurfürstendamm at the end of that year, and to do so in a predominantly theatrical rather than an orthodoxly operatic production. Actors were engaged rather than singers, with the fortunate result that Weill had to write a new setting for Jenny's Arietta in scene 5 to allow for Lenya's vocal limitations (it is now the accepted one). Brecht and Neher were nominated as directors, while the conductor was Schönberg's brother-in-law Alexander Zemlinsky, previously Klemperer's number two at the Kroll. Many cuts were made, including the crane duet, the Benares Song, 'God in Mahagonny' and the chorus 'Lasst euch nicht verführen'; the whole scale was reduced and shortened; the orchestra was cut down. To Theodor Adorno, though he had come to think an opera house the proper place for this work, it was the tightest, clearest and musically strongest performance yet, while Lenya too has written of it as something quite unforgettable. This in spite of the fact that Brecht and Weill were on bad terms throughout: so much so indeed that Aufricht underwrote the almost simultaneous première of the former's didactic play *The Mother* in order to distract him from the rehearsals, leaving the more amicable Neher in charge.

· · · · ·

Though there was no irreparable quarrel between the two men, there was from mid-1930 onwards a growing divergence which discouraged any further work of the originality of *Mahagonny*, as well as some specific disagreement about *Mahagonny* itself. In his edition of the writings of Kurt Weill David Drew has attributed this to what he terms 'the time-honoured rivalry of words and music', suggesting in particular that Brecht was riled by the one-sidedly 'musical' slant of the programme note to the Leipzig première. Whether or not this was the cause, he left the compilation of the 'prompt-book' entirely to his two partners, even though Universal-Edition had announced that he too would take part in it; and he also acted quite unilaterally where the publication of the text was concerned. This seems to have taken place some time in the winter of 1930–31 (the relevant number of his *Versuche* being actually dated 1930), and it showed a number of variations from the version composed by Weill. Among these was the changing of the German name Johann previously proposed for the hero Jimmy, so as to turn the four lumberjacks into Paul, Heinrich, Jakob and Josef.

More significantly perhaps, the 'Notes on the Opera' which Brecht wrote for this publication in August 1930 not only differ from Weill's views but indicate a considerable disappointment with the way in which *Mahagonny* had turned out. Meant as an epic opera of a new kind, it had finished up as a 'culinary' one, so Brecht felt: that is to say it resembled the conventional *opera whose* ingredients, instead of being kept separate, are cooked together for the *benefit of an* audience of musical gastronomes. In fact this was not a criticism of the *work* itself so much as of its presentation, which had been left in the first place to the established opera houses. For what Brecht was concerned with, and had doubtless imagined Weill to be concerned with too, was not just the writing of 'an opera' but the transformation of the audience and of the whole theatrical and operatic 'apparatus': that Establishment, in fact, which he now realised to be socially and economically based. The trouble, then, was not so much a basic incompatibility between the two men – for after all they spent their summer holidays together at Le Lavandou in 1931 and supported each other in the *Threepenny Opera* film lawsuit that autumn – as a sense on Brecht's part that Weill, once so full of promise for him, had let him down.

And there was indeed some inconsistency between the collaborators' original concept of the staging and the actual results. Thus the provisions of the 'prompt-book' (whose foreword by Weill appeared two months before the Leipzig première) suggest that the set must be made 'so simple as to be equally well transferable from the theatre to any old platform', with neither emotion, stylisation nor any kind of irony or caricature being added to the bald, almost concert-like delivery of the material with its carefully built-in gests. This extreme economy of approach, reflecting possibly the lessons of the first *Lehrstücke* as well as the experience of the *Songspiel* of 1927, was intended to make very clear the montage structure of the work. At the same time it rested on a systematic concept of 'gestic' writing, acting and composition which was actually formulated in the first place by Weill. Indeed his essay 'On the Gestic Nature of Music', which first appeared in *Die Musik* as early as March 1929 – some two years before Brecht started writing of 'the gest' – plainly reflects the work on *Mahagonny*. This principle of identifying the successive attitudes expressed in a work or a scene or a song, and then communicating them individually in all the separate media involved, underlay the whole Weill–Brecht–Neher collaboration. Each point had to be distinctly made from their three different directions in such a way that the audience could follow the cumulative argument without abandoning what Weill termed 'the calm posture of a thinking being'.

Nothing in the available contemporary accounts suggests that these demands ever came near to being fulfilled, not even in the Aufricht production of 1931. And so Brecht may well have blamed Weill for his willingness to listen to the powerful chiefs of Universal-Edition who had done so much to establish the modern repertoire at the Kroll-Oper and elsewhere, instead of seeking that new audience which goes to the theatre 'naïvely'. He could equally well, for that matter, have blamed himself, for once the libretto was off his hands he seems to have left Weill, and in a lesser degree Neher, to settle the question of where and how it was to be staged. Whatever the reason, the salient fact is that from then on he apparently lost all interest in what, after all, remains a powerful, funny, unusually concise and often quite beautiful text. Simply to read, it is one of his finest works. Yet after the 1931 production he virtually ignored it, never (for instance) once mentioning it in the *Journals* that set out his achievements, reflections and preoccupations between 1938 and the end of his life. Certainly he did not view it with anything like the affection which he felt for *The Threepenny Opera*, though the latter was a far less original piece of writing.

·   ·   ·

The great difference between *The Threepenny Opera* and either *Mahagonny* or *Happy End* was its enormous success, which kept it running in different parts of Germany until the Nazis took over and in other countries longer still. This did not immediately tempt Brecht to tinker with the text of the play (as he continued to do with *Man equals Man*), but when Warner Brothers and Tobis, acting through producers called Nero-Film, contracted in May 1930 to make a film version he started looking at it with changed – and changing – eyes. Though sound film was then in its infancy, the prospects seemed good: G. W. Pabst was to be the director, Lania (of Piscator's old collective) to write the script; Carola Neher would play Polly, Lenya Jenny; while Brecht and Weill were given a say respectively in the script and the music. Two parallel versions would be made, one German and one French. That summer, accordingly, Brecht wrote Lania the treatment called 'Die Beule', 'The Bruise', which in effect ignores all that had remained of *The Beggar's Opera* and uses the characters and the Victorian London setting to point a radically changed moral. Everything now is on a larger scale – the gang is 120 strong, Peachum heads a Begging Trust – and a higher social level, with peers, a general and a magistrate at Macheath's wedding in the ducal manège. The gang and the beggars this time are engaged in a war whose symbol is the bruise inflicted by the former on a beggar called Sam. Peachum accordingly uses the beggars to disfigure the smartly repainted slum streets through which the Queen is to pass; he interviews Brown with seven lawyers behind him, and secures Macheath's arrest after a bucolic picnic and a chase in which a car full of policemen pursues a car full of whores. There is no escape and no second arrest. Under Polly's direction the gang has simply taken over the National Deposit Bank and converted itself into a group of solemn financiers. Both they and Mrs Peachum now become uneasy about the dangers of unleashing the poor; while Brown has a terrible dream, in which thousands of poor people emerge from under one of the Thames bridges as a great flood, sweeping through the streets and public buildings. So the 'mounted Messengers' this time are the bankers who arrive to bail Macheath out; and rather than disappoint the crowds Peachum hands over Sam to be hanged instead. The social façades are maintained as Macheath joins the reunited bourgeoisie awaiting the arrival of their Queen.

This scheme, on which Neher and the Bulgarian director Slatan Dudow also collaborated, was plainly unwelcome to the producers, and the fact that Brecht only met the agreed August deadline by communicating it to Lania orally did not improve matters. Though Lania needed him to continue working the Nero firm chose to dismiss Brecht at this stage, and brought in the Communist film critic Béla Balázs to help complete the script. A lawsuit followed, which Brecht lost, and thereafter he had no words too bad for Pabst's film, which meanwhile went obstinately ahead, to be shown in Berlin on 19 February 1931. Though the long theoretical essay which Brecht thereafter wrote on the 'Threepenny Lawsuit', as he termed it, is an illuminating work, not least for its links with the ideas of his new friend Walter Benjamin, the modern reader should not allow its downright condemnation to put him off the film. For in fact not only did the latter capture aspects of the original (for instance Carola Neher's interpretation of Polly) that necessarily elude any modern production, but it also incorporates a surprising proportion of Brecht's changes to the story. These, however, continued to itch Brecht, so that while leaving the play itself as it had been in the 1928 production (with all its last-minute decisions and improvisations) he was soon planning its further development in The Threepenny Novel, his one substantial work of fiction, which he was to hand in to its Dutch publisher some months after leaving Germany in 1933. Engel, when he came again to direct the play at the Theater am Schiffbauerdamm for the Berliner Ensemble in 1960, after Brecht's death, wondered at first if he could not incorporate some of the ideas from 'The Bruise' and the novel, but soon decided that they were too divergent from the play. Brecht for his part wrote some topical versions of the songs (p. 305 ff.) for other directors in the immediate post-war years, but it is not clear if and when they were used, and certainly he never mad...

them a permanent part of the text; indeed they hardly merit it. All the same, his discussions in connection with Giorgio Strehler's Milan production in the last year of his life (pp. 320–5) show that he regarded *The Threepenny Opera* as no inviolable museum piece. For he envisaged a new framework, and welcomed Strehler's updating of the story to the era of the Keystone Kops.

·   ·   ·   ·

Like *Man equals Man*, *The Threepenny Opera* presents a problem to earnest-minded interpreters, since it is hard to reconcile its flippancies with Brecht's status as a Communist playwright, while its repeated successes in the commercial theatres of bourgeois society – from Berlin of the 1920s to New York of the 1970s – take some explaining away. The trouble here is not only that when Brecht actually wrote his share of this play he was only beginning to explore Marxism and had barely begun to relate to the class struggle (as the leading Communist Party critic Alfred Kemény pointed out), but that the issue was subsequently confused by Brecht's writing all his own notes and interpretations *after* adopting a more committed position in 1929. His remarks moreover are too easily taken out of context and at their face value: his insistence, for instance, that the play is a critique of bourgeois society and not merely of the *Lumpenproletariat* was only a retort – quite unsubstantiated – to that ill-disposed critic in the party's daily *Die Rote Fahne* who had accused him of the contrary, referred to him as 'the Bohemian Bert Brecht' and dismissed the whole work as a money-spinner containing 'Not a vestige of modern social or political satire'. Just like Piscator's productions of the previous season *The Threepenny Opera* undoubtedly appealed to the fashionable Berlin public and subsequently to the middle classes throughout Germany, and if it gave them an increasingly cynical view of their own institutions it does not seem to have prompted either them or any other section of society to try to change these for the better. The fact was simply that 'one has to have seen it', as the elegant and cosmopolitan Count Kessler noted in his diary after doing so with a party that included an ambassador and a director of the Dresdner Bank.

Brecht himself had far too much affection for this work to admit the ineffectiveness of its message, even after he had tacitly confirmed such accusations by going over to austerer, explicitly didactic forms. Even years later he could still view it through something of a pink cloud, as indicated by his wishful replies to Giorgio Strehler on p. 322. Yet the most favourable criticisms at the time were concerned less with its attack on 'bourgeois morality' and capitalist property rights as being based on theft than with its establishment of a highly original new theatrical genre. Thus Herbert Ihering, who from the first had been Brecht's leading supporter among the Berlin critics, while welcoming this 'new form, open to every possibility, every kind of content', pointed out that 'this content, however, has still to come'. Part of the common over-estimation of the play's social purpose and impact is due most probably to the intense dislike felt for it by the German nationalist reaction which began gaining ground within a year of the première and was soon to bring the Nazis their first great electoral successes. It was a time of growing polarisation in German political and cultural life, and if the Berlin theatre continued to move leftwards, dragging part of the cinema with it, there was now much less hesitation on the part of the authorities and the great middlebrow public to voice their dislike of anything 'alien' and 'decadent' in the arts. Not only was Weill a leading target for such campaigns, largely on racialist grounds, but the brothel scene and the cynicism of the songs were certainly enough to qualify Brecht too, whether or not he represented any kind of serious threat. A great wave of irrational feeling was building up, and in so far as it was directed against *The Threepenny Opera* its political aspects were quite deceptive. Thus that shrewd observer Kurt Tucholsky could write in spring 1930 that the battle was a sham one because the work itself was unrealistic. 'This writer can be compared to a man cooking soup on a burning house. It isn't he who caused the fire.'

Yet if its political significance is often overrated today *The Threepenny Opera* remains revolutionary in a less obvious but equally disturbing sense. For, like *The Little Mahagonny* before it, it struck almost instinctively at the whole hierarchical order of the arts, with opera on its Wagnerian pinnacle at the top, and reshuffled highbrow and lowbrow elements to form a new kind of musical theatre which would upset every accepted notion of what was socially and culturally proper. This was what the best critics immediately recognised, Ihering writing that the success of *The Threepenny Opera* was of immense importance:

> A theatre that is not smart, not geared to 'society', has broken through to the audience.

Far more so the musicians; thus Klemperer included the wind suite from the music in his concerts and is reported to have seen the 1928 production ten times, while Heinrich Strobel compared it with *The Soldier's Tale* as 'showing the way' and Theodor Adorno judged it th most important event since Berg's *Wozzeck*. In many ways the char of values which it implied has proved harder for later societies to assimilate than have the somewhat random gibes at business, religious hypocrisy, individual charity, romantic marriage and the judicial system which make up the political content of the text. Particularly when seen in conjunction with Brecht's and Walter Benjamin's current thinking about the 'apparatus' of the arts, it suggested a complete cultural and sociological re-evaluation which would alter all the existing categories, starting with those of opera and operetta (for it was neither), as well as the corresponding techniques of acting, singing and so forth. Today, though certainly poverty, slums, corrupt business practices and biassed justice continue to exist in our most prosperous societies, we no longer feel that *The Threepenny Opera* has anything all that acute to say about them. But the implications of the new form for singers, musicians, voice teachers and above all for institutionalised opera are still far from fully digested. And because Brecht and his friends did not yet manage to capture the 'apparatus' of which they spoke this held good for Communist as well as for capitalist society.

*   *   *

If the problem with *The Threepenny Opera* is that its interpreters tend to take the social criticisms too seriously, those of *The Rise and Fall of the City of Mahagonny* may fail to take its content seriously enough. This is partly due to the fact that the translation by W. H. Auden and Chester Kallman, for all its verbal felicities, needs to be treated with some reservation. A few minor misunderstandings have been corrected, but they also made a dubious decision to return to a modified form of the original 'American' names as found in the piano score which they used. For while it is true that an American audience hearing them for the first time might find that they help make the text more relevant to its own society, to everybody who knows that the work emanated from the Berlin of the 1920s – i.e., for almost anyone directing or conducting it – they conjure up just that modish *Amerikanismus* which Brecht and Weill wanted to discard. Of course the collaborators themselves had somewhat undermined this good intention by their deliberate return to the 'American' milieu in *The Seven Deadly Sins*, which the New York revival of 1958 further emphasised by consciously setting it in the 1920s. But there remains a considerable risk that if *Mahagonny* is staged in English in this spirit it will become dated, historical, fashionably nostalgic and that much ~asier for us to stomach.

The Seven Deadly Sins was a comparatively slight work that was written in exile in May 1933, some three months after Hitler came to power. It was commissioned by a short-lived Paris-based company called Les Ballets 1933 backed by the surrealist picture collector Edward James, with his Viennese wife Tilly Losch as its principal dancer; their choreographer was George Balanchine. Fairly clearly the commission was prompted by the success of Weill's concert there the previous December, when *Der Jasager* and a very trimmed-down version of *Mahagonny*, with Lenya among the singers, were included in a series called 'Concerts de la Sérénade'. So Brecht joined Weill in Paris that spring and supplied a libretto which was essentially a cycle of songs for Lenya in the old pseudo-American vein. As performed at the Théâtre des Champs-Elysées, with Lenya and Losch as the two Annas, this fell comparatively flat – Serge Lifar calling it 'de la pourriture de ballet' – though it made a great impression on Constant Lambert, who conducted the subsequent performance at the Savoy Theatre in London. To Brecht himself however this excursion into the past seems to have been of little interest, for he subsequently paid no attention to his script and made no attempt to get it published. He made just one amendment: the addition of the words 'of the petty bourgeoisie' to the title; the German phrase being *des Kleinbürgers*, the same words as he added to the title of the early one-act play *The Wedding*.

To return to *Mahagonny*, the unpleasant truth is that this work's message, unlike that of *The Threepenny Opera*, remains as valid as ever in a society like our own. For we too live in a consumer civilisation: one that has been intensified, refurbished and in many ways enriched, but remains every bit as money-conscious as that of Brecht's Suckerville, the 'city of nets'. We too have our idealists who feel that once 'Don'ts are not permitted here' the Golden Age will return and all social and economic problems fade into the background. We too are just as loud in our protests against just as muddled a list of things. And so the message must come direct to us, not altered through a blue and angelic 'period' haze.

The important thing, then, in staging this work is to forget all about the Berlin Cabarets on the one hand and the marching storm-troopers on the other, and treat it as simply and directly as its original conception. For Mahagonny is localised neither in Weimar Germany nor in a pseudo-America but in any society which lives in great cities and becomes obsessed with pleasure and the problem of how to pay for it. Its teaching is far closer to that of the great Bible-thumping revivalists than to the idiosyncratic attitudes of Mr Norris and Herr Issyvoo on which our present picture of pre-Hitler Berlin is so largely based; its choruses do not recall the husky voice of Marlene Dietrich much as the *Dies Irae*. Its warnings therefore are likely to be relevant as long as such societies depend on commercialised distractions, vices and entertainments, where even their permissiveness remains subsidiary to the rule that everything must be paid for. The point is summed up in one of the inter-scene inscriptions which Auden and Kallman for some reason failed to translate: 'SO GREAT IS THE REGARD FOR MONEY IN OUR TIME.' Only when this no longer applies will *Mahagonny* be truly a 'period' work. To present it as such today is an evasion.

THE EDITORS

This introduction is based on the three separate introductions to those plays in the Methuen hardback edition of the Collected Plays. Among further developments worth noting are some that concern the rôle of Brecht's collaborators Kurt Weill and Caspar Neher. Basing itself on the bowdlerised version of the original *Threepenny Opera* libretto which Weill's publishers issued in the autumn of 1928, the Kurt Weill Foundation has more than once tried to insist on the exclusion from English-language productions of lines 10–17 on p. 166 (starting 'You see before you') in Macheath's last speech on the gallows, on the grounds that they were a slightly later addition by Brecht. They are however part of the spoken dialogue to a 'play with music'; there is no musical pretext for excising them; we have no evidence that Weill himself ever argued for their removal; and their alleged 'Marxism' is hardly the business of a US-based charitable foundation.

Neher's designs shown by the Arts Council of Great Britain in 1986 indicate that the projection screens right and left of the stage for the same play were not meant for titles and inscriptions as seen in photographs of the original production, but for coloured drawings with handwritten comments and quotations. For the 1931 production of *Man equals Man* Neher drew giant soldiers – hence perhaps Brecht's notion of putting two of them on stilts – and once or twice gave Galy Gay a brown skin. This suggests the possibility of making him an Indian rather than the 'Irishman' of our text.

JOHN WILLETT, 1994

Chronology

1898	10 February: Eugen Berthold Friedrich Brecht born in Augsburg.
1917	Autumn: Bolshevik revolution in Russia. Brecht to Munich university.
1918	Work on his first play, *Baal*. In Augsburg Brecht is called up as medical orderly till end of year. Elected to Soldiers' Council as Independent Socialist (USPD) following Armistice.
1919	Brecht writing second play *Drums in the Night*. In January Spartacist Rising in Berlin. Rosa Luxemburg murdered. April–May: Bavarian Soviet. Summer: Weimer Republic constituted. Birth of Brecht's illegitimate son Frank Banholzer.
1920	May: death of Brecht's mother in Augsburg.
1921	Brecht leaves university without a degree. Reads Rimbaud.
1922	A turning point in the arts. End of utopian Expressionism; new concern with technology. Brecht's first visit to Berlin, seeing theatres, actors, publishers and cabaret. He writes 'Of Poor BB' on the return journey. Autumn: becomes a dramaturg in Munich. Première of *Drums in the Night*, a prize-winning national success. Marries Marianne Zoff, an opera singer.
1923	Galloping German inflation stabilised by November currency reform. In Munich Hitler's new National Socialist party stages unsuccessful 'beer-cellar putsch'.
1924	'Neue Sachlichkeit' exhibition at Mannheim gives its name to the new sobriety in the arts. Brecht to Berlin as assistant in Max Reinhardt's Deutsches Theater.
1925	Field-Marshal von Hindenburg becomes President. Elisabeth Hauptmann starts working with Brecht. Two seminal films: Chaplin's *The Gold Rush* and Eisenstein's *The Battleship Potemkin*. Brecht writes birthday tribute to Bernard Shaw.
1926	Première of *Man equals Man* in Darmstadt. Now a freelance; starts reading Marx. His first book of poems, the *Devotions*, includes the 'Legend of the Dead Soldier'.
1927	After reviewing the poems and a broadcast of *Man equals Ma*· Kurt Weill approaches Brecht for a libretto. Result is the t

of *Mahagonny*, whose 'Songspiel' version is performed in a boxing-ring at Hindemith's Baden-Baden music festival in July. In Berlin he helps adapt *The Good Soldier Schweik* for Piscator's high-tech theatre.

1928   August 31: première of *The Threepenny Opera* by Brecht and Weill, based on Gay's *The Beggar's Opera*.

1929   Start of Stalin's policy of 'socialism in one country'. Divorced from Marianne, Brecht now marries the actress Helene Weigel. May 1: Berlin police break up banned KPD demonstration, witnessed by Brecht. Summer: Brecht writes two didactic music-theatre pieces with Weill and Hindemith, and neglects *The Threepenny Opera*'s successor *Happy End*, which is a flop. From now on he stands by the KPD. Autumn: Wall Street crash initiates world economic crisis. Cuts in German arts budgets combine with renewed nationalism to create cultural backlash.

1930   Nazi election successes; end of parliamentary government. Unemployed 3 million in first quarter, about 5 million at end of the year. March: première of the full-scale *Mahagonny* opera in Leipzig Opera House.

1931   German crisis intensifies. Aggressive KPD arts policy: agitprop theatre, marching songs, political photomontage. In Moscow the Comintern forms international associations of revolutionary artists, writers, musicians and theatre people.

1932   Première of Brecht's agitational play *The Mother* (after Gorky) with Eisler's music. *Kuhle Wampe*, his militant film with Eisler, is held up by the censors. He meets Sergei Tretiakov at the film's première in Moscow. Summer: the Nationalist Von Papen is made Chancellor. He denounces 'cultural bolshevism', and deposes the SPD-led Prussian administration.

1933   January 30: Hitler becomes Chancellor with Papen as his deputy. The Prussian Academy is purged; Goering becomes Prussian premier. A month later the Reichstag is burnt down, the KPD outlawed. The Brechts instantly leave via Prague; at first homeless. Eisler is in Vienna, Weill in Paris, where he agrees to compose a ballet with song texts by Brecht: *The Seven Deadly Sins*, premièred there in June. In Germany Nazi students burn books; all parties and trade unions banned; first measures against the Jews. Summer: Brecht in Paris works on anti-Nazi publications. With the advance on his *Threepenny Novel*, he buys a house on Fyn island, Denmark, overlooking the Svendborg Sound, where the family will spend the next six years. Margarete Steffin, a young Berlin Communist, goes with them. Autumn: he meets the Danish Communist actress Ruth Berlau, a doctor's wife.

1934 Spring: suppression of Socialist rising in Austria. Eisler stays with Brecht to work on *Round Heads and Pointed Heads* songs. Summer: Brecht misses the first Congress of Soviet Writers, chaired by Zhdanov along the twin lines of Socialist Realism and Revolutionary Romanticism. October: in London with Eisler.

1935 Italy invades Ethiopia. Hitler enacts the Nuremberg Laws against the Jews. March–May: Brecht to Moscow for international theatre conference. Meets Kun and Knorin of Comintern Executive. Eisler becomes president of the International Music Bureau. At the 7th Comintern Congress Dimitrov calls for all antifascist parties to unite in Popular Fronts against Hitler and Mussolini. Autumn: Brecht with Eisler to New York for Theatre Union production of *The Mother*.

1936 Soviet purges lead to arrests of many Germans in USSR, most of them Communists; among them Carola Neher and Ernst Ottwalt, friends of the Brechts. International cultural associations closed down. Official campaign against 'Formalism' in the arts. Mikhail Koltsov, the Soviet journalist, founds *Das Wort* as a literary magazine for the German emigration, with Brecht as one of the editors. Popular Front government in Spain resisted by Franco and other generals, with the support of the Catholic hierarchy. The Spanish Civil War becomes a great international cause.

1937 Summer: in Munich, opening of Hitler's House of German Art. Formally, the officially approved art is closely akin to Russian 'Socialist Realism'. In Russia Tretiakov is arrested as a Japanese spy, interned in Siberia and later shot. October: Brecht's Spanish war play *Señora Carrar's Rifles*, with Weigel in the title part, is performed in Paris, and taken up by antifascist and amateur groups in many countries.

1938 January: in Moscow Meyerhold's avant-garde theatre is abolished. March: Hitler takes over Austria without resistance. It becomes part of Germany. May 21: première of scenes from Brecht's *Fear and Misery of the Third Reich* in a Paris hall. Autumn: Munich Agreement, by which Britain, France and Italy force Czechoslovakia to accept Hitler's demands. In Denmark Brecht writes the first version of *Galileo*. In Moscow Koltsov disappears into arrest after returning from Spain.

1939   March: Hitler takes over Prague and the rest of the Czech
        territories. Madrid surrenders to Franco; end of the Civil War.
        Eisler has emigrated to New York. April: the Brechts leave
        Denmark for Stockholm. Steffin follows. May: Brecht's
        Svendborg Poems published. His father dies in Germany.
        Denmark accepts Hitler's offer of a Non-Aggression Pact.
        August 23: Ribbentrop and Molotov agree Nazi-Soviet Pact.
        September 1: Hitler attacks Poland and unleashes Second
        World War. Stalin occupies Eastern Poland, completing its
        defeat in less than three weeks. All quiet in the West.
        Autumn: Brecht writes *Mother Courage* and the radio play
        Lucullus in little over a month. November: Stalin attacks
        Finland.

1940   Spring: Hitler invades Norway and Denmark. In May his
        armies enter France through the Low Countries, taking Paris
        in mid-June. The Brechts hurriedly leave for Finland, taking
        Steffin with them. They aim to travel on to the US, where
        Brecht has been offered a teaching job in New York at the New
        School. July: the Finnish writer Hella Wuolijoki invites them
        to her country estate, which becomes the setting for *Puntila*,
        the comedy she and Brecht write there.

1941   April: première of *Mother Courage* in Zurich. May: he gets US
        visas for the family and a tourist visa for Steffin. On 15th they
        leave with Berlau for Moscow to take the Trans-Siberian
        railway. In Vladivostok they catch a Swedish ship for Los
        Angeles, leaving just nine days before Hitler, in alliance with
        Finland, invades Russia. June: Steffin dies of tuberculosis in a
        Moscow sanatorium, where they have had to leave her. July:
        once in Los Angeles, the Brechts decide to stay there in the
        hope of film work. December: Japanese attack on Pearl Harbor
        brings the US into the war. The Brechts become 'enemy
        aliens'.

1942   Spring: Eisler arrives from New York. He and Brecht work on
        Fritz Lang's film *Hangmen Also Die*. Brecht and Feuchtwanger
        write *The Visions of Simone Machard*; sell rights to MGM. Ruth
        Berlau takes a job in New York. August: the Brechts rent a
        pleasant house and garden in Santa Monica. Autumn: Ger-
        mans defeated at Stalingrad and El Alamein. Turning point of
        World War 2.

  943   Spring: Brecht goes to New York for three months – first visit
        since 1935 – where he stays with Berlau till May and plans a
        wartime *Schweik* play with Kurt Weill. In Zurich the Schau-

spielhaus gives world premières of *The Good Person of Szechwan* and *Galileo*. November: his first son Frank is killed on the Russian front.

1944   British and Americans land in Normandy (June); Germans driven out of France by end of the year. Heavy bombing of Berlin, Hamburg and other German cities. Brecht works on *The Caucasian Chalk Circle*, and with H. R. Hays on *The Duchess of Malfi*. His son by Ruth Berlau, born prematurely in Los Angeles, lives only a few days. Start of collaboration with Charles Laughton on English version of *Galileo*.

1945   Spring: Russians enter Vienna and Berlin. German surrender; suicide of Hitler; Allied military occupation of Germany and Austria, each divided into four Zones. Roosevelt dies; succeeded by Truman; Churchill loses elections to Attlee. June: *Private Life of the Master Race* (wartime adaptation of *Fear and Misery* scenes) staged in New York. August: US drops atomic bombs on Hiroshima and Nagasaki. Japan surrenders. Brecht and Laughton start discussing production of *Galileo*.

1946   Ruth Berlau taken to hospital after a violent breakdown in New York. Work with Auden on *Duchess of Malfi*, which is finally staged there in mid-October – not well received. The Brechts have decided to return to Germany. Summer: A. A. Zhdanov reaffirms Stalinist art policies: Formalism bad, Socialist Realism good. Eisler's brother Gerhart summoned to appear before the House Un-American Activities Committee. November: the Republicans win a majority in the House. Cold War impending.

1947   FBI file on Brecht reopened in May. Rehearsals begin for Los Angeles production of *Galileo*, with Laughton in the title part and music by Eisler; opens July 31. Brecht's HUAC hearing October 30; a day later he leaves the US for Zurich.

1948   In Zurich renewed collaboration with Caspar Neher. Production of *Antigone* in Chur, with Weigel. Berlau arrives from US. Summer: *Puntila* world première at Zurich Schauspielhaus. Brecht completes his chief theoretical work, the *Short Organum*. Travel plans hampered because he is not allowed to enter US Zone (which includes Augsburg and Munich). Russians block all land access to Berlin. October: the Brechts to Berlin via Prague, to establish contacts and prepare production of *Mother Courage*.

1949   January: success of *Mother Courage* leads to establishment c the Berliner Ensemble. Collapse of Berlin blockade in M followed by establishment of West and East German states. Eisler, Dessau and Elisabeth Hauptmann arrive from US and join the Ensemble.

1950   Brecht gets Austrian nationality in connection with plan to involve him in Salzburg Festival. Long drawn-out scheme for *Mother Courage* film. Spring: he and Neher direct Lenz's *The Tutor* with the Ensemble. Autumn: he directs *Mother Courage* in Munich; at the end of the year *The Mother* with Weigel, Ernst Busch and the Ensemble.

1951   Selection of *A Hundred Poems* is published in East Berlin. Brecht beats off Stalinist campaign to stop production of Dessau's opera version of *Lucullus*.

1952   Summer: at Buckow, east of Berlin, Brecht starts planning a production of *Coriolanus* and discusses Eisler's project for a *Faust* opera.

1953   Spring: Stalin dies, aged 73. A 'Stanislavsky conference' in the East German Academy, to promote Socialist Realism in the theatre, is followed by meetings to discredit Eisler's libretto for the *Faust* opera. June: quickly suppressed rising against the East German government in Berlin and elsewhere. Brecht at Buckow notes that 'the whole of existence has been alienated' for him by this. Khrushchev becomes Stalin's successor.

1954   January: Brecht becomes an adviser to the new East German Ministry of Culture. March: the Ensemble at last gets its own theatre on the Schiffbauerdamm. July: its production of *Mother Courage* staged in Paris. December: Brecht awarded a Stalin Peace Prize by the USSR.

1955   August: Shooting at last begins on *Mother Courage* film, but is broken off after ten days and the project abandoned. Brecht in poor health.

1956   Khrushchev denounces Stalin's dictatorial methods and abuses of power to the Twentieth Party Congress in Moscow. A copy of his speech reaches Brecht. May: Brecht in the Charité hospital to shake off influenza. August 14: he dies in the Charité of a heart infarct.

1957   *The Resistible Rise of Arturo Ui, The Visions of Simone Machard* and *Schweyk in the Second World War* produced for the first time in Stuttgart, Frankfurt and Warsaw respectively.

Man equals Man

The transformation of the porter Galy Gay in the military cantonment of Kilkoa during the year nineteen hundred and twenty five

Collaborators: E. BURRI, S. DUDOW, E. HAUPTMANN,
  C. NEHER, B. REICH

Translators: GERHARD NELLHAUS and (for scene 1)
  BERTOLT BRECHT

Characters
URIAH SHELLEY ⎫
JESSE MAHONEY ⎬ *four privates in a machine-gun section*
POLLY BAKER   ⎪ *of the British Army in India*
JERAIAH JIP   ⎭
CHARLES FAIRCHILD, *known as Bloody Five, a Sergeant*
GALY GAY, *an Irish porter*
GALY GAY'S WIFE
MR WANG, *bonze of a Tibetan pagoda*
ᴬH SING, *his sacristan*
  OKADIA BEGBICK, *canteen proprietress*
  ꜱldiers

Kilkoa

Galy Gay and Galy Gay's wife

GALY GAY *sits one morning upon his chair and tells his wife*: Dear wife, I have decided in accordance with our income to buy a fish today. That would be within the means of a porter who drinks not at all, smokes very little and has almost no vices. Do you think I should buy a big fish or do you require a small one?

WIFE: A small one.

GALY GAY: Of what kind should the fish be that you require?

WIFE: I would say a good flounder. But please look out for the fishwives: they are lustful and always chasing men, and you have a soft nature, Galy Gay.

GALY GAY: That is true but I hope they would not bother with a penniless porter from the harbour.

WIFE: You are like an elephant which is the unwieldiest beast in the animal kingdom, but he runs like a freight train once he gets started. And then there are those soldiers who are the worst people in the world and who are said to be swarming at the station like bees. They are sure to be hanging around in numbers at the market place and you must be thankful if they don't break in and murder people. What's more they are dangerous for a man on his own because they always go around in fours.

GALY GAY: They would not want to harm a simple porter from the harbour.

WIFE: One can never tell.

GALY GAY: Then put the water on for the fish, for I am beginning to get an appetite and I guess I shall be back in ten minutes.

2

Street outside the Pagoda of the Yellow God

Four soldiers stop outside the pagoda. Military marches are heard as troops move into the town.

JESSE: Party, halt! Kilkoa! This here is Her Majesty's town of Kilkoa where they are concentrating the army for a long-predicted war. Here we are, along with a hundred thousand other soldiers, all of us thirsting to restore order on the northern frontier.

JIP: That demands beer. *He collapses.*

POLLY: Just as the powerful tanks of our Queen must be filled with petrol if we are to see them rolling over the damned roads of this oversized Eldorado so can the soldier only function if he drinks beer.

JIP: How much beer have we left?

POLLY: There are four of us. We still have fifteen bottles. So we must get hold of another twenty-five bottles.

JESSE: That demands money.

URIAH: Some people object to soldiers, but just one pagoda like this contains more copper than a strong regiment needs to march from Calcutta to London.

POLLY: Our friend Uriah's suggestion with respect to a pagoda which, though rickety and covered with flyshit, may well be bursting with copper surely merits our sympathetic attention.

JIP: All I know, Polly, is I've got to have more to drink.

URIAH: Calm down, sweetheart. This Asia has a hole for us to crawl through.

JIP: Uriah, Uriah, my mother always used to say: Do what you like, my darlingest Jeraiah, but remember pitch always sticks. And this place stinks of pitch.

JESSE: The door isn't properly shut. Watch out, Uriah, you bet there's some devilry behind it.

URIAH: Nobody's going through this open door.

JESSE: Right, what are windows for?

URIAH: Take your belts and make a long line to fish for the collection boxes with. That's it.

They attack the windows. Uriah smashes one, looks inside and starts fishing.

POLLY: Catch anything?

URIAH: No, but my helmet's fallen in.

JESSE: Bloody hell, you can't go back to camp with no helmet.

URIAH: Oh boy, am I catching things! This is a shocking establishment. Just look. Snares. Mantraps.

JESSE: Let's pack it in. This isn't an ordinary temple, it's a trap.

URIAH: Temple equals temple. I've got to get my helmet out of there.

JESSE: Can you reach it?

URIAH: No.

JESSE: Perhaps I can get this latch to lift.

POLLY: Don't damage the temple, though.

JESSE: Ow! Ow! Ow!

URIAH: What's up now?

JESSE: Hand's got stuck.

POLLY: Let's call it off.

JESSE *indignantly*: Call it off? I need my hand back.

URIAH: My helmet's in there too.

POLLY: Then we'll have to go through the wall.

JESSE: Ow! Ow! Ow! *He pulls his hand out. It is covered with blood.* They'll have to pay for this hand. I'm not calling it off after that. Give us a ladder, come on!

URIAH: Wait! Hand over your paybooks first. A soldier's paybook must never be damaged. You can replace a man anytime, but a paybook is sacred if anything is.

They hand over their paybooks to him.

POLLY: Polly Baker.

JESSE: Jesse Mahoney.

JIP *crawling up*: Jeraiah Jip.

URIAH: Uriah Shelley. All from the Eighth Regiment. Stationed at Kankerdan, machine-gun section. Shooting will be avoided so that no visible damage is done to the temple. Forward!

Uriah, Jesse and Polly climb into the pagoda.

JIP *calls after them*: I'll mount guard. Then at least I won't have gone in. *The yellow face of Wang, the bonze, appears at a small window above.* How do you do? Are you the honourable owner? Delightful part of the world, this.

URIAH *within*: Hand me your knife, Jesse, so I can force these collection boxes open.

Wang smiles, and Jip smiles too.

JIP *to the bonze*: It is just awful, belonging to a troupe of hippopotamuses like that. *The face disappears.* Come on out. There's a man wandering around upstairs.

Electric bells are heard at intervals within.

URIAH: Watch where you step. What is it, Jip?

JIP: A man upstairs.

URIAH: A man? Everybody out! Hoy!

THE THREE *within, shouting and cursing*: Get your foot out of the way! – Let go! Now I can't move my foot. My boot's gone too – Don't weaken, Polly. Never! – It's my tunic now, Uriah! – What's a tunic? This temple must be wiped out. Now what? – Bloody hell, my trousers are stuck. That's what comes of being in a hurry. That idiot Jip.

JIP: Find anything? Whisky? Rum? Gin? Brandy? Ale?

JESSE: Uriah's ripped his trousers on a bamboo hook, and the boot on Polly's good foot is stuck in a mantrap.

POLLY: And Jesse's tangled up in electric wire.

JIP: That's just what I expected. Next time you go into a building why not use the front door?

Jip goes in through the door. The three climb out above, pale, bleeding and ragged.

POLLY: This calls for vengeance.

URIAH: This temple doesn't fight fair. Filthy, I call it.

POLLY: I want to see blood.

JIP *from within*: Hey!

POLLY *bloodthirstily advances on to the roof, but his boot gets stuck*: Now my other boot's gone.

URIAH: Now I shall shoot the place up.

The three climb down and aim their machine-gun at the pagoda.

POLLY: Fire!

They fire.

JIP *within*: Ow! What are you doing?

The three look up, horrified.

POLLY: Where are you?

JIP *within*: Here. You've gone and shot me through the finger.

JESSE: What the devil are you up to in that rat trap, you fool?

JIP *appearing in the doorway*: I wanted to get the money. Here it is.

URIAH *joyfully*: Trust the biggest rumpot of us all to get it first go off. *Aloud*: Come out of that door at once.

JIP *sticks his head out of the door*: Where did you say?

URIAH: Out of that door at once!

JIP: Oh, what's this?

POLLY: What's up with him?

JIP: Look!

URIAH: Now what?

JIP: My hair! Oh, my hair! I can't go forwards and I can't go back! Oh, my hair! It's stuck fast to something. Uriah, see what's sticking to my hair. Oh, Uriah, get me free! I'm hanging by the hair.

Polly tiptoes over to Jip and looks down at his hair.

POLLY: His hair is stuck to the door frame.

URIAH *shouts*: Your knife, Jesse, so as I can cut him free!

Uriah cuts him free, Jip lurches forward.

POLLY *amused*: And now he's got a bald patch.

They examine Jip's head.

JESSE: A bit of the skin came off too.

URIAH *looks at the two of them, then icily*: A bald patch will give us away.

JESSE *with a venomous look*: A walking 'Wanted' notice!
Uriah, Jesse and Polly confer among themselves.

URIAH: We'll go back to camp and get a pair of scissors, then come back this evening and crop all his hair off so the bald patch can't be seen. *He gives back the paybooks.* Jesse Mahoney!

JESSE *taking his paybook*: Jesse Mahoney!

URIAH: Polly Baker!

POLLY *taking his paybook*: Polly Baker!

URIAH: Jeraiah Jip! *Jip tries to get up.* I'll hold on to yours. *He points to a palanquin in the courtyard.* Sit in that leather box and wait till dark.
Jip crawls into the palanquin. The other three walk off dejectedly shaking their heads. When they have left, Wang the bonze appears in the doorway of the pagoda and takes some of the hair stuck to it which he examines.

3

Country Road between Kilkoa and the Camp

Sergeant Fairchild appears from behind a shed and nails a poster to it.

FAIRCHILD: It is many moons since I, Bloody Five, known also as Tiger of Kilkoa, the Human Typhoon, a sergeant in the British Army, experienced anything as marvellous as this. *Points at the poster.* Pagoda of the Yellow God broken into. Roof of said Pagoda riddled with bullets. What have we in the way of a clue? Four ounces of hair stuck to pitch. If the roof is riddled with bullets then there must be a machine-gun section involved; if there are four ounces of hair at the scene of the crime then there must be a man who is four ounces short. So if there is a machine-gun section containing a man with a bald patch then those are the offenders. It is all plain as a pikestaff. But who is this coming? *He steps behind the shed. The three approach and observe the poster with alarm. Then they go dejectedly on their way. But Fairchild appears from behind the shed and blows a police whistle. They stop.*

FAIRCHILD: Have none of you seen a man with a bald patch?

POLLY: No.

FAIRCHILD: Just look at you. Take your helmets off. Where is your fourth man?

URIAH: Why, Sergeant, he's relieving himself.

FAIRCHILD: Then we'll just wait for him and find out if he has seen a man with a bald patch. *They wait.* He seems to take a lot of relieving.

JESSE: Yes, sergeant.

They go on waiting.

POLLY: Perhaps he went a different way?

FAIRCHILD: It would be better for you, let me tell you, if you had summarily shot one another in your mothers' wombs than if you turn up at my roll call tonight without your fourth man. *Exit.*

POLLY: Let's hope that wasn't our new sergeant. If that rattle-snake is taking tonight's roll-call we might as well line up against the wall straight away.

URIAH: Before they sound the roll-call we'll have to have a fourth man.

POLLY: Here's a man coming now. Let's have a quiet look at him. *They hide behind the shed. Widow Begbick comes down the street. Galy Gay is following her, carrying her basket of cucumbers.*

BEGBICK: What are you moaning about? You're being paid by the hour, aren't you?

GALY GAY: That'll be three hours then.

BEGBICK: You'll get your money. This is a road that hardly anyone uses. A woman might have a hard time resisting a man that wished to embrace her.

GALY GAY: In your profession as a canteen owner always involved with soldiers, who are the worst people in the world, you must know certain holds.

BEGBICK: Ah, sir, you should never say such things to a woman. Certain words put women in a state when their blood gets aroused.

GALY GAY: I am only a simple porter from the harbour.

BEGBICK: It will be roll-call for the new lot in a few minutes. You can hear the drums already. At this hour there's not a soul on the road.

GALY GAY: If it's really as late as all that I'll have to turn around and hurry back to the town of Kilkoa, for I still have a fish to buy.

BEGBICK: Would you mind my asking you, Mr – I hope I've got the name correctly – Galy Gay, whether the profession of porter demands exceptional strength?

GALY GAY: I could never have imagined that unforeseen events would once again delay me for almost four hours from quickly buying a fish and returning home, but I run like an express train once I get started.

BEGBICK: Yes, there is quite a difference between buying a fish to eat and helping a lady to carry her basket. But possibly the lady might be in a position to express her gratitude in a manner that would be more enjoyable than the eating of a fish.

GALY GAY: I must confess I would like to go and buy a fish.

BEGBICK: How can you be such a materialist?

GALY GAY: You know, I am a funny sort of person. Sometimes I know even before I get up: today I want a fish. Or I want a curry. When that happens the world can come to an end, but I just have to get a fish or a curry as the case may be.

BEGBICK: I understand, sir. But isn't it too late? The shops are closed and they are out of fish.

GALY GAY: You see, I am a man with great powers of imagination; I get fed up with a fish, for instance, even before I have set eyes on it. People set out to buy a fish, and first of all they buy that fish and secondly they carry that fish home, and thirdly they cook that fish till it is done, and fourthly they devour that fish, then at night after they have drawn a thick black line under their digestion they are still preoccupied with the same depressing fish, just because they are the sort who have no power of imagination.

BEGBICK: I see, you're only thinking of yourself all the time. *Pause*. Hm. If you are only thinking of yourself I suggest you take your fish money and buy this cucumber, which I will let you have as a favour. The cucumber is worth more, but you can keep the difference in return for carrying my basket.

GALY GAY: But I do not require a cucumber.

BEGBICK: I would never have expected you to humiliate me so.

GALY GAY: It is just that the water for the fish has already been put on.

BEGBICK: I see. Have it your own way. Have it your own way.

GALY GAY: No, no, believe me, I'd be only too glad to oblige you.

BEGBICK: Not another word, talking only makes it worse.

GALY GAY: Far be it from me to disappoint you. If you are still prepared to let me have the cucumber, here is the money.

URIAH *to Jesse and Polly*: That is a man who can't say no.

GALY GAY: Careful, there are soldiers about.

BEGBICK: God knows what they are doing around here at this hour. It is almost time for roll-call. Quick, hand me my basket, why should I go on wasting any more time standing here gossiping with you? But I would be happy to welcome you as a visitor to my beer waggon at the camp, for I am the widow Begbick, and my beer waggon is famous from Hyderabad to Rangoon. *She takes her packages and leaves.*

URIAH: That's our man.

JESSE: Someone who can't say no.

POLLY: And he even has red hair like old Jip.

The three set out.

JESSE: Nice evening tonight.

GALY GAY: Yes, sir.

JESSE: It's a funny thing, sir, but something tells me you come from Kilkoa.

GALY GAY: Kilkoa? Why, yes. That's where my cabin is, so to speak.

JESSE: I'm exceptionally glad to hear that, Mr . . .

GALY GAY: Galy Gay.

JESSE: You've got a cabin there, haven't you?

GALY GAY: Oh, have you met me already, as you know that? Or my wife perhaps?

JESSE: You're called, why yes, you're called . . . half a moment . . . Galy Gay.

GALY GAY: Perfectly true, that's my name.

JESSE: I knew it right away. You see, that's the way I am. For instance, I bet you're married. But why are we standing around like this, Mr Galy Gay? These are my friends Polly and Uriah. Won't you smoke a pipe with us in our canteen?

Pause. Galy Gay looks at them suspiciously.

GALY GAY: Many thanks. Unfortunately my wife is waiting for me in Kilkoa. Besides, I haven't personally got a pipe, absurd as that may seem to you.

JESSE: A cigar then. No, you can't refuse, it's such a nice evening.

GALY GAY: Well, in that case I can't say no.

POLLY: And you shall have your cigar.

Exeunt all four.

4

Canteen of the Widow Leokadja Begbick

Soldiers are singing 'The Song of Widow Begbick's Drinking Truck'.

SOLDIERS:
In Widow Begbick's drinking truck
You smokes and swigs and sleeps your time away.
You buys your beer and tries your luck
From Jubbulpore to Mandalay.
   From Halifax to Hindustan
   Horse, foot and guns, the service man
   Wants what the widow has to sell.
   It's toddy, gum and hi, hi, hi
   Bypassing heaven and skirting hell.
   Shut your big mouth, Tommy, keep your hair on,
     Tommy
   As you slide down Soda Mountain into Whisky Dell.

In Widow Begbick's drinking tank
You always gets the things that you likes best.
That's where the Indian Army drank
When you was drinking at Mummy's breast.
   From Halifax to Hindustan
   Horse, foot and guns, the service man
   Wants what the widow has to sell.
   It's toddy, gum and hi, hi, hi
   Bypassing heaven and skirting hell.
   Shut your big mouth, Tommy, keep your hair on,
     Tommy
   As you slide down Soda Mountain into Whisky Dell.

And when it's war in Cooch Behar
We'll stock ourselves with gum and smokes and beer

And climb on Begbick's drinking car
To show those wogs who's master here.
  From Halifax to Hindustan
  Horse, foot and guns, the service man
  Wants what the widow has to sell.
  It's toddy, gum and hi, hi, hi
  Bypassing heaven and skirting hell.
  Shut your big mouth, Tommy, keep your hair on,
    Tommy
  As you slide down Soda Mountain into Whisky Dell.

BEGBICK *entering*: Good evening, you military gentlemen. I
am the Widow Begbick and this is my beer waggon which
gets hooked on to the great troop trains and goes rolling
over the entire Indian railway system; and because you
can travel and drink beer and sleep in it at one and the same
time it is called 'Widow Begbick's Beer Waggon' and everybody from Hyderabad to Rangoon knows that it has been
a refuge to many an affronted soldier.
In the doorway stand the three soldiers with Galy Gay. They
thrust him back.
URIAH: Is this the Eighth Regiment canteen?
POLLY: Are we addressing the owner of the canteen, the
world-famous Widow Begbick? We are the machine-gun
section of the Eighth Regiment.
BEGBICK: Only three of you? Where is your fourth man?
They enter without answering, pick up two tables and carry them
to the left where they build a kind of partition. The other soldiers
look on in astonishment.
JESSE: What kind of a man is the sergeant?
BEGBICK: Not nice.
POLLY: It is most disagreeable that the sergeant should not
be nice.
BEGBICK: They call him Bloody Five, alias The Tiger of
Kilkoa, the Human Typhoon. He has an unnatural sense
of smell, he can smell criminal activity.

Jesse, Polly and Uriah look at one another.

URIAH: Indeed.

BEGBICK *to her guests*: This is the famous MG section which swung the battle of Hyderabad and is known as The Shower.

SOLDIERS: From now on they're part of our lot. Their crimes are said to follow them like shadows. *A soldier brings in a 'Wanted' notice which he nails up.* And right on their tail comes another of those signs.

The guests have stood up and slowly leave the canteen. Uriah whistles.

GALY GAY *entering*: I've been to this kind of establishment before. Printed menus. They have a whopping one at the Siam Hotel, gold on white. I bought one once. If you've got the right contacts you can get anything. One thing on it is Chicauqua sauce. And that's just a side dish. Chicauqua sauce!

JESSE *pushing Galy Gay towards the partition*: My dear sir, you are in a position to do three poor soldiers in distress a little service with no inconvenience to yourself.

POLLY: Our fourth man has been delayed taking leave of his wife, and if there are not four of us at roll-call we shall all be thrown into the black dungeons of Kilkoa.

URIAH: So it would help if you would put on one of our uniforms. You'd only need to be present when they number off the new arrivals and answer to his name. Just to keep the record straight.

JESSE: That's all.

POLLY: A cigar more or less that you might feel like smoking at our expense would not be worth mentioning.

GALY GAY: It is not that I am reluctant to oblige you, but unfortunately I have to hurry home. I have bought a cucumber for dinner and therefore cannot do exactly as I would like.

JESSE: Thank you. Frankly, it is what I expected of you. That's the point: you cannot do exactly as you would like.

You would like to go home, but you cannot. Thank you, sir, for justifying the confidence we placed in you the instant we set eyes on you. Your hand, sir.

He seizes Galy Gay's hand. Uriah motions him imperiously to go into the corner behind the tables. As soon as he is in the corner all three rush him and undress him except for his shirt.

URIAH: Permit us, for the said purpose, to clothe you in the noble garb of the glorious British Army. *He rings. Begbick appears.* Widow Begbick, can a man speak freely in these parts? We need a complete uniform. *Begbick produces a box and tosses it to Uriah. Uriah throws it to Polly.*

POLLY *to Galy Gay*: Here is the noble garb we purchased for you.

JESSE *showing him the trousers*: Put this garb on, brother Galy Gay.

POLLY *to Begbick*: It's because he lost his uniform.

The three of them dress Galy Gay.

BEGBICK: I see. He lost his uniform.

POLLY: Yes, a Chinese in the bath house managed to abstract our friend Jip's service dress.

BEGBICK: I see: in the bath house?

JESSE: As a matter of fact, Widow Begbick, we're having a bit of a lark.

BEGBICK: I see: a lark?

POLLY: Isn't that right, my dear sir? Isn't it all a bit of a lark?

GALY GAY: Yes, it's a sort of a bit of a – cigar. *He laughs. The three laugh too.*

BEGBICK: How helpless a weak woman is against four such strong men. Let no one ever say the Widow Begbick hindered a man from changing his trousers.

She goes to the rear and writes on a slate: 1 pair of trousers, 1 tunic, 1 pair of puttees etc.

GALY GAY: What's all this about?

JESSE: It's all about nothing, really.

GALY GAY: Won't it be dangerous if it gets found out?

POLLY: Not in the least. And in your case, once equals never.

GALY GAY: True enough. Once equals never. Or so they say.

BEGBICK: That uniform will be five shillings an hour.

POLLY: Sheer bloody extortion, three's the limit.

JESSE *at the window*: Rain clouds are coming up fast. If it rains now the palanquin will get wet, and if the palanquin gets wet they'll take it into the pagoda, and if they take it into the pagoda Jip will be discovered, and if Jip is discovered we're sunk.

GALY GAY: Too small. I'll never get into it.

POLLY: You see, he can't get into it.

GALY GAY: And the boots pinch horribly.

POLLY: Everything's too small. Unusable! Two bob.

URIAH: Shut up, Polly. Four bob because everything's too small and particularly because the boots pinch so. Don't they?

GALY GAY: To the highest degree. They pinch quite particularly.

URIAH: The gentleman isn't such a crybaby as you, you see, Polly.

BEGBICK *comes up to Uriah, leads him to the rear and points at the 'Wanted' sign*: This poster has been up all round the camp for the last hour, stating that a military crime has been perpetrated in this town. The guilty parties have not yet been identified. And if the uniform costs no more than five shillings it's because I'm not having the whole company dragged into this crime.

POLLY: Four shillings is a lot of money.

URIAH *coming forward*: Be quiet, Polly. Ten bob.

BEGBICK: Anything that might besmirch the company's honour can generally be cleaned up in Widow Begbick's Drinking Car.

JESSE: By the way, Widow Begbick, do you think it'll rain?

BEGBICK: To answer that one I'd have to take a look at the sergeant, Bloody Five. It's well known throughout the army that when it rains he gets into the most appalling states of sensuality and is outwardly and inwardly transformed.

JESSE: You see, this lark of ours absolutely depends on its not raining.

BEGBICK: Not a bit of it. Once it starts raining Bloody Five, from being the most dangerous man in the British Army, becomes harmless as a kitten. As soon as he gets one of his fits of sensuality he is blind to everything going on around him.

A SOLDIER *calls into the room*: All out for roll call; it's that pagoda business, there's supposed to be a man missing. So they're calling the roll and checking paybooks.

URIAH: His paybook!

GALY GAY *kneels down and wraps up his old clothes*: I take good care of my things, you see.

URIAH *to Galy Gay*: Here's your paybook. All you have to do is to call out our comrade's name, very clearly and as loud as possible. Nothing to it.

POLLY: And our lost comrade's name is Jeraiah Jip. Jeraiah Jip!

GALY GAY: Jeraiah Jip!

URIAH *to Galy Gay as they walk off*: It's a pleasure to meet well-bred persons who know how to conduct themselves in any situation.

GALY GAY *stops just inside the door*: And what is in it for me?

URIAH: A bottle of beer. Come on.

GALY GAY: Gentlemen, my profession of porter obliges me to look after my own interests in any situation. I was thinking of two boxes of cigars and four or five bottles of beer.

JESSE: But we need you for that roll call.

GALY GAY: Exactly.

POLLY: All right. Two boxes of cigars and three or four bottles of beer.

GALY GAY: Three boxes and five bottles.

JESSE: I don't get it. You just said two boxes.

GALY GAY: If you're going to take that line it will be five boxes and eight bottles.

A bugle call.

URIAH: Time we were out of here.

JESSE: Right. It's a deal if you come along with us straight away.

GALY GAY: Right.

URIAH: And what is your name?

GALY GAY: Jip! Jeraiah Jip!

JESSE: So long as it doesn't rain.

POLLY *comes back; to Begbick*: Widow Begbick, we understand the sergeant becomes very sensual when it rains. And now it's going to rain. See to it that he's blind to whatever goes on around him for the next few hours, or else we risk getting found out. *Exit.*

BEGBICK *looking after them*: That man's not called Jip, I happen to know. That's a porter called Galy Gay from Kilkoa, and at this very instant a man who is by no means a soldier is forming up under the eyes of Bloody Five. *She takes a mirror and goes to the rear*. I'll stand here where Bloody Five is sure to see me, and lure him in.

Second bugle call. Enter Fairchild. Begbick looks at him seductively in the mirror and sits down in a chair.

FAIRCHILD: Don't cast such devouring glances at me, you white-washed Babylon. Things are bad enough already. Three days ago I took to my bunk and began washing in cold water. On Thursday my unbridled sensuality forced me to proclaim a state of siege against myself. It is a particularly disagreeable situation for me since only today I sniffed out a crime virtually without precedent in military history.

BEGBICK:

Follow, o Bloody Five, thine own great nature
Unobserved! For who will learn it?
And in the pit of my arm, in my hair
Learn who thou art. And in the crook of my knee forget

Thy fortuitous name.
Pathetic discipline! Poverty-stricken Order!
Therefore, Bloody Five, I entreat thee come
To me in this night of tepid rainfall
Exactly as thou fearest to: as man
A contradiction. As must-but-don't-want-to.
Come now as man. Just as nature made thee
With no tin hat. Confused and savage and tied up in thyself
And defenceless victim of thy instincts
And helpless slave of thine own strength.
Come, then, as man.

FAIRCHILD: Never. The collapse of Mankind started when
the first of these Zulus left a button undone. The Infantry
Training Manual is a book chock-a-block with weak-
nesses, but it is the one thing a man can fall back on,
because it stiffens the backbone and takes over responsibility towards God. Verily a hole should be dug in the
ground and dynamite put in it so as to blow up the entire
planet; then they might just begin to realise one means
business. It's all plain as a pikestaff. But will you, Bloody
Five, be able to last out this rainy night without the
widow's flesh?

BEGBICK: So when you come to me tonight I want you to
wear a black suit and have a bowler hat on your head.

A VOICE OF COMMAND: Machine-gunners fall in for roll
call!

FAIRCHILD: Now I must sit by this door post so as to keep
an eye on this scum they're counting. *Sits down.*

VOICES OF THREE SOLDIERS *outside*: Polly Baker. – Uriah
Shelley. – Jesse Mahoney.

FAIRCHILD: Ha, and now there will be a slight pause.

GALY GAY'S VOICE *outside*: Jeraiah Jip!

BEGBICK: Correct.

FAIRCHILD: They're up to something again. Insubordination without. Insubordination within. *He stands up and
starts to leave.*

BEGBICK *calls after him*: But let me inform you, Sergeant, that before the black rains of Nepal have fallen for three nights you will take a more lenient view of human failings, for you are perhaps the most sex-ridden individual under the sun. You will hobnob with insubordination, and the desecrators of the temple will gaze deep into your eyes, for your own crimes will be as numberless as the sands of the sea.

FAIRCHILD: Ho, we'd take action in that case, my dear, believe me, we'd take action in exemplary fashion against that insubordinate little Bloody Five. The whole thing's plain as a pikestaff. *Exit.*

FAIRCHILD'S VOICE *outside*: Eight men up to the navel in hot sand for non-regulation haircuts!

Enter Uriah, Jesse and Polly with Galy Gay. Galy Gay steps forward.

URIAH: Scissors, please, Widow Begbick.

GALY GAY *to the audience*: This sort of little favour, man to man, can't do any harm. You scratch my back and I'll scratch yours, that's the idea. Now I'll drink a glass of beer as if it were water and tell myself: you've done these gentlemen a good turn. And all that counts in this world is to take a chance now and then and say 'Jeraiah Jip' the way another man would say 'Good evening', and be the way people want you to be, because it's so easy.

Begbick brings a pair of scissors.

URIAH: Time we looked for Jip.

JESSE: That's a nasty storm blowing up.

The three turn to Galy Gay.

URIAH: I am afraid we're in a great hurry, sir.

JESSE: We've still got to crop a gentleman's hair, you see.

They turn to the door. Galy Gay runs after them.

GALY GAY: Couldn't I help you with that too?

URIAH: No, we have no further need of you, sir. *To Begbick*: Five boxes of cheap cigars and eight bottles of brown ale for this man. *On the way out*: There are some people

who will keep sticking their noses into everything. Give them a finger and they'll have your whole hand.
The three hurry out.

GALY GAY:
Now I could go away, but
Should a man go away when he is sent away?
Perhaps once he has gone
He may be needed again? And can a man go away
When he is needed. Unless it has to be
A man should not go away.
Galy Gay goes to the rear and sits down in a chair by the door. Begbick takes beer bottles and cigar boxes and places them in a circle on the ground in front of Galy Gay.

BEGBICK: Haven't we met somewhere? *Galy Gay shakes his head.* Aren't you the man who carried my basket of cucumbers for me? *Galy Gay shakes his head.* Isn't your name Galy Gay?

GALY GAY: No.
Exit Begbick shaking her head. It grows dark. Galy Gay falls asleep on his chair. Rain falls. Begbick is heard singing to soft music.

BEGBICK:
Often as you may see the river sluggishly flowing
Each time the water is different.
What's gone can't go past again. Not one drop
Ever flows back to its starting point.

5
Interior of the Pagoda of the Yellow God

Wang the bonze and his sacristan

SACRISTAN: It is raining.

WANG: Bring in our leather palanquin out of the rain. *The sacristan goes out.* Now the last of our takings have been stolen. And now the rain is coming in on my head through those bullet holes. *The sacristan drags in the palanquin. Groans from within.* What's that? *He looks inside.* I knew it must be a white man as soon as I saw what a disgusting state the palanquin was in. Oh, he's wearing a uniform. And he's got a bald spot, this thief. They've simply cut his hair off. What shall we do with him? Since he is a soldier he must be without brains. A soldier of his Queen, coated with sicked-up drinks, more helpless than an infant hen, too drunk to recognise his own mother. We can hand him to the police. What's the good of that? Once the money has gone what's the good of justice? And all he can do is grunt. *Furiously*: Heave him out, you cheese-hole, and stuff him in the prayer-box, but make sure his head is on top. Our best answer is to make a god of him. *The sacristan puts Jip into the prayer box.* Get me some paper. We must hang out paper flags at once. We must immediately paint posters for all we are worth. No false economies: I want it to be a big operation, with posters that can't be overlooked. What's the good of a god that doesn't get talked about? *A knock at the door.* Who is calling on me at this hour?

POLLY: Three soldiers.

WANG: Those will be his comrades. *He admits the three.*

POLLY: We are looking for a gentleman, or more specifically a soldier, who is sleeping in a leather box that once stood outside this rich and distinguished temple.

WANG: May his awakening be a pleasant one.

POLLY: That box however has disappeared.

WANG: I understand your impatience, which originates in uncertainty; for I too am looking for some men, about three all told, specifically soldiers, and I cannot find them.

URIAH: That will be extremely difficult. I'd say you might as well give up. But we thought you might know something about that leather box.

WANG: Unhappily not. The unpleasant fact is that all you honourable soldiers wear the same clothes.

JESSE: That is not unpleasant. Inside the said leather box just now is sitting a man who is very ill.

POLLY: Having moreover lost a certain amount of hair through his illness he is in urgent need of help.

URIAH: Might you have seen such a man?

WANG: Unhappily not. I did however find hair such as you mention. But a sergeant in your army took it away with him. He wished to give it back to the honourable soldier. *Jip groans inside the prayer box.*

POLLY: What is that, sir?

WANG: That is my cow who is slumbering.

URIAH: Your cow does not seem to slumber very well.

POLLY: This is the palanquin we stuffed Jip into. Permit us to inspect it.

WANG: It will be best if I tell you the whole truth. It is not the same palanquin.

POLLY: It's as full of sick as a slop pail on the third day of Christmas. Jesse, it's obvious Jip was here.

WANG: He couldn't have been in that, now, could he? Nobody would get into such a filthy palanquin. *Jip groans loudly.*

URIAH: We've got to have our fourth man. Even if it means murdering our own grandmother.

WANG: I fear the man you are looking for is not here. But to make it clear to you that the man who in your opinion is here but of whose presence I have no knowledge is not your man, allow me to explain the entire situation by means of a drawing. Permit your unworthy servant to delineate four criminals by means of chalk. *He draws on the door of the prayer box.*

One of them has a face, so you can see who he is, but three of them have no faces. You cannot recognise them. Now the man with the face has got no money, so he is not a thief. Those with the money however have got no faces, so you cannot know them. Unless they are together, that is. But once they are together the three faceless ones will grow faces, and other people's money will be found on them. You will never make me believe that a man who might be here is your man.

The three threaten him with their weapons, but at a sign from Wang the sacristan appears with Chinese worshippers.

JESSE: We shall not disturb your night's rest any longer, sir. Besides, your tea doesn't agree with us. Your drawing, to be sure, is very clever. Come along.

WANG: It grieves me to see you depart.

URIAH: Do you really believe that when our comrade wakes up, no matter where, wild horses will prevent him from coming back to us?

WANG: Wild horses possibly not, but a small portion of domestic horse, who knows?

URIAH: Once he's shaken the beer out of his head he'll be back. *The three leave amid deep bows.*

JIP *inside the prayer box*: Hey!

Wang draws the attention of the worshippers to his god.

6

The Canteen

Late at night. Galy Gay is sitting in his chair, still asleep. The three soldiers appear in the window.

POLLY: He's still sitting there. Like an Irish mammoth, isn't he?

URIAH: Perhaps he didn't want to leave on account of the rain.

JESSE: Who can say? Anyhow we're going to need him again now.

POLLY: Don't you think that Jip will be back?

JESSE: Uriah, I know that Jip will not be back.

POLLY: We can hardly tell this porter the same old tale again.

JESSE: What do you think, Uriah?

URIAH: I think I'll have a kip.

POLLY: But suppose this porter now gets up and walks out of that door our heads will be hanging by a mere thread.

JESSE: Definitely. But I'm turning in now too. You can't expect too much of a fellow.

POLLY: Perhaps it's best if we all have a kip. It's too depressing and it's really all the fault of the rain.

Exeunt the three.

7

Interior of the Pagoda of the Yellow God

Towards morning. Large posters on all sides. The sound of an old gramophone and of a drum. Religious ceremonies of some importance appear to be going on in the background.

WANG *approaches the prayer box; to the sacristan*: Roll those camel-dung balls quicker, you trash! *Close to the prayer box*: Is the honourable soldier still asleep?

JIP *inside*: Shall we be de-training soon, Jesse? This truck is shaking so dreadfully, and it's as cramped as a water closet.

WANG: Honourable soldier, you must not imagine that you are in a railway truck. If anything is shaking it is the beer in your honourable head.

JIP *inside*: Nonsense. Who's that singing in the gramophone? Can't it stop?

WANG: Come on out, honourable soldier, eat a piece of meat from a cow.

JIP *inside*: Is it all right for me to have a piece of meat, Polly? *He pounds on the sides of the prayer box.*

WANG *running to the rear*: Quiet, you wretches! The god you can hear knocking on the walls of the holy prayer box is asking for five taels. Grace is being shown unto you. Take a collection, Mah Sing.

JIP *inside*: Uriah, Uriah, where am I?

WANG: Knock a little more, honourable soldier, on the other wall, honourable general, with both your feet, emphatically.

JIP *inside*: Hey, what is this? Where am I? Where are you? Uriah, Jesse, Polly!

WANG: Your grovelling servant is desirous of knowing what food and strong drinks the honourable soldier wishes to call for.

JIP *inside*: Hey, who's that? What is that voice that sounds like a fat rat talking?

WANG: That moderately fat rat, colonel, is your friend Wang from Tientsin.

JIP *inside*: What town am I in now?

WANG: A wretched town, exalted patron, a hole known as Kilkoa.

JIP *inside*: Let me out!

WANG *to the rear*: When you have finished rolling the camel dung into balls, lay them out on a dish, beat the drum and light them. *To Jip*: At once, honourable soldier, if only you promise not to run away.

JIP *inside*: Open up, you voice of a muskrat, open up, do you hear!

WANG: Wait, wait, ye faithful! Stay where you are for just one instant. The god will speak to you in three thunderclaps. Count them carefully. Four, no, five. Too bad: he only wishes you to sacrifice five taels. *Taps on the prayerbox; in a friendly tone*: Honourable soldier, here is a beefsteak for your mouth.

JIP *inside*: Oh, now I feel it, my insides are utterly corroded. I must have rinsed them in pure alcohol. Oh, it may be that I have had too much to drink and now I am having to eat the same amount.

WANG: You may eat a whole cow, honourable soldier, and a beefsteak already awaits you. But I fear you will run away, honourable soldier. Do you promise me that you will not run away?

JIP *inside*: Let's have a look at it first. *Wang lets him out.* How did I get here?

WANG: Through the air, honourable general. You came through the air.

JIP: Where was I when you found me?

WANG: Deigning to rest in an old palanquin, Exalted One.

JIP: And where are my comrades? Where is the Eighth Regiment? Where is our machine-gun section? Where are those twelve troop trains and four elephant parks? Where is the whole British Army? Where have they all gone, you grinning yellow spittoon?

WANG: Somewhere beyond the Punjab Mountains a month ago. But here is a beefsteak.

JIP: What? And me? Where was I? What was I doing when they were moving off?

WANG: Beer, much beer, one thousand bottles, and making money too.

JIP: Didn't people come asking for me?

WANG: Unfortunately not.

JIP: That is disagreeable.

WANG: But if they should come now, looking for a man in the uniform of a white soldier, should I bring them to you, honourable Minister of War?

JIP: That is not necessary.

WANG: If you don't want to be disturbed, Johnny, just step into this box, Johnny, in case anyone comes who offends your eye.

JIP: Where's that beefsteak? *Sits down and eats.* It's far too small. What is that ghastly noise?
To the sound of drumming the smoke from the camel-dung balls rises to the ceiling.

WANG: That is the prayers of the faithful who are down on their knees back there.

JIP: It's from a tough part of the cow. Who are they praying to?

WANG: That is their secret.

JIP *eating more quickly*: This is a good beefsteak, but it is wrong that I should be sitting here. Polly and Jesse are sure to have waited for me. They may still be waiting. It's as soft as butter. It is bad of me to be eating. I can hear Polly telling Jesse: Jip will definitely be back. As soon as he's sobered up, Jip will be back. Uriah may not exactly burst himself waiting, because Uriah is a bad man, but Jesse and Polly will say: Jip will be back. No question but this is an appropriate meal for me after all that liquor. If only Jesse didn't have such blind faith in his old friend Jip; but as it is he's saying: Jip won't let us down, and of course that's hard for me to bear. It's all wrong that I should be sitting here, but this is good meat.

8

The Canteen

Early morning. Galy Gay is still asleep in his chair. The three are eating breakfast.

POLLY: Jip will be back.

JESSE: Jip won't let us down.

POLLY: As soon as he's sobered up, Jip will be back.

URIAH: You never can tell. Anyway we won't let this porter out of our hands so long as Jip is still out on the tiles.

JESSE: He never left.

POLLY: He must be frozen stiff. He spent the whole night on that wooden chair.

URIAH: But we had a good night's sleep and are in fine shape again.

POLLY: And Jip will be back. That much is clear to my sound, well-rested military mind. As soon as Jip wakes up he'll want his beer, and then Jip will be back.

Enter Wang. He goes to the bar and rings. Enter Widow Begbick.

BEGBICK: I'm not serving native undesirables, nor yellow ones neither.

WANG: For a white man: ten bottles of good light beer.

BEGBICK: For a white man ten bottles of light beer. *She gives him the ten bottles.*

WANG: Yes, for a white man. *Exit Wang, bowing to all. Jesse, Polly and Uriah exchange looks.*

URIAH: Jip won't be back now. We must take some beer on board. Widow Begbick, in future you will keep twenty beers and ten whiskies permanently at action stations. *Begbick pours beer and goes out. The three drink and observe the sleeping Galy Gay.*

POLLY: But how do we manage it, Uriah? All we have is Jip's paybook.

URIAH: That's enough. That'll give us a new Jip. People are taken much too seriously. One equals no one. Anything less than two hundred at a time is not worth mentioning. Of course anybody can be of a different opinion. An opinion is of no consequence whatever. Any level-headed man can level-headedly adopt two or three different opinions.

JESSE: They can stuff their 'personalities'.

POLLY: But what's he going to say if we turn him into Private Jeraiah Jip?

URIAH: His kind change of their own accord, you know. Throw him into a pond, and two days later he'll have webs growing between his fingers. That's because he's got nothing to lose.

JESSE: Never mind what he says, we've got to have a fourth man. Wake him up.

POLLY *wakes Galy Gay*: Dear sir, what a piece of luck that you didn't leave. Circumstances have arisen which prevented our friend Jeraiah Jip from reporting here on time.

URIAH: Are you of Irish extraction?

GALY GAY: I think so.

URIAH: That is a help. I trust you are not over forty, Mr Galy Gay?

GALY GAY: I am not as old as that.

URIAH: Brilliant. Have you by any chance got flat feet?

GALY GAY: Somewhat.

URIAH: That settles it. Your fortune is made. For the time being you can remain here.

GALY GAY: Unhappily my wife is expecting me in connection with a fish.

POLLY: We understand your hesitations: they are honourable and worthy of an Irishman. But we like your appearance.

JESSE: And what's more, it fits the bill. There may perhaps be an opening for you to become a soldier.

Galy Gay is silent.

URIAH: The soldier's life is extremely pleasant. Every week they give us a handful of money and all we have to do in

return is to foot it round India gazing at these highways
and pagodas. Kindly take a look at the comfortable leather
sleeping bags that are issued to a soldier free of charge.
Cast your eye on this rifle bearing the trademark of the
firm of Everett and Co. Mostly we amuse ourselves fishing,
with tackle bought for us by Mum, as we laughingly call
the army, while a number of military bands take it in turn
to provide music. For the remainder of the day you smoke
in your bungalow or idly observe the golden palaces of one
of those Rajahs, whom you may also shoot if you feel so
inclined. The ladies expect a great deal from us soldiers,
but never money, and that, you must admit, is yet another
attraction. *Galy Gay is silent.*

POLLY: The soldier's life in wartime is particularly pleasant.
Only in battle does a man attain his full stature. Do you
realise that you are living in momentous times? Before
each infantry attack the soldier is given a large glass of
spirits free of charge, after which his courage is boundless,
positively boundless.

GALY GAY: I realise that the soldier's life is a pleasant
one.

URIAH: Definitely. So this means you can keep your military
uniform with its pretty brass buttons and have a right to be
called Mr at any moment: Mr Jip.

GALY GAY: You cannot wish to cause unhappiness to a poor
porter.

JESSE: Why not?

URIAH: You mean you want to leave?

GALY GAY: Yes, I am leaving now.

JESSE: Polly, go and get his clothes.

POLLY *with the clothes*: What's the reason for your not wanting
to be Jip, then?
Fairchild appears at the window.

GALY GAY: The fact that I am Galy Gay. *He goes to the door.*
The three look at one another.

URIAH: Just wait a minute longer.

POLLY: Have you ever heard the saying: More haste, less speed?

URIAH: You are up against the sort of men who don't like accepting free gifts from strangers.

JESSE: Whatever your name is, you should get something for having been so obliging.

URIAH: It all boils down – all right, keep your hand on the doorknob – to a bit of business.

Galy Gay stops short.

JESSE: This bit of business is as good as anything Kilkoa has to offer, aren't I right, Polly? You know, if we could manage to get our hands on that . . .

URIAH: It is our duty to offer you a chance to get in on this stupendous bit of business.

GALY GAY: Business? Did I hear you say business?

URIAH: Possibly. But you've no time for that, have you?

GALY GAY: There's having time and having time.

POLLY: Oh, you'd have time all right. If you knew what this bit of business was you'd have time all right. After all, Lord Kitchener had time to conquer Egypt.

GALY GAY: I should think so. You mean it's a big bit of business?

POLLY: For the Maharajah of Peshawar it might be. But it might not be all that big perhaps for a big man like you.

GALY GAY: What would I have to contribute in this bit of business?

JESSE: Nothing.

POLLY: At the most you might have to sacrifice your moustache, which could possibly provoke undesirable notoriety.

GALY GAY: I see. *He takes his things and starts for the door.*

POLLY: What an utter elephant!

GALY GAY: Elephant? Elephants are a goldmine of course. If you've got an elephant you'll never end up in the work-house. *Excitedly takes a chair and sits down in the centre of the group.*

URIAH: Elephant? You bet we've got an elephant.

GALY GAY: Would your elephant be such as to be instantly available?

POLLY: An elephant! That's something he seems extremely keen on.

GALY GAY: So you have an elephant available?

POLLY: Who ever heard of a bit of business involving an unavailable elephant?

GALY GAY: Well, in that case, Mr Polly, I too would be glad to get my cut of this.

URIAH *hesitantly*: The only trouble is the Devil of Kilkoa.

GALY GAY: The devil of Kilkoa, what's that?

POLLY: Speak quieter. You're speaking the name of the Human Typhoon, Bloody Five, our sergeant.

GALY GAY: What does he do to get such names?

POLLY: Oh, nothing. Occasionally when a man gives the wrong name at roll call he bundles him up in six feet of canvas and dumps him in among the elephants.

GALY GAY: So you need a man with a head on his shoulders.

URIAH: You have that head, Mr Galy Gay.

POLLY: A head like that has something in it.

GALY GAY: Nothing to speak of. But I do know a riddle that might be of interest to educated persons like yourselves.

JESSE: You are in fact surrounded by expert riddle-guessers.

GALY GAY: It goes like this: what's white, is a mammal, and can see as well behind as in front?

JESSE: That's a hard one.

GALY GAY: You'll never guess this riddle. I couldn't guess it myself. A mammal. White. Sees as well behind as in front. A blind white horse.

URIAH: It's a prodigious riddle.

POLLY: And you just keep all that in your head?

GALY GAY: As a rule, because I'm no good at writing. But I fancy I'm the right man for any bit of business.

The three go to the bar. Galy Gay takes a box of his cigars and hands it round.

URIAH: Matches!

GALY GAY *while lighting their cigars*: Gentlemen, permit me to prove to you that you have selected no bad associate for your bit of business. Do you happen to have some heavy objects handy?

JESSE *points to some weights and clubs lying along the wall by the door*: There you are.

GALY GAY *taking the heaviest weight and lifting it*: I'm a member of the Kilkoa Wrestling Club, you see.

URIAH *handing him a bottle of beer*: Anyone can tell that from the way you behave.

GALY GAY *drinking*: Yes, we wrestlers have our own way of behaving. There are certain rules. For instance, when a wrestler comes into a room full of people, he hoists his shoulders on entering, raises his arms to shoulder height, then lets them dangle and saunters into the room. *He drinks*. Join up with me and you can rob a bank.

FAIRCHILD *enters*: There's a woman out here who is looking for an individual called Galy Gray.

GALY GAY: Galy Gay! Galy Gay's the name of the individual she's looking for.

Fairchild looks at him for a moment, then fetches Mrs Galy Gay.

GALY GAY *to the three*: Don't worry, she's a gentle soul, being as how she's from a province where nearly everyone is friendly. You can rely on me. Galy Gay has tasted blood.

FAIRCHILD: Come in, Mrs Gray. There's a man here who knows your husband. *He comes back with Galy Gay's wife.*

MRS GALY GAY: Excuse a humble woman, gentlemen, and pardon the way I am dressed, I was in such a hurry. Ah, there you are, Galy Gay. But are you really you in that army uniform?

GALY GAY: No.

MRS GALY GAY: I can't make you out. How do you come to be in uniform? It doesn't suit you a bit, ask anybody. You're a strange man, Galy Gay.

URIAH: She isn't right in the head.

MRS GALY GAY: It's not easy being married to someone who cannot say no.

GALY GAY: I wonder who she's talking to.

URIAH: Sounds like insults to me.

FAIRCHILD: In my opinion Mrs Gray is extremely lucid in the head. Please go on talking, Mrs Gray. Your voice is more grateful to my ears than a coloratura soprano.

MRS GALY GAY: I don't know what you're up to this time with your big ideas, but you'll come to no good end. Come along now. Why don't you say something? Have you got a sore throat?

GALY GAY: I do believe you are addressing all that to me. You've mistaken me for someone else, let me tell you, and what you're saying about him is stupid and tactless.

MRS GALY GAY: What's that? Mistaken you? Have you been drinking? He can't stand drink, you see.

GALY GAY: I'm no more your Galy Gay than I'm the Army Commander.

MRS GALY GAY: I put the water on around this time yesterday, but you never brought the fish.

GALY GAY: What's this about a fish? You are talking as if you had lost your wits, and in front of all these gentlemen too!

FAIRCHILD: This is a most remarkable case. It conjures up such frightful thoughts that cold shivers go running down my spine. Does any of you know this woman? *The three shake their heads*. How about you?

GALY GAY: I've seen many things in my life, from Ireland to Kilkoa, but I never before set eyes on this woman.

FAIRCHILD: Tell the woman your name.

GALY GAY: Jeraiah Jip.

MRS GALY GAY: This is the limit! All the same, sergeant, now I come to look at him I almost get the feeling that he is somehow different from my husband Galy Gay the porter, somehow different though I couldn't put my finger on it.

FAIRCHILD: We'll soon put our finger on it, never you mind. *He goes out with Mrs Galy Gay.*

GALY GAY *dances to the centre of the stage, singing*:

> O moon of Alabama
> You must go under soon!
> Our dear old good old mamma
> Would like a brand-new moon.

He goes up to Jesse beaming. All over Ireland the Galy Gays are famous for banging the nail home in any situation.

URIAH *to Polly*: Before the sun has set seven times this man must be another man.

POLLY: Can it really be done, Uriah? Changing one man into another?

URIAH: Yes, one man is like the other. Man equals man.

POLLY: But Uriah, the army can move off any minute, you know.

URIAH: Of course the army can move off any minute. But you can see this canteen is still here, can't you? Don't you realise that the gunners are still holding race meetings? Let me tell you that God would never agree to ruin our sort by getting the army on the move this very day. He'd certainly think twice about that.

POLLY: Listen.

Drums and bugles give the signal for departure. The three fall in and stand to attention.

FAIRCHILD *offstage, shouting*: The Army will move to the northern frontiers! Starting time zero two one zero hours tonight!

Interlude

Spoken by the Widow Leokadja Begbick.

> Herr Bertolt Brecht maintains man equals man
> – A view that has been around since time began.
> But then Herr Brecht points out how far one can
> Manoeuvre and manipulate that man.
> Tonight you are going to see a man reassembled like a car
> Leaving all his individual components just as they are.
> He has some kind friends by whom he is pressed
> Entirely in his own interest
> To conform with this world and its twists and turns
> And give up pursuing his own fishy concerns.
> So whatever the purpose of his various transformations
> He always lives up to his friends' expectations.
> Indeed if we people were to let him out of our sight
> They could easily make a butcher of him overnight.
> Herr Bertolt Brecht hopes you'll feel the ground on which
>   you stand
> Slither between your toes like shifting sand
> So that the case of Galy Gay the porter makes you aware
> Life on this earth is a hazardous affair.

9
The Canteen

The sounds of an army breaking camp. A loud voice is heard from backstage.

THE VOICE: War has broken out as predicted. The Army will move to the northern frontier. The Queen calls on her

troops to take their guns and elephants and board the
trains, and orders those trains to head for the northern
frontier. Your General therefore commands you to be seated
in those trains before the moon is up.

Widow Begbick sits behind her bar, smoking.

BEGBICK:

In Yehoo, the city that is always crowded and
Where no one stays, they sing
A song of the Flow of Things
Which starts with:

She sings:

Don't try to hold on to the wave
That's breaking against your foot: so long as
You stand in the stream fresh waves
Will always keep breaking against it.

*She stands up, takes a stick and starts pushing back the canvas
awnings.*

I was seven years in one place, had a roof over
My head
And was not alone.
But the man who kept me fed and who was unlike anyone
   else
One day
Lay unrecognisable beneath a dead man's shroud.
All the same that evening I ate my supper
And soon I let off the room in which we had
Embraced one another
And the room kept me fed
And now that it no longer feeds me
I continue to eat.
I said:

Sings:

> Don't try to hold on to the wave
> That's breaking against your foot: so long as
> You stand in the stream fresh waves
> Will always keep breaking against it.

She sits down at the bar again. The three enter with several other soldiers.

URIAH *in the centre*: My friends, war has broken out. The period of disorder is over. So no more allowances can be made for private inclinations. Galy Gay, the porter from Kilkoa, has accordingly to be transformed in double quick time into the soldier Jeraiah Jip. To this end we shall get him involved in a bit of business, as is normal in our day and age, which will mean constructing an artificial elephant. Polly, take this pole and the elephant's head that's hanging on that wall, while you, Jesse, take this bottle and pour it whenever Galy Gay wants to check if the elephant can make water. And I shall spread this map over the two of you. *They build an artificial elephant.* We'll present him with this elephant and bring along a buyer, and then if he sells the elephant we'll arrest him and say: How do you come to be selling a WD elephant? At that point he will surely think it better to be Jeraiah Jip, a soldier proceeding to the northern frontier, than Galy Gay, a criminal with some chance of actually being shot.

A SOLDIER: Do you people really imagine he's going to take that thing for an elephant?

JESSE: Is it all that bad?

URIAH: He'll take it for an elephant all right, let me tell you. He'd take this beer bottle for an elephant if somebody points at it and says: I want to buy that elephant.

SOLDIER: Then you need a buyer.

URIAH *calling out*: Widow Begbick! *Begbick steps forward.* Will you play the buyer?

BEGBICK: Yes, because my beer waggon is going to get left behind unless somebody helps me to pack it up.

URIAH: Just tell the man who's about to come in that you want to buy this elephant, then we'll help pack up your canteen. And you must pay cash.

BEGBICK: Right. *She goes back to her place.*

GALY GAY *enters*: Has the elephant arrived?

URIAH: Mr Gay, your bit of business is under way. It concerns the unregistered army surplus elephant Billy Humph. The deal consists in auctioning him off unobtrusively – only to private bidders of course.

GALY GAY: That is entirely clear. Who is auctioning him off?

URIAH: Someone who signs as owner.

GALY GAY: Who is to sign as owner?

URIAH: Would you care to sign as owner, Mr Gay?

GALY GAY: Have we a buyer?

URIAH: Yes.

GALY GAY: My name, of course, must not be mentioned.

URIAH: Right. Would you care to smoke a cigar?

GALY GAY *suspiciously*: Why?

URIAH: Just to keep you from worrying, as the elephant has a slight cold.

GALY GAY: Where is the buyer?

BEGBICK *comes forward*: Oh, Mr Galy Gay, I am looking for an elephant. Would you have one, by any chance?

GALY GAY: Widow Begbick, I might have one for you.

BEGBICK: But first of all take my wall down, the gunners will soon be here.

THE SOLDIERS: Yes, Widow Begbick.

The soldiers take down one wall of the canteen. The elephant is dimly visible.

JESSE *to Begbick*: I tell you, Widow Begbick, if you take the long view what is happening here is an historic event. For what is happening here? Personality itself is being put

under the microscope, we are getting under the skin of the
colourful character. Steps are being taken. Technology
intervenes. At the lathe or at the conveyor belt great men
and little men are the same, even in stature. Personality!
Remember that the ancient Assyrians, Widow Begbick,
depicted personality as a tree branching out. Like this,
branching out! After which, Widow Begbick, it branches
in again. How does Copernicus put it? What turns? The
earth turns. The earth, in other words the human race.
According to Copernicus. I.e., man is not in the centre.
Take a look at him, now. Is that what is supposed to stand
in the centre? It's antediluvian. Man is nothing. Modern
science has proved that everything is relative. What does
that mean? Table, bench, water, shoehorn – all relative.
You, Widow Begbick, me – relative. Look into my eyes,
Widow Begbick, it's an historic moment. Man is in the
centre, but only relatively speaking. *Both go off.*

No. I

URIAH *calls out*: Number One: The Elephant Deal. The
MG section transfers an elephant to the man whose name
must not be mentioned.

GALY GAY: One more swig from the cherry brandy bottle,
one more puff at the Corona Corona, then the plunge into
life.

URIAH *introduces the elephant to Galy Gay*: Billy Humph, champion of Bengal, elephant in Her Majesty's service.

GALY GAY *sees the elephant and is alarmed*: Is this the WD
elephant?

A SOLDIER: He's got a bad cold, as you can see from his
scarf.

GALY GAY *worried, walks round the elephant*: His scarf isn't the
worst thing about him.

BEGBICK: I am the buyer. *She points to the elephant.* Sell me that elephant.

GALY GAY: Do you truly want to buy this elephant?

BEGBICK: It makes no difference how big or small he is; it's just that I've wanted to buy an elephant ever since I was a child.

GALY GAY: Is he truly what you imagined?

BEGBICK: When I was a child I wanted an elephant as big as the Hindu Kush, but today this one will do.

GALY GAY: Well, Widow Begbick, if you truly wish to buy this elephant I am the owner.

A SOLDIER *comes running from the rear*: Psst . . . psst . . . Bloody Five is going round the camp checking all railway trucks.

THE SOLDIERS: The Human Typhoon!

BEGBICK: Stay here; nobody's taking this elephant off me. *Begbick and the soldiers hurry off.*

URIAH *to Galy Gay*: Look after the elephant for a moment, will you? *Hands him the rope.*

GALY GAY: But what about me, Mr Uriah, where am I supposed to go?

URIAH: Just stay there. *He runs off after the other soldiers. Galy Gay holds the rope by the extreme end.*

GALY GAY *alone*: My mother used to say: No one knows anything for sure. But you know nothing whatsoever. This morning, Galy Gay, you went out to buy a small fish and now you have got a large elephant, and nobody knows what will happen tomorrow. It's no concern of yours so long as you get your cheque.

URIAH *looks in*: So help me, he's not even looking at the elephant. He's keeping as far from it as he can. *Fairchild is seen passing by in the background.* The Tiger of Kilkoa was just passing by.

Uriah, Begbick and the rest of the soldiers reappear.

No. II

URIAH *calls out*: And now for Number Two: the Elephant Auction. The man whose name must not be mentioned sells the elephant.

Galy Gay fetches a bell; Begbick puts a wooden bucket upside down in mid-stage.

A SOLDIER: Got any more doubts about that elephant, mate?

GALY GAY: As somebody is buying him I have no doubts.

URIAH: That's it: if somebody is buying him he must be all right.

GALY GAY: I can't say no to that. Elephant equals elephant, particularly when he is being bought.

He mounts the bucket to auction off the elephant, who is standing beside him in the centre of the group.

GALY GAY: Let's get on with the sale. I hereby invite bids for Billy Humph, the champion of Bengal. He was born, as sure as you see him standing here, in the southern Punjab. Seven Rajahs stood by his cradle. His mother was white. He is sixty-five years old. That's no great age. Thirteen hundredweight, he weighs, and a forest that has to be cleared is to him like a blade of grass in the wind. Billy Humph, as you see him now, represents a small goldmine for his eventual possessor.

URIAH: And here comes Widow Begbick with the cheque.

BEGBICK: Does this elephant belong to you?

GALY GAY: Like my own foot.

A SOLDIER: Billy must be pretty old, to judge from his uncommonly stiff deportment.

BEGBICK: So you will have to bring the price down a little.

GALY GAY: His cost was two hundred rupees ex works, and he will be worth that until he goes to his grave.

BEGBICK *examines him*: Two hundred rupees with a belly sagging like that?

GALY GAY: In my view he is nevertheless the thing for a widow.

BEGBICK: Very well. But is he in good health? *Billy Humph makes water.* That will do. I see that he is a healthy elephant. Five hundred rupees.

GALY GAY: Five hundred rupees. Going, going, gone at five hundred rupees. Widow Begbick, you will take over this elephant from me as its previous owner, and settle by cheque.

BEGBICK: Your name?

GALY GAY: Is not to be mentioned.

BEGBICK: Kindly lend me a pencil, Mr Uriah, so that I may make out a cheque to this gentleman who wishes his name not to be mentioned.

URIAH *aside to the soldiers*: Arrest him when he takes the cheque.

BEGBICK: Here is your cheque, man whose name is not to be mentioned.

GALY GAY: And here, Widow Begbick, is your elephant.

A SOLDIER *laying his hand on Galy Gay's shoulder*: In the name of the British Army, what are you up to?

GALY GAY: Me? Nothing. *He laughs foolishly.*

THE SOLDIER: What is that elephant you have got there?

GALY GAY: Which elephant do you mean?

THE SOLDIER: The one behind you, broadly speaking. No prevaricating, now.

GALY GAY: I know not the elephant.

SOLDIERS: Cor!

A SOLDIER: We can testify that this gentleman said the elephant belonged to him.

BEGBICK: He said it belonged to him like his own foot.

GALY GAY *starts to go*: Unfortunately I have to go as my wife is expecting me urgently. *He forces his way through the group.* I'll be back to discuss the matter with you. Good night. *To Billy, who is following him*: You stay here, Billy, don't be so pig-headed. That's sugar cane growing over there.

URIAH: Halt! Cover that criminal with your service pistols, yes, a criminal, that's what he is.

Polly, inside Billy Humph, laughs loudly. Uriah hits him.

URIAH: Shut up, Polly!

The front canvas slips, leaving Polly visible.

POLLY: Damnation!

Galy Gay, now utterly bewildered, looks at Polly. Then he looks from one to the other. The elephant runs away.

BEGBICK: What is going on? That's no elephant, it's just men and tarpaulin. The whole thing's phoney. Such a phoney elephant for my genuine money!

URIAH: Widow Begbick, the criminal will forthwith be bound with cords and flung into the latrine.

The soldiers bind Galy Gay and put him into a pit so that only his head is visible. The artillery is heard rolling by.

BEGBICK: The gunners are loading up. When are you lot going to pack my canteen? You know, it is not just your man that has got to be dismantled but my canteen too.

All the soldiers begin packing up the canteen. Before they have finished Uriah chases them away. Begbick comes forward with a basket loaded with dirty tarpaulins, kneels beside a small trapdoor and washes them. Galy Gay listens to her song.

In this way I too had a name
And those who heard that name in the city said 'It's a
    good name'
But one night I drank four glasses of schnapps
And one morning I found chalked on my door
A bad word.
Then the milkman took back my milk again.
My name was finished.
Like linen that once was white and gets dirty
And can go white once more if you wash it
But hold it up to the light, and look: it's not
The same linen.
So don't speak your name so distinctly. What is the point?

Considering that you are always using it to name a differ-
ent person.
And wherefore such loud opinions, forget them.
What were they, did you say? Never remember
Anything longer than its own duration.

She sings:

Don't try to hold on to the wave
That's breaking against your foot: so long as
You stand in the stream fresh waves
Will always keep breaking against it.

She goes off. Uriah and the soldiers come in from the rear.

No. III

URIAH *calls out*: And now comes Number Three: the Trial
of the Man Whose Name is Not to be Mentioned. Form a
circle round the criminal and interrogate him and do not
stop until you know the naked truth.

GALY GAY: May I have permission to say something?

URIAH: You have said a lot tonight, mister. Does anyone
know what the man was called who put the elephant up for
auction?

A SOLDIER: He was called Galy Gay.

URIAH: Can anyone testify to that?

THE SOLDIERS: We can testify to that.

URIAH: What has the accused got to say on that point?

GALY GAY: He was someone whose name was not to be mentioned.

The soldiers grumble.

A SOLDIER: I heard him say he was Galy Gay.

URIAH: Isn't that you?

GALY GAY *slyly*: Well, supposing I were Galy Gay, perhaps I might be the man you are looking for.

URIAH: Then you are not Galy Gay?

GALY GAY *under his breath*: No, I am not.

URIAH: And perhaps you were not even present when Billy Humph was put up for auction?

GALY GAY: No, I was not present.

URIAH: But you saw that it was someone called Galy Gay who conducted the sale?

GALY GAY: Yes, I can testify to that.

URIAH: So now you are saying that you were present after all?

GALY GAY: I can testify to that.

URIAH: Did you all hear? Do you see the moon? The moon has risen, and here he is up to his neck in this crooked elephant business. As for Billy Humph, wasn't there something a bit wrong with him?

JESSE: There certainly was.

A SOLDIER: The man called it an elephant, but it was nothing of the sort, just made of paper.

URIAH: In other words he was selling a phoney elephant. Which of course carries the death penalty. What have you to say to that?

GALY GAY: Perhaps another elephant might not have taken him for an elephant. It is very hard to keep all this straight, your Honour.

URIAH: Indeed it is extremely complicated, but I think you will have to be shot none the less, because your behaviour has been highly suspicious. *Galy Gay is silent.* Come to think of it, I have heard of a soldier by the name of Jip who even answered to that name at sundry roll calls, while trying to make people think his name was Galy Gay. Are you by any chance the Jip in question?

GALY GAY: No, certainly not.

URIAH: So you are not called Jip? Then what is your name? No answer? Then you are a man whose name is not to be mentioned. Are you by any chance the man at the elephant auction whose name was not to be mentioned? What? Again no answer? That is immensely suspicious, almost enough to get you convicted. What is more, the criminal who sold the elephant is said to have been a man with a moustache, and you have got a moustache. Come on, men, all this calls for discussion. *He goes to the rear with the soldiers. Two of them stay with Galy Gay.*

URIAH *as he leaves*: Now he doesn't want to be Galy Gay any more.

GALY GAY *after a pause*: Can you two hear what they are saying?

A SOLDIER: No.

GALY GAY: Are they saying that I am this Galy Gay?

SECOND SOLDIER: They are saying it's no longer all that certain.

GALY GAY: Better remember: one man equals no man.

SECOND SOLDIER: Anybody know who this war's against?

FIRST SOLDIER: If they need cotton it'll be Tibet, and if they need wool it'll be Pamir.

JESSE *arriving*: Surely that's Galy Gay sitting tied up here?

FIRST SOLDIER: Hey, you, answer him.

GALY GAY: I think you're mistaking me for someone else, Jesse. Take a good look at me.

JESSE: Ha, aren't you Galy Gay? *Galy Gay shakes his head.* Leave us for a moment; he has just been sentenced to death, so I have to speak to him.
The two soldiers go to the rear.

GALY GAY: Has it come to that? Oh, Jesse, help me, you are a great soldier.

JESSE: How did it happen?

GALY GAY: Well, Jesse, it's like this: I don't know. There we were, smoking and drinking, and I talked my soul away.

JESSE: I heard them say it's someone called Galy Gay who's supposed to be killed.

GALY GAY: Out of the question.

JESSE: Ha, aren't you Galy Gay?

GALY GAY: Wipe the sweat from my face, Jesse.

JESSE *does so*: Look me straight in the eye, I'm your friend Jesse. Aren't you Galy Gay from Kilkoa?

GALY GAY: No, you must have got it wrong.

JESSE: There were four of us when we left Kankerdan. Were you with us then?

GALY GAY: Yes, at Kankerdan I was with you.

JESSE *goes to the rear to the other soldiers*: The moon is not yet up, and he is already wanting to be Jip.

URIAH: All the same, I think we'd better put a little more fear of death into him.

The artillery is heard rolling by.

BEGBICK *enters*: That's the gunners, Uriah. Help me fold up the awnings. And the rest of you, carry on taking it down. *The soldiers go on loading sections of the canteen into the waggon. Just one plank wall remains standing. Uriah and Begbick fold the tarpaulins.*

I spoke to many people and listened
Carefully and heard many opinions
And heard many say of many things: 'That is for sure'.
But when they came back they spoke differently from the
   way they spoke earlier
And it was something else of which they said: 'That is for
   sure'.
At that I told myself: of all sure things
The surest is doubt.

Uriah goes to the rear. So does Begbick with her laundry basket, passing Galy Gay. She sings:

Don't try to hold on to the wave
That's breaking against your foot: so long as
You stand in the stream fresh waves
Will always keep breaking against it.

GALY GAY: Widow Begbick, may I ask you to get a pair of scissors and cut my moustache off?

BEGBICK: What for?

GALY GAY: I know what for all right.

Begbick cuts off his moustache, wraps it in a cloth and takes it to the waggon. The soldiers reappear.

No. IV

URIAH *calls out*: And now for Number Four: the Execution of Galy Gay in the military cantoment at Kilkoa.

BEGBICK *comes up to him*: Mr Uriah, I have something for you here. *She whispers something in his ear and gives him the cloth with the moustache in it.*

URIAH *goes to the latrine pit where Galy Gay is*: Has the accused man anything further to say?

GALY GAY: Your Honour, they tell me the criminal who sold the elephant was a man with a moustache, and I have no moustache.

URIAH *silently showing him the open cloth with the moustache*: And what is this? You've really convicted yourself this time, my man, because cutting off that moustache of yours just shows your guilty conscience. Come now, man without a name, and hear the verdict of the Kilkoa court-martial which says that you are to be shot by a firing squad of five. *The soldiers drag Galy Gay out of the latrine pit.*

GALY GAY *shouting*: You can't do that to me.

URIAH: You'll find that we can, though. Listen carefully, my man: first because you stole and sold a WD elephant – which is theft –, secondly because you sold an elephant which was no elephant – which is fraud –, and thirdly because you are unable to produce any kind of name or identity document and may well be a spy – which is high treason.

GALY GAY: Oh, Uriah, why are you treating me like this?

URIAH: Come along now and conduct yourself as a good soldier like the army taught you. Quick march! Get moving so they can shoot you.

GALY GAY: Oh, do not be so hasty. I am not the man you are looking for. I have never met him. My name is Jip, I can swear it is. What is an elephant compared to a man's life? I didn't see that elephant, it was just a rope I was holding. Don't go away, please. I'm someone quite different. I am not Galy Gay. I am not.

JESSE: Oh yes you are, and nobody else. Under the three rubber trees of Kilkoa Galy Gay will see his blood flowing. Get moving, Galy Gay.

GALY GAY: O God! Wait a minute, there has to be an official record listing the charges and showing that I didn't do it and that my name is not Galy Gay. Every detail must be weighed. You can't rush this sort of thing when a man is about to be slaughtered.

JESSE: Quick march!

GALY GAY: What do you mean, quick march? I am not the man you're looking for. All I wanted was to buy a fish, but where do you find fish around here? What are those guns rolling by? What is that battle music blaring away? No, I am not budging. I'll cling to the grass. The whole thing must stop. And why is no one here when a man is being slaughtered?

BEGBICK: Once they start loading the elephants if you lot aren't ready you can be written off. *She goes off.*
Galy Gay is led back and forth; he strides like the protagonist in a tragedy.

JESSE: Make way for the criminal whom the court martial has condemned to death.

SOLDIERS: Look, there's someone who's going to be shot. Perhaps it's a pity, he's not old yet. – And he doesn't know how he got into this.

URIAH: Halt! Would you like to relieve yourself one last time?

GALY GAY: Yes.

URIAH: Guard him closely.

GALY GAY: They say that once the elephants arrive the soldiers will have to leave, so I must take my time to allow the elephants to get here.

SOLDIERS: Hurry up!

GALY GAY: I can't. Is that the moon?

SOLDIERS: Yes. – It's getting late.

GALY GAY: Isn't that the Widow Begbick's bar where we always used to drink?

URIAH: No, my boy. This is the rifle range and here is the 'Johnny don't wet yourself' wall. Hey! Get fell in over there, you lot! And load your rifles. There should be five of them.

SOLDIERS: It's so hard to see in this light.

URIAH: Yes, it is very hard.

GALY GAY: Wait a moment, this won't do. You people must be able to see when you shoot.

URIAH *to Jesse*: Take that paper lantern and hold it beside him. *He blindfolds Galy Gay. In a loud voice*: Load your rifles! *Under his breath*: What are you doing, Polly? That's a live round you're putting in. Take it out.

POLLY: So sorry, I almost really loaded. And that could almost have led to a real disaster.

The elephants are heard passing in the background. The soldiers stand for a moment as if transfixed.

BEGBICK *off, calls*: The elephants!

URIAH: It's all no use. He has got to be shot. I'll count up to three. One!

GALY GAY: All right, Uriah, enough is enough. The elephants have arrived, haven't they? Am I supposed to go on standing here, Uriah? But why are you all keeping so horribly still?

URIAH: Two!

GALY GAY *laughing*: You're a queer cuss, Uriah. I can't see you, because you blindfolded me. But your voice sounds just like if you were dead serious about it.

URIAH: And one more makes . . .

GALY GAY: Whoah, don't say three, or you'll regret it. If you shoot now you're bound to hit me. Whoah! No, not yet. Listen to me. I confess! I confess I don't know what has been happening to me. Believe me, and don't laugh: I'm a man who doesn't know who he is. But I am not Galy Gay, that much I do know. I'm not the man who is supposed to be shot. Who am I, though? Because I've forgotten. Last night when it rained I still knew. It did rain last night, didn't it? I beseech you, when you look over here or where this voice is coming from, it's me, I beseech you. Call up that place, say Galy Gay or something to it, be merciful, give me a bit of meat. Where it goes in will be Galy Gay, and likewise where it comes out. Or at the very least if you come across a man who has forgotten who he is, that'll be me. And it's him I am beseeching you to let go.

Uriah has whispered something in Polly's ear; then Polly runs up behind Galy Gay and raises a big club over his head

URIAH: Once equals never! Three!

Galy Gay lets out a scream.

URIAH: Fire!

Galy Gay falls down in a faint.

POLLY: Whoah! He fell of his own accord.

URIAH *shouts*: Fire! So that he can hear he's dead.

The soldiers fire into the air.

URIAH: Leave him there and get ready to move off.

Galy Gay is left lying as all the others exeunt.

No. IVa

Begbick and the three are sitting outside the packed waggon at a table with five chairs. To one side lies Galy Gay covered with a sack.

JESSE: Here's the sergeant coming. Can you stop him poking his nose into our business, Widow Begbick?

Fairchild is seen approaching in civilian clothes.

BEGBICK: Yes, because that is a civilian coming. *To Fairchild, who is standing in the doorway*: Come and join us, Charles.

FAIRCHILD: There you sit, you Gomorrah! *Standing over Galy Gay*: And what is this sozzled carcass? *Silence. He pounds on the table.* Atten – shun!

URIAH *from behind knocks his hat down over his ears*: Stop your gob, civvy!
Laughter.

FAIRCHILD: Go ahead, mutiny, you sons of a gun! Observe my suit and laugh! Tear up my name that is famous from Calcutta to Cooch Behar! Give me a drink and then I'll shoot you!

URIAH: Come on, Fairchild old boy, show us what a brilliant shot you are.

FAIRCHILD: No.

BEGBICK: Nine women out of every ten fall for these top-class riflemen.

POLLY: Get cracking, Fairchild.

BEGBICK: You really should, for my sake.

FAIRCHILD: O thou Babylon! Here I place one egg – here. How many paces shall I make it?

POLLY: Four.

FAIRCHILD *takes ten paces, which Begbick counts aloud*: Here I have one perfectly ordinary service revolver. *He fires.*

JESSE *goes over to the egg*: The egg is untouched.

POLLY: Utterly.

URIAH: If anything it's got bigger.

FAIRCHILD: Strange. I thought I could hit it.
Loud laughter.

FAIRCHILD: Give me a drink. *He drinks.* I shall squash you all like bedbugs as sure as my name is Bloody Five.

URIAH: How did you actually come by the name Bloody Five?

JESSE *seated again*: Give us a demonstration.

FAIRCHILD: Shall I tell the story, Mrs Begbick?

BEGBICK: Eight women out of every nine would find this gory man divine.

FAIRCHILD: Right: here we have the River Chadze. There stand five Hindus. Hands tied behind their backs. Then along comes me with an ordinary service revolver, waves it in their faces a bit and says: this revolver has been misfiring. It has got to be tested. Like this. Then I fire – bang! down you go, that man there! – and so on four times more. That's all there was to it, gentlemen. *He sits down.*

JESSE: So that is how you came by your great name, which has made this widow your slave for life? From a human point of view, of course, one might regard your conduct as unbecoming and say you are simply a swine.

BEGBICK: Are you a monster?

FAIRCHILD: I would be very sorry if you took it like that. Your opinion means a lot to me.

BEGBICK: But do you accept it as final?

FAIRCHILD *looking deeply into her eyes*: Absolutely.

BEGBICK: In that case, my dear man, my opinion is that I must get my canteen packed up and have no more time for private matters, for now I can hear the lancers trotting past as they take their horses to be loaded.

The lancers are heard riding by.

POLLY: Are you still insisting on your own selfish desires, sir, even though the lancers are loading their horses and you have been told that for military reasons this canteen has to be packed up?

FAIRCHILD *bellowing*: Yes, I am. Give me a drink.

POLLY: All right, but we'll soon settle your hash, my boy.

JESSE: Sir, not all that far from here a man clad in British Army service dress is lying under a rough tarpaulin. He is recuperating after a hard day's work. A mere twenty-four hours ago he was still – from a military point of view – a babe in arms. His wife's voice frightened him. Without guidance he was incapable of buying a fish. In return for a cigar he was prepared to forget his father's name. Some

people took him in hand, because they happened to know
of a place for him. Since then, admittedly at the cost of
painful trials, he has become a man who will play his part
in the battles to come. You on the other hand have declined
into a mere civilian. At a time when the army is off to
restore order on the northern frontier, a move that demands beer, you big shitheap are deliberately hindering
the proprietress of an army canteen from getting her beer
waggon entrained.

POLLY: How can you hope to check our names at the last
roll-call and enter all four of them in your sergeant's notebook as per regulations?

URIAH: How can you possibly hope to face a company thirsting to confront its countless enemies given the state you're
in? Get up!

Fairchild rises unsteadily.

POLLY: Call that getting up?

He gives Fairchild a kick in the bottom, which makes him fall down.

URIAH: Is this what they used to call the Human Typhoon?
Chuck that wreck into the bushes or he'll demoralise the
company.

The three start dragging Fairchild to the rear.

A SOLDIER *rushes in and stops at the rear*: Is Sergeant Charles
Fairchild here? The General says he is to hurry up and get
his company fallen in at the goods station.

FAIRCHILD: Don't tell him it's me.

JESSE: There is no such sergeant here.

No. V

*Begbick and the three contemplate Galy Gay, who is still lying under
the sack.*

URIAH: Widow Begbick, we have reached the end of our
assemblage. We believe that our man has now been recon-
structed.

POLLY: I'd say all he needs now is a human voice.

JESSE: Have you got a human voice for this kind of eventuality, Widow Begbick?

BEGBICK: Yes, and something for him to eat. Take this crate here and write 'Galy Gay' on it in black chalk and then put a cross. *They do so.* Then form a funeral procession and bury him. The whole operation must not last more than nine minutes, as it's already a minute past two.

URIAH *calls out*: Number Five: Obsequies and Interment of Galy Gay, last of the personalities, in the year nineteen hundred and twenty-five. *The soldiers enter, doing up their packs.* Pick up that crate there and form a neat funeral procession. *The soldiers form up at the rear with the crate.*

JESSE: And I shall step up to him and say: You are to deliver a funeral oration for Galy Gay. *To Begbick*: He won't eat anything.

BEGBICK: That kind eats even when he's nobody.
She takes her basket over to Galy Gay, removes his sack and gives him food.

GALY GAY: More!
She gives him more; then she signals to Uriah and the procession comes downstage.

GALY GAY: Who's that they're carrying?

BEGBICK That is someone who was shot at the last minute.

GALY GAY: What is he called?

BEGBICK: Wait a moment. Unless I am mistaken he was called Galy Gay.

GALY GAY: And what's to happen to him now?

BEGBICK: To whom?

GALY GAY: To this Galy Gay fellow.

BEGBICK: Now they're going to bury him.

GALY GAY: Was he a good man or a bad one?

BEGBICK: Oh, he was a dangerous man.

GALY GAY: Yes, he was shot, wasn't he; I was present.
The procession passes. Jesse stops and speaks to Galy Gay.

JESSE: Surely that is Jip? Jip, you must get up at once and

give the address at this fellow Galy Gay's funeral, as you
probably knew him better than any of us.

GALY GAY: Hey, are you actually able to see me down here?
Jesse points at him. Yes, that's right. And what am I doing
now? *He bends his arm.*

JESSE: Bending your arm.

GALY GAY: So I've bent my arm twice now. And now?

JESSE: Now you are walking like a soldier.

GALY GAY: Do you people walk the same way?

JESSE: Exactly the same way.

GALY GAY: And how will you address me when you want
something?

JESSE: Jip.

GALY GAY: Try saying: Jip, walk around.

JESSE: Jip, walk around. Walk around under the rubber
trees and rehearse your funeral oration for Galy Gay.

GALY GAY *slowly walks over to the crate*: Is this the crate he's
in?
*He walks around the procession as they hold up the crate. He
walks faster and faster and tries to run away. Begbick holds him
back.*

BEGBICK: Are you looking for something? The Army's one
remedy for all diseases, up to and including cholera, is
castor oil. No soldier has any disease that castor oil won't
cure. Would you like some castor oil?

GALY GAY *shakes his head*:

My mother on her calendar marked the day
When I came out, and the thing that cried was me.
This bundle of flesh, nails and hair
Is me, is me.

JESSE: Yes, Jeraiah Jip, Jeraiah Jip from Tipperary.

GALY GAY: Someone who carried cucumbers for tips.
Swindled by an elephant, he had to sleep quickly on a
wooden chair for lack of time, because the fish water was

boiling in his hut. Nor had the machine-gun yet been cleaned, for they presented him with a cigar and five rifle barrels of which one was missing. Oh, what was his name?

URIAH: Jip. Jeraiah Jip.

Sounds of train whistling.

SOLDIERS: The trains are whistling. – Now it's every man for himself. *They fling down the crate and run off.*

JESSE: The convoy leaves in six minutes. He'll have to come as he is.

URIAH: Listen, Polly, and you too, Jesse. Fellow-soldiers! We are three survivors, and now that they have started sawing through the hair by which the three of us are suspended over the precipice you had better listen carefully to what I say beneath the last wall of Kilkoa at approximately two o'clock in the morning. The man we want must be allowed a little time, since it is for all eternity that he will be changing. Therefore I, Uriah Shelley, am now drawing my service revolver and threatening you with instant death if any of you moves.

POLLY: But if he looks inside the crate we are sunk.

Galy Gay sits down beside the crate.

GALY GAY:

I could not, without instant death
Gaze into a crate at a drained face
Of some person once familiar to me from the water's surface
Into which a man looked who, so I realise, died.
Therefore I am unable to open this crate
Because this fear is in the both of me, for perhaps
I am the Both which has just come about
On our earth's transformable top surface:
A chopped-off batlike thing hanging
Betwixt rubber trees and hut, a night bird
A thing that would gladly be cheerful.
One man equals no man. Some one has to call him.

Therefore
I would gladly have looked into this chest
As the heart clings to its parents.

Given a forest, which would still be there
If no one walked through it, and the very man
Who walked through where a forest once was:
How do they recognise one another?
When he sees his own footprints among the reeds
With water spurting into them, does that puddle mean any-
    thing to him?
What is your opinion?

By what sign does Galy Gay know himself
To be Galy Gay?
Suppose his arm was cut off
And he found it in the chink of a wall
Would Galy Gay's eye know Galy Gay's arm
And Galy Gay's foot cry out: This is the one!?
Therefore I am not looking into this chest.
Moreover in my opinion the difference
Between yes and no is not all that great.
And if Galy Gay were not Galy Gay
Then he would be the drinking son of some mother who
Would be some other man's mother if she
Were not his, and thus would anyway drink.
And would have been produced in March, not in Septem-
    ber
Unless instead of March he had
Been produced only in September of this year, or already
In September the year before
Which represents that one small year's difference
That turns one man into another man.
And I, the one I and the other I
Are used and accordingly usable.
And since I never gazed at that elephant

I shall close an eye to what concerns myself
And shed what is not likeable about me and thereby
Be pleasant.

Noise of moving trains.

GALY GAY: And what trains are those? Where are they off to?
BEGBICK: This army is heading straight into the fire-belching cannon of the battles that have been planned for the
north. Tonight a hundred thousand will march in a single
direction. That direction is from south to north. When a
man gets caught up in such a stream he seeks out two to
march beside him, one right and one left. He looks for a
rifle and a haversack and an identity disc to go round his
neck and a number on that identity disc so that when they
find him they can tell what unit he belonged to, so he can
be given his place in a mass grave. Have you got an identity
disc?
GALY GAY: Yes.
BEGBICK: What's on it?
GALY GAY: Jeraiah Jip.
BEGBICK: Well, Jeraiah Jip, better have a wash, for you look
like a rubbish heap. Make yourself ready. The army is leaving for the northern frontier. The fire-belching cannon
of the northern battlefields are awaiting it. The army is
thirsting to restore order in the populous cities of the
north.
GALY GAY *washing*: Who is the enemy?
BEGBICK: Up to now it has not been announced which
country we are making war on. But it begins to look more
and more like Tibet.
GALY GAY: You know something, Widow Begbick: One
man equals no man, until some one calls him.
The soldiers march in with their packs.
SOLDIERS: Everyone on board! – Get entrained! – Are you
all present and correct?

URIAH: In one moment. Your funeral oration, Comrade Jip, your funeral oration!

GALY GAY *goes to the coffin*: Therefore raise up Widow Begbick's crate which contains this mysterious corpse, lifting it two feet high and plunging it six feet deep in the Kilkoa soil here, and listen to his funeral oration rendered by Jeraiah Jip from Tipperary, a very difficult job as I am unprepared. But never mind: here lies Galy Gay, a man who was shot. He set out to buy a small fish one morning, had acquired a large elephant by that evening and was shot in the course of the same night. Do not imagine, dearly beloved brethren, that he was of no consequence during his lifetime. Indeed he owned a straw hut on the fringes of the town as well as various other things which had best be passed over in silence. It was no great crime that he committed, good man that he was. And they can say what they like, and it was really an oversight, and I was much too drunk, gentlemen, but Man equals Man and that is why they had to shoot him. And now the wind is perceptibly cooler as it always is before dawn, and I think we should get away from here, it's an uneasy place in other ways too. *He steps away from the coffin;* But why have you people got all your kit?

POLLY: You see, this morning we are to board the waggons going to the northern frontier.

GALY GAY: Well, why haven't I got all my kit?

JESSE: Well, why hasn't he got all his kit?
Soldiers bring his equipment.

JESSE: Here's your stuff, captain.
Some soldiers carry a large bundle wrapped in straw mats to the train.

URIAH: He took his time, the swine. But we'll get him yet. *Pointing to the bundle:* That was the Human Typhoon. *All go off.*

10

In the Moving Train

*Just before dawn. The company are asleep in their hammocks. Jesse,
Uriah and Polly are sitting up on guard. Galy Gay is sleeping.*

JESSE: The world is dreadful. Men cannot be relied on.

POLLY: The vilest and weakest thing alive is man.

JESSE: Through dust and water we have footed it down every
road in this oversized country from the mountains of the
Hindu Kush to the great plains of the southern Punjab; yet
from Benares to Calcutta, by sun and moon, we have seen
nothing but treachery. This man whom we took under our
wing and who has swiped our blankets and ruined our
night's sleep is like a leaky oil can. Yes and no are the same
to him, he says one thing today another tomorrow. Ah,
Uriah, we have tried and failed. Let us go to Leokadja
Begbick, who is sitting up with the sergeant to save him
from falling off his bunk, and ask her to lie down with this
man so that he feels good and asks no questions. Old as
she is there is still warmth in her, and once a man is lying
with a woman he knows all the answers. Get up, Polly.
They go over to Widow Begbick.

JESSE: Come in, Widow Begbick, we are at a loss what to do,
and are frightened of falling asleep, and here we are with
this man who is ill. So you lie down with him, pretend he's
spent the night with you, and make him feel good.

BEGBICK *enters half asleep*: I'll do it for seven weeks' pay.

URIAH: You shall have all we earn for seven weeks.
Begbick lies down with Galy Gay. Jesse covers them with papers.

GALY GAY *waking up*: What is it that's shaking so?

URIAH *to the others*: That is the elephant nibbling at your hut,
you sniveller.

GALY GAY: What is it that's hissing so?

URIAH *to the others*: That is the fish boiling in the water, you pleasant man.

GALY GAY *gets up with difficulty and looks out of the window*: A woman, sleeping bags. Telegraph poles. It's a train.

JESSE: Pretend you are all asleep.

The three pretend to be asleep.

GALY GAY *goes up to a sleeping bag*: Hey, you.

SOLDIER: What do you want?

GALY GAY: Where are you people going?

SOLDIER *opening one eye*: To the front. *Goes back to sleep.*

GALY GAY: These are soldiers. *Looks out of the window again, then wakes another.* Mr Soldier, what is the time? *No answer.* Almost morning. What day of the week is it?

SOLDIER: Between Thursday and Friday.

GALY GAY: I must get off. Hey, you, the train must be stopped.

SOLDIER: This train doesn't stop.

GALY GAY: If this train doesn't stop and everyone's sleeping I'd better lie down too and sleep till it does stop. *Sees Widow Begbick.* There's a woman lying beside me. Who is this woman who lay beside me in the night?

JESSE: Hullo, mate, good morning.

GALY GAY: Oh, I'm so glad to see you, Mr Jesse.

JESSE: Aren't you living it up? Lying there with a woman beside you and letting everybody see.

GALY GAY: Isn't it remarkable? Positively indecent, eh? But a man is a man, you know. He is not always master of himself. For instance, here am I waking up, and there's a woman lying beside me.

JESSE: Why, so there is.

GALY GAY: And would you believe that there are times when I don't know a woman who is lying beside me like this in the morning? To be perfectly frank and speaking as man to man, I don't know this woman. And, Mr Jesse, as one man to another, would you be able to tell me who she is?

JESSE: Oh you line-shooter! This time of course it's Widow

Leokadja Begbick. Duck your head in a pail of water and you'll know your lady friend all right. I don't suppose you know your own name, then, either?

GALY GAY: I do.

JESSE: All right, what is your name?

GALY GAY *is silent.*

JESSE: So you know your name?

GALY GAY: Yes.

JESSE: That's good. A man needs to know who he is when he is off to the war.

GALY GAY: Is there a war?

JESSE: Yes, the Tibetan War.

GALY GAY: The Tibetan. But suppose just for the moment a man didn't know who he is, that would be funny when he is off to the war, wouldn't it? Now you mentioned Tibet, sir, that's a place I always wanted to see. I used to know a man had a wife came from the province of Sikkim, which is on the Tibetan frontier. They are good people there, she used to say.

BEGBICK: Jippie, where are you?

GALY GAY: Who is she talking to?

JESSE: I think she is talking to you.

GALY GAY: Here.

BEGBICK: Come and give us a kiss, Jippie.

GALY GAY: I don't mind if I do, but I think you have got me a bit muddled with someone else.

BEGBICK: Jippie!

JESSE: This gentleman claims his head is not quite clear; he says he doesn't know you.

BEGBICK: Oh, how can you humiliate me so in front of this gentleman?

GALY GAY: If I duck my head in this pail of water I'll know you right away. *He sticks his head into the pail of water.*

BEGBICK: Do you know me now?

GALY GAY *lying:* Yes.

POLLY: Then you also know who you yourself are?

GALY GAY *slyly*: Didn't I know that?

POLLY: No, because you were out of your mind and claimed to be someone else.

GALY GAY: Who was I, then?

JESSE: You're not getting much better, I see. What's more I still think you are a public menace, because last night when we called you by your right name you turned as dangerous as any murderer.

GALY GAY: All I know is that my name is Galy Gay.

JESSE: Listen to that, you people, he's starting all over again. You'd better call him Galy Gay like he says, or he'll throw another fit.

URIAH: Oh bollocks. Mr Jip from Ireland, consider yourself free to play the wild man right up to the point where you get tied to a post outside the canteen and the night rain comes down. We who have been your mates since the battle of the River Chadze would sell our shirts to make things easier for you.

GALY GAY: No need for that about the shirts.

URIAH: Call him anything he wants.

JESSE: Shut up, Uriah. Would you care for a glass of water, Galy Gay?

GALY GAY: Yes, that is my name.

JESSE: Of course, Galy Gay. How could you be called anything else? Just take it easy, lie down. Tomorrow they will put you in hospital, in a nice comfortable bed with plenty of castor oil, and that will relieve you, Galy Gay. Tread delicately, all of you, our friend Jip, I mean Galy Gay, is unwell.

GALY GAY: Let me tell you, gentlemen, the situation is beyond me. But when it is a matter of carrying a cabin trunk, never mind how heavy it is, they say every cabin trunk is supposed to have its soft spot.

POLLY *ostensibly aside to Jesse*: Just keep him away from that pouch around his neck, or he'll read his real name in his paybook and throw another fit.

JESSE: Oh, how good a paybook is! How easily one forgets
things! Therefore we soldiers, being unable to carry everything at once in our heads, have a pouch on a cord round
each man's neck containing a paybook with his name in it.
Because if a man spends too much time thinking about his
name it is not good.

GALY GAY *goes to the rear, looks gloomily at his paybook and
returns to his corner.* In future I shall give up thinking. I shall
just sit on my bottom and count the telegraph poles.

THE VOICE OF SERGEANT FAIRCHILD: O misery, o
awakening! Where is my name that was famous from Calcutta to Couch Behar? Even the uniform I wore is gone.
They bundled me into a train like a calf going to the
slaughterhouse. They stopped my mouth with a civilitic
hat and the whole train knows that I am no longer Bloody
Five. I will go and fix this train so that it can be tossed on
to a rubbish dump like a twisted stovepipe. That is plain
as a pikestaff.

JESSE: Bloody Five! Wake up, Widow Begbick!
Fairchild enters in soiled civilian clothes.

GALY GAY: Have you been having trouble with your name?

FAIRCHILD: You are the most melancholy specimen of
them all, and I shall start by crushing you. Tonight I am
going to chop you all up ready for the cannery. *He sees the
Widow Begbick sitting there; she smiles.* I'll be damned! There
you are still, you Gomorrah! What have you done to me
that I am no longer Bloody Five? Get away from me!
Begbick laughs. What are these clothes I'm wearing? Do you
call them suitable? And what is this head I've got? Do you
suppose that's pleasant? Am I to lie down with you again,
you Sodom?

BEGBICK: If you want to, do.

FAIRCHILD: I do not want to! Get away from me! The eyes
of this country are upon me. I used to be a big gun. My
name is Bloody Five. The pages of the history books are
criss-crossed with that name, in triplicate.

BEGBICK: Then don't if you don't want to.

FAIRCHILD: Don't you realise that my manhood makes me weak when you sit there like that?

BEGBICK: Then pluck out your manhood, my boy.

FAIRCHILD: No need to tell me twice. *He goes out.*

GALY GAY *cries out after him*: Stop! Don't take any steps on account of your name! A name is an uncertain thing, you can't build on it.

FAIRCHILD: That is plain as a pikestaff. That is the answer. There we have a rope. There we have a service pistol. That's where we draw the line. Mutineers will be shot. That is plain as a pikestaff. 'Johnny Bowlegs, pack your kit.' No girl in this world will ever cost me a penny again. That is plain as a pikestaff. And I shall remain cool as a cucumber. I accept full responsibility. I have to do it if I am to go on being Bloody Five.

A shot is heard.

GALY GAY *who has been standing in the doorway for some time laughs.* Fire!

SOLDIERS *in the waggons on either side*: Did you hear that scream? – Who was screaming? – Somebody must have got hurt. They've all stopped singing, even up at the front of the train. – Listen.

GALY GAY: I know who screamed and I know why. On account of his name this gentleman has done something extremely bloody to himself. He has shot off his manhood. Witnessing that was a great stroke of luck for me. Now I realise where such stubbornness gets you and what a bloody thing it is when a man is never satisfied with himself and makes so much fuss about his name. *He runs over to Widow Begbick.* Don't get the idea that I don't know you. I know you very well indeed. And anyway it doesn't matter. But tell me quickly, how far away is the town where we met?

BEGBICK: Many days' march, and it gets further every minute.

GALY GAY: How many days' march?

BEGBICK: At the instant when you asked it was at least a hundred days' march.

GALY GAY: And how many men are there here travelling to Tibet?

BEGBICK: A hundred thousand. One equals no one.

GALY GAY: Of course. A hundred thousand. And what do they eat?

BEGBICK: Dried fish and rice.

GALY GAY: Everybody the same?

BEGBICK: Everybody the same.

GALY GAY: Of course. Everybody the same.

BEGBICK: They all have hammocks to sleep in, each man his own, and denims for summer.

GALY GAY: And in the winter?

BEGBICK: Khaki in winter.

GALY GAY: And women?

BEGBICK: The same.

GALY GAY: Women the same.

BEGBICK: And now, do you also know who you are?

GALY GAY: Jeraiah Jip, that's my name. *He runs over to the three others and shows them his name in his paybook.*

JESSE *and the others smile*: Right. You know how to keep putting your name across, don't you, comrade Jip?

GALY GAY: How about food?
Polly brings him a dish of rice.

GALY GAY: Yes, it is most important that I eat. *Eats.* How many days' march did you say this train covers in one minute?

BEGBICK: Ten.

POLLY: Just look how he's making himself at home. How he stares at everything and counts the telegraph poles and gloats at the speed we are going.

JESSE: I cannot bear the sight of him. It is truly loathsome when a mammoth, just because a couple of rifles are shoved under his nose, chooses to turn into a louse rather than be decently gathered to the bosom of his forebears.

URIAH: On the contrary, it's a sign of vitality. So long as Jip doesn't come after us now singing 'For man equals man, since time began' I think we will be over the hump.

A SOLDIER: What's that noise in the air?

URIAH *with a nasty smile*: That is the roaring of the artillery, for we are nearing the hills of Tibet.

GALY GAY: Isn't there some more rice?

11

Deep in Remote Tibet Lies the Mountain Fortress of Sir El-Djowr

And on a hilltop Jeraiah Jip sits waiting amid the thunder of guns

VOICES FROM BELOW: This is as far as we can go. – This is the fortress of Sir El-Djowr which blocks the pass into Tibet.

GALY GAY'S VOICE *behind the hill*: At the double! Or we'll be too late. *He appears, carrying a gun tripod on his shoulder.* Out of the train and straight into battle. That's what I like. A gun takes some living up to.

JIP: Haven't you seen a machine-gun section with only three men in it?

GALY GAY *charging on irresistibly like a war elephant*: There's no such thing, soldier. Our section consists of four men, for instance. One man to the right of you, one to the left and one behind you, after which it's proper for it to get through any pass.

BEGBICK *appears, carrying a gun barrel on her back*: Don't run so fast, Jippie. The trouble is, you've got a heart like a lion. *The three soldiers appear, groaning as they drag their machine-gun.*

JIP: Hullo, Uriah, hullo, Jesse, hullo, Polly! Here I am again. *The three soldiers pretend not to see him.*

JESSE: We must get this machine-gun set up at once.

URIAH: The gunfire's so noisy already you can't hear yourself speak.

POLLY: We must keep a particularly sharp eye on the fortress of Sir El-Djowr.

GALY GAY: And I want to have first shot. Something is holding us up, it must be taken out. All these gentlemen here can't be kept waiting. It won't hurt the mountain. Jesse, Uriah, Polly! The battle is starting, and I already feel the urge to sink my teeth in the enemy's throat. *And he and Widow Begbick together assemble the gun.*

JIP: Hullo, Jesse, hullo, Uriah, hullo, Polly! How are you all? Long time no see. I was a bit held up, you know. I hope you haven't had any trouble on my account. I couldn't make it sooner. I'm really glad to be back. But why don't you say something?

POLLY: How can we be of service to you, sir? *Polly puts a dish of rice on the gun for Galy Gay.* Won't you eat your rice ration? The battle will be starting soon.

GALY GAY: Gimme! *He eats.* Yes: first I eat my rice ration, then I get my correct apportionment of whisky, and while I am eating and drinking I can study this mountain fortress and try to find its soft spot. After that it will be a piece of cake.

JIP: Your voice has completely changed, Polly, but you still like to have your joke. Me, I was employed in a flourishing business, but I had to leave. For your sakes, of course. You aren't angry, are you?

URIAH: This is where I fear we must inform you that you seem to have come to the wrong address.

POLLY: We don't even know you.

JESSE: It is of course possible that we have met somewhere. But the army has vast reserves of manpower, sir.

GALY GAY: I should like another rice ration. You have not handed your ration over yet, Uriah.

JIP: You people really have become very different, you know.

URIAH: That is quite possible, that's army life for you.

JIP: But I am Jip, your comrade.

The three laugh. When Galy Gay also begins to laugh the others stop.

GALY GAY: One more ration. I'm ravenous now we're going into battle, and I like this fortress better and better.

Polly gives him a third dish.

JIP: Who is that gobbling up your rations?

URIAH: Mind your own business.

JESSE: You know, you couldn't possibly be old Jip. Old Jip would never have betrayed and abandoned us. Old Jip would never have let himself be held up. So you cannot be old Jip.

JIP: I certainly am.

URIAH: Prove it! Prove it!

JIP: Is there really not one of you who will admit he knows me? Then listen to me and mark my words. You are extremely hard-hearted men and your end can already be foreseen. Give me back my paybook.

GALY GAY *goes up to Jip with his last dish of rice*: You must be making a mistake. *Turns back to the others.* He's not right in the head. *To Jip:* Have you been going without food a lot? Would you like a glass of water? *To the others:* We shouldn't upset him. *To Jip:* Don't you know who you belong to? Never mind. Just sit down quietly over here till we have decided the battle. And please don't get any closer to the roar of the guns, as it demands great moral strength. *To the three:* He has no idea what's what. *To Jip:* Of course you need a pay-book. Nobody's going to let you run around without a pay-book, are they? Ah yes, Polly, look in the ammunition box where we keep the little megaphone and fish out Galy Gay's old papers, you remember, that fellow you used to tease me about. *Polly runs over to the box.* Anybody who has lived in the lowlands where the tiger asks the jaguar about his teeth knows how important it is to have something on you in black and white, because, you see, these days they are always trying to take your name away,

and I know what a name is worth. O my children, when
you called me Galy Gay that time, why didn't you just call
me Nobody? Such larks are dangerous. They could have
turned out very badly. But I always say let bygones be
bygones. *He hands Jip the papers.* Here is that paybook, take
it. Is there anything else you want?

JIP: You're the best of this lot. At least you've got a heart.
But the rest of you will have my curse.

GALY GAY: To save you people having to listen to too much
of that I'm going to make a bit of a noise with this gun for
you . . . Show us how it works, Widow Begbick.
The two of them aim the gun at the fortress and start loading.

JIP: The icy wind of Tibet shall shrivel your bones to the
marrow, you devils, never again shall you hear the harbour
bell in Kilkoa, but shall march to the end of the world and
back, over and over again. The Devil himself, your master,
will have no use for you once you are old, and you will
have to go on marching night and day through the Gobi
desert and the waving green rye fields of Wales, and that
shall be your recompense for betraying a comrade in need.
Exit.

The three are silent.

GALY GAY: All set. And now I shall do it with five shots.
The first shot is fired.

BEGBICK *smoking a cigar*: You are one of those great soldiers
who made the army so dreaded in bygone days. Five such
men were a threat to any woman's life.
The second shot is fired.

I have proof that during the battle of the River Chadze it
was by no means the worst elements in the company that
dreamed of my kisses. One night with Leokadja Begbick
was something for which men would sacrifice their whisky
and save their shillings from two weeks' pay. They had
names like Genghis Khan, famous from Calcutta to Couch
Behar.
The third shot is fired.

One embrace from their beloved Irishwoman set their blood
to rights. You can read in *The Times* how staunchly they
fought in the battles of Bourabay, Kamatkura and Daguth.
The fourth shot is fired.

GALY GAY: Something that's no longer a mountain is tum-
bling down.

Smoke begins to pour from the fortress of Sir El-Djowr.

POLLY: Look!

Enter Fairchild.

GALY GAY: This is tremendous. Leave me alone now I've
tasted blood.

FAIRCHILD: What do you think you are doing? Take a look
over there. Right, I am now going to bury you up to the
neck in that anthill to stop you shooting the whole Hindu
Kush to pieces. My hand is steady as a rock. *He aims his
service pistol at Galy Gay.* It's not shaking at all. There, it is
plain as a pikestaff. You are now looking at the world for
the last time.

GALY GAY *loading enthusiastically*: One more shot! Just one
more. Just number five.

The fifth shot is fired. A cry of joy is heard from the valley below:
'The fortress of Sir El-Djowr that was blocking the pass
into Tibet has fallen. The army is advancing into Tibet.'

FAIRCHILD: Right. Once more I hear the familiar step of
the Army on the march, and now I propose to take a few
steps of my own. *Steps up to Galy Gay.* Who are you?

VOICE OF A SOLDIER *from below*: Who is the man who over-
threw the fortress of Sir El-Djowr?

GALY GAY: One moment. Polly, pass me that little megaphone out of the ammunition box, so I can tell them who it
is. *Polly fetches the megaphone and hands it to Galy Gay.*

GALY GAY *through the megaphone*: It was me, one of you,
Jeraiah Jip!

JESSE: Three cheers for Jeraiah Jip, the human fighting-
machine!

POLLY: Look!

*The fortress has begun to burn. A thousand horrified voices cry out
in the distance.*

DISTANT VOICE: Flames are now engulfing the mountain
fortress of Sir El-Djowr, in which seven thousand refugees
from Sikkim province had found shelter, peasants, artisans
and shopkeepers, most of them friendly, hard-working
people.

GALY GAY: Oh. But what is that to me? The one cry and the
other cry.

And already I feel within me
The desire to sink my teeth
In the enemy's throat
Ancient urge to kill
Every family's breadwinner
To carry out the conquerors'
Mission.

Hand me your paybooks.
They do so.

POLLY: Polly Baker.
JESSE: Jesse Mahoney.
URIAH: Uriah Shelley.
GALY GAY: Jeraiah Jip. At ease! We are now crossing the
frontier of frozen Tibet.
Exeunt all four.

The Elephant Calf
An interlude for the foyer

Translator: JOHN WILLETT

Theatre

A few rubber trees above a trestle stage. Chairs in front of it.

POLLY *before the curtain*: In order that the act of the drama may have its full effect on you, you are invited to smoke like chimneys. Our artistes are the best in the world, our drinks over proof, our seats comfortable, bets on the story's outcome can be placed at the bars, acts will end and the curtain fall according to how the betting goes. Kindly do not take shots at the pianist, he is doing his best. Anyone who doesn't get the plot first go off needn't bother, it's incomprehensible. If you insist on seeing something full of meaning you should go to the gents. Ticket money will be refunded under no circumstances. Here is our comrade Jip, whose privilege it is to play the Elephant Calf, Jackie Pall. If that should strike you as impossibly difficult then all I can say is that stage artistes have got to be able to do absolutely anything.

SOLDIER *in audience*: Hear hear.

POLLY: Presenting Jesse Mahoney as the Elephant Calf's mother, with Uriah Shelley, the famous international turf expert, as the Moon. It will furthermore be your good fortune to see my humble self in the important role of the Banana Tree.

SOLDIERS: Get started, can't you? Fancy charging ten cents for rubbish like that.

POLLY: Permit me to inform you that we are absolutely impervious to crude interjections of that sort. The play is mostly about a crime committed by the Elephant Calf. I'm just telling you so that we don't have to keep interrupting.

URIAH *behind the curtain*: Alleged to have been committed.

POLLY: Quite right. That's because the only part I've read is my own. The Elephant Calf is innocent, you see.

SOLDIERS *slow clapping*: Get on with the show, get on with the show.

POLLY: All right, all right. *Steps behind the curtain.* You know I'm not sure we didn't charge too much for admission. What do you blokes think?

URIAH: Much too late to worry about that now. We just have to jump in at the deep end.

POLLY: It's such a feeble play, that's the difficulty. I'm sure you can't really remember, Jesse, how things went in the real theatre, and I rather think, Jesse, that what you've forgotten is the most important part of it. Here, half a mo', I've been taken short. *The curtain rises.* I am the Banana Tree.

SOLDIER: High time too.

POLLY: The arbiter of the jungle. I have been standing here on a parched savannah in South Punjab, yea ever since elephants were first invented. Now and then, but mainly in the evening, the Moon cometh to me to lay a complaint against an Elephant Calf, let's say.

URIAH: You're going too fast. You're half way there. It's ten cents, you know. *Enters.*

POLLY: Greetings, Moon, whence comest thou at this late hour?

URIAH: I have heard a good one about an Elephant Calf —

POLLY: Art laying a complaint against it?

URIAH: Aye, of course.

POLLY: So the Elephant Calf hath perpetrated a crime?

URIAH: It is precisely as thou supposest, indeed this is an instance of thy perspicacity from which naught can be hid.

POLLY: O, you've seen nothing yet. Hath not the Elephant Calf murdered his mother?

URIAH: Indeed he hath.

POLLY: Well, that's terrible.

URIAH: Appalling it is.

POLLY: If only I could find my specs.

URIAH: I just happen to have a pair on me, if they should fit you.

POLLY: They would fit all right if only they had lenses in them. Look, no lenses.

URIAH: Better than nothing, anyway.

POLLY: It's not a laughing matter.

URIAH: Aye, it is passing strange. Therefore I lay a complaint against the Moon, or rather the Elephant Calf.

Enter the Elephant Calf, slowly.

POLLY: Ah, here is that agreeable Elephant Calf. Whence comest thou, eh?

GALY GAY: I am the Elephant Calf. Seven Rajahs stood around my cradle. What are you laughing at, Moon?

URIAH: Keep talking, Elephant Calf.

GALY GAY: My name is Jackie Pall. I am taking a walk.

POLLY: They tell me thou didst beat thy mother to death.

GALY GAY: No, I just broke her milk jug to pieces.

URIAH: On her head, on her head.

GALY GAY: No, Moon, on a stone, on a stone.

POLLY: And I tell thee thou didst do it, as sure as I am a Banana Tree.

URIAH: And as sure as I am the Moon I shall prove it, and my first proof is this woman here.

Enter Jesse as the Elephant Calf's mother.

POLLY: Who's that?

URIAH: It's his mother.

POLLY: Isn't that rather peculiar?

URIAH: Not in the least.

POLLY: All the same it does strike me as peculiar her being there.

URIAH: Not me.

POLLY: Then she may as well stay, but of course you will have to prove it.

URIAH: Thou art the judge.

POLLY: All right, Elephant Calf, prove that thou didst not murder thy Mother.

SOLDIER *in the audience*: Hey, with her standing there . . .

URIAH *to the audience*: That's just the point.

SOLDIER: Even the start's a load of tripe. With his mother standing there. How on earth can the rest of the play be worth bothering about?

JESSE: I am the Elephant Calf's Mother, and I bet my little Jackie can prove quite conclusively that he's no murderer. Eh, Jackie?

URIAH: And I bet that he cannot and will not.

POLLY *bellows*: Curtain!

The audience goes silently to the bar and loudly and aggressively orders cocktails.

POLLY *behind the curtain*: That went very nicely, not a single boo.

GALY GAY: I'd like to know why nobody applauded?

JESSE: Perhaps they found it too gripping.

POLLY: But it's so interesting.

URIAH: If only we had a few chorus girls to flash their bums at them they'd tear up the seats. Get out in front, we must have a go at the betting lark.

POLLY *before the curtain*: Gentlemen . . .

SOLDIERS: Here, none of that. Let's have a proper interval. Give us time for a drink. A fellow needs it in this place.

POLLY: We just wanted to see if we could get you to lay a bet or two, on one of the two parties, that is, Mother versus Moon.

SOLDIERS: Bloody cheek. So that's their way of squeezing extra cash out of us. Just you wait till they get going. You ain't seen nothing yet.

POLLY: All right. Bets on the Mother, this side. *Nobody moves.* For the Moon, over here. *Nobody moves.*

URIAH *behind the curtain*: Have they placed their bets?

POLLY: Not so as you'd notice. They say that the best part's still to come, which I find most disturbing.

JESSE: They're drinking so appallingly, it's as if they couldn't sit through the rest otherwise.

URIAH: Sock them with a bit of music, that'll cheer them up.

POLLY *steps through the curtain*: Now for a few discs. *Withdraws. Curtain up.* Step forth, Moon, Mother and Elephant Calf, and ye shall learn the complete explanation of this mysterious crime, and you lot out there too. How dost thou hope to conceal the fact that thou, Jackie Pall, didst stab thine honourable Mother to death?

GALY GAY: How could I have done, seeing as how I am but a defenceless maiden?

POLLY: Art thou? Then let me put it to thee, Jackie Pall, that thou art by no means a maiden, as thou claimest. Now hark ye to my first major proof I recall a strange incident in my childhood in Whitechapel —

SOLDIER: South Punjab. *Roars of laughter.*

POLLY: — in South Punjab, when a fellow dressed up as a girl so as not to have to go off to the war. Up came the sergeant and tossed a round in his lap, and because he didn't move his legs apart, like a girl would to catch it in her skirt, the sergeant could tell he was a man, and the same thing here. *They do it.* There you are, now you all know the Elephant Calf's a man. Curtain! *Curtain. Feeble applause.*

POLLY: It's a smash hit, hear that? Curtain up! Take a bow! *Curtain. Applause stops.*

URIAH: They're positively nasty. It's all no use. The whole thing's hopeless.

JESSE: We must simply pack it in and refund their money. It's a matter of to be lynched or not to be lynched, that is the question; the situation is absolutely critical. Have a look out front.

URIAH: What, refund their money? Not on your life. There isn't a theatre in the world could stand that.

SOLDIERS: Tomorrow we'll be moving off to Tibet, eh, Georgie, may be the last time you ever sit under the rubber trees swigging four-cent cocktails. It's not particularly good weather for a war, or else it would be quite nice here, apart from this show.

SOLDIER: How about entertaining giving us a bit of a song, like 'Johnny Bowlegs, pack your kit and trek' say?

SOLDIERS: Bravo. *Sing 'Janny mit dem Hoppelbein'*.

URIAH: They've started their own singing now. We must get going again.

POLLY: I wish I were out there with them, 'Johnnys'' one of my favourite songs. Why couldn't we give them something like that? *Curtain up*. Now that . . . *He is competing with the singing*. Now that the Elephant Calf . . .

SOLDIER: Still going on about that Elephant Calf!

POLLY: As I was saying, now that the . . .

SOLDIER: Acting unpaid lance-calf.

POLLY: . . . That the animal in question has been exposed as a swindler by my first major proof, we move on to the second, even majorer proof.

SOLDIER: Can't we skip that one, Polly?

URIAH: Don't let them rattle you, Polly.

POLLY: I suggest that thou art a murderer, Elephant Calf. Therefore prove thine inability to murder, let's say, the Moon.

SOLDIER: That's not right. It's for the Banana Tree to do the proving.

POLLY: But that's just it. Now watch out. We've reached a particularly crucial point of the drama. As I was saying, thou must prove thine inability to murder, let's say, the Moon. Climb up this creeper of mine and take a knife with thee. *Galy Gay does so. The Moon holds the top of the rope ladder*.

SOLDIERS *quieten a few who want to continue singing*: Quiet! It's a tricky climb, you know, what with not being able to see out of that elephant's head.

JESSE: So long as he doesn't choose this moment to piss. Give it all you've got, Uriah. *Uriah gives a cry*.

URIAH: Oh, oh, oh!

POLLY: What's the matter, Moon, wherefore thy cries?

URIAH: Because it hurteth so. Emphatically this is a murderer climbing towards me.

GALY GAY: Hang the ladder on a branch, Uriah, I'm awfully weary.

URIAH: Oh, he is tearing my hand off. My hand! My hand! He is tearing off my hand.

POLLY: There you are, there you are.

Galy Gay has Uriah's artificial hand in his hands and shows it to the audience.

JESSE: That's bad, Jackie. I would not have thought it of thee. Thou art no child of mine.

URIAH *holds up stump of his hand*: I attest him to be a murderer.

POLLY: Behold the bleeding stump with which he attesteth; nor hast thou proved that it is impossible for thee to commit a murder, Elephant Calf, for now thou hast furthermore so handled the Moon that it must needs bleed to death before first light. Curtain! *Curtain. He immediately comes forward.* If anyone's interested in betting it can be done at the bar.

SOLDIERS *go to place bets*: A cent on the Moon, half a cent on the Elephant Calf.

URIAH: Look, they're starting to nibble. Now, Jesse, it's all yours with the sorrowing Mother's speech. *Curtain up.*

JESSE:
Do you all know what a mother is?
Ah, her heart is tender as no other is.
Tender your mother's heart as you lay in her
Tender the mother's hand that fed you dinner
Tender the mother's eye that watched you play
Tender the mother's foot that led the way
Laughter.
And when a mother's heart sinks beneath the sod
Laughter.
A noble soul goes shooting up to God.

Laughter.

Hear a mother, hear a mother weeping:

Laughter.

Mine is the bosom where this calf lay sleeping.

Stormy, prolonged laughter.

SOLDIERS: Encore! That alone's worth ten cents. Bravo! Hurrah! Three cheers for the Mother. Hip, hip, hooray!

Curtain falls.

URIAH: Carry on! It's a hit! Get on stage!

Curtain up.

POLLY: I have demonstrated that thou art a man capable of committing a murder. Now I put it to thee, Elephant Calf: art of the opinion that this is thy mother?

SOLDIERS: It's a damned unfair business, what they're performing up there, it absolutely goes against nature, it does. But very deep, very philosophical. They'll have some sort of happy ending up their sleeve, you bet. Quiet!

POLLY: Far be it from me to suggest, of course, that any child in the world would touch a hair of the head of the mother that bore him in any country under traditional British rule. *Hear, hear.* Rule Britannia! *All sing 'Rule Britannia'.* I thank you gentlemen. So long as this moving ditty resounds from rough masculine throats all will be well with England and her traditions. But on with the show! In as much as thou, O Elephant Calf, didst truly murder this universally beloved woman and great artiste – *Hear, hear* – it cannot possibly be the case that thou, Jackie Pall, art son or daughter of this celebrated lady – *Hear, hear* – moreover whatever a Banana Tree suggests he also proves. *Applause.* So take a piece of billiard chalk, thou Moon of Cooch Behar, and draw a firm circle in the centre of the stage. Thereupon take an ordinary rope in thy hand and wait until this profoundly stricken Mother steps into the middle of thy doubtless most incompetently drawn circle. Place the rope delicately round her white neck.

SOLDIERS: Round her lovely white mother's neck, round her lovely white mother's neck.

POLLY: Exactly. But thou, the alleged Jackie Pall, take the other end of this judicial rope and place thyself outside the circle over against the Moon. There; and now I ask thee, woman, didst thou give birth to a murderer? Art silent? Well, then. I just wanted to show you, gentlemen, that the mother herself, whom you see represented here, turns her back on her fallen child. But soon I shall show you even more, for soon the terrible sun of justice will be focussing its rays into the most hidden depths of this affair.

SOLDIERS: Don't overdo it, Polly. Sh!

POLLY: For the last time, Jackie Pall, dost persist in suggesting that thou art this wretched woman's son?

GALY GAY: Yes.

POLLY: Well, well. So thou art her son? A moment ago thou didst claim to be her daughter, but thou art not all that exact in thy statements. We shall now proceed, gentlemen, to our last and most important patent super-proof, which will not only surpass anything you have seen so far, but is guaranteed to give you total satisfaction. If thou, Jackie Pall, art this mother's child, then thou willst have been given the strength to pull thine alleged mother out of the circle to thy side. That's clear enough.

SOLDIERS: Crystal clear. Clear as a shithouse window. Hey, wait. He's got it all wrong. Just you stick to the truth, Jackie.

POLLY: When I count three, pull. *All count*. Go! *Galy Gay pulls Jesse out of the circle to his side.*

JESSE: Hey! Stop! Goddam! What d'you think you're up to? My neck!

SOLDIERS: What about it? Pull, Jackie! Stop! He's as blue as a fish out of water.

JESSE: Help!

GALY GAY: My side! my side!

POLLY: How about that, eh? Did you ever see such crude

behaviour? Now shall unnatural deception reap its reward. For thou hast clearly made a terrible mistake. By thy crude tugging hast thou proved, not what thou intendedst, but merely that under no circumstances cans't thou be son or daughter of this wretchedly tormented Mother. Thou hast made plain the truth, Jackie Pall.

SOLDIERS: Oho! Bravo! Stinking! Nice family, I don't think. Pack it in, Jackie, you've had it. Always tell the truth, Jackie.

POLLY: All right, gentlemen, I think that should do. That ought to look after our patent super-proof, I'd think. Now listen carefully, gentlemen, and I'd like those gentlemen to listen who saw fit to make a disturbance at the start of our show, and those who backed this miserable proof-riddled Elephant Calf with their good pence: this Elephant Calf is a murderer. The Elephant Calf, which is not the daughter of this honourable mother, as it suggested, but the son, as I have proved, and not the son either, as you saw, but simply no child whatsoever of this matron, whom it simply murdered, even though here she stands in full view of you all, acting as if nothing had happened, which is perfectly natural, even though previously unheard-of, as I can prove, and in fact I can now prove everything and am suggesting a great deal more and won't let myself be put off but insist on getting my certificate and even prove that, for I put it to you: what is anything without proof? *Steadily increasing applause.* Without proof men aren't men but orangutans, as proved by Darwin, and what about Progress, and just bat an eyelid, thou wretched little nonentity of a lie-sodden Elephant Calf, phoney to the very marrow, then I'll absolutely prove – in fact this is really the point of the whole thing, gentlemen – that this here Elephant Calf is no Elephant Calf whatsoever, but none other than Jeraiah Jip from Tipperary.

SOLDIERS: Hooray.

GALY GAY: It won't wash.

POLLY: And why not? Why won't it wash?

GALY GAY: Because it's not in the book. Take that back.

POLLY: Anyway, you're a murderer.

GALY GAY: That's a lie.

POLLY: But I can prove it. Prove it, prove it, prove it.

Galy Gay hurls himself with a groan at the Banana Tree whose base gives way under the force of his attack.

POLLY *falling*: See that? See that?

URIAH: All right, now you are a murderer.

POLLY *groaning*: And I proved it.

Curtain.

URIAH: Straight into the song, now.

The four players quickly take up positions before the curtain and sing.

    What a bit of all right in Uganda
    Seven cents a seat on the verandah
    And the poker games we played with that old tiger –
    No, I've never played as well as that.
    When we bet the hide off old Pa Krueger
    He bet nothing but his battered hat.
      How peacefully the moon shone in Uganda!
      Through the cool night we sat about
      Until sunrise
      And then pulled out.
      A man needs money to be able
      To sit at the poker table
      With a tiger in disguise.
      (Seven cents a seat on the verandah.)

SOLDIERS: Is it all over? It's a bloody travesty of justice. Call that a proper ending? You can't leave off like that. Keep the curtain up. Play on.

POLLY: What do you mean? We've come to the end of the script. Be reasonable, the play's over.

SOLDIERS: I never heard such a piece of cheek in all my life.

It's an absolute utter outrage, it offends every decent human instinct. *A compact group climbs on the stage and says seriously*: We want our money back. Either the Elephant Calf comes to a proper conclusion or else every single cent piece of ours must be on your table in two seconds, you Moon of Cooch Behar.

POLLY: It is our earnest submission that what we performed was the absolute truth.

SOLDIERS: All right, just you wait. We'll give you absolute truth.

POLLY: The fact is that you've no notion of art and no idea how artists should be treated.

SOLDIERS: Don't waste your breath.

GALY GAY: I wouldn't like you blokes to imagine I wouldn't stick up for what you've just seen, get me?

POLLY: Bravo, boss.

GALY GAY: Don't let's beat about the bush. Whichever of you is keenest to get his money back, let me just say I'd like to invite that particular phenomenon to step outside straight away for eight rounds with the four-ounce gloves.

SOLDIERS: Go on Towneley, see if you can wipe the floor with that Elephant Calf's little trunk.

GALY GAY: And now I fancy we'll see if what we performed was the absolute truth, or if it was good or bad theatre, my friends.

All off to the fight.

The Threepenny Opera
after John Gay: The Beggar's Opera

Collaborators: ELISABETH HAUPTMANN, KURT WEILL

Translators: RALPH MANHEIM, JOHN WILLETT

Characters
MACHEATH, *called Mac the Knife*
JONATHAN JEREMIAH PEACHUM, *proprietor of the Beggar's Friend Ltd*
CELIA PEACHUM, *his wife*
POLLY PEACHUM, *his daughter*
BROWN, *High Sheriff of London*
LUCY, *his daughter*
LOW-DIVE JENNY
SMITH
THE REVEREND KIMBALL
FILCH
A BALLAD SINGER
THE GANG
Beggars
Whores
Constables

PROLOGUE

The Ballad of Mac the Knife

Fair in Soho.

The beggars are begging, the thieves are stealing, the whores are whoring. A ballad singer sings a ballad.

See the shark with teeth like razors.
All can read his open face.
And Macheath has got a knife, but
Not in such an obvious place.

See the shark, how red his fins are
As he slashes at his prey.
Mac the Knife wears white kid gloves which
Give the minimum away.

By the Thames's turbid waters
Men abruptly tumble down.
Is it plague or is it cholera?
Or a sign Macheath's in town?

On a beautiful blue Sunday
See a corpse stretched in the Strand.
See a man dodge round the corner . . .
Mackie's friends will understand.

And Schmul Meier, reported missing
Like so many wealthy men:
Mac the Knife acquired his cash box.
God alone knows how or when.

Peachum goes walking across the stage from left to right with his wife and daughter.

Jenny Towler turned up lately
With a knife stuck through her breast
While Macheath walks the Embankment
Nonchalantly unimpressed.

Where is Alfred Gleet the cabman?
Who can get that story clear?
All the world may know the answer
Just Macheath has no idea.

And the ghastly fire in Soho –
Seven children at a go –
In the crowd stands Mac the Knife, but he
Isn't asked and doesn't know.

And the child-bride in her nightie
Whose assailant's still at large
Violated in her slumbers –
Mackie, how much did you charge?

Laughter among the whores. A man steps out from their midst and walks quickly away across the square.

LOW-DIVE JENNY: That was Mac the Knife!

ACT ONE

I

To combat the increasing callousness of mankind, J. Peachum, a man of business, has opened a shop where the poorest of the poor can acquire an exterior that will touch the hardest of hearts.

Jonathan Jeremiah Peacham's outfitting shop for beggars.

PEACHUM'S MORNING HYMN

You ramshackle Christian, awake!
Get on with your sinful employment
Show what a good crook you could make.
The Lord will cut short your enjoyment.

Betray your own brother, you rogue
And sell your old woman, you rat.
You think the Lord God's just a joke?
He'll give you His Judgement on that.

PEACHUM *to the audience:* Something new is needed. My business is too hard, for my business is arousing human sympathy. There are a few things that stir men's souls, just a few, but the trouble is that after repeated use they lose their effect. Because man has the abominable gift of being able to deaden his feelings as well, so to speak. Suppose, for instance, a man sees another man standing on the corner with a stump for an arm; the first time he may be shocked enough to give him tenpence, but the second time it will only be fivepence, and if he sees him a third time he'll hand him over to the police without batting an eyelash. It's the same with the spiritual approach. *A large sign saying 'It is more blessed to give than to receive' is lowered from the grid.* What good are the most beautiful, the most poignant sayings, painted on the most enticing little signs, when they get expended so quickly? The Bible has four or five sayings that stir the heart; once a man has expended them, there's nothing for it but starvation. Take this one, for instance – 'Give and it shall be given unto you' – how threadbare it is after hanging here a mere three weeks. Yes, you have to keep on offering something new. So it's back to the good old Bible again, but how long can it go on providing?

Knocking. Peachum opens. Enter a young man by the name of Filch.

FILCH: Messrs Peachum & Co.?

PEACHUM: Peachum.

FILCH: Are you the proprietor of The Beggar's Friend Ltd.? I've been sent to you. Fine slogans you've got there! Money in the bank, those are. Got a whole library full of them, I suppose? That's what I call really something. What chance has a bloke like me got to think up ideas like that; and how can business progress without education?

PEACHUM: What's your name?

FILCH: It's this way, Mr Peachum, I've been down on my luck since a boy. Mother drank, father gambled. Left to my own resources at an early age, without a mother's tender hand, I sank deeper and deeper into the quicksands of the big city. I've never known a father's care or the blessings of a happy home. So now you see me . . .

PEACHUM: So now I see you . . .

FILCH *confused:* . . . bereft of all support, a prey to my baser instincts.

PEACHUM: Like a derelict on the high seas and so on. Now tell me, derelict, which district have you been reciting that fairy story in?

FILCH: What do you mean, Mr Peachum?

PEACHUM: You deliver that speech in public, I take it?

FILCH: Well, it's this way, Mr Peachum, yesterday there was an unpleasant little incident in Highland Street. There I am, standing on the corner quiet and miserable, holding out my hat, no suspicion of anything nasty . . .

PEACHUM *leafs through a notebook:* Highland Street. Yes, yes, right. You're the bastard that Honey and Sam caught yesterday. You had the impudence to be molesting passers-by in District 10. We let you off with a thrashing because we had reason to believe you didn't know what's what. But if you show your face again it'll be the chop for you. Got it?

FILCH: Please, Mr Peachum, please. What can I do, Mr Peachum? The gentlemen beat me black and blue and then they gave me your business card. If I took off my coat, you'd think you were looking at a fish on a slab.

PEACHUM: My friend, if you're not flat as a kipper, then my men weren't doing their job properly. Along come these young whipper-snappers who think they've only got to hold out their paw to land a steak. What would you say if someone started fishing the best trout out of your pond?

FILCH: It's like this, Mr Peachum – I haven't got a pond.

PEACHUM: Licences are delivered to professionals only. *Points in a businesslike way to a map of the city.* London is divided into fourteen districts. Any man who intends to practise the craft of begging in any one of them needs a licence from Jonathan Jeremiah Peachum & Co. Why, anybody could come along – a prey to his baser instincts.

FILCH: Mr Peachum, only a few shillings stand between me and utter ruin. Something must be done. With two shillings in my pocket I . . .

PEACHUM: One pound.

FILCH: Mr Peachum!

Points imploringly at a sign saying 'Do not turn a deaf ear to misery!' Peachum points to the curtain over a showcase, on which is written: 'Give and it shall be given unto you!'

FILCH: Ten bob.

PEACHUM: Plus fifty per cent of your take, settle up once a week. With outfit seventy per cent.

FILCH: What does the outfit consist of?

PEACHUM: That's for the firm to decide.

FILCH: Which district could I start in?

PEACHUM: Baker Street. Numbers 2 to 104. That comes even cheaper. Only fifty per cent, including the outfit.

FILCH: Very well. *He pays.*

PEACHUM: Your name?

FILCH: Charles Filch.

PEACHUM: Right. *Shouts.* Mrs Peachum! *Mrs Peachum enters.* This is Filch. Number 314. Baker Street district. I'll do his entry myself. Trust you to pick this moment to apply, just before the Coronation, when for once in a lifetime there's a chance of making a little something. Outfit C. *He opens a linen curtain before a showcase in which there are five wax dummies.*

FILCH: What's that?

PEACHUM: Those are the five basic types of misery, those most likely to touch the human heart. The sight of such types puts a man into the unnatural state where he is willing to part with money. Outfit A: Victim of vehicular progress. The merry paraplegic, always cheerful – *He acts it out.* – always carefree, emphasised by arm-stump. Outfit B: Victim of the Higher Strategy. The Tiresome Trembler, molests passers-by, operates by inspiring nausea – *He acts it out.* – attenuated by medals. Outfit C: Victim of advanced Technology. The Pitiful Blind Man, the Cordon Bleu of Beggary.

He acts it out, staggering toward Filch. The moment he bumps into Filch, Filch cries out in horror. Peachum stops at once, looks at him with amazement and suddenly roars.

He's *sorry* for me! You'll never be a beggar as long as you live! You're only fit to be begged from! Very well, outfit D! Celia, you've been drinking again. And now you can't see straight. Number 136 has complained about his outfit. How often do I have to tell you that a gentleman doesn't put on filthy clothes? The only thing about it that could inspire pity was the stains and they should have been added by just ironing in candle wax. Use your head! Have I got to do everything myself? *To Filch:* Take off your clothes and put this on, but mind you, look after it!

FILCH: What about my things?

PEACHUM: Property of the firm. Outfit E: young man who has seen better days or, if you'd rather, never thought it would come to this.

FILCH: Oh, you use them again? Why can't I do the better days act?

PEACHUM: Because nobody can make his own suffering sound convincing, my boy. If you have a bellyache and say so, people will simply be disgusted. Anyway, you're not here to ask questions but to put these things on.

FILCH: Aren't they rather dirty? *After Peachum has given him a penetrating look.* Excuse me, sir, please excuse me.

MRS PEACHUM: Shake a leg, son, I'm not standing here holding your trousers till Christmas.

FILCH *suddenly emphatic:* But I'm not taking my shoes off! Absolutely not. I'd sooner pack the whole thing in. They're the only present my poor mother ever gave me, I may have sunk pretty low, but never . . .

MRS PEACHUM: Stop drivelling. We all know your feet are dirty.

FILCH: Where am I supposed to wash my feet? In mid-winter?

Mrs Peachum leads him behind a screen, then she sits down on the left and starts ironing candle wax into a suit.

PEACHUM: Where's your daughter?

MRS PEACHUM: Polly? Upstairs.

PEACHUM: Has that man been here again? The one who's always coming round when I'm out?

MRS PEACHUM: Don't be so suspicious, Jonathan, there's no finer gentleman. The Captain takes a real interest in our Polly.

PEACHUM: I see.

MRS PEACHUM: And if I've got half an eye in my head, Polly thinks he's very nice too.

PEACHUM: Celia, the way you chuck your daughter around anyone would think I was a millionaire. Wanting to marry her off? The idea! Do you think this lousy business of ours would survive a week if those ragamuffins our customers had nothing better than *our* legs to look at? A husband! He'd have us in his clutches in three shakes! In his clutches! Do you think your daughter can hold her tongue in bed any better than you?

MRS PEACHUM: A fine opinion of your daughter you have.

PEACHUM: The worst. The very worst. A lump of sensuality, that's what she is.

MRS PEACHUM: If so, she didn't get it from you.

PEACHUM: Marriage! I expect my daughter to be to me as bread to the hungry. *He leafs in the Book.* It even says so in the Bible somewhere. Anyway marriage is disgusting. I'll teach her to get married.

MRS PEACHUM: Jonathan, you're just a barbarian.

PEACHUM: Barbarian! What's this gentleman's name?

MRS PEACHUM: They never call him anything but 'the Captain'.

PEACHUM: So you haven't even asked him his name? Interesting.

MRS PEACHUM: You don't suppose we'd ask for a birth certificate when such a distinguished gentleman invites Polly and me to the Cuttlefish Hotel for a little hop.

PEACHUM: Where?

MRS PEACHUM: To the Cuttlefish Hotel for a little hop.

PEACHUM: Captain? Cuttlefish Hotel? Hm, hm, hm . . .

MRS PEACHUM: A gentleman who has always handled me and my daughter with kid gloves.

PEACHUM: Kid gloves!

MRS PEACHUM: Honest, he always does wear gloves, white ones: white kid gloves.

PEACHUM: I see. White gloves and a cane with an ivory handle and spats and patent-leather shoes and a charismatic personality and a scar . . .

MRS PEACHUM: On his neck. Isn't there anyone you don't know?

Filch crawls out from behind the screen.

FILCH: Mr Peachum, couldn't you give me a few tips, I've always believed in having a system and not just shooting off my mouth any old how.

MRS PEACHUM: A system!

PEACHUM: He can be a half-wit. Come back this evening at six, we'll teach you the rudiments. Now piss off!

FILCH: Thank you very much indeed, Mr Peachum. Many thanks. *Goes out.*

PEACHUM: Fifty per cent! – And now I'll tell you who this

gentleman with the gloves is – Mac the *Knife! He runs up the stairs to Polly's bedroom.*

MRS PEACHUM: God in Heaven! Mac the Knife! Jesus! Gentle Jesus meek and mild – Polly! Where's Polly?
Peachum comes down slowly.

PEACHUM: Polly? Polly's not come home. Her bed has not been slept in.

MRS PEACHUM: She'll have gone to supper with that wool merchant. That'll be it, Jonathan.

PEACHUM: Let's hope to God it is the wool merchant!
Mr and Mrs Peachum step before the curtain and sing. Song lighting: golden glow. The organ is lit up. Three lamps are lowered from above on a pole, and the signs say:

THE 'NO THEY CAN'T' SONG

No, they can't
Bear to be at home all tucked up tight in bed.
It's fun they want
You can bet they've got some fancy notions brewing up
    instead.

So that's your Moon over Soho
That is your infernal 'd'you feel my heart beating?' line.
That's the old 'wherever you go I shall be with you,
    honey'
When you first fall in love and the moonbeams shine.

No, they can't
See what's good for them and set their mind on it.
It's fun they want
So they end up on their arses in the shit.

Then where's your Moon over Soho?
What's come of your infernal 'd'you feel my heart beat-
    ing?' bit?
Where's the old 'wherever you go I shall be with you,
    honey'?
When you're no more in love, and you're in the shit?

2

Deep in the heart of Soho the bandit Mac the
Knife is celebrating his marriage to Polly
Peachum, the beggar king's daughter.

Bare stable.

MATTHEW, *known as Matt of the Mint, holds out his revolver and
searches the stable with a lantern:* Hey, hands up, anybody
that's here!
*Macheath enters and makes a tour of inspection along the foot-
lights.*
MACHEATH: Well, is there anybody?
MATTHEW: Not a soul. Just the place for our wedding.
POLLY *enters in wedding dress:* But it's a stable!
MAC: Sit on the feed-bin for the moment, Polly. *To the audi-
ence:* Today this stable will witness my marriage to Miss
Polly Peachum, who has followed me for love in order to
share my life with me.
MATTHEW: All over London they'll be saying this is the most
daring job you've ever pulled, Mac, enticing Mr Peachum's
only child from his home.
MAC: Who's Mr Peachum?
MATTHEW: He'll tell you he's the poorest man in Lon-
don.
POLLY: But you can't be meaning to have our wedding here?
Why, it is a common stable. You can't ask the vicar to a
place like this. Besides, it isn't even ours. We really
oughtn't to start our new life with a burglary, Mac. Why,
this is the biggest day of our life.
MAC: Dear child, everything shall be done as you wish. We
can't have you embarrassed in any way. The trimmings will
be here in a moment.
MATTHEW: That'll be the furniture.
Large vans are heard driving up. Half a dozen men come in, carry-

*ing carpets, furniture, dishes, etc., with which they transform the
stable into an exaggeratedly luxurious room.*[1]*

MAC: Junk.

*The gentlemen put their presents down left, congratulate the bride
and report to the bridegroom.*[2]

JAKE *known as Crook-fingered Jake*: Congratulations! At 14
Ginger Street there were some people on the second floor.
We had to smoke them out.

BOB *known as Bob the Saw*: Congratulations! A copper got done
in the Strand.

MAC: Amateurs.

NED: We did all we could, but three people in the West End
were past saving. Congratulations!

MAC: Amateurs and bunglers.

JIMMY: An old gent got hurt a bit, but I don't think it's anything serious. Congratulations.

MAC: My orders were: avoid bloodshed. It makes me sick to
think of it. You'll never make business men! Cannibals,
perhaps, but not business men!

WALTER *known as Dreary Walt*: Congratulations. Only half an
hour ago, Madam, that harpsichord belonged to the
Duchess of Somerset.

POLLY: What is this furniture anyway?

MAC: How do you like the furniture, Polly?

POLLY *in tears*: Those poor people, all for a few sticks of
furniture.

MAC: And what furniture! Junk! You have a perfect right to
be angry. A rosewood harpsichord along with a renaissance
sofa. That's unforgivable. What about a table?

WALTER: A table?

They lay some planks over the bins.

POLLY: Oh, Mac, I'm so miserable! I only hope the vicar
doesn't come.

MATTHEW: Of course he'll come. We gave him exact
directions.

WALTER *introduces the table*: A table!

MAC *seeing Polly in tears*: My wife is very much upset. Where
are the rest of the chairs? A harpsichord and the happy

* These numbers refer to the 'Hints for actors' in the Notes p. 93 ff.

couple has to sit on the floor! Use your heads! For once
I'm having a wedding, and how often does that happen?
Shut up, Dreary! And how often does it happen that I leave
you to do something on your own? And when I do you
start by upsetting my wife.

NED: Dear Polly . . .

MAC *knocks his hat off his head³*: 'Dear Polly'! I'll bash your
head through your kidneys with your 'dear Polly', you
squirt. Have you ever heard the like? 'Dear Polly!' I suppose you've been to bed with her?

POLLY: Mac!

NED: I swear . . .

WALTER: Dear madam, if any items of furniture should be
lacking, we'll be only too glad to go back and . . .

MAC: A rosewood harpsichord and no chairs. *Laughs.* Speaking as a bride, what do you say to that?

POLLY: It could be worse.

MAC: Two chairs and a sofa and the bridal couple has to sit on
the floor.

POLLY: Something new, I'd say.

MAC *sharply*: Get the legs sawn off this harpsichord! Go on!

FOUR MEN *saw the legs off the harpsichord and sing:*

Bill Lawgen and Mary Syer
Were made man and wife a week ago.
When it was over and they exchanged a kiss
He was thinking 'Whose wedding dress was this?'
While his name was one thing she'd rather like to
know.
Hooray!

WALTER: The finished article, madam: there's your bench.

MAC: May I now ask the gentlemen to take off those filthy
rags and put on some decent clothes? This isn't just anybody's wedding, you know. Polly, may I ask you to look
after the fodder?

POLLY: Is this our wedding feast? Was the whole lot stolen,
Mac?

MAC: Of course. Of course.

POLLY: I wonder what you will do if there's a knock at the door and the sheriff steps in.

MAC: I'll show you what your husband will do in that situation.

MATTHEW: It couldn't happen today. The mounted police are all sure to be in Daventry. They'll be escorting the Queen back to town for Friday's Coronation.

POLLY: Two knives and fourteen forks! One knife per chair.

MAC: What incompetence! That's the work of apprentices, not experienced men! Haven't you any sense of style? Fancy not knowing the difference between Chippendale and Louis Quatorze.

The gang comes back. The gentlemen are now wearing fashionable evening dress, but unfortunately their movements are not in keeping with it.

WALTER: We only wanted to bring the most valuable stuff. Look at that wood! Really first class.

MATTHEW: Ssst! Ssst! Permit us, Captain . . .

MAC: Polly, come here a minute.

Mac and Polly assume the pose of a couple prepared to receive congratulations.

MATTHEW: Permit us, Captain, on the greatest day of your life, in the full bloom of your career, or rather the turning point, to offer you our heartiest and at the same time most sincere congratulations, etcetera. That posh talk don't half make me sick. So to cut a long story short – *Shakes Mac's hand.* – keep up the good work, old mate.

MAC: Thank you, that was kind of you, Matthew.

MATTHEW *shaking Polly's hand after embracing Mac with emotion*: It was spoken from the heart, all right! So as I was saying, keep it up, old china, I mean – *Grinning* – the good work of course.

Roars of laughter from the guests. Suddenly Mac with a deft movement sends Matthew to the floor.

MAC: Shut your trap. Keep that filth for Kitty, she's the kind of slut that appreciates it.

POLLY: Mac, don't be so vulgar.

MATTHEW: Here, I don't like that. Calling Kitty a slut . . . *Stands up with difficulty.*

MAC: Oh, so you don't like that?

MATTHEW: And besides, I never use filthy language with her. I respect Kitty too much. But maybe you wouldn't understand that, the way you are. You're a fine one to talk about filth. Do you think Lucy didn't tell me the things you've told her? Compared to that, I'm driven snow.
Mac looks at him.

JAKE: Cut it out, this is a wedding. *They pull him away.*

MAC: Fine wedding, isn't it, Polly? Having to see trash like this around you on the day of your marriage. You wouldn't have thought your husband's friends would let him down. Think about it.

POLLY: I think it's nice.

ROBERT: Blarney. Nobody's letting you down. What's a difference of opinion between friends? Kitty's as good as the next girl. But now bring out your wedding present, mate.

ALL: Yes, hand it over!

MATTHEW *offended:* Here.

POLLY: Oh, a wedding present. How kind of you, Mr Matt of the Mint. Look, Mac, what a lovely nightgown.

MATTHEW: Another bit of filth, eh, Captain?

MAC: Forget it. I didn't mean to hurt your feelings on this festive occasion.

WALTER: What do you say to this? Chippendale!
He unveils an enormous Chippendale grandfather clock.

MAC: Quatorze.

POLLY: It's wonderful. I'm so happy. Words fail me. You're so unbelievably kind. Oh, Mac, isn't it a shame we've no flat to put it in?

MAC: Hm, it's a start in the right direction. The great thing is to get started. Thank you kindly, Walter. Go on, clear the stuff away now. Food!

JAKE *while the others start setting the table:* Trust me to come empty-handed again. *Intensely to Polly:* Believe me, young lady, I find it most distressing.

POLLY: It doesn't matter in the least, Mr Crook-finger Jake.

JAKE: Here are the boys flinging presents right and left, and me standing here like a fool. What a situation to be in! It's always the way with me. Situations! It's enough to make your hair stand on end. The other day I meet Low-Dive Jenny; well, I say, you old cow . . .

Suddenly he sees Mac standing behind him and goes off without a word.

MAC *leads Polly to her place:* This is the best food you'll taste today, Polly. Gentlemen!

All sit down to the wedding feast.[4]

NED *indicating the china:* Beautiful dishes, Savoy Hotel.

JAKE: The plover's eggs are from Selfridge's. There was supposed to be a bucket of foie gras. But Jimmy ate it on the way, he was mad because it had a hole in it.

WALTER: We don't talk about holes in polite society.

JIMMY: Don't bolt your eggs like that, Ned, not on a day like this.

MAC: Couldn't somebody sing something? Something splendiferous?

MATTHEW *choking with laughter:* Something splendiferous? That's a first-class word. *He sits down in embarrassment under Mac's withering glance.*

MAC *knocks a bowl out of someone's hand:* I didn't mean us to start eating yet. Instead of seeing you people wade straight into the trough, I would have liked something from the heart. That's what other people do on this sort of occasion.

JAKE: What, for instance?

MAC: Am I supposed to think of everything myself? I'm not asking you to put on an opera. But you might have arranged for something else besides stuffing your bellies and making filthy jokes. Oh well, it's a day like this that you find out who your friends are.

POLLY: The salmon is marvellous, Mac.

NED: I bet you've never eaten anything like it. You get that every day at Mac the Knife's. You've landed in the honey pot all right. That's what I've always said: Mac is the right match for a girl with a feeling for higher things. As I was saying to Lucy only yesterday.

POLLY: Lucy? Mac, who is Lucy?

JAKE *embarrassed:* Lucy? Oh, nothing serious, you know.

Matthew has risen; standing behind Polly, he is waving his arms to shut Jake up.

POLLY *sees him:* Do you want something? Salt perhaps . . .? What were you saying, Mr Jake?

JAKE: Oh, nothing, nothing at all. The main thing I wanted to say really was nothing at all. I'm always putting my foot in it.

MAC: What have you got in your hand, Jake?

JAKE: A knife, Boss.

MAC: And what have you got on your plate?

JAKE: A trout, Boss.

MAC: I see. And with the knife you are eating the trout, are you not? It's incredible. Did you ever see the like of it, Polly? Eating his fish with a knife! Anybody who does that is just a plain swine, do you get me, Jake? Think about it. You'll have your hands full, Polly, trying to turn trash like this into a human being. Have you boys got the least idea what that is?

WALTER: A human being or a human pee-ing?

POLLY: Really, Mr Walter!

MAC: So you won't sing a song, something to brighten up the day? Has it got to be a miserable gloomy day like any other? And come to think of it, is anybody guarding the door? I suppose you want me to attend to that myself too? Do you want me on this day of days to guard the door so you lot can stuff your bellies at my expense?

WALTER *sullenly:* What do you mean at your expense?

JIMMY: Stow it, Walter boy. I'm on my way. Who's going to come here anyway? *Goes out.*

JAKE: A fine joke on a day like this if all the wedding guests were pulled in.

JIMMY *rushes in:* Hey, Captain. The cops!

WALTER: Tiger Brown!

MATTHEW: Nonsense, it's the Reverend Kimball.
Kimball enters.

ALL *roar:* Good evening, Reverend Kimball!

KIMBALL: So I've found you after all. I find you in a lowly hut, a humble place but your own.

MAC: Property of the Duke of Devonshire.

POLLY: Good evening, Reverend. Oh, I'm so glad that on the happiest day of our life you . . .

MAC: And now I request a rousing song for the Reverend Kimball.

MATTHEW: How about Bill Lawgen and Mary Syer?

JAKE: Good. Bill Lawgen might be just the thing.

KIMBALL: Be nice if you'd do a little number, boys.

MATTHEW: Let's have it, gentlemen.

Three men rise and sing hesitantly, weakly and uncertainly:

WEDDING SONG FOR THE LESS WELL-OFF

Bill Lawgen and Mary Syer
Were made man and wife a week ago
(Three cheers for the happy couple: hip, hip, hooray!)
When it was over and they exchanged a kiss
He was thinking 'Whose wedding dress was this?'
While his name was one thing she'd rather like to know.
Hooray!

Do you know what your wife's up to? No!
Do you like her sleeping round like that? No!
Three cheers for the happy couple: Hip, hip, hooray!
Billy Lawgen told me recently
Just one part of her will do for me.
The swine.
Hooray!

MAC: Is that all? Penurious!

MATTHEW *chokes again:* Penurious is the word, gentlemen.

MAC: Shut your trap!

MATTHEW: Oh, I only meant no gusto, no fire, and so on.

POLLY: Gentlemen, if none of you wishes to perform, I myself will sing a little song; it's an imitation of a girl I saw once in some twopenny-halfpenny dive in Soho. She was washing the glasses, and everybody was laughing at her, and then she turned to the guests and said things like the things I'm going to sing to you. Right. This is a little bar, I want you to think of it as filthy. She stood behind it morning and night. This is the bucket and this is the rag she washed the glasses with. Where you are sitting, the customers were sitting laughing at her. You can laugh too, to make it exactly the same; but if you don't want to, you don't have to. *She starts pretending to wash glasses, muttering to herself.* Now, for instance, one of them – it might be you – *Pointing at Walter* – says: Well, when's your ship coming in, Jenny?

WALTER: Well, when's your ship coming in, Jenny?

POLLY: And another says – you, for instance: Still washing up glasses, Jenny the pirate's bride?

MATTHEW: Still washing up glasses, Jenny the pirate's bride?

POLLY: Good. And now I'll begin.

Song lighting: golden glow. The organ is lit up. Three lamps are lowered from above on a pole, and the signs say:

PIRATE JENNY

Now you gents all see I've the glasses to wash.
When a bed's to be made I make it.
You may tip me with a penny, and I'll thank you very
    well
And you see me dressed in tatters, and this tatty old hotel
And you never ask how long I'll take it.
But one of these evenings there will be screams from the
    harbour
And they'll ask: what can all that screaming be?
And they'll see me smiling as I do the glasses
And they'll say: how she can smile beats me.
    And a ship with eight sails and
    All its fifty guns loaded
    Has tied up at the quay.

They say: get on, dry your glasses, my girl
And they tip me and don't give a damn.
And their penny is accepted, and their bed will be made
(Although nobody is going to sleep there, I'm afraid)
And they still have no idea who I am.
But one of these evenings there will be explosions from
    the harbour,
And they'll ask: what kind of a bang was that?

And they'll see me as I stand beside the window
And they'll say: what has she got to smile at?
    And that ship with eight sails and
    All its fifty guns loaded
    Will lay siege to the town.

Then you gents, you aren't going to find it a joke
For the walls will be knocked down flat
And in no time the town will be rased to the ground.
Just one tatty old hotel will be left standing safe and
    sound
And they'll ask: did someone special live in that?
Then there'll be a lot of people milling round the hotel
And they'll ask: what made them let that place alone?
And they'll see me as I leave the door next morning
And they'll say: don't tell us she's the one.
    And that ship with eight sails and
    All its fifty guns loaded
    Will run up its flag.

And a hundred men will land in the bright midday sun
Each stepping where the shadows fall.
They'll look inside each doorway and grab anyone they
    see
And put him in irons and then bring him to me
And they'll ask: which of these should we kill?
In that noonday heat there'll be a hush round the harbour
As they ask which has got to die.
And you'll hear me as I softly answer: the lot!
And as the first head rolls I'll say: hoppla!
    And that ship with eight sails and
    All its fifty guns loaded
    Will vanish with me.

MATTHEW: Very nice. Cute, eh? The way the missus puts it
across!
MAC: What do you mean nice? It's not nice, you idiot! It's
art, it's not nice. You did that marvellously, Polly. But it's
wasted on trash like this, if you'll excuse me, your Rever-

ence. *In an undertone to Polly:* Anyway, I don't like you play-acting; let's not have any more of it.

Laughter at the table. The gang is making fun of the parson.

What you got in your hand, your Reverence?

JAKE: Two knives, Captain.

MAC: What you got on your plate, your Reverence?

KIMBALL: Salmon, I think.

MAC: And with that knife you are eating the salmon, are you not?

JAKE: Did you ever see the like of it, eating fish with a knife? Anybody who does that is just a plain . . .

MAC: Swine. Do you understand me, Jake? Think about it.

JIMMY *rushing in:* Hey, Captain, coppers. The sheriff in person.

WALTER: Brown. Tiger Brown!

MAC: Yes, Tiger Brown, exactly. It's Tiger Brown himself, the Chief Sheriff of London, pillar of the Old Bailey, who will now enter Captain Macheath's humble abode. Think about it.

The bandits creep away.

JAKE: It'll be the drop for us!

Brown enters.

MAC: Hullo, Jackie.

BROWN: Hullo, Mac! I haven't much time, got to be leaving in a minute. Does it have to be somebody else's stable? Why, this is breaking and entering again!

MAC: But Jackie, it's such a good address. I'm glad you could come to old Mac's wedding. Let me introduce my wife, née Peachum. Polly, this is Tiger Brown, what do you say, old man? *Slaps him on the back.* And these are my friends, Jackie, I imagine you've seen them all before.

BROWN *pained:* I'm here unofficially, Mac.

MAC: So are they. *He calls them. They come in with their hands up.* Hey, Jake.

BROWN: That's Crook-fingered Jake. He's a dirty dog.

MAC: Hey, Jimmy; hey, Bob; hey, Walter!

BROWN: Well, just for today I'll turn a blind eye.

MAC: Hey, Ned; hey, Matthew.

BROWN: Be seated, gentlemen, be seated.

ALL: Thank you, sir.

BROWN: I'm delighted to meet my old friend Mac's charming
wife.

POLLY: Don't mention it, sir.

MAC: Sit down, you old bugger, and pitch into the whisky! –
Polly and gentlemen! You have today in your midst a man
whom the king's inscrutable wisdom has placed high above
his fellow men and who has none the less remained my
friend throughout the storms and perils, and so on. You
know who I mean, and you too know who I mean, Brown.
Ah, Jackie, do you remember how we served in India together, soldiers both of us? Ah, Jackie, let's sing the
Cannon Song right now.

They sit down on the table.

*Song lighting: golden glow. The organ is lit up. Three lamps are
lowered from above on a pole, and the signs say:*

THE CANNON SONG

John was all present and Jim was all there
And Georgie was up for promotion.
Not that the army gave a bugger who they were
When confronting some heathen commotion.
    The troops live under
    The cannon's thunder
    From the Cape to Cooch Behar.
    Moving from place to place
    When they come face to face
    With a different breed of fellow
    Whose skin is black or yellow
    They quick as winking chop him into beefsteak
        tartare.

Johnny found his whisky too warm
And Jim found the weather too balmy
But Georgie took them both by the arm
And said: never let down the army.
    The troops live under
    The cannon's thunder

From the Cape to Cooch Behar.
Moving from place to place
When they come face to face
With a different breed of fellow
Whose skin is black or yellow
They quick as winking chop him into beefsteak
tartare.

John is a write-off and Jimmy is dead
And they shot poor old Georgie for looting
But young men's blood goes on being red
And the army goes on recruiting.
The troops live under
The cannon's thunder
From the Cape to Cooch Behar.
Moving from place to place
When they come face to face
With a different breed of fellow
Whose skin is black or yellow
They quick as winking chop him into beefsteak
tartare.

MAC: Though life with its raging torrent has carried us boyhood friends far apart, although our professional interests
are very different, some people would go so far as to say
diametrically opposed, our friendship has come through
unimpaired. Think about it. Castor and Pollux, Hector and
Andromache, etcetera. Seldom have I, the humble bandit,
well, you know what I mean, made even the smallest haul
without giving him, my friend, a share, a substantial share,
Brown, as a gift and token of my unswerving loyalty, and
seldom has he, take that knife out of your mouth, Jake, the
all-powerful police chief, staged a raid without sending me,
his boyhood friend, a little tip-off. Well, and so on and so
forth, it's all a matter of give and take. Think about it. *He
takes Brown by the arm.* Well, Jackie, old man, I'm glad
you've come, I call that real friendship. *Pause, because Brown
has been looking sadly at a carpet.* Genuine Shiraz.
BROWN: From the Oriental Carpet Company.

MAC: Yes, we never go anywhere else. Do you know, Jackie, I had to have you here today, I hope it's not awkward for you in your position?

BROWN: You know, Mac, that I can't refuse you anything. I must be going, I've really got so much on my plate; if the slightest thing should go wrong at the Queen's Coronation . . .

MAC: See here, Jackie, my father-in-law is a revolting old bastard. If he tries to make trouble for me, is there anything on record against me at Scotland Yard?

BROWN: There's nothing whatsoever on record against you at Scotland Yard.

MAC: I knew it.

BROWN: I've taken care of that. Good night.

MAC: Aren't you fellows going to stand up?

BROWN *to Polly:* Best of luck. *Goes out accompanied by Mac.*

JAKE *who along with Matthew and Walter has meanwhile been conferring with Polly:* I must admit I couldn't repress a certain alarm a while ago when I heard Tiger Brown was coming.

MATTHEW: You see, dear lady, we have contacts in the highest places.

WALTER: Yes, Mac always has some iron in the fire that the rest of us don't even suspect. But we have our own little iron in the fire. Gentlemen, it's half-past nine.

MATTHEW: And now comes the *pièce de résistance*.

All go upstage behind the carpet that conceals something. Mac enters.

MAC: I say, what's going on?

MATTHEW: Hey, Captain, another little surprise.

Behind the curtain they sing the Bill Lawgen song softly and with much feeling. But at 'his name was one thing she'd rather like to know' Matthew pulls down the carpet and all go on with the song, bellowing and pounding on the bed that has been disclosed.

MAC: Thank you, friends, thank you.

WALTER: And now we shall quietly take our leave.

The gang go out.

MAC: And now the time has come for softer sentiments. Without them man is a mere beast of burden. Sit down, Polly.

Music.

MAC: Look at the moon over Soho.

POLLY: I see it, dearest. Feel my heart beating, my beloved.

MAC: I feel it, beloved.

POLLY: Where'er you go I shall be with you.

MAC: And where you stay, there too shall I be.

BOTH:

> And though we've no paper to say we're wed
> And no altar covered with flowers
> And nobody knows for whom your dress was made
> And even the ring is not ours –
> The platter off which you've been eating your bread
> Give it one brief look; fling it far.
> For love will endure or not endure
> Regardless of where we are.

3

To Peachum, conscious of the hardness of the world, the loss of his daughter means utter ruin.

Peachum's Outfitting Emporium for Beggars.

To the right Peachum and Mrs Peachum. In the doorway stands Polly in her coat and hat, holding her travelling bag.

MRS PEACHUM: Married? First you rig her fore and aft in dresses and hats and gloves and parasols, and when she's cost as much as a sailing ship, she throws herself in the garbage like a rotten pickle. Are you really married?
Song lighting: golden glow. The organ is lit up. Three lamps are lowered from above on a pole and the signs say:

IN A LITTLE SONG POLLY GIVES HER PARENTS TO
UNDERSTAND THAT SHE HAS MARRIED THE
BANDIT MACHEATH:

I once used to think, in my innocent youth
(And I once was as innocent as you)
That someone someday might come my way
And then how should I know what's best to do?
And if he'd got money
And seemed a nice chap
And his workday shirts were white as snow
And if he knew how to treat a girl with due respect
I'd have to tell him: No.
    That's where you must keep your head screwed on
    And insist on going slow.
    Sure, the moon will shine throughout the night
    Sure, the boat is on the river, tied up tight.
    That's as far as things can go.
    Oh, you can't lie back, you must stay cold at heart
    Oh, you must not let your feelings show.
    Oh, whenever you feel it might start
    Ah, then your only answer's: No.

The first one that came was a man of Kent
And all that a man ought to be.
The second one owned three ships down at Wapping
And the third was crazy about me.
And as they'd got money
And all seemed nice chaps
And their workday shirts were white as snow
And as they knew how to treat a girl with due respect
Each time I told them: No.
    That's where I still kept my head screwed on
    And I chose to take it slow.
    Sure, the moon could shine throughout the night
    Sure, the boat was on the river, tied up tight
    That's as far as things could go.
    Oh, you can't lie back, you must stay cold at heart

Oh, you must not let your feelings show.
Oh, whenever you feel it might start
Ah, then your only answer's: No.

But then one day, and that day was blue
Came someone who didn't ask at all
And he went and hung his hat on the nail in my little
    attic
And what happened I can't quite recall.
And as he'd got no money
And was not a nice chap
And his Sunday shirts, even, were not like snow
And as he'd no idea of treating a girl with due respect
I could not tell him: No.
    That's the time my head was not screwed on
    And to hell with going slow.
    Oh, the moon was shining clear and bright
    Oh, the boat kept drifting downstream all that night
    That was how it simply had to go.
    Yes, you must lie back, you can't stay cold at heart
    In the end you have to let your feelings show.
    Oh, the moment you know it must start
    Ah, then's no time for saying: No.

PEACHUM: So she's associating with criminals. That's lovely. That's delightful.

MRS PEACHUM: If you're immoral enough to get married, did it have to be a horse-thief and a highwayman? That'll cost you dear one of these days! I ought to have seen it coming. Even as a child she had a swollen head like the Queen of England.

PEACHUM: So she's really got married!

MRS PEACHUM: Yes, yesterday, at five in the afternoon.

PEACHUM: To a notorious criminal. Come to think of it, it shows that the fellow is really audacious. If I give away my daughter, the sole prop of my old age, why, my house will cave in and my last dog will run off. I'd think twice about giving away the dirt under my fingernails, it would mean risking starvation. If the three of us can get through the winter on one log of wood, maybe we'll live to see the new year. Maybe.

MRS PEACHUM: What got into you? This is our reward for all we've done, Jonathan. I'm going mad. My head is swimming. I'm going to faint. Oh! *She faints*. A glass of Cordial Médoc.

PEACHUM: You see what you've done to your mother. Quick! Associating with criminals, that's lovely, that's delightful! Interesting how the poor woman takes it to heart. *Polly brings in a bottle of Cordial Médoc.* That's the only consolation your poor mother has left.

POLLY: Go ahead, give her two glasses. *My* mother can take twice as much when she's not quite herself. That will put her back on her feet. *During the whole scene she looks very happy.*

MRS PEACHUM *wakes up:* Oh, there she goes again, pretending to be so loving and sympathetic!
Five men enter.[5]

BEGGAR: I'm making a complaint, see, this thing is a mess, it's not a proper stump, it's a botch-up, and I'm not wasting my money on it.

PEACHUM: What do you expect? It's as good a stump as any other; it's just that you don't keep it clean.

BEGGAR: Then why don't I take as much money as the others? Naw, you can't do that to me. *Throws down the stump.* If I wanted crap like this, I could cut off my real leg.

PEACHUM: What do you fellows want anyway? Is it my fault if people have hearts of flint? I can't make you five stumps. In five minutes I can turn any man into such a pitiful wreck it would make a dog weep to see him. Is it my fault if people don't weep? Here's another stump for you if one's not enough. But look after your equipment!

BEGGAR: This one will do.

PEACHUM *tries a false limb on another:* Leather is no good, Celia; rubber is more repulsive. *To the third:* That swelling is going down and it's your last. Now we'll have to start all over again. *Examining the fourth:* Of course natural scabies is never as good as the artificial kind. *To the fifth:* You're a sight! You've been eating again. I'll have to make an example of you.

BEGGAR: Mr Peachum, I really haven't eaten anything much. I'm just abnormally fat, I can't help it.

PEACHUM: Nor can I. You're fired. *Again to the second beggar:* My dear man, there's an obvious difference between 'tugging at people's heart strings' and 'getting on people's nerves'. Yes, artists, that's what I need. Only an artist can tug at anybody's heart strings nowadays. If you fellows performed properly, your audience would be forced to applaud. You just haven't any ideas! Obviously I can't extend your engagement.

The beggars go out.

POLLY: Look. Is he particularly handsome? No. But he makes a living. He can support me. He is not only a first-class burglar but a far-sighted and experienced stick-up man as well. I've been into it, I can tell you the exact amount of his savings to date. A few successful ventures and we shall be able to retire to a little house in the country just like that Mr Shakespeare father admires so much.

PEACHUM: It's quite simple. You're married. What does a girl do when she's married? Use your head. Well, she gets divorced, see. Is that so hard to figure out?

POLLY: I don't know what you're talking about.

MRS PEACHUM: Divorce.

POLLY: But I love him. How can I think of divorce?

MRS PEACHUM: Really, have you no shame?

POLLY: Mother, if you've ever been in love . . .

MRS PEACHUM: In love! Those damn books you've been reading have turned your head. Why, Polly, everybody's doing it.

POLLY: Then I'm an exception.

MRS PEACHUM: Then I'm going to tan your behind, you exception.

POLLY: Oh yes, all mothers do that; but it doesn't help because love goes deeper than a tanned behind.

MRS PEACHUM: Don't strain my patience.

POLLY: I won't let my love be taken away from me.

MRS PEACHUM: One more word out of you and you'll get a clip on the ear.

POLLY: But love is the finest thing in the world.

MRS PEACHUM: Anyway, he's got several women, the black-guard. When he's hanged, like as not half a dozen widows will turn up, each of them like as not with a brat in her arms. Oh, Jonathan!

PEACHUM: Hanged, what made you think of that, that's a good idea. Run along, Polly. *Polly goes out.* Quite right. That'll earn us forty pounds.

MRS PEACHUM: I see. Report him to the sheriff.

PEACHUM: Naturally. And besides, that way we get him hanged free of charge . . . Two birds with one stone. Only we've got to find out where he's holed up.

MRS PEACHUM: I can tell you that, my dear, he's holed up with his tarts.

PEACHUM: But they won't turn him in.

MRS PEACHUM: Just let me attend to that. Money rules the world. I'll go to Turnbridge right away and talk to the girls. Give us a couple of hours, and after that if he meets a single one of them he's done for.

POLLY *has been listening behind the door*: Dear Mama, you can spare yourself the trip. Mac will go to the Old Bailey of his own accord sooner than meet any of those ladies. And even if he did go to the Old Bailey, the sheriff would serve him a cocktail; they'd smoke their cigars and have a little chat about a certain shop in this street where a little more goes on than meets the eye. Because, Papa dear, the sheriff was very cheerful at my wedding.

PEACHUM: What's this sheriff called?

POLLY: He's called Brown. But you probably know him as Tiger Brown. Because everyone who has reason to fear him calls him Tiger Brown. But my husband, you see, calls him Jackie. Because to him he's just dear old Jackie. They're boyhood friends.

PEACHUM: Oh, so they're friends, are they? The sheriff and Public Enemy No. 1, ha, they must be the only friends in this city.

POLLY *poetically*: Every time they drank a cocktail together, they stroked each other's cheeks and said: 'If you'll have the same again, I'll have the same again.' And every time one of them left the room, the other's eyes grew moist and he said: 'Where'er you go I shall be with you.' There's nothing on record against Mac at Scotland Yard.

PEACHUM: I see. Between Tuesday evening and Thursday morning Mr Macheath, a gentleman who has assuredly been married many times, lured my daughter from her home on pretext of marriage. Before the week is out, he will be taken to the gallows on that account, and deservedly so. 'Mr Macheath, you once had white kid gloves, a cane with an ivory handle, and a scar on your neck, and frequented the Cuttlefish Hotel. All that is left is your scar, undoubtedly the least valuable of your distinguishing marks, and today you frequent nothing but prison cells, and within the foreseeable future no place at all . . .'

MRS PEACHUM: Oh, Jonathan, you'll never bring it off. Why, he's Mac the Knife, whom they call the biggest criminal in London. He takes what he pleases.

PEACHUM: Who's Mac the Knife? Get ready, we're going to see the Sheriff of London. And you're going to Turnbridge.

MRS PEACHUM: To see his whores.

PEACHUM: For the villainy of the world is great, and a man needs to run his legs off to keep them from being stolen from under him.

POLLY: I, Papa, shall be delighted to shake hands with Mr Brown again.

All three step forward and sing the first finale. Song lighting. On the signs is written:

FIRST THREE-PENNY FINALE
CONCERNING THE INSECURITY OF THE HUMAN CONDITION

POLLY:
Am I reaching for the sky?
All I'm asking from this place is
To enjoy a man's embraces.
Is that aiming much too high?
PEACHUM *with a Bible in his hand:*
Man has a right, in this our brief existence
To call some fleeting happiness his own

Partake of worldly pleasures and subsistence
And have bread on his table rather than a stone.
Such are the basic rights of man's existence.
But do we know of anything suggesting
That when a thing's a right one gets it? No!
To get one's rights would be most interesting
But our condition's such it can't be so.

MRS PEACHUM:

How I want what's best for you
How I'd teach you airs and graces
Show you things and take you places
As a mother likes to do.

PEACHUM:

Let's practise goodness: who would disagree?
Let's give our wealth away: is that not right?
Once all are good His Kingdom is at hand
Where blissfully we'll bask in His pure light.
Let's practise goodness: who would disagree?
But sadly on this planet while we're waiting
The means are meagre and the morals low.
To get one's record straight would be elating
But our condition's such it can't be so.

POLLY AND MRS PEACHUM:

So that is all there is to it.
The world is poor, and man's a shit.

PEACHUM:

Of course that's all there is to it.
The world is poor, and man's a shit.
Who wouldn't like an earthly paradise?
Yet our condition's such it can't arise.
Out of the question in our case.
Let's say your brother's close to you
But if there's not enough for two
He'll kick you smartly in the face.
You think that loyalty's no disgrace?
But say your wife is close to you
And finds she's barely making do
She'll kick you smartly in the face.
And gratitude: that's no disgrace

But say your son is close to you
And finds your pension's not come through
He'll kick you smartly in the face.
And so will all the human race.

POLLY AND MRS PEACHUM:

That's what you're all ignoring
That's what's so bloody boring.
The world is poor, and man's a shit
And that is all there is to it.

PEACHUM:

Of course that's all there is to it
The world is poor, and man's a shit.
We should aim high instead of low
But our condition's such this can't be so.

ALL THREE:

Which means He has us in a trap:
The whole damn thing's a load of crap.

PEACHUM:

The world is poor, and man's a shit
And that is all there is to it.

ALL THREE:

That's what you're all ignoring
That's what's so bloody boring.
That's why He's got us in a trap
And why it's all a load of crap.

ACT TWO

4

Thursday afternoon: Mac the Knife takes leave of his wife and flees from his father-in-law to the heaths of Highgate.

The stable.

POLLY *enters:* Mac! Mac, don't be frightened.

MAC *lying on the bed:* Well, what's up? Polly, you look a wreck.

POLLY: I've been to see Brown, my father went too, they decided to pull you in; my father made some terrible threats and Brown stood up for you, but then he weakened, and now he thinks too that you'd better stir yourself and make yourself scarce for a while, Mac. You must pack right away.

MAC: Pack? Nonsense. Come here, Polly. You and I have got better things to do than pack.

POLLY: No, we mustn't now. I'm so frightened. All they talked about was hanging.

MAC: I don't like it when you're moody, Polly. There's nothing on record against me at Scotland Yard.

POLLY: Perhaps there wasn't yesterday, but suddenly today there's an awful lot. You – I've brought the charges with me, I don't even know if I can get them straight, the list goes on so. You've killed two shopkeepers, more than thirty burglaries, twenty-three hold-ups, and God knows how many acts of arson, attempted murder, forgery and perjury, all within eighteen months. You're a dreadful man. And in Winchester you seduced two sisters under the age of consent.

MAC: They told me they were over twenty. What did Brown say?

He stands up slowly and goes whistling to the right along the footlights.

POLLY: He caught up with me in the corridor and said there was nothing he could do for you now. Oh, Mac! *She throws herself on his neck.*

MAC: All right, if I've got to go away, you'll have to run the business.

POLLY: Don't talk about business now, Mac, I can't bear it. Kiss your poor Polly again and swear that you'll never never be . . .

Mac interrupts her brusquely and leads her to the table where he pushes her down in a chair.

MAC: Here are the ledgers. Listen carefully. This is a list of the personnel. *Reads.* Hm, first of all, Crook-finger Jake, a year and a half in the business. Let's see what he's brought in. One, two, three, four, five gold watches, not much, but clean work. Don't sit on my lap, I'm not in the mood right now. Here's Dreary Walter, an unreliable sod. Sells stuff on the side. Give him three weeks, grace, then get rid of him. Just turn him in to Brown.

POLLY *sobbing:* Just turn him in to Brown.

MAC: Jimmy II, cheeky bastard; good worker but cheeky. Swipes bed sheets right out from under ladies of the best society. Give him a rise.

POLLY: I'll give him a rise.

MAC: Robert the Saw: small potatoes, not a glimmer of genius. Won't end on the gallows, but he won't leave any estate either.

POLLY: Won't leave any estate either.

MAC: In all other respects you will carry on exactly the same as before. Get up at seven, wash, have your weekly bath and so on.

POLLY: You're perfectly right, I'll have to grit my teeth and look after the business. What's yours is mine now, isn't it, Mackie? What about your chambers, Mac? Should I let them go? I don't like having to pay the rent.

MAC: No, I still need them.

POLLY: What for, it's just a waste of our money!

MAC: Oh, so you think I won't be coming back at all, do you?

POLLY: What do you mean? You can rent other rooms, Mac . . . Mac, I can't go on. I keep looking at your lips and then I don't hear what you say. Will you be faithful to me, Mac?

MAC: Of course I'll be faithful, I'll do as I'm done by. Do you think I don't love you? It's only that I see farther ahead than you.

POLLY: I'm so grateful to you, Mac. Worrying about me when they're after you like bloodhounds . . .

Hearing the word 'bloodhounds' he goes stiff, stands up, goes to the right, throws off his coat and washes his hands.

MAC *hastily:* You will go on sending the profits to Jack Poole's banking house in Manchester. Between ourselves it's only a matter of weeks before I go over to banking altogether. It's safer and it's more profitable. In two weeks at the most the money will have to be taken out of this business, then off you go to Brown and give the list to the police. Within four weeks all that human scum will be safely in the cells at the Old Bailey.

POLLY: Why, Mac! How can you look them in the eye when you've written them off and they're as good as hanged? How can you shake hands with them?

MAC: With who? Robert the Saw, Matt of the Mint, Crook-fingered Jake? Those gaol-birds?

Enter the gang.

MAC: Gentlemen, it's a pleasure to see you.

POLLY: Good evening, gentlemen.

MATTHEW: I've got hold of the Coronation programme, Captain. It looks to me like we're going to be very busy in the next few days. The Archbishop of Canterbury is arriving in half an hour.

MAC: When?

MATTHEW: Five thirty. We'd better be shoving off, Captain.

MAC: Yes, you'd better be shoving off.

ROBERT: What do you mean: you?

MAC: For my part, I'm afraid I'm obliged to take a little trip.

ROBERT: Good God, are they out to nab you?

MATTHEW: It would be just now, with the Coronation coming up! A Coronation without you is like porridge without a spoon.

MAC: Shut your trap! In view of that, I am temporarily handing over the management of the business to my wife.

He pushes her forward and goes to the rear where he observes her.

POLLY: Well, boys, I think the Captain can go away with an easy mind. We'll swing this job, you bet. What do you say, boys?

MATTHEW: It's no business of mine. But at a time like this I'm not so sure that a woman . . . I'm not saying anything against you, Ma'am.

MAC *from upstage:* What do you say to that, Polly?

POLLY: You shit, that's a fine way to start in. *Screaming.* Of course you're not saying anything against me! If you were, these gentlemen would have ripped your pants off long ago and tanned your arse for you. Wouldn't you, gentlemen? *Brief pause, then all clap like mad.*

JAKE: Yes, there's something in that, you can take her word for it.

WALTER: Hurrah, the missus knows how to lay it on! Hurrah for Polly!

ALL: Hurrah for Polly!

MAC: The rotten part of it is that I won't be here for the Coronation. There's a gilt-edged deal for you. In the day time nobody's home and at night the toffs are all drunk. That reminds me, you drink too much, Matthew. Last week you suggested it was you set the Greenwich Children's Hospital on fire. If such a thing occurs again, you're out. Who set the Children's Hospital on fire?

MATTHEW: I did.

MAC *to the others:* Who set it on fire?

THE OTHERS: You, Mr Macheath.

MAC: So who did it?

MATTHEW *sulkily:* You, Mr Macheath. At this rate our sort will never rise in the world.

MAC *with a gesture of stringing up:* You'll rise all right if you think you can compete with me. Who ever heard of one of those professors at Oxford College letting some assistant put his name to his mistakes? He puts his own.

ROBERT: Ma'am, while your husband is away, you're the boss. We settle up every Thursday, ma'am.

POLLY: Every Thursday, boys.

The gang goes out.

MAC: And now farewell, my heart. Look after your complexion, and don't forget to make up every day, exactly as if I were here. That's very important, Polly.

POLLY: And you, Mac, promise me you won't look at another woman and that you'll leave town right away. Believe me, it's not jealousy that makes your little Polly say that; no, it's very important, Mac.

MAC: Oh, Polly, why should I go round drinking up the empties? I love only you. As soon as the twilight is deep enough I'll take my black stallion from somebody's stable and before you can see the moon from your window, I'll be the other side of Highgate Heath.

POLLY: Oh, Mac, don't tear the heart out of my body. Stay with me and let us be happy.

MAC: But I must tear my own heart out of my body, for I must go away and no one knows when I shall return.

POLLY: It's been such a short time, Mac.

MAC: Does it have to be the end?

POLLY: Oh, last night I had a dream. I was looking out the window and I heard laughter in the street, and when I looked out I saw our moon and the moon was all thin like a worn-down penny. Don't forget me, Mac, in strange cities.

MAC: Of course I won't forget you, Polly. Kiss me, Polly.

POLLY: Goodbye, Mac.

MAC: Goodbye, Polly. *On his way out:*

> For love will endure or not endure
> Regardless of where we are.

POLLY *alone:* He never will come back. *She sings:*

> Nice while it lasted, and now it is over
> Tear out your heart, and goodbye to your lover!
> What's the use of grieving, when the mother that bore you
> (Mary, pity women!) knew it all before you?

The bells start ringing.

POLLY:
>Into this London the Queen now makes her way.
>Where shall we be on Coronation Day?

Interlude

Mrs Peachum and Low-Dive Jenny step out before the curtain.

MRS PEACHUM: So if you see Mac the Knife in the next few days, run to the nearest constable and turn him in; it'll earn you ten shillings.

JENNY: Shall we see him, though, if the constables are after him? If the hunt is on, he won't go spending his time with us.

MRS PEACHUM: Take it from me, Jenny, even with all London at his heels, Macheath is not the man to give up his habits. *She sings:*

THE BALLAD OF SEXUAL OBSESSION

>There goes a man who's won his spurs in battle
>The butcher, he. And all the others, cattle.
>The cocky sod! No decent place lets him in.
>Who does him down, that's done the lot? The women.
>Want it or not, he can't ignore that call.
>Sexual obsession has him in its thrall.
>>He doesn't read the Bible. He sniggers at the law
>>Sets out to be an utter egoist
>>And knows a woman's skirts are what he must resist
>>So when a woman calls he locks his door.
>>So far, so good, but what's the future brewing?
>>As soon as night falls he'll be up and doing.

>Thus many a man watched men die in confusion:
>A mighty genius, stuck on prostitution!
>The watchers claimed their urges were exhausted
>But when they died who paid the funeral? Whores did.
>Want it or not, they can't ignore that call.
>Sexual obsession has them in its thrall.

Some fall back on the Bible. Some stick to the law
Some turn to Christ and some turn anarchist
At lunch you pick the best wine on the list
Then meditate till half-past four.
At tea: what high ideals you are pursuing!
Then soon as night falls you'll be up and doing.

5

Before the Coronation bells had died away, Mac
the Knife was sitting with the whores of Turnbridge! The whores betray him. It is Thursday
evening.

Whorehouse in Turnbridge.

*An afternoon like any other; the whores, mostly in their shifts, are
ironing clothes, playing draughts, or washing: a bourgeois idyll.*
*Crook-fingered Jake is reading the newspaper. No one pays any
attention to him. He is rather in the way.*

JAKE: He won't come today.
WHORE: No?
JAKE: I don't think he'll ever come again.
WHORE: That would be a pity.
JAKE: Think so? If I know him, he's out of town by now.
This time he's really cleared out.
*Enter Macheath, hangs his hat on a nail, sits down on the sofa
behind the table.*
MAC: My coffee!
VIXEN *repeats admiringly:* 'My coffee!'
JAKE *horrified:* Why aren't you in Highgate?
MAC: It's my Thursday. Do you think I can let such trifles
interfere with my habits? *Throws the warrant on the floor.*
Anyhow, it's raining.

JENNY *reads the warrant*: In the name of the King, Captain Macheath is charged with three . . .

JAKE *takes it away from her*: Am I in it too?

MAC: Naturally, the whole team.

JENNY *to the other whore*: Look, that's the warrant. *Pause.* Mac, let's see your hand. *He gives her his hand.*

DOLLY: That's right, Jenny, read his palm, you do it so well. *Holds up an oil lamp.*

MAC: Coming into money?

JENNY: No, not coming into money.

BETTY: What's that look for, Jenny? It gives me the shivers.

MAC: A long journey?

JENNY: No, no long journey.

VIXEN: What *do* you see?

MAC: Only the good things, not the bad, please.

JENNY: Oh well, I see a narrow dark place and not much light. And then I see a big T, that means a woman's treachery. And then I see . . .

MAC: Stop. I'd like some details about that narrow dark place and the treachery. What's this treacherous woman's name?

JENNY: All I see is it begins with a J.

MAC: Then you've got it wrong. It begins with a P.

JENNY: Mac, when the Coronation bells start ringing at Westminster, you'll be in for a sticky time.

MAC: Go on! *Jake laughs uproariously.* What's the matter? *He runs over to Jake, and reads.* They've got it wrong, there were only three of them.

JAKE *laughs*: Exactly.

MAC: Nice underwear you've got there.

WHORE: From the cradle to the grave, underwear first, last and all the time.

OLD WHORE: I never wear silk. Makes gentlemen think you've got something wrong with you.
Jenny slips stealthily out the door.

SECOND WHORE *to Jenny*: Where are you going, Jenny?

JENNY: You'll see. *Goes out.*

DOLLY: But homespun underwear can put them off too.

OLD WHORE: I've had very good results with homespun underwear.

VIXEN: It makes the gentleman feel they're at home.

MAC *to Betty:* Have you still got the black lace trimming?

BETTY: Still the black lace trimming.

MAC: What kind of lingerie do you have?

SECOND WHORE: Oh, I don't like to tell you. I can't take anybody to my room because my aunt is so crazy about men, and in doorways, you know, I just don't wear any. *Jake laughs.*

MAC: Finished?

JAKE: No, I just got to the rapes.

MAC *back to the sofa:* But where's Jenny? Ladies, long before my star rose over this city . . .

VIXEN: 'Long before my star rose over this city . . .'

MAC: . . . I lived in the most impecunious circumstances with one of you dear ladies. And though today I am Mac the Knife, my good fortune will never lead me to forget the companions of my dark days, especially Jenny, whom I loved the best of all. Now listen, please.

While Mac sings, Jenny stands to the right outside the window and beckons to Constable Smith. Then Mrs Peachum joins her. The three stand under the street lamp and watch the house.

BALLAD OF IMMORAL EARNINGS

There was a time, now very far away
When we set up together, I and she.
I'd got the brain, and she supplied the breast.
I saw her right, and she looked after me –
A way of life then, if not quite the best.
And when a client came I'd slide out of our bed
And treat him nice, and go and have a drink instead
And when he paid up I'd address him: Sir
Come any night you feel you fancy her.
That time's long past, but what would I not give
To see that whorehouse where we used to live?
Jenny appears in the door, with Smith behind her.

JENNY:
That was the time, now very far away
He was so sweet and bashed me where it hurt.

And when the cash ran out the feathers really flew
He'd up and say: I'm going to pawn your skirt.
A skirt is nicer, but no skirt will do.
Just like his cheek, he had me fairly stewing
I'd ask him straight to say what he thought he was doing
Then he'd lash out and knock me headlong down the
    stairs.
I had the bruises off and on for years.

BOTH:

That time's long past, but what would I not give
To see that whorehouse where we used to live?

BOTH *together and alternating*:

That was the time, now very far away [8]

MAC:

Not that the bloody times seem to have looked up.

JENNY:

When afternoons were all I had for you

MAC:

I told you she was generally booked up.
(The night's more normal, but daytime will do.)

JENNY:

Once I was pregnant, so the doctor said.

MAC:

So we reversed positions on the bed.

JENNY:

He thought his weight would make it premature.

MAC:

But in the end we flushed it down the sewer.
That could not last, but what would I not give
To see that whorehouse where we used to live?
*Dance. Mac picks up his sword stick, she hands him his hat, he
is still dancing when Smith lays a hand on his shoulder.*

SMITH: Coming quietly?

MAC: Is there only one way out of this dump?

    *Smith tries to put the handcuffs on Macheath; Mac gives him a
    push in the chest and he reels back. Mac jumps out of the window.
    Outside stands Mrs Peachum with constables.*

MAC *with poise, very politely*: Good afternoon, ma'am.

MRS PEACHUM: My dear Mr Macheath. My husband says the

greatest heroes in history have tripped over this humble threshold.

MAC: May I ask how your husband is doing?

MRS PEACHUM: Better, thank you. I'm so sorry, you'll have to be bidding the charming ladies goodbye now. Come, constable, escort the gentleman to his new home. *He is led away. Mrs Peachum through the window:* Ladies, if you wish to visit him, you'll invariably find him in. From now on the gentleman's address will be the Old Bailey. I knew he'd be round to see his whores. I'll settle the bill. Goodbye, ladies. *Goes out.*

JENNY: Wake up, Jake, something has happened.

JAKE *who has been too immersed in his reading to notice anything:* Where's Mac?

JENNY: The rozzers were here.

JAKE: Good God! And me just reading, reading, reading . . . Well, I never! *Goes out.*

6

Betrayed by the whores, Macheath is freed from prison by the love of yet another woman.

The cells in the Old Bailey.
A cage.

Enter Brown.

BROWN: If only my men don't catch him! Let's hope to God he's riding out beyond Highgate Heath, thinking of his Jackie. But he's so frivolous, like all great men. If they bring him in now and he looks at me with his faithful friendly eyes, I won't be able to bear it. Thank God, anyway, the moon is shining; if he is riding across the heath, at least he won't stray from the path. *Sounds backstage.* What's that? Oh, my God, they're bringing him in.

MAC *tied with heavy ropes, accompanied by six constables, enters with head erect.* Well, flatfeet, thank God we're home again. *He notices Brown who has fled to the far corner of the cell.*

BROWN *after a long pause, under the withering glance of his former friend:* Oh, Mac, it wasn't me . . . I did everything . . . don't look at me like that, Mac . . . I can't stand it . . . Your silence is killing me. *Shouts at one of the constables:* Stop tugging at that rope, you swine . . . Say something, Mac. Say something to your poor Jackie . . . A kind word in his tragic . . . *Rests his head against the wall and weeps.* He doesn't deem me worthy even of a word. *Goes out.*

MAC: That miserable Brown. The living picture of a bad conscience. And he calls himself a chief of police. It was a good idea not shouting at him. I was going to at first. But just in time it occurred to me that a deep withering stare would send much colder shivers down his spine. It worked. I looked at him and he wept bitterly. That's a trick I got from the Bible.

Enter Smith with handcuffs.

MAC: Well, Mr Warder, I suppose these are the heaviest you've got? With your kind permission I should like to apply for a more comfortable pair. *He takes out his cheque book.*

SMITH: Of course, Captain, we've got them here at every price. It all depends how much you want to spend. From one guinea to ten.

MAC: How much would none at all be?

SMITH: Fifty.

MAC *writes a cheque:* But the worst of it is that now this business with Lucy is bound to come out. If Brown hears that I've been carrying on with his daughter behind his friendly back, he'll turn into a tiger.

SMITH: You've made your bed, now lie on it.

MAC: I bet the little tart is waiting outside right now. I can see happy days between now and the execution.

Is this a life for one of my proud station?
I take it, I must frankly own, amiss.
From childhood up I heard with consternation:

One must live well to know what living is!
Song lighting: golden glow. The organ is lit up. Three lamps are lowered on a pole, and the signs say:

BALLADE OF GOOD LIVING[9]

I've heard them praising single-minded spirits
Whose empty stomachs show they live for knowledge
In rat-infested shacks awash with ullage.
I'm all for culture, but there are some limits.
The simple life is fine for those it suits.
I don't find, for my part, that it attracts.
There's not a bird from here to Halifax
Would peck at such unappetising fruits.
What use is freedom? None, to judge from this.
One must live well to know what living is.

The dashing sort who cut precarious capers
And go and risk their necks just for the pleasure
Then swagger home and write it up at leisure
And flog the story to the Sunday papers –
If you could see how cold they get at night
Sullen, with chilly wife, climbing to bed
And how they dream they're going to get ahead
And see the future stretching out of sight –
Now tell me, who would choose to live like this?
One must live well to know what living is.

There's plenty that they have. I know I lack it
And ought to join their splendid isolation
But when I gave it more consideration
I told myself: my friend, that's not your racket.
Suffering ennobles, but it can depress.
The paths of glory lead but to the grave.
You once were poor and lonely, wise and brave.
You ought to try to bite off rather less.
The search for happiness boils down to this:
One must live well to know what living is.

Enter Lucy.

LUCY: You dirty dog, you – how can you look me in the face after all there's been between us?

MAC: Have you no bowels, no tenderness, my dear Lucy, seeing a husband in such circumstances?

LUCY: A husband! You monster! So you think I haven't heard about your goings-on with Miss Peachum! I could scratch your eyes out!

MAC: Seriously, Lucy, you're not fool enough to be jealous of Polly?

LUCY: You're married to her, aren't you, you beast?

MAC: Married! It's true, I go to the house, I chat with the girl. I kiss her, and now the silly jade goes about telling everyone that I'm married to her. I am ready, my dear Lucy, to give you satisfaction – if you think there is any in marriage. What can a man of honour say more? He can say nothing more.

LUCY: Oh, Mac, I only want to become an honest woman.

MAC: If you think marriage with me will . . . all right. What can a man of honour say more? He can say nothing more.
Enter Polly.

POLLY: Where is my dear husband? Oh, Mac, there you are. Why do you turn away from me? It's your Polly. It's your wife.

LUCY: Oh, you miserable villain!

POLLY: Oh, Mackie in prison! Why didn't you ride across Highgate Heath? You told me you weren't going to see those women any more. I knew what they'd do to you; but I said nothing, because I believed you. Mac, I'll stay with you till death us do part. – Not one kind word, Mac? Not one kind look? Oh, Mac, think what your Polly must be suffering to see you like this.

LUCY: Oh, the slut.

POLLY: What does this mean, Mac? Who on earth is that? You might at least tell her who I am. Please tell her I'm your wife. Aren't I your wife? Look at me. Tell me, aren't I your wife?

LUCY: You low-down sneak! Have you got two wives, you monster?

POLLY: Say something, Mac. Aren't I your wife? Haven't I done everything for you? I was innocent when I married you know that. Why, you even put me in charge of the gang, and I've done it all the way we arranged, and Jake wants me to tell you that he . . .

MAC: If you two would kindly shut your traps for one minute I'll explain everything.

LUCY: No, I won't shut my trap, I can't bear it. It's more than flesh and blood can stand.

POLLY: Yes, my dear, naturally the wife has . . .

LUCY: The wife!!

POLLY: . . . the wife is entitled to some preference. Or at least the appearance of it, my dear. All this fuss and bother will drive the poor man mad.

LUCY: Fuss and bother, that's a good one. What have you gone and picked up now? This messy little tart! So this is your great conquest! So this is your Rose of old Soho!
Song lighting: golden glow. The organ is lit up. Three lamps are lowered on a pole and the signs say:

JEALOUSY DUET

LUCY:
Come on out, you Rose of Old Soho!
Let us see your legs, my little sweetheart!
I hear you have a lovely ankle
And I'd love to see such a complete tart.
They tell me that Mac says your behind is so provoking.

POLLY:
Did he now, did he now?

LUCY:
If what I see is true he must be joking.

POLLY:
Is he now, is he now?

LUCY:
Ho, it makes me split my sides!

POLLY:
Oh, that's how you split your side?

LUCY:

Fancy you as Mackie's bride!

POLLY:

Mackie fancies Mackie's bride.

LUCY:

Ha ha ha! Catch him sporting
With something that the cat brought in.

POLLY:

Just you watch your tongue, my dear.

LUCY:

Must I watch my tongue, my dear?

BOTH:

Mackie and I, see how we bill and coo, man
He's got no eye for any other woman.
The whole thing's an invention
You mustn't pay attention
To such a bitch's slanders.
Poppycock!

POLLY:

Oh, they call me Rose of Old Soho
And Macheath appears to find me pretty.

LUCY:

Does he now?

POLLY:

They say I have a lovely ankle
And the best proportions in the city.

LUCY:

Little whippersnapper!

POLLY:

Who's a little whippersnapper?
Mac tells me that he finds my behind is most provoking.

LUCY:

Doesn't he? Doesn't he?

POLLY:

I do not suppose that he is joking.

LUCY:

Isn't he, isn't he?

POLLY:

Ho, it makes me split my sides!

LUCY:

Oh, that's how you spill your shit?

POLLY:

Being Mackie's only bride!

LUCY:

Are you Mackie's only bride?

POLLY *to the audience:*

Can you really picture him sporting
With something that the cat brought in?

LUCY:

Just you watch your tongue, my dear.

POLLY:

Must I watch my tongue, my dear?

BOTH:

Mackie and I, see how we bill and coo, man
He's got no eye for any other woman.
The whole thing's an invention
You cannot pay attention
To such a bitch's slanders.
Poppycock!

MAC: All right, Lucy. Calm down. You see it's just a trick of Polly's. She wants to come between us. I'm going to be hanged and she wants to parade as my widow. Really, Polly, this isn't the moment.

POLLY: Have you the heart to disclaim me?

MAC: And have you the heart to go on about my being married? Oh, Polly, why do you have to add to my misery? *Shakes his head reproachfully:* Polly! Polly!

LUCY: It's true, Miss Peachum. You're putting yourself in a bad light. Quite apart from the fact that it's uncivilised of you to worry a gentleman in his situation!

POLLY: The most elementary rules of decency, my dear young lady, ought to teach you, it seems to me, to treat a man with a little more reserve when his wife is present.

MAC: Seriously, Polly, that's carrying a joke too far.

LUCY: And if, my dear lady, you start raising a row here in this prison, I shall be obliged to send for the screw to show you the door. I'm sorry, my dear Miss Peachum.

POLLY: Mrs, if you please! Mrs Macheath. Just let me tell you this, young lady. The airs you give yourself are most unbecoming. My duty obliges me to stay with my husband.

LUCY: What's that? What's that? Oh, she won't leave! She stands there and we throw her out and she won't leave! Must I speak more plainly?

POLLY: You – you just hold your filthy tongue, you slut, or I'll knock your block off, my dear young lady.

LUCY: You've been thrown out, you interloper! I suppose that's not clear enough. You don't understand nice manners.

POLLY: You and your nice manners! Oh, I'm forgetting my dignity! I shouldn't stoop to . . . no, I shouldn't.
She starts to bawl.

LUCY: Just look at my belly, you slut! Did I get that from out of nowhere? Haven't you eyes in your head?

POLLY: Oh! So you're in the family way! And you think that gives you rights? A fine lady like you, you shouldn't have let him in!

MAC: Polly!

POLLY *in tears:* This is really too much. Mac, you shouldn't have done that. Now I don't know what to do.
Enter Mrs Peachum.

MRS PEACHUM: I knew it. She's with her man. You little trollop, come here immediately. When they hang your man, you can hang yourself too. A fine way to treat your respectable mother, making her come and get you out of jail. And he's got two of them, what's more – the Nero!

POLLY: Leave me here, mama; you don't know . . .

MRS PEACHUM: You're coming home this minute.

LUCY: There you are, it takes your mama to tell you how to behave.

MRS PEACHUM: Get going.

POLLY: Just a second. I only have to . . . I only have to tell him something . . . Really . . . it's very important.

MRS PEACHUM *giving her a box on the ear:* Well, this is important too. Get going!

POLLY: Oh, Mac! *She is dragged away.*

MAC: Lucy, you were magnificent. Of course I felt sorry for her. That's why I couldn't treat the slut as she deserved. Just for a moment you thought there was some truth in what she said. Didn't you?

LUCY: Yes, my dear, so I did.

MAC: If there were any truth in it, her mother wouldn't have put me in this situation. Did you hear how she laid into me? A mother might treat a seducer like that, not a son-in-law.

LUCY: It makes me happy to hear you say that from the bottom of your heart. I love you so much I'd almost rather see you on the gallows than in the arms of another. Isn't that strange?

MAC: Lucy, I should like to owe you my life.

LUCY: It's wonderful the way you say that. Say it again.

MAC: Lucy, I should like to owe you my life.

LUCY: Shall I run away with you, dearest?

MAC: Well, but you see, if we run away together, it won't be easy for us to hide. As soon as they stop looking, I'll send for you post haste, you know that.

LUCY: What can I do to help you?

MAC: Bring me my hat and cane.

Lucy comes back with his hat and cane and throws them into his cage.

Lucy, the fruit of our love which you bear beneath your heart will hold us forever united.

Lucy goes out.

SMITH *enters, goes into the cell, and says to Mac:* Let's have that cane.

After a brief chase, in which Smith pursues Mac with a chair and a crow bar, Mac jumps over the bars. Constables run after him. Enter Brown.

BROWN *off:* Hey, Mac! – Mac, answer me, please. It's Jackie. Mac, please be a good boy, answer me, I can't stand it any longer. *Comes in.* Mackie! What's this? He's gone, thank God.

He sits down on the bed.

Enter Peachum.

PEACHUM *to Smith:* My name is Peachum. I've come to col-

lect the forty pounds reward for the capture of the bandit
Macheath. *Appears in front of the cage.* Excuse me! Is that
Mr Macheath? *Brown is silent.* Oh. I suppose the other
gentleman has gone for a stroll? I come here to visit a
criminal and who do I find sitting here but Mr Brown!
Tiger Brown is sitting here and his friend Macheath is not
sitting here.

BROWN *groaning:* Oh, Mr Peachum, it wasn't my fault.

PEACHUM: Of course not. How could it be? You'd never
have dreamt . . . considering the situation it'll land you in
. . . it's out of the question, Brown.

BROWN: Mr Peachum, I'm beside myself.

PEACHUM: I believe you. Terrible, you must feel.

BROWN: Yes, it's this feeling of helplessness that ties one's
hands so. Those fellows do just as they please. It's dreadful,
dreadful.

PEACHUM: Wouldn't you care to lie down awhile? Just close
your eyes and pretend nothing has happened. Imagine
you're on a lovely green meadow with little white clouds
overhead. The main thing is to forget all about those
ghastly things, those that are past, and most of all, those
that are still to come.

BROWN *alarmed:* What do you mean by that?

PEACHUM: I'm amazed at your fortitude. In your position I
should simply collapse, crawl into bed and drink hot tea.
And above all, I'd find someone to lay a soothing hand on
my forehead.

BROWN: Damn it all, it's not my fault if the fellow escapes.
There's not much the police can do about it.

PEACHUM: I see. There's not much the police can do about
it. You don't believe we'll see Mr Macheath back here
again? *Brown shrugs his shoulders.* In that case your fate will
be hideously unjust. People are sure to say – they always do
– that the police shouldn't have let him escape. No, I can't
see that glittering Coronation procession just yet.

BROWN: What do you mean?

PEACHUM: Let me remind you of a historical incident which,
though it caused a great stir at the time, in the year 1400 BC,
is unknown to the public of today. On the death of the

Egyptian king Rameses II, the police captain of Nineveh, or was it Cairo, committed some minor offence against the lower classes of the population. Even at that time the consequences were terrible. As the history books tell us, the coronation procession of Semiramis, the new Queen, 'developed into a series of catastrophes thanks to the unduly active participation of the lower orders'. Historians still shudder at the cruel way Semiramis treated her police captain. I only remember dimly, but there was some talk of snakes she fed on his bosom.

BROWN: Really?

PEACHUM: The Lord be with you, Brown. *Goes out.*

BROWN: Now only the mailed fist can help. Sergeants! Report to me at the double!

Curtain. Macheath and Low-Dive Jenny step before the curtain and sing to song lighting:

SECOND THREEPENNY FINALE
WHAT KEEPS MANKIND ALIVE?

You gentlemen who think you have a mission
To purge us of the seven deadly sins
Should first sort out the basic food position
Then start your preaching: that's where it begins.
You lot, who preach restraint and watch your waist as
      well
Should learn for all time how the world is run:
However much you twist, whatever lies you tell
Food is the first thing. Morals follow on.
So first make sure that those who now are starving
Get proper helpings when we do the carving.
        What keeps mankind alive? The fact that millions
        Are daily tortured, stifled, punished, silenced,
            oppressed.
        Mankind can keep alive thanks to its brilliance
        In keeping its humanity repressed.
        For once you must try not to shirk the facts:
        Mankind is kept alive by bestial acts.

You say that girls may strip with your permission.
You draw the lines dividing art from sin.
So first sort out the basic food position
Then start your preaching: that's where we begin.
You lot, who bank on your desires and our disgust
Should learn for all time how the world is run:
Whatever lies you tell, however much you twist
Food is the first thing. Morals follow on.
So first make sure that those who now are starving
Get proper helpings when we do the carving.

What keeps mankind alive? The fact that millions
Are daily tortured, stifled, punished, silenced,
    oppressed.
Mankind can keep alive thanks to its brilliance
In keeping its humanity repressed.
For once you must try not to shirk the facts:
Mankind is kept alive by bestial acts.

ACT THREE

7

That night Peachum prepares his campaign. He plans to disrupt the Coronation procession by a demonstration of human misery.

Peachum's Outfitting Emporium for Beggars.

The beggars paint little signs with inscriptions such as 'I gave my eye for my king', etc.

PEACHUM: Gentlemen, at this moment, in our eleven branches from Drury Lane to Turnbridge, one thousand four hundred and thirty-two gentlemen are working on signs like these with a view to attending the Coronation of our Queen.

MRS PEACHUM: Get a move on! If you won't work, you can't beg. Call yourself a blind man and can't even make a proper K? That's supposed to be child's writing, anyone would think it was an old man's.

A drum rolls.

BEGGAR: That's the Coronation guard presenting arms. Little do they suspect that today, the biggest day in their military careers, they'll have us to deal with.

FILCH *enters and reports:* Mrs Peachum, there's a dozen sleepy-looking hens traipsing in. They claim there's some money due them.

Enter the whores.

JENNY: Madam . . .

MRS PEACHUM: Hm, you do look as if you'd fallen off your perches. I suppose you've come to collect the money for that Macheath of yours? Well, you'll get nothing, you understand, nothing.

JENNY: How are we to understand that, Ma'am?

MRS PEACHUM: Bursting in here in the middle of the night! Coming to a respectable house at three in the morning! With the work you do, I should think you'd want some sleep. You look like sicked-up milk.

JENNY: Then you won't give us the stipulated fee for turning in Macheath, ma'am?

MRS PEACHUM: Exactly. No thirty pieces of silver for you.

JENNY: Why not, ma'am?

MRS PEACHUM: Because your fine Mr Macheath has scattered himself to the four winds. And now, ladies, get out of my parlour.

JENNY: Well, I call that the limit. Just don't you try that on us. That's all I've got to say to you. Not on us.

MRS PEACHUM: Filch, the ladies wish to be shown the door. *Filch goes towards the ladies, Jenny pushes him away.*

JENNY: I would be grateful if you would be so good as to hold your filthy tongue. If you don't, I'm likely to . . . *Enter Peachum.*

PEACHUM: What's going on, you haven't given them any money, I hope? Well, ladies how about it? Is Mr Macheath in jail, or isn't he?

JENNY: Don't talk to me about Mr Macheath. You're not fit to black his boots. Last night I had to let a customer go because it made me cry into my pillow thinking how I had sold that gentleman to you. Yes, ladies, and what do you think happened this morning? Less than an hour ago, just after I had cried myself to sleep, I heard somebody whistle, and out on the street stood the very gentleman I'd been crying about, asking me to throw down the key. He wanted to lie in my arms and make me forget the wrong I had done him. Ladies, he's the last sportsman left in London. And if our friend Suky Tawdry isn't here with us now, it's because he went on from me to her to console her too.

PEACHUM *muttering to himself:* Suky Tawdry . . .

JENNY: So now you know that you're not fit to black that gentleman's boots. You miserable sneak.

PEACHUM: Filch, run to the nearest police station, tell them Mr Macheath is at Miss Suky Tawdry's place. *Filch goes out.* But ladies, what are we arguing for? The money will be paid out, that goes without saying. Celia dear, you'd do better to make the ladies some coffee instead of slanging them.

MRS PEACHUM *on her way out:* Suky Tawdry! *She sings the third stanza of the Ballad of Sexual Obsession:*

There stands a man. The gallows loom above him.
They've got the quicklime mixed in which to shove him.
They've put his neck just under where the noose is
And what's he thinking of, the idiot? Floozies.
They've all but hanged him, yet he can't ignore that call.
Sexual obsession has him in its thrall.
    She's sold him down the river heart and soul
    He's seen the dirty money in her hand
    And bit by bit begins to understand:
    The pit that covers him is woman's hole.
    Then he may rant and roar and curse his ruin –
    But soon as night falls he'll be up and doing.

PEACHUM: Get a move on, you'd all be rotting in the sewers of Turnbridge if in my sleepless nights I hadn't worked out how to squeeze a penny out of your poverty. I discovered that though the rich of this earth find no difficulty in creating misery, they can't bear to see it. Because they are weaklings and fools just like you. They may have enough to eat till the end of their days, they may be able to wax their floors with butter so that even the crumbs from their tables grow fat. But they can't look on unmoved while a man is collapsing from hunger, though of course that only applies so long as he collapses outside their own front door. *Enter Mrs Peachum with a tray full of coffee cups.*

MRS PEACHUM: You can come by the shop tomorrow and pick up your money, but only once the Coronation's over.

JENNY: Mrs Peachum, you leave me speechless.

PEACHUM: Fall in. We assemble in one hour outside Buckingham Palace. Quick march.

The beggars fall in.

FILCH *dashes in:* Cops! I didn't even get to the police station. The police are here already.

PEACHUM: Hide, gentlemen! *To Mrs Peachum:* Call the band together. Shake a log. And if you hear me say 'harmless', do you understand, *harmless* . . .

MRS PEACHUM: Harmless? I don't understand a thing.

PEACHUM: Naturally you don't understand. Well, if I say *harmless* . . . *Knocking at the door.* Thank God, that's the answer, *harmless,* then you play some kind of music. Get a move on!

Mrs Peachum goes out with the beggars. The beggars, except for the girl with the sign 'A Victim of Military Tyranny', hide with their things upstage right behind the clothes rack. Enter Brown and constables.

BROWN: Here we are. And now, Mr Beggar's Friend, drastic action will be taken. Put the derbies on him, Smith. Ah, here are some of those delightful signs. *To the girl:* 'A Victim of Military Tyranny' – is that you?

PEACHUM: Good morning, Brown, good morning. Sleep well?

BROWN: Huh?

PEACHUM: Morning, Brown.

BROWN: Is he saying that to me? Does he know one of you? I don't believe I have the pleasure of your acquaintance.

PEACHUM: Really? Morning, Brown.

BROWN: Knock his hat off. *Smith does so.*

PEACHUM: Look here, Brown, since you're passing by, *passing,* I say, Brown, I may as well ask you to put a certain Macheath under lock and key, it's high time.

BROWN: The man's mad. Don't laugh, Smith. Tell me, Smith, how is it possible that such a notorious criminal should be running around loose in London?

PEACHUM: Because he's your pal, Brown.

BROWN: Who?

PEACHUM: Mac the Knife. Not me. I'm no criminal. I'm a poor man, Brown. You can't abuse me, Brown, you've got the worst hour in your life ahead of you. Care for some coffee? *To the whores:* Girls, give the chief of police a sip, that's no way to behave. Let's all be friends. We are all law-abiding people. The law was made for one thing alone, for the exploitation of those who don't understand it, or are prevented by naked misery from obeying it. And anyone who wants a crumb of this exploitation for himself must obey the law strictly.

BROWN: I see, then you believe our judges are corruptible?

PEACHUM: Not at all, sir, not at all. Our judges are absolutely incorruptible: it's more than money can do to make them give a fair verdict.

A second drum roll.

The troops are marching off to line the route. The poorest of the poor will move off in half an hour.

BROWN: That's right, Mr Peachum. In half an hour the poorest of the poor will be marched off to winter quarters in the Old Bailey. *To the constables:* All right, boys, round them all up, all the patriots you find here. *To the beggars:* Have you fellows ever heard of Tiger Brown? Tonight, Peachum, I've hit on the solution, and I believe I may say, saved a friend from mortal peril. I'll simply smoke out your whole nest. And lock up the lot of you for – hm, for what? For begging on the street. You seem to have intimated your intention of embarrassing me and the Queen with these beggars. I shall simply arrest the beggars. Think about it.

PEACHUM: Excellent, but . . . what beggars?

BROWN: These cripples here. Smith, we're taking these patriots along with us.

PEACHUM: I can save you from a hasty step; you can thank the Lord, Brown, that you came to me. You see, Brown, you can arrest these few, they're harmless, *harmless* . . .

Music starts up, playing a few measures of the 'Song of the Insufficiency of Human Endeavour'.

BROWN: What's that?

PEACHUM: Music. They're playing as well as they can. The Song of Insufficiency. You don't know it? Think about it.

Song lighting: golden glow. The organ is lit up. Three lamps are lowered from above on a pole and the signs say:

SONG OF THE INSUFFICIENCY OF HUMAN ENDEAVOUR

Mankind lives by its head
Its head won't see it through
Inspect your own. What lives off that?
At most a louse or two.
    For this bleak existence
    Man is never sharp enough.
    Hence his weak resistance
    To its tricks and bluff.

Aye, make yourself a plan
They need you at the top!
Then make yourself a second plan
Then let the whole thing drop.
    For this bleak existence
    Man is never bad enough
    Though his sheer persistence
    Can be lovely stuff.

Aye, race for happiness
But don't you race too fast.
When all start chasing happiness
Happiness comes in last.
    For this bleak existence
    Man is never undemanding enough.
    All his loud insistence
    Is a load of guff.

PEACHUM: Your plan, Brown, was brilliant but hardly realistic. All you can arrest in this place is a few young fellows celebrating their Queen's Coronation by arranging a little fancy dress party. When the real paupers come along – there aren't any here – there will be thousands of them. That's the point: you've forgotten what an immense number of poor people there are. When you see them standing

outside the Abbey, it won't be a festive sight. You see, they
don't look good. Do you know what grogblossom is,
Brown? Yes, but how about a hundred and twenty noses
all flushed with grogblossom? Our young Queen's path
should be strewn with blossom, not with grogblossom.
And all those cripples at the church door. That's something
one wishes to avoid, Brown. You'll probably say the police
can handle us poor folk. You don't believe that yourself.
How will it look if six hundred poor cripples have to be
clubbed down at the Coronation? It will look bad. It will
look disgusting. Nauseating. I feel faint at the thought of it,
Brown. A small chair, if you please.

BROWN *to Smith:* That's a threat. See here, you, that's blackmail. We can't touch the man, in the interests of public
order we simply can't touch him. I've never seen the like
of it.

PEACHUM: You're seeing it now. Let me tell you something.
You can behave as you please to the Queen of England.
But you can't tread on the toes of the poorest man in
England, or you'll be brought down, Mr Brown.

BROWN: So you're asking me to arrest Mac the Knife? Arrest
him? That's easy to say. You have to find a man before you
can arrest him.

PEACHUM: If you say that, I can't contradict you. So I'll find
your man for you; we'll see if there's any morality left.
Jimmy, where is Mr Macheath at this moment?

JENNY: 21 Oxford Street, at Suky Tawdry's.

BROWN: Smith, go at once to Suky Tawdry's place at 21
Oxford Street, arrest Macheath and take him to the Old
Bailey. In the meantime, I must put on my gala uniform.
On this day of all days I must wear my gala uniform.

PEACHUM: Brown, if he's not on the gallows by six
o'clock . . .

BROWN: Oh, Mac, it was not to be. *Goes out with constables.*

PEACHUM *calling after him:* Think about it, eh, Brown?
Third drum roll.
Third drum roll. Change of objective. You will head for the
dungeons of the Old Bailey.
The beggars go out.

Peachum sings the fourth stanza of the 'Song of Human Insufficiency':

Man could be good instead
So slug him on the head
If you can slug him good and hard
He may stay good and dead.
　　For this bleak existence
　　Man's not good enough just yet.
　　You'll need no assistance.
　　Slug him on the head.

Curtain. Jenny steps before the curtain with a hurdy-gurdy and sings the

SOLOMON SONG

You saw sagacious Solomon
You know what came of him.
To him complexities seemed plain.
He cursed the hour that gave birth to him
And saw that everything was vain.
How great and wise was Solomon!
But now that time is getting late
The world can see what followed on.
It's wisdom that had brought him to this state –
How fortunate the man with none!

You saw the lovely Cleopatra
You know what she became.
Two emperors slaved to serve her lust.
She whored herself to death and fame
Then rotted down and turned to dust.
How beautiful was Babylon!
But now that time is getting late
The world can see what followed on.
It's beauty that had brought her to this state –
How fortunate the girl with none!

You saw the gallant Caesar next
You know what he became.
They deified him in his life
Then had him murdered just the same.
And as they raised the fatal knife
How loud he cried 'You too, my son!'
But now that time is getting late
The world can see what followed on.
It's courage that had brought him to this state –
How fortunate the man with none!

You know the ever-curious Brecht
Whose songs you liked to hum.
He asked, too often for your peace
Where rich men get their riches from.
So then you drove him overseas.
How curious was my mother's son!
But now that time is getting late
The world can see what followed on.
Inquisitiveness brought him to this state –
How fortunate the man with none!

And now look at this man Macheath
The sands are running out.
If only he'd known where to stop
And stuck to crimes he knew all about
He surely would have reached the top.
But one fine day his heart was won.
So now that time is getting late
The world can see what followed on.
His sexual urges brought him to this state –
How fortunate the man with none!

8

Property in dispute.[10]

A young girl's room in the Old Bailey.

Lucy.

SMITH *enters:* Miss, Mrs Polly Macheath wishes to speak with you.

LUCY: Mrs Macheath? Show her in.

Enter Polly.

POLLY: Good morning, madam. Madam, good morning.

LUCY: What is it, please?

POLLY: Do you recognise me?

LUCY: Of course I know you.

POLLY: I've come to beg your pardon for the way I behaved yesterday.

LUCY: Very interesting.

POLLY: I have no excuse to offer for my behaviour, madam, but my misfortunes.

LUCY: I see.

POLLY: Madam, you must forgive me. I was stung by Mr Macheath's behaviour. He really should not have put us in such a situation, and you can tell him so when you see him.

LUCY: I . . . I . . . shan't be seeing him.

POLLY: Of course you will see him.

LUCY: I shall not see him.

POLLY: Forgive me.

LUCY: But he's very fond of you.

POLLY: Oh no, you're the only one he loves. I'm sure of that.

LUCY: Very kind of you.

POLLY: But, madam, a man is always afraid of a woman who loves him too much. And then he's bound to neglect and avoid her. I could see at a glance that he is more devoted to you than I could ever have guessed.

LUCY: Do you mean that sincerely?

POLLY: Of course, certainly, very sincerely, madam. Do believe me.

LUCY: Dear Miss Polly, both of us have loved him too much.

POLLY: Perhaps. *Pause*. And now, madam, I want to tell you how it all came about. Ten days ago I met Mr Macheath for the first time at the Cuttlefish Hotel. My mother was there too. Five days later, about the day before yesterday, we were married. Yesterday I found out that he was wanted by the police for a variety of crimes. And today I don't know what's going to happen. So you see, madam, twelve days ago I couldn't have imagined ever losing my heart to a man. *Pause*.

LUCY: I understand, Miss Peachum.

POLLY: Mrs Macheath.

LUCY: Mrs Macheath.

POLLY: To tell the truth, I've been thinking about this man a good deal in the last few hours. It's not so simple. Because you see, Miss, I really can't help envying you for the way he behaved to you the other day. When I left him, only because my mother made me, he didn't show the slightest sign of regret. Maybe he has no heart and nothing but a stone in his breast. What do you think, Lucy?

LUCY: Well, my dear Miss, I really don't know if Mr Macheath is entirely to blame. You should have stuck to your own class of people, dear Miss.

POLLY: Mrs Macheath.

LUCY: Mrs Macheath.

POLLY: That's quite true – or at least, as my father always advised me, I should have kept everything on a strict business footing.

LUCY: Definitely.

POLLY *weeping*: But he's my only possession in all the world.

LUCY: My dear, such a misfortune can befall the most intelligent woman. But after all, you are his wife on paper. That should be a comfort to you. Poor child, I can't bear to see you so depressed. Won't you have a little something?

POLLY: What?

LUCY: Something to eat.

POLLY: Oh yes, please, a little something to eat. *Lucy goes out.*
Polly aside: The hypocritical strumpet.

LUCY *comes back with coffee and cake:* Here. This ought to do it.

POLLY: You really have gone to too much trouble, madam.
Pause. She eats. What a lovely picture of him you've got.
When did he bring it?

LUCY: Bring it?

POLLY *innocently:* I mean when did he bring it up here to you?

LUCY: He didn't bring it.

POLLY: Did he give it to you right here in this room?

LUCY: He never was in this room.

POLLY: I see. But there wouldn't have been any harm in that.
The paths of fate are so dreadfully crisscrossed.

LUCY: Must you keep talking such nonsense? You only came
here to spy.

POLLY: Then you know where he is?

LUCY: Me? Don't you know?

POLLY: Tell me this minute where he is.

LUCY: I have no idea.

POLLY: So you don't know where he is. Word of honour?

LUCY: No, I don't know. Hm, and you don't either?

POLLY: No. This is terrible. *Polly laughs and Lucy weeps.* Now
he has two commitments. And he's gone.

LUCY: I can't stand it any more. Oh, Polly, it's so dreadful.

POLLY *gaily:* I'm so happy to have found such a good friend
at the end of this tragedy. That's something. Would you
care for a little more to eat? Some more cakes?

LUCY: Just a bit! Oh, Polly, don't be so good to me. Really,
I don't deserve it. Oh, Polly, men aren't worth it.

POLLY: Of course men aren't worth it, but what else can we
do?

LUCY: No! Now I'm going to make a clean breast of it. Will
you be very cross with me, Polly?

POLLY: About what?

LUCY: It's not real!

POLLY: What?

LUCY: This here! *She indicates her belly.* And all for that crook!

POLLY *laughs:* Oh, that's magnificent! Is it a cushion? Oh, you
really are a hypocritical strumpet! Look – you want

Mackie? I'll make you a present of him. If you find him you
can keep him. *Voices and steps are heard in the corridor.* What's
that?

LUCY *at the window:* Mackie! They've caught him once more.

POLLY *collapses:* This is the end.

Enter Mrs Peachum.

MRS PEACHUM: Ha, Polly, so this is where I find you. You
must change your things, your husband is being hanged.
I've brought your widow's weeds. *Polly changes into the
widow's dress.* You'll be a lovely widow. But you'll have to
cheer up a little.

9

Friday morning. 5 am. Mac the Knife, who has
been with the whores again, has again been betrayed by whores. He is about to be hanged.

Death cell.

*The bells of Westminster ring. Constables bring Macheath shackled
into the cell.*

SMITH: Bring him in here. Those are the bells of Westminster. Stand up straight, I'm not asking you why you
look so worn out. I'd say you were ashamed. *To the constables:* When the bells of Westminster ring for the third
time, that will be at six, he's got to have been hanged. Make
everything ready.

A CONSTABLE: For the last quarter of an hour all the streets
around Newgate have been so jammed with people of all
classes you can't get through.

SMITH: Strange! Then they already know?

CONSTABLE: If this goes on, the whole of London will know
in another quarter of an hour. All the people who would
otherwise have gone to the Coronation will come here. And
the Queen will be riding through empty streets.

SMITH: All the more reason for us to move fast. If we're through by six, that will give people time to get back to the Coronation by seven. So now, get going.

MAC: Hey, Smith, what time is it?

SMITH: Haven't you got eyes? Five oh-four.

MAC: Five oh-four.

Just as Smith is locking the cell door from outside, Brown enters.

BROWN, *his back to the cell, to Smith:* Is he in there?

SMITH: You want to see him?

BROWN: No, no, no, for God's sake. I'll leave it all to you. *Goes out.*

MAC *suddenly bursts into a soft unbroken flow of speech:* All right, Smith, I won't say a word, not a word about bribery, never fear. I know all about it. If you let yourself be bribed, you'd have to leave the country for a start. You certainly would. You'd need enough to live on for the rest of your life. A thousand pounds, eh? Don't say anything! In twenty minutes I'll tell you whether you can have your thousand pounds by noon. I'm not saying a word about feelings. Go outside and think it over carefully. Life is short and money is scarce. And I don't even know yet if I can raise any. But if anyone wants to see me, let them in.

SMITH *slowly:* That's a lot of nonsense, Mr Macheath. *Goes out.*

MAC *sings softly and very fast the 'Call from the Grave':*
Hark to the voice that's calling you to weep.
Macheath lies here, not under open sky
Not under treetops, no, but good and deep.
Fate struck him down in outraged majesty.
God grant his dying words may reach a friend.
The thickest walls encompass him about.
Is none of you concerned to know his fate?
Once he is gone the bottles can come out
But do stand by him while it's not too late.
D'you want his punishment to have no end?[11]

Matthew and Jake appear in the corridor. They are on their way to see Macheath. Smith stops them.

SMITH: Well, son. You look like a soused herring.

MATTHEW: Now the captain's gone it's my job to put our girls in pod, so they can throw themselves on the mercy of

the court. It's a job for a horse. I've got to see the Captain.
Doth continue towards Mac.

MAC: Five twenty-five. You took your time.

JAKE: Yes, but, you see, we had to -. .[12]

MAC: You see, you see. I'm being hanged, man! But I've no
time to waste arguing with you. Five twenty-eight. All
right: How much can you people draw from your savings
account right away?

MATTHEW: From our . . . at five o'clock in the morning?

JAKE: Has it really come to this?

MAC: Can you manage four hundred pounds?

JAKE: But what about us? That's all there is.

MAC: Who's being hanged, you or me?

MATTHEW *excitedly:* Who was lying around with Suky
Tawdry instead of clearing out? Who was lying around
with Suky Tawdry, us or you?

MAC: Shut your trap. I'll soon be lying somewhere other than
with that slut. Five-thirty.

JAKE: Matt, if that's how it is, we'll just have to do it.

SMITH: Mr Brown wishes to know what you'd like for your
. . . repast.

MAC: Don't bother me. *To Matthew:* Well, will you or won't
you? *To Smith:* Asparagus.

MATTHEW: Don't you shout at me. I won't have it.

MAC: I'm not shouting at you. It's only that . . . well,
Matthew, are you going to let me be hanged?

MATTHEW: Of course I'm not going to let you be hanged.
Who said I was? But that's the lot. Four hundred pounds is
all there is. No reason why I shouldn't say that, is there?

MAC: Five thirty-eight.

JAKE: We'll have to run, Matthew, or it'll be no good.

MATTHEW: If we can only get through. There's such a crowd.
Human scum! *Both go out.*

MAC: If you're not here by five to six, you'll never see me
again. *Shouts:* You'll never see me again . . .

SMITH: They've gone. Well, how about it? *Makes a gesture of
counting money.*

MAC: Four hundred. *Smith goes out shrugging his shoulders. Mac,
calling after him:* I've got to speak to Brown.

SMITH *comes back with constables:* Got the soap?

CONSTABLE: Yes, but not the right kind.

SMITH: You can set the thing up in ten minutes.

CONSTABLE: But the trap doesn't work.

SMITH: It's got to work. The bells have gone a second time.

CONSTABLE: What a shambles!

MAC *sings:*

Come here and see the shitty state he's in.
This really is what people mean by bust.
You who set up the dirty cash you win
As just about the only god you'll trust
Don't stand and watch him slipping round the bend!
Go to the Queen and say that her subjects need her
Go in a group and tell her of his trouble
Like pigs all following behind their leader.
Say that his teeth are wearing down to rubble.
D'you want his punishment to have no end?

SMITH: I can't possibly let you in. You're only number sixteen. Wait your turn.

POLLY: What do you mean, number sixteen? Don't be a bureaucrat. I'm his wife. I've got to see him.

SMITH: Not more than five minutes, then.

POLLY: Five minutes! That's perfectly ridiculous. Five minutes! How's a lady to say all she's got to say? It's not so simple. This is goodbye forever. There's an exceptional amount of things for man and wife to talk about at such a moment . . . where is he?

SMITH: What, can't you see him?

POLLY: Oh yes, of course. Thank you.

MAC: Polly!

POLLY: Yes, Mackie, here I am.

MAC: Oh yes, of course!

POLLY: How are you? Are you quite worn out? It's hard.

MAC: But what are you going to do now? What will become of you?

POLLY: Don't worry, the business is doing very well. That's the least part of it. Are you very nervous, Mackie? . . . By the way, what was your father? There's so much you still haven't told me. I just don't understand. Your health has always been excellent.

MAC: Polly, can't you help me to get out?

POLLY: Oh yes, of course.

MAC: With money, of course. I've arranged with the warder . . .

POLLY *slowly:* The money has gone off to Manchester.

MAC: And you have got none on you?

POLLY: No, I have got nothing on me. But you know, Mackie, I could talk to somebody, for instance . . . I might even ask the Queen in person. *She breaks down.* Oh, Mackie!

SMITH *pulling Polly away:* Well, have you raised those thousand pounds?

POLLY: All the best, Mackie, look after yourself, and don't forget me! *Goes out.*

Smith and a constable bring in a table with a dish of asparagus on it.

SMITH: Is the asparagus tender?

CONSTABLE: Yes. *Goes out.*

BROWN *appears and goes up to Smith:* Smith, what does he want me for? It's good you didn't take the table in earlier. We'll take it right in with us, to show him how we feel about him. *They enter the cell with the table. Smith goes out. Pause.* Hello, Mac. Here's your asparagus. Won't you have some?

MAC: Don't you bother, Mr Brown. There are others to show me the last honours.[13]

BROWN: Oh, Mackie!

MAC: Would you have the goodness to produce your accounts? You don't mind if I eat in the meantime, after all it is my last meal. *He eats.*

BROWN: I hope you enjoy it. Oh, Mac, you're turning the knife in the wound.

MAC: The accounts, sir, if you please, the accounts. No sentimentality.

BROWN *with a sigh takes a small notebook from his pocket:* I've got them right here, Mac. The accounts for the past six months.

MAC *bitingly:* Oh, so all you came for was to get your money before it's too late.

BROWN: You know that isn't so . . .

MAC: Don't worry, sir, nobody's going to cheat you. What do

I owe you? But I want a detailed bill, if you don't mind. Life has made me distrustful . . . in your position you should be able to understand that.

BROWN: Mac, when you talk that way I just can't think.

A loud pounding is heard rear.

SMITH *off:* All right, that'll hold.

MAC: The accounts, Brown.

BROWN: Very well, if you insist. Well, first of all the rewards for murderers arrested thanks to you or your men. The Treasury paid you a total of . . .

MAC: Three instances at forty pounds a piece, that makes a hundred and twenty pounds. One quarter for you comes to thirty pounds, so that's what we owe you.

BROWN: Yes . . . yes . . . but really, Mac, I don't think we ought to spend our last . . .

MAC: Kindly stop snivelling. Thirty pounds. And for the job in Dover eight pounds.

BROWN: Why only eight pounds, there was . . .

MAC: Do you believe me or don't you believe me? Your share in the transactions of the last six months comes to thirty-eight pounds.

BROWN *wailing:* For a whole lifetime . . . I could read . . .

BOTH: Your every thought in your eyes.

MAC: Three years in India – John was all present and Jim was all there – five years in London, and this is the thanks I get. *Indicating how he will look when hanged.*

Here hangs Macheath who never wronged a flea
A faithless friend has brought him to this pass.
And as he dangles from the gallowstree
His neck finds out how heavy is his arse.

BROWN: If that's the way you feel about it, Mac . . . The man who impugns my honour, impugns me. *Runs furiously out of the cage.*

MAC: Your honour . . .

BROWN: Yes, my honour. Time to begin, Smith! Let them in! *To Mac:* Excuse me, would you?

SMITH *quickly to Macheath:* I can still get you out of here, in another minute I won't be able to. Have you got the money?

MAC: Yes, as soon as the boys get back.

SMITH: There's no sign of them. The deal is off.

People are admitted. Peachum, Mrs Peachum, Polly, Lucy, the whores, the parson, Matthew and Jake.

JENNY: They weren't anxious to let us in. But I said to them: If you don't get those pisspots you call heads out of my way, you'll hear from Low-Dive Jenny.

PEACHUM: I am his father-in-law. I beg your pardon, which of the present company is Mr Macheath?

MAC *introduces himself:* I'm Macheath.

PEACHUM *walks past the cage, and like all who follow him stations himself to the right of it:* Fate, Mr Macheath, has decreed that though I don't know you, you should be my son-in-law. The occasion of this first meeting between us is a very sad one. Mr Macheath, you once had white kid gloves, a cane with an ivory handle, and a scar on your neck, and you frequented the Cuttlefish Hotel. All that is left is your scar, no doubt the least valuable of your distinguishing marks. Today you frequent nothing but prison cells, and within the foreseeable future no place at all . . .

Polly passes the cage in tears and stations herself to the right.

MAC: What a pretty dress you're wearing.

Matthew and Jake pass the cage and station themselves on the right.

MATTHEW: We couldn't get through because of the terrible crush. We ran so hard I was afraid Jake was going to have a stroke. If you don't believe us . . .

MAC: What do my men say? Have they got good places?

MATTHEW: You see, Captain, we thought you'd understand. You see, a Coronation doesn't happen every day. They've got to make some money while there's a chance. They send you their best wishes.

JAKE: Their very best wishes.

MRS PEACHUM *steps up to the cage, stations herself on the right:* Mr Macheath, who would have expected this a week ago when we were dancing at a little hop at the Cuttlefish Hotel.

MAC: A little hop.

MRS PEACHUM: But the ways of destiny are cruel here below.

BROWN *at the rear to the parson:* And to think that I stood shoulder to shoulder with this man in Azerbaidjan under a hail of bullets.

JENNY *approaches the cage:* We Drury Lane girls are frantic. Nobody's gone to the Coronation. Everybody wants to see you. *Stations herself on the right.*

MAC: To see me.

SMITH: All right. Let's go. Six o'clock. *Lets him out of the cage.*

MAC: We mustn't keep anybody waiting. Ladies and gentlemen. You see before you a declining representative of a declining social group. We lower middle-class artisans who toil with our humble jemmies on small shopkeepers' cash registers are being swallowed up by big corporations backed by the banks. What's a jemmy compared with a share certificate? What's breaking into a bank compared with founding a bank? What's murdering a man compared with employing a man? Fellow citizens, I hereby take my leave of you. I thank you for coming. Some of you were very close to me. That Jenny should have turned me in amazes me greatly. It is proof positive that the world never changes. A concatenation of several unfortunate circumstances has brought about my fall. So be it – I fall.

Song lighting: golden glow. The organ is lit up. Three lamps are lowered on a pole, and the signs say:

BALLAD IN WHICH MACHEATH BEGS ALL MEN FOR FORGIVENESS

You fellow men who live on after us
Pray do not think you have to judge us harshly
And when you see us hoisted up and trussed
Don't laugh like fools behind your big moustaches
Or curse at us. It's true that we came crashing
But do not judge our downfall like the courts.
Not all of us can discipline our thoughts –
Dear fellows, your extravagance needs slashing.
Dear fellows, we've shown how a crash begins.
Pray then to God that He forgive my sins.

The rain washes away and purifies.
Let it wash down the flesh we catered for
And we who saw so much, and wanted more –
The crows will come and peck away our eyes.
Perhaps ambition used too sharp a goad
It drove us to these heights from which we swing
Hacked at by greedy starlings on the wing
Like horses' droppings on a country road.
O brothers, learn from us how it begins
And pray to God that He forgive our sins.

The girls who flaunt their breasts as bait there
To catch some sucker who will love them
The youths who slyly stand and wait there
To grab their sinful earnings off them
The crooks, the tarts, the tarts' protectors
The models and the mannequins
The psychopaths, the unfrocked rectors
I pray that they forgive my sins.

Not so those filthy police employees
Who day by day would bait my anger
Devise new troubles to annoy me
And chuck me crusts to stop my hunger.
I'd call on God to come and choke them
And yet my need for respite wins:
I realise that it might provoke them
So pray that they forgive my sins.

**Someone must take a huge iron crowbar
And stave their ugly faces in
All I ask is to know it's over
Praying that they forgive my sins.**

SMITH: If you don't mind, Mr Macheath.
MRS PEACHUM: Polly and Lucy, stand by your husband in
   his last hour.
MAC: Ladies, whatever there may have been between us . . .
SMITH *leads him away:* Get a move on!

Procession to the Gallows.
All go out through doors left. These doors are on projection screens.
Then all re-enter from the other side of the stage with dark lan-
terns. When Macheath is standing at the top of the gallows steps
Peachum speaks.

Dear audience, we now are coming to
The point where we must hang him by the neck
Because it is the Christian thing to do
Proving that men must pay for what they take.

But as we want to keep our fingers clean
And you're the people we can't risk offending
We thought we'd better do without this scene
And substitute instead a different ending.

Since this is opera, not life, you'll see
Justice give way before humanity.
So now, to stop our story in its course
Enter the royal official on his horse.

THIRD THREEPENNY FINALE
APPEARANCE OF THE DEUS EX MACHINA

CHORUS:

Hark, who's here?
A royal official on horseback's here!
Enter Brown on horseback as deus ex machina.

BROWN: I bring a special order from our beloved Queen to
have Captain Macheath set at liberty forthwith – *All cheer.* –
as it's the coronation, and raised to the hereditary peerage.
Cheers. The castle of Marmarel, likewise a pension of ten
thousand pounds, to be his in usufruct until his death. To
any bridal couples present Her Majesty bids me to convey
her gracious good wishes.

MAGI

Reprieved! Reprieved! I was sure of it.
When you're most despairing
The clouds may be clearing

POLLY: Reprieved, my dearest Macheath is reprieved. I am so
happy.

MRS PEACHUM: So it all turned out nicely in the end. How
nice and easy everything would be if you could always
reckon with saviours on horseback.

PEACHUM: Now please remain all standing in your places,
and join in the hymn of the poorest of the poor, whose most
arduous lot you have put on stage here today. In real life the
fates they meet can only be grim. Saviours on horseback are
seldom met with in practice. And the man who's kicked
about must kick back. Which all means that injustice should
be spared from persecution.

All come forward, singing to the organ:

Injustice should be spared from persecution:
Soon it will freeze to death, for it is cold.
Think of the blizzards and the black confusion
Which in this vale of tears we must behold.

The bells of Westminster are heard ringing for the third time.

The Rise and Fall of the City of Mahagonny

Opera

Collaborators: E. HAUPTMANN, C. NEHER, K. WEILL

Translators: W. H. AUDEN and CHESTER KALLMAN

Characters
JIMMY ⎫
BILLY ⎬ *Lumberjacks*
JAKE ⎪
JOE ⎭
LADYBIRD BEGBICK
TRINITY MOSES
FATTY THE BOOKIE
JENNY
Men and Girls of Mahagonny

Founding of the City of Mahagonny

A large lorry in very bad condition comes to a stop in a desolate place.

FATTY: What's up? We must go on.

MOSES: But the truck has broken down.

FATTY: Then we can't go on.

Pause

MOSES: But we must go on.

FATTY: But there's nothing there but desert.

MOSES: Then we can't go on.

Pause

FATTY: Then we must go back.

MOSES: But the sheriffs are waiting back there; they know our faces only too well.

FATTY: Then we can't go back.

They sit on the running-board and light cigarettes.

MOSES: Further up the coast we might strike a gold-field.

FATTY: Maybe. But the coast is too long.

MOSES: Then we can't even go there.

FATTY: But we might strike a gold-field.

MOSES: Maybe. But the coast is too long.

MADAM LADYBIRD BEGBICK *appearing in the window of the driver's cabin*: Are we stuck?

MOSES: Yes.

BEGBICK: Good! Why don't we stay here? As I always say: If you can't get to the top, stay at the bottom. Listen to me.

The people we've met who have seen the gold-fields agree that the rivers don't like parting with their gold at all. It's back-breaking work. That's hardly in our line. But I took a good look at the faces of those fellows and they'll part with their gold all right, I assure you. Men are easier to manage than rivers. This is the spot for us. Any objections? Then that's settled.

In this empty waste is our town founded
And its name is Mahagonny
Which means Suckerville!

FATTY AND MOSES: Suckerville!

BEGBICK:
We will make it a snare
Plump little birds will be eager to enter.
Everywhere men must labour and sorrow
Only here is it fun.
For the deepest craving of man is
Not to suffer but do as he pleases.
That is our golden secret.
Gin and whisky
Girls for the asking.
We'll have a seven-day week: every day a day of leisure;
And the raging typhoon will never bother us here.
No one shall suffer from the blues,
They'll smoke and dream of all the promises of nightfall
And every other day we'll have boxing
With mayhem and knockouts though the fighting is fair.
Stick that fishing-rod in the ground and run up this bit of
Linen so that the ships returning from the gold-coast
Can see us as they pass.
Set the bar up there
Beside that tamarack.

There is our town
This shall be our centre
This is the . . . *As-You-Like-It Tavern.*
The red Mahogonny pennant is run up on a long fishing-pole.

FATTY AND MOSES:

Why, though, do we need a Mahogonny?
Because this world is a foul one
With neither charity
Nor peace nor concord
Because there's nothing
To build any trust upon.

2

Within a few weeks a city had arisen and the first sharks and harpies were making themselves at home

Jenny and six girls enter carrying large suitcases. They sit on their suitcases and sing the Alabama Song.

Oh, show us the way
To the next whisky-bar.
Oh, don't ask why!
For we must find the next whisky-bar.
For if we don't find the next whisky-bar
I tell you we must die!
Oh, Moon of Alabama
We now must say good-bye.
We've lost our good old mama
And must have whisky
Oh, you know why.

Oh, show us the way to the next pretty boy
Oh, don't ask why, oh, don't ask why!
For we must find the next pretty boy
For if we don't find the next pretty boy
I tell you we must die!
Oh, Moon of Alabama
We now must say good-bye.
We've lost our good old mama
And must have boys
Oh, you know why!

Oh, show us the way to the next little dollar!
Oh, don't ask why, oh, don't ask why!
For we must find the next little dollar
For if we don't find the next little dollar
I tell you, we must die!
Oh, Moon of Alabama
We now must say good-bye.
We've lost our good old mama
And must have dollars
Oh, you know why.
They go out with their suitcases.

3

News of the founding of a new Jerusalem reached the big cities

On the backcloth appears a projection showing a view of a metropolis and a photomontage of men's faces.

MEN:
   We dwell in large dark cities: miles of sewers below them;
   Thick over them, smoke; in them nothing at all.
   No peace, no joy: here is no soil to grow them;
   Here we quickly fade. More slowly they also shall fall.
   Fatty and Moses enter with placards.

FATTY: Far from the hullaballoo . . .

MOSES: – The big express-trains never bother us –

FATTY: . . . Lies our Joytown, Mahagonny.

MOSES: They just were asking where you've been so long.

FATTY: We live in an age that produces many city-dwellers
   city life does not content: all are flocking to Mahagonny,
   the Joytown.

MOSES: Chips and chippies are cheaper!

FATTY:
   Here in all your cities there is so much noise
   So much ill-temper and discord
   And nothing to build your trust upon.

MOSES: For yours is a foul world.

FATTY AND MOSES:
   But once you puff with fellow
   Mahagonny-dwellers
   Smoke-rings white as snow

Soon you'll feel your parchment-yellow
Cheeks glow.
Sky-blue reflections turn
Gold in your drink:
Should San Francisco burn
All there for which you yearn
Must, good or evil, churn
Down the same sink.

MEN *offstage*:
We dwell in large dark cities: miles of sewers below them;
Thick over them, smoke; in them nothing at all.
No peace, no joy: here is no soil to grow them;
Here we quickly fade. More slowly they also shall fall.

FATTY: Then off to Mahagonny!

MOSES: They just were asking where you've been so long.

4

The next few years saw the discontented from every country making their way towards Mahagonny

Jim, Jake, Bill and Joe enter carrying suitcases.

Off to Mahagonny
Where all the winds refresh
Where gin and whisky rivers flow
Past horse- and woman-flesh!
Green and lovely
Moon of Alabama
Shine for us!

Underneath our shirts we've got
Money and we've got a lot
That should smear some smile across
Your big and stupid face.

Off to Mahagonny
Where all the trade-winds blow
Where steaks are cut and blood runs out
But no one runs the show!
Green and lovely
Moon of Alabama
Shine for us!
Underneath our shirts we've got
Money and we've got a lot
That should smear some smile across
Your big and stupid face.

Off to Mahagonny
On swift and even keel
Where civ-civ-il-i-sation
Will lose its scab and heal.
Green and lovely
Moon of Alabama
Shine for us!
Underneath our shirts we've got
Money and we've got a lot
That should smear some smile across
Your big and stupid face.
The men go out.

5

One day there came to Mahagonny among others a man called Jimmy Gallagher. We are going to tell you his story.

A quay near Mahagonny. Jim, Jake, Bill and Joe are standing before a signpost that reads: To Mahagonny. A price-list hangs on the signpost.

JIM:
When you arrive some place the first time
You're a bit out of focus to begin with.

JAKE: You don't know where to go or how to go.

BILL: Who to order around.

JOE: Who to take off your hat to.

JIM:
It's inconvenient
When you arrive some place the first time.
Lady Begbick enters carrying a large notebook.

BEGBICK:
Gentlemen, welcome.
Just make yourselves comfy. *Consulting her notebook.*
So you're the famous Jimmy Gallagher!
We hear tell of your knife tricks, Jimmy.
At your bedtime you must always have
English-made gin and bitters.

JIM: Pleased to meet you.

BEGBICK: Lady – that's short for Ladybird – Begbick.
They shake hands.
And for your arrival, John Jacob Smith
We've put on our party clothes.

JAKE: Nice to know you.

BEGBICK: And you're known as Billy?

JIM *introducing him*: Bookkeeping Billy.

BEGBICK: Then you must be Joe?

JIM *introducing him*: Alaskawolf Joe.

BEGBICK:

And just to show how glad we are to have you
Prices will be cut till further notice.
She makes changes on the price-list.

BILL AND JOE *shaking hands with her*: Thanks a million.

BEGBICK: Now you'll want to look into our latest crop of
cuties . . .
*Moses brings in pictures of the girls and sets them up. The pictures
are like the covers of the old penny-dreadfuls.*

Gentlemen, every man carries an image of the ideal in his
heart: one man's voluptuous is another man's skinny. The
way this one can wriggle her hips should make her just
about perfect for you, Joe.

JAKE: Maybe that one over there would suit me.

JOE: Actually, I had something a little darker in mind.

BEGBICK: What about you, Billy?

BILL: Me? I pass.

BEGBICK: And you, Jim?

JIM:

No, pictures don't say nothing to me. I have to pinch them
     and pat them to know if it's really going to be love.
Come out, you beauties of Mahagonny!
We've got the dough, let's see your stuff.

JAKE, BILL AND JOE:

Seven years we worked Alaska:
That means frost-bite, that means dough.
Come out, you beauties of Mahagonny!
We like to pay for what we like.

JENNY AND GIRLS:

Here we are to help you melt Alaska:

Did you freeze there, but make the dough?

JIM: Well, hello, you beauties of Mahagonny!

JENNY AND GIRLS:

We are the cuties of Mahagonny:

By paying well, you'll get whatever you like.

BEGBICK *pointing to Jenny*:

That's the girl for you, John Jacob Smith:

And if her behind doesn't have bounce in it

Your fifty dollars won't be worth their weight in toilet
paper.

JAKE: Thirty dollars . . .

BEGBICK *to Jenny, shrugging her shoulders*: Thirty dollars?

JENNY:

Have you thought at all, John Jacob Smith

Have you thought what you can buy with thirty dollars
now?

Ten silk step-ins and no change.

My home is Havana.

From my mother I get my white blood.

She often said to me

'My lamb, don't sell yourself

The way your mother used to

For a buck or two.

You can see what that life has done to her.'

Have you thought of that, John Jacob Smith?

JAKE: For that, twenty dollars.

BEGBICK: Thirty, sir. We don't bargain. Thirty.

JAKE: Out of the question.

JIM:

Well, maybe I'll take her.

You, what's your name?

JENNY:

Jenny Jones from Oklahoma

I've been hereabouts for seven weeks now.

I was down there in the larger cities.

I'm game for all things that I am asked to do.

I know you Jimmies, Jimmies, Jimmies from Alaska well:

You have it worse in winter than the dead have

But you get rich in hell.

In leather jackets and your wallets stuffed with greenbacks

You come to see what Mahagonny has to sell.

But this time's not like other Jims:

They all went crazy for my limbs

Those limbs belong to you now, baby.

It wasn't love before to me

So clasp your hand about my knee

And drink from my glass too now, baby.

JIM: Good. I'll take you.

JENNY: Bottoms up, handsome.

They are on the point of moving off to Mahagonny when some people arrive from that direction, carrying suitcases.

JOE: But who are these people?

THE PEOPLE WITH SUITCASES:

Has the ship left?

No thank God! It's still at anchor!

They crowd off hurriedly to the quay.

BEGBICK *shouting after them*: Bird-brains! Wool-heads! Look at them scuttling off to the ship like a pack of rats! And their pig-skin wallets are still fat with moola! Sons-of-bitches! Blue-nosed baboons!

JAKE:

I don't get it, why they're going.

From a fun place, you don't run.

Do you think that something stinks there?

BEGBICK:

You boys now, *you're* not going;
You're coming along to Mahagonny.
Call it a favour to me
If you accept another cut in prices.
She puts a new price-list up over the other.

JOE:

In this Mahagonny that we'd put so high a price on
Things are too cheap. That disturbs me.

BILL: To me the place looks too expensive.

JAKE: And you, Jimmy, do you think the place looks good?

JIM: When we're there, it will be good.

JENNY: I used to be so blue before.

THE SIX GIRLS: I used to be so blue before.

JENNY AND THE SIX GIRLS:

I never could be true before:
It wasn't you before now, baby.

JENNY, THE SIX GIRLS, BEGBICK, JIM, JAKE, BILL, JOE:

We know these Jimmies, Jimmies, Jimmies from Alaska
well:

JENNY AND THE SIX GIRLS: They have it worse in
winter than the dead have.

JIM, JAKE, BILL, JOE:

But we got rich in hell.
But we got rich in hell.
In leather jackets and their wallets stuffed with greenbacks
They come to see what Mahagonny has to sell.
Exeunt for Mahagonny.

6

Instructions

Street map of Mahagonny. Jim and Jenny walking.

JENNY:
One thing I have learned when I meet a gent for the first time, that's to ask him what he is used to. Tell me then exactly how you would like me.

JIM:
As you are, you're exactly my type. If you would call me Jimmy I'd imagine you liked me a little.

JENNY:
Tell me, Jimmy, how would you like my hair done: combed straight or with a wave?

JIM:
They both would look fine to me . . . whatever's the mood you're in.

JENNY:
What are your feelings about underclothes, friend? Should I wear step-ins when I'm dressed or a dress with nothing under?

JIM: Nothing under.

JENNY: As you like it, Jimmy.

JIM: But what would you like?

JENNY: Let's say it's much too soon for me to tell you.

7

Every great undertaking has its ups and downs

On the backcloth is a projection giving statistics about crime and currency fluctuation in Mahagonny. Seven different price-lists. Inside the As-You-Like-It Tavern, Fatty and Moses are sitting at the bar. Begbick rushes in wearing white make-up.

BEGBICK:
  Fatty, we're ruined! Moses, we're ruined! Haven't you noticed? People are leaving! They're rushing down to the quay with their bags. I saw them there.

FATTY: What should keep them here – a sprinkling of bars and a deluge of silence?

MOSES: And a fine lot of men they are! They hook a minnow and they're happy; they puff smoke on the porch and they're satisfied.

BEGBICK, FATTY, MOSES:
  Our lovely Mahagonny
  Has not brought in the business.

BEGBICK: Whisky's down to twelve dollars a quart today.

FATTY: By tomorrow it's sure to drop to eight.

MOSES: And sure never to rise again!

BEGBICK, FATTY, MOSES:
  Our lovely Mahagonny
  Has not brought in the business.

BEGBICK: I've lost all idea what to do. Everybody wants something from me and I've already given them everything. What more can I give to keep them from deserting us?

BEGBICK, FATTY, MOSES:

Our lovely Mahagonny
Has not brought in the business.

BEGBICK:

I, too, was once with a man who took me and put my
Back to the wall:
There we stood and talked for a while
And it was love that we spoke of.
Once all the money went
Talk like that lost its tenderness.

FATTY AND MOSES:

Ready money
Makes you tender.

BEGBICK:

It's nineteen years back that the misery of struggling for
survival began, and it's sapped me dry. This was to be my
last big scheme – Mahagonny, Suckerville. But the suckers
refuse to get caught.

BEGBICK, FATTY, MOSES:

Our lovely Mahagonny
Has not brought in the business.

BEGBICK:

All that's left is to retreat quickly
To follow our steps backwards through a thousand cities
To travel in time backwards through nineteen years, boys.
Pack your luggage! Pack your luggage!
We've got to go back!

FATTY:

Sure, Lady Begbick. Sure, Lady Begbick, we'll go back.
But it's *you* they're waiting for. *Reading from a newspaper.*
'In Pensacola yesterday the county sheriffs arrived in force
and split to pick up Ladybird Begbick's trail. They made a
systematic search of every house and rode off together . . .'

BEGBICK: God! Now nothing will save us!

FATTY AND MOSES:

Dear Lady Begbick,
It's a fact that crime has never paid well
And those dealing in vice do not
Live to grow old!

BEGBICK:

With just a few dollars!
Yes, with just a few dollars
That we might have made in this enterprise
Planned as a snare, which wasn't a snare
I could manage to hold the sheriffs off.
But weren't there some newcomers today?
They looked like money to me.
And maybe they'll spend it with us.

8

Seek and ye shall not find

The quay near Mahagonny. Coming away from Mahagonny, like the people with suitcases in scene 5, Jimmy enters followed by his friends, who are trying to hold him back.

JAKE: Jimmy, what's the hurry?

JIM: What's there to keep me?

BILL: Why that look on your face?

JIM: I'm sick of seeing the word 'Forbidden'.

JOE: But the gin and whisky are so cheap.

JIM: Too cheap.

BILL: And it's so peaceful here.

JIM: Too peaceful.

JAKE: When you feel like eating fish, you can catch one.

JIM: I don't like fishing.

JOE: You can smoke.

JIM: You can smoke.

BILL: You can sleep.

JAKE: You can go swimming.

JIM *copying him*: You can go pick yourself a banana.

JOE: You can look at the water.

Jim shrugs his shoulders.

BILL: You can forget.

JIM: But it won't quite do.

JAKE, BILL, JOE:

Soft and agreeable is the stillness
And enchanting is the concord.

JIM: But they won't quite do.

JAKE, BILL, JOE:

Noble is the simple existence
And Nature's wonders are sublime beyond compare.

JIM:

But they won't quite do.
I think I will eat my old felt hat
The flavour, at least, will be new:
And why shouldn't a man eat his old felt hat
When he's nothing, when he's nothing, when he's nothing
  else to do?

You've learned to mix your cocktails every way
You've seen the moonlight shining on the wall:
The bar is shut, the bar of Mandalay:
And why does nothing make sense at all?
You tell me, please, why nothing makes sense at all.
I think I will set out for Arkansas:

It may not be much, it's true.
But why shouldn't a man go to Arkansas
When he's nothing, when he's nothing, when he's nothing
      else to do?

You've learned to mix your cocktails every way
You've seen the moonlight shining on the wall:
The bar is shut, the bar of Mandalay:
And why does nothing make sense at all?
You tell me, please, why nothing makes sense at all.

JAKE, BILL, JOE:
    Why, Jimmy, must you blow your top?
    This *is* the bar of Mandalay.

JOE: Jimmy says he will eat his hat.

BILL: But why, why should you want to eat your hat?

JAKE, BILL, JOE:
    You mustn't eat your hat, Jimmy!
    We won't let you do that, Jimmy!
    Hat-eating goes too far –
    Eating hats in a bar!
    Shouting.
    We'll give you a beating
    Jimmy! Hat-eating
    'S not what mankind was born for.

JIM *calmly*: You tell me! What is it man was born for?

JOE: Well, now you've said your little piece, you can come
    along with us like a good boy, home to Mahagonny.
    They take him back to Mahagonny.

9

Under a wide-open sky, in front of the As-You-Like-It Tavern, the Men of Mahagonny, including the Four Friends, are sitting on rocking chairs, smoking and drinking. They are listening to a piano, and dreamily watching a white cloud which travels back and forth across the sky. Around them are printed notices bearing such inscriptions as 'Kindly take care of my furniture. L.B.' 'Wipe your shoes before entering. L.B.' 'Do not put your feet on the table. L.B.' 'No spitting. L.B.' 'Ashtrays have been provided: use them. L.B.' 'Do not pick your teeth in public. L.B.' 'Do not throw razor blades down the W.C. L.B.' 'Please refrain from using indecent language and singing indecent songs. L.B.' 'Keep this establishment as we like it and it will be as-you-like-it.'

JIM:

    Deep in the woods of ice-bound Alaska
    Seven winters I toiled with three buddies together
    Cutting down trees and hauling logs through the snow
    And I lived on raw meat and saved my earnings:
    Seven years it's taken to get me
    Here where I now am.

    There in a riverside hut for seven winters
    Carving our curses with our knives in the table
    Talking of nothing but where we would go to
    Of just where we would go to when we'd saved enough
        money
    Hungered, thirsted, sweated, shivered to
    Get where we now are.

    When our time was over, we picked up our savings.

Out of all towns we had to choose from, we chose
    Mahagonny
Made our way here without stopping to rest
By the shortest route.
And what does it all add up to?
That no fouler place could exist
Nor any duller one be found on earth than
Here where we now are.
He jumps to his feet.
What's the big idea? You think you can treat us like this?
You've got a second think coming. Come out of there, you
As-You-Like-It slut! It's Jimmy Gallagher talking . . . from
Alaska . . . He doesn't like it here!

BEGBICK *coming out of the Tavern*: What don't you like here?

JIM: Your dungheap.

BEGBICK: I seem to keep hearing 'dungheap'. Did anyone by
  chance say
  'Dungheap'?

JIM: You heard me. I said *Dungheap*.
The cloud shakes and goes quickly off.
Seven winters, seven winters hauling logs and cutting down
  trees . . .

THE SIX GIRLS, JAKE, BILL, JOE: He spent in cutting down
  trees . . .

JIM: And the rivers, and the rivers, and the rivers jammed
  with floating ice . . .

JAKE: Be quiet, Jim.

THE SIX GIRLS, JAKE, BILL, JOE: The rivers jammed with
  floating ice . . .

JIM:
  Hungered, thirsted, sweated, shivered, Slaving like a beast
    to get here
  But I do not like it here, for

Nothing's going on.

JENNY:

Listen, Jimmy! Listen, Jimmy!

Please be good and put that knife away.

JIM: Hold me, hold me back!

JAKE, BILL, JOE: Please be good and put that knife away.

JENNY:

Listen, Jimmy!

Be a good boy, Jimmy, and behave.

JIM:

Seven years of felling timber

Seven years of cold and squalor

Seven years of bitter toil and

This is all you have to offer:

BEGBICK, FATTY, MOSES: You have quiet, concord, whisky, women.

JIM: Quiet! Concord! Whisky! Women!

JENNY, JAKE, BILL, JOE: Put your knife back in your belt now!

CHORUS: Qui-et! Qui-et!

BEGBICK, FATTY, MOSES: You can sleep here, smoke here, fish here, swim here.

JIM: Sleeping! Smoking! Fishing! Smoking!

JENNY, THE SIX GIRLS, JAKE, BILL, JOE:

Jimmy, put that knife away!

Jimmy, put that knife away!

CHORUS: Qui-et! Qui-et!

BEGBICK, FATTY, MOSES:

We know these Jimmies from Alaska.

We know these Jimmies from Alaska.

JIM:

Hold me, hold me back! Or there will be trouble.

Hold me, hold me back!

JAKE, BILL, JOE:
Hold him, hold him back! Or there will be trouble.
Hold him, hold him back!

CHORUS:
We know these Jimmies, Jimmies, Jimmies from Alaska
well:
They have it worse in winter than the dead have.
But you get rich in hell. But you get rich in hell.

BEGBICK, FATTY, MOSES: Why can't stupid swine like these
remain forever in Alaska? All they ever want to do is spoil
the fun of peace and concord. Throw the bastard out! He's
had enough.

JIM:
Hold me, hold me back or there'll be trouble!
For there's no life here!
For there's no life here!
He stands on a table.
No, not all your bars in Mahagonny
Will ever make a man happy:
There's too much charity
And too much concord
And there is too much
To build all his trust upon.
All the lights go out. Everyone remains as he is in the dark.

10

In enormous letters on the backcloth appears: TYPHOON!, *and then:*
A HURRICANE THREATENS MAHAGONNY.

ALL:
No! Not utter destruction!

Our golden Joytown will be lost!
For the raging storm hangs over the mountains:
We shall die, drown in the waters of death.
We face utter destruction
A black, horrible end!

O is there no wall to shelter us now?
O is there no cavern which will hide us?
We face utter destruction
A black, horrible end!

11

During this dreadful night an untutored lumberjack called Jimmy Gallagher had a vision in which the laws of human happiness were revealed to him

The night of the hurricane. Sitting on the ground leaning against the wall are Jenny, Begbick, Jim, Jake, Bill and Joe. All are in despair, but Jim is smiling. From backstage can be heard the voices of men in procession as they pass behind the wall.

THE MEN OF MAHAGONNY *off*:
  Stout be your hearts though dark be the night
  Stand though the sun and the moon take to flight:
  Hence with idle wailing
  Tears are unavailing;
  Face the fury of the storm and fight!
JENNY *softly and sadly*:
  Oh, Moon of Alabama

We now must say good-bye.
We've lost our good old mama
And must have whisky
Oh, you know why.

JAKE:
Why try to escape it?
It's no use.
To run away
Cannot save you.
The best thing we can do
Is to sit here
And face it
Until the end comes.

THE MEN OF MAHAGONNY *off*:
Stout be your hearts though dark be the night
Stand though the sun and the moon take to flight:
Hence with idle wailing
Tears are unavailing;
Face the fury of the storm and fight!
Jim laughs.

BEGBICK: What's the laugh for?

JIM:
So, then – that's how it is!
Quiet and concord do not exist.
But the big typhoons have existence.
So do earthquakes. You can ignore neither.
And the same is true of mankind:
It must destroy and bring ruin.
You're afraid of raging hurricanes?
You think that typhoons are shocking?
Wait till a man is out to have his fun.

In the distance: 'Stout be your hearts . . .' etc.

JAKE: Be quiet, Jim.

JOE: You talk too much.

BILL: Relax and smoke and forget.

JIM:

> You may build a tower taller than Everest:
> Man will come and smash it to bits.
> He'll do it for the hell of it.
> The straightest way shall be made crooked
> And the high place brought down to dust.
> We need no raging hurricane
> We need no bolt from the blue:
> There's no havoc which they might have done
> That we cannot better do.

In the distance: 'Stout be your hearts . . .' etc.

BEGBICK:

> Bad is the hurricane.
> Even worse the typhoon.
> But the worst of all is man.

JIM *to Begbick:*

> Listen! You've had placards put up
> Upon which was written:
> *This is prohibited.*
> *That you mustn't do.*
> That sort of thing spoils any happiness.
> Boys! In that corner there is a placard.
> It says there: *It is henceforth forbidden*
> *To sing any cheerful songs.*
> But before two o'clock strikes
> You will hear Jimmy Gallagher
> Singing a cheerful song
> To show you that
> Nothing is forbidden.

JOE:

We need no raging hurricane
We need no bolt from the blue;
There's no havoc which they might have done
That we cannot better do.

JENNY:

Be quiet, Jim. You talk too much.
Come outside with me: make love to me.

JIM:

No. I've more to say.

Dreams have all one ending:
To wake and be coldly sure
To see the dark descending
To hear the wind portending
A night that shall endure.

Life, our only treasure
Runs out before you know.
The deepest draught of pleasure
Will seem too short a measure
When you are told to go.

Daily we grow older.
We have but little time
So leave the dead to moulder
To be alive is nobler
To flee from life, a crime.

Take not as your teacher
The tyrant or the slave.
And do not dread the preacher:
The end for every creature

Is nothing but the grave.
He comes to the front of the stage.

If you see a thing
You can only have for cash
Then fork out your cash:
If someone is passing by who has cash
Knock him on the head and take all his cash:
Yes, do it!

If you fancy a lovely home
Then enter a home
And pick yourself a bed:
If the housewife comes, make a twosome with her
If the roof begins leaking, get away!
Yes, do it!

If one morning a thought occurs
New to your mind
Think that, like all thinking
It'll cost you cash and ruin your home:
Think it, though! Think it, though!
Yes, do it!

For the sake of good order
The good of the state
For humanity's future
And for your personal satisfaction
Do it!

All have risen. They are now holding their heads high. Jim returns
to them and they congratulate him.
THE MEN OF MAHAGONNY *offstage*:
    Hence with idle wailing

Tears are unavailing;
Face the fury of the storm and fight!

BEGBICK *beckons Jim and goes into a corner with him*: So you think I was wrong to forbid anything.

JIM: Yes. Now I'm cheerful, I feel like tearing down all your precious notices. Even the walls will have to go. The hurricane won't pay you for them, but I will. Here. Take this.

BEGBICK *to all*:
Let each one do just what he likes,
The storm will soon do it too:
So when a raging hurricane strikes
There's nothing we may not do.

JIM, JAKE, BILL, JOE:
Clap your hands when a hurricane strikes:
Who cares for being immortal?
When a man can do just what he likes
Who's afraid of the storm at his portal?
Let it say
Any day:
Do you think you're immortal?
Fatty and Moses rush in excitedly.

FATTY AND MOSES:
Destroyed is Pensacola!
Destroyed is Pensacola!
And the hurricane roars
On its raging way to Mahagonny!

BEGBICK *exultantly*:
Pensacola!
Pensacola!
The sharp-eyed sheriffs are swallowed up
The just alike with the unjust have been brought to
nothing:
It must have taken them all!

JIM:
    You are free, I say, if you dare!
    You may do all tonight that's prohibited.
    Soon the hurricane will do it as well, so
    Sing, as an example, for that's prohibited.

THE MEN OF MAHAGONNY *quite close behind the wall*: Be
    quiet! Be quiet!

JIM WITH JENNY AND JOE:
    Come on, sing with us!
    Sing with us, sing any cheerful song.
    If it's prohibited
    Sing it with us!

JIM *jumping on to the wall*:
    As you make your bed, so you lie on it
    The bed can be old or brand-new;
    So if someone must kick, why, that's my part
    And another get kicked, that part's for you!

ALL:
    As you make your bed, so you lie on it
    The bed can be old or brand-new;
    So if someone must kick, that is my part,
    And another get kicked, that's for you!
    *Lights out. On the backcloth is a map on which an arrow indi-
    cating the path of the hurricane moves slowly towards Mahagonny.*

CHORUS *distant*: Stout be your hearts though dark be the
    night!

12

*In a dim light, the Men and Girls of Mahagonny are waiting on a
country road outside the city. As at the end of scene 11, the projection*

on the backcloth shows an arrow moving slowly towards Mahagonny.
Every so often during the orchestral introduction a loudspeaker makes
announcements: 'The hurricane is now approaching Atsena at a speed
of one hundred and twenty miles an hour.'

Second loudspeaker announcement: 'Atsena totally destroyed. No
reports coming through. Communications with Atsena impossible to
re-establish.'

Third loudspeaker announcement: 'The hurricane's speed is increas-
ing; it is now making straight for Mahagonny. All lines to Maha-
gonny are now down.
In Pensacola 11,000 are reported dead.'

All are watching the arrow horror-struck. Suddenly, a minute's
distance from Mahagonny, the arrow stops. Dead silence. Then the
arrow makes a rapid half-circle around Mahagonny and moves on.
Loudspeaker:
'The hurricane has veered in a circle round Mahagonny and is con-
tinuing on its course.'

MEN AND GIRLS:
   O wonderful salvation!
   Our lovely city stands unharmed.
   The raging hurricane veered away in a new direction
   And pale death said to the waters: Go back.
   Rejoice in our salvation!

From now on the phrase 'do it', which they had
been taught in that night of horror, became the
motto of the people of Mahagonny

13

A year later. Mahagonny is booming.

Men step on to the apron and sing.

CHORUS:
>One means to eat all you are able;
>Two, to change your loves about;
>Three means the ring and gaming table;
>Four, to drink until you pass out.
>Moreover, better get this clear
>That Don'ts are not permitted here.
>Moreover, better get it clear
>That Don'ts are not permitted here!
>*The Men return to the stage and take part in what follows. On the signs at the back of the stage in enormous letters is the word* 'EATING'. *A number of the Men, including Jim, are seated at tables laden with joints of meat. Jake, now known as Guzzler, is seated at a centre table eating incessantly. On each side of him, a Musician is playing.*

GUZZLER JAKE:
>Two calves never made a man fatter:
>So serve me a third fatted calf.
>All is only half:
>I wish it were me on my platter.

JIM AND JAKE:
>Always insist on the whole
>Never be content with half!

SOME OF THE MEN:
>Jake Smith! You're a stout soul!
>Eat away! Don't give up! One more calf!

JAKE:

Watch me! Watch me! Would you have guessed
How much one person can eat?
In the end I shall have a rest.
To forget is sweet.
More please! Give me more . . .
He topples over dead.
The Men form a half-circle behind and remove their hats.

MEN:

Smith lies dead in his glory
Smith lies dead in his happiness
Smith lies dead with a look on his face
Of insatiable craving
For Smith went the whole hog
And Smith has fulfilled himself:
A man without fear.
They put their hats on.

MEN *moving along the apron*: Next we change our loves about.

14

The word 'LOVING' in enormous letters is seen on the signs at the back. On a platform, a bare room has been set up. In the middle of this room sits Begbick with a Girl seated on her left and a Man on her right. Below the platform the Men of Mahagonny are queueing up. Background music.

BEGBICK *turning to the man next to her*:

Spit out your chewing-gum, boy.
See that your hands aren't dirty.

Give the girl time:
A short conversation's polite.
MEN *without looking up*:
Spit out your chewing gum, boys.
See that your hands aren't dirty.
Give the girl time:
A short conversation's polite.
The room slowly darkens.

Get to it soon!
Play that Mandalay immortal tune:
Love's not dependent on time for a lover.
Lovers, make haste
Lovers, don't waste
What in seconds is over:
Mandalay won't glow
Forever below
Such a moon.

Lovers, stop waiting
Hurry, the juicy moon
Is green and slowly setting.
The room has gradually grown light again. The man's chair is now empty. Begbick turns to the Girl.
BEGBICK:
By itself, ready money
Won't or can't make you tender.
MEN *without looking up*:
By itself, ready money
Won't or can't make you tender.
The room grows dark again.
Get to it soon!
Play that Mandalay immortal tune:

Love's not dependent on time for a lover.
Lovers, make haste
Lovers, don't waste
What in seconds is over:
Mandalay won't glow
Forever below
Such a moon.

Lovers, stop waiting,
Hurry, the juicy moon
Is green and slowly setting.
The room grows light again. Another Man enters, hangs his hat on the wall, and sits in the empty chair. The room slowly darkens again.

MEN:
Mandalay won't glow
Forever below
Such a moon.
When the stage grows light again, Jim and Jenny are seated on two chairs some distance from one another. He is smoking, she is putting on make-up.

JENNY:
See there two cranes veer by one with another.

JIM:
The clouds they pierce have been their lot together

JENNY:
Since from their nest and by their lot escorted

JIM:
From one life to a new life they departed

JENNY:
At equal speed with equal miles below them

BOTH:
And at each other's side alone we see them:

JENNY:
> That so the crane and cloud may share the lovely –
> The lonely sky their passage heightens briefly;

JIM:
> That neither one may tarry back nor either

JENNY:
> Mark but the ceaseless lolling of the other
> Upon the wind that goads them imprecisely
> As on their bed of wind they lie more closely.

JIM:
> What though the wind into the void should lead them
> While they live and let nothing yet divide them:

JENNY:
> So for that while no harm can touch their haven

JIM:
> So for that while they may be from all places driven
> Where storms are lashing or the hunt beginning:

JENNY:
> So on through sun and moon's only too similar shining
> In one another lost, they find their power

JIM:
> And fly from?

JENNY:
> Everyone.

JIM:
> And bound for where?

JENNY:
> For nowhere.

JIM:
> Do you know what time they have spent together?

JENNY:
> A short time.

JIM:
And when they will veer asunder?

JENNY:
Soon.

BOTH:
So love to lovers keeps eternal noon.
Men move along the apron.

MEN:
One means to eat all you are able;
Two, to change your loves about;
Three means the ring and gaming table;
Four, to drink until you pass out.
Moreover, better get it clear
That Don'ts are not permitted here.
(So long as you have money).

15

The Men go back upstage, where a boxing ring is being set up in front of a background displaying the word 'FIGHTING'. On a platform to one side, a brass band is playing.

JOE *standing on a chair*:
We have the honour today to present the greatest
Fight ever: to be won by a straight Kayo –
The famous bruiser, Trinity Moses
Versus me, the – Alaskawolf Joe.

FATTY:
What! You're challenging Trinity Moses!
Boy! You'd best be making your will.

That's no fight. It's murder. When that man
Enters the ring, he's out to kill.

JOE:

That may be so, but the bid's worth making:
All that I earned in Alaska I'm staking
For I believe that I shall win through.
May all those who have known me longest
Bet upon Joe to prove the strongest.
Jimmy, I'm counting above all on you!
All those who believe more in brains than in brawn
That Jack may be small but the giant is slow –
Victory nearest when hope seems forlorn –
Will lay their bets on Alaskawolf Joe.

MEN:

All those who believe more in brains than in brawn
That Jack may be small but the giant is slow –
Victory nearest when hope seems forlorn –
Will lay their bets upon Alaskawolf Joe!
Joe has gone over to Bill.

BILL:

Joe, we're close as friends, you know –
But it goes against the grain so
Chucking money down the drain, so . . .
I've put my money on Moses, Joe.
Joe goes to Jim.

JIM:

Joe, my brother in work and in play
And my closest friend of any
I am betting on you today
All I have, Joe, every penny.

JOE:

Jim, when you say that, before me
Far Alaska rises up

Those seven winters of bitter weather
When we felled timber, we two together.

JIM:

Joe, my oldest friend, I tell you
All I prize I would give up:
Those seven winters of bitter weather
When we felled timber, we two together.

JOE:

Jim, when you told me you'd dare it
Our Alaska came in view;
The seven winters of bitter weather
When we felled timber, we two together.

JIM:

Joe, I'd sooner lose, I swear it
Than betray that life we knew:
The seven winters of bitter weather
When we felled timber, we two together.
Alaska I see and pair it
Ever, Joe, only with you!

JOE:

You'll win your money, I swear it!
I'll do all a man can do!
The boxing ring is set up by now. Moses enters it.

MEN:

Give three cheers for Trinity Moses!
Good old Moses! Give him hell, man!

A WOMAN'S VOICE *screaming*:

This is murder!

MOSES:

I regret it.

MEN:

Hit him so's he won't forget it!

REFEREE *introducing the fighters*:

(Our) Trinity Moses, two hundred pounds.

Alaskawolf Joe, one-eighty . . .

MAN *shouting*:

Coffee grounds!

Last preparations for the bout.

JIM *from below*:

How you feeling?

JOE *in the ring*:

All set.

JIM:

Keep your end up.

JOE:

You bet.

The fight begins.

MEN *alternately*:

Let's go! Fight, boys!

Shit! Quit stalling!

Now, Joe! No clinches! Foul! Get at it!

More blood! Neat one! Nail him! he's had it!

Watch it! Perfect! Hey! he's falling!

Trinity Moses and Joe are boxing in time to the music.

MEN *together*:

Moses, keep slugging

Make him swallow dirt!

Moses, beat him up, man!

Land them where they hurt!

Moses, a left hook

Now a right as well!

Sock him in the kidney!

Moses, give him hell!

Joe drops to the canvas.

REFEREE *starts counting him out, then*:

    The man's dead.

    A burst of laughter from the Men. The crowd breaks up.

MEN *dispersing*:

    A Kayo's a Kayo. He couldn't take it.

REFEREE:

    The winner: Trinity Moses!

MOSES:

    I regret it.

    Exit.

BILL *to Jim: they are alone in the ring together*:

    I said he wouldn't make it.

    I warned him he'd get it.

    He has.

JIM *softly*:

    So long, Joe.

    The Men move along the apron.

MEN:

    One means to eat all you are able;

    Two, to change your loves about;

    Three means the ring and gaming table;

    Four, to drink until you pass out.

    Moreover, better get it clear

    That Don'ts are not permitted here.

    Moreover, better get it clear

    That Don'ts are not permitted here!

16

Men are back on the main stage. The signs in the background display the word 'DRINKING'. The Men sit down, put their feet up on the table and drink. Downstage Jim, Bill and Jenny are playing billiards.

JIM:
    Drinks on me. The gang is my guest.
    I just want to show
    That it's easy work at best
    To be knocked out like Joe.
    Lady Begbick, set them up for all the gents!

MEN:
    Good for Jimmy! It's a pleasure! It makes sense!

    Mahagonny sure was swell
    Daily rates were twenty dollars;
    Those who raised more special hell
    Had to pay a little extra:
    Then they all were steady callers
    At Mahagonny's luxury saloon,
    So they all lost their shirts and collars
    But at least they saw the moon.

    Both at sea and on land
    Everyone who gets around is sure to get a skinning:
    That's the reason everybody
    Strips his own skin from his body
    And when pelts are bought on every hand
    With dollars, thinks he's winning!

JIM:
    Lady Begbick, set them up again for all the gents!

MEN:

Good old Jimmy! Double whiskys! No expense!

Both at sea and on land
Skins are up for sale and their consumption is extensive:
Who's to pay when everybody
Feeds the tiger in his body?
For those yellow pelts go cheaply and
The whisky comes expensive!

Mahagonny sure was swell
Daily rates were twenty dollars;
Those who raised more special hell
Had to pay a little extra:
Then they all were steady callers
At Mahagonny's luxury saloon
So they all lost their shirts and collars
But at least they saw the moon.

BEGBICK:

Time to settle the bill, gentlemen.

JIM *softly*:

Jenny, come here. Jenny
I'm out of money.
We'd better beat it from here;
It sure makes no difference to where.
Loudly addressing everyone, pointing to the billiard table:
Gentlemen, climb on this clipper with me!
With all of us aboard, we'll put to sea!
Again softly:
Spend this ocean trip at my side, Jenny
For the deck will tremble like the earth quaking.
You as well, Billy. Don't desert me now.
We'll go sailing back to old Alaska, buddies

For this is not the place for us.

Loudly.

Now or never we will hoist our sails and head for our
   Alaska!

*With part of the bar-rail, a curtain and various other objects in
the room, a 'ship' is constructed on the billiard-table, which Jim,
Bill and Jenny 'board'. There they take up sailor-like poses.*

JIM:

Pour cognac down the toilet and flush it
And latch your salmon-pink persian-blinds:
Alaska's our goal; we won't have to rush it
We'll get there on relaxed behinds.

The Men remain seated below watching them, vastly amused.

MEN:

Ahoy, Jimmy! Was Columbus greater?
Ahoy there, how that guy can handle the sails!
Jenny, get undressed. It's too hot. The Equator!
Stay buttoned, Billy. The Gulf Stream gales!

JENNY: O God! Isn't that a typhoon to starboard?

MEN *with the hearty solemnity of a Glee Club*:

Lo! black as pitch
The heavens are heavy with menace!

The Men, whistling, howling and moaning, make storm 'effects'.

JENNY, BILL *bawling out*:

Our ship is not a silk settee!
Stormy the night and rampant the sea!
O deck so shaky! O dark so quick!
O S-O-S! Six of us three are sick!

MEN:

Death now is nigh!
Now black as pitch the sky . . .

JENNY *clinging anxiously to the 'mast'*: It might be best to sing
'Stormy the Night' to keep up our courage.

BILL: 'Stormy the Night' is a wonderful tonic when your courage begins to get shaky.

JIM: Then we'd better sing it at once.

JENNY, JIM, BILL:

Stormy the night and the white-caps high
'Courage', the Captain said:
Hark! like his echo the ship-bell rings –
Lo! there's a reef ahead!

JENNY: Go faster but go cautiously. Under no circumstances sail against the wind or try out anything new.

MEN:

Listen
Hear how the wind in the rigging moans.
Look now
See where the heavens are pitch-black with menace!

BILL: Shouldn't we lash ourselves to the mast if the violence of the storm increases?

JIM:

No, that is no menace, faithful shipmates
That's the black forest of Alaska.
Disembark.
We shall at last have peace.
He climbs down and calls:
Ahoy! Is that Alaska?

MOSES *slipping over to him*:

Come on, cough up the money!

JIM *deeply disappointed*:

No, it's Mahagonny.
The Men cluster around Jim, raising their glasses.

MEN:

Jimmy, old boy, you're a regular fellow
Standing us the drinks that make us mellow,
So with the same drinks we offer a toast:

Long life to Jimmy, the perfect host!

BEGBICK:

Well, it's time for paying – pet!

JIM:

Look, Lady Begbick, but what can I do now
If I'm not able to pay you yet?
My money, I notice, all is through now.

BEGBICK:

What! you don't want to pay now?

JENNY:

Jimmy, you must have a little more.
Why don't you go through your pockets again?

JIM:

I was telling you before . . .

MOSES:

What! the gentleman won't pay now?
What's that? No money? He really said it?
Do you realise what that means, my friend?

FATTY:

Sweetheart, this is your unhappy end.
All except Jenny and Bill have drawn away from Jim.

BEGBICK *to them*:

Couldn't *you* give him a little credit? *Bill walks away without
a word.* And you, Jenny?

JENNY:

Me?

BEGBICK:

You. Why not?

JENNY:

Don't make me laugh.
What will they ask a girl to do next?

BEGBICK:

Wouldn't you even consider putting up half?

JENNY:
No! If you have to have the precise text.
MOSES:
Put them on!
While Jim is being put in irons, Jenny comes downstage and walks up and down the apron singing:
JENNY:
Let me tell you what my mother called me –
A bad word – yessir, that's what.
She swore I would end on a morgue-slab
Or an even more unhealthy spot.
Well, things like that don't cost much to say,
But what *I* say is: Wait around and see!
The talk doesn't matter two hoots
For you won't make those things happen to me!
We're human, not brutes.
As you make your bed, so you lie on it:
The proverb is old but it's true.
So if someone must kick, why, that's my part
And another get kicked, that part's for you!

Have you heard yet what some guy told me?
'There's one thing can't be bought –
That's true love, the crown of existence.'
Also 'Give tomorrow no thought'.
Well, such things don't cost much to say
But what's mankind got to do with love
When each one gets older each day
And shorter grows the time we must make use of?
We're human, not brutes!
As you make your bed, so you lie on it:
The proverb is old but it's true.
So if someone must kick, why, that's my part

And another get kicked, that part's for you.

MOSES:

You'll observe this miserable wreck
Who ordered drinks and couldn't pay his check.
Why, there's gall in that to choke one!
What man's viler than a broke one?
Jim is taken out.
This is a capital offence!
A thousand pardons for the disturbance, gents.
All take their places again, drinking and playing billiards.

MEN:

Stay-at-homes do very well
Don't need daily twenty dollars;
Those who also marry tell
How they save a little extra:
So today they all are callers
At the Lord-and-Shepherd's second-class saloon;
They keep clean there in shirts and collars
Stamping in time with the music.
But they never see the moon.
They lean back slowly and put their feet up on the tables again.
Downstage men move along the apron and then go back to go off upstage.
One means to eat all you are able;
Two, to change your loves about;
Three means the ring and gaming table;
Four, to drink until you pass out.
Moreover, better get it clear
That Don'ts are not permitted here!

17

Jim lies in irons. It is night.

JIM:
   If the sky must lighten
   Then a new goddam day begins.
   But the sky still is covered up in darkness.
   Let the dark
   Last forever
   Day must not
   Break at all.

I'm still afraid they soon will be here.

I'll lie and sink in roots below me
When I hear them.
They'll have to tear my roots up with me
If they want me to go.
Let the dark
Last forever
Day must not break at all.

That's the kind of poker hand
They dealt you;
Play it out.
What you lived of life
Was good enough for you.
What it brings now –
That's the hand you're stuck with.

Surely the sky won't ever lose its darkness.
It begins to grow light.
It must not lighten.
There must be no sunrise.
That means a new goddam day begins.

18

Every city has its own notion of what is just, and Mahagonny's was no sillier than that of any other place

A courtroom in a tent. In the centre, a table and three chairs. Behind them rise tiers of benches on which the Public is sitting, reading newspapers, chewing gum and smoking. The set suggests an operating theatre. Begbick is in the judge's chair, Fatty in that of the defence attorney. On the prisoner's bench, to one side, sits a man. Moses, the prosecutor, is standing at the entrance.

MOSES:
   Have the folks here all paid their admissions?
   Three tickets still to go, at only five each!
   Two absolutely first-class tri-als –
   Five dollars buys a seat for both!
   Where could you find such a bargain?
   A measly fine to watch Justice in action!
   When no one else comes in, he resumes his place as prosecutor.
   First comes the case of Toby Higgins.

   The man on the prisoner's bench rises.
   He is charged with premeditated murder

Done to test a newly purchased revolver.
Never yet
Has there been a crime so fraught
With brutal baseness.
Toby Higgins, you have outraged
Every decent feeling known.
Yea, the naked soul of sorely wounded Righteousness
Cries out for its retribution.
I therefore must now as prosecutor move
Owing to the stubborn unrepentance this defendant –
This abyss of mean obscene corruption – still displays
That we let the Law take its course unhindered . . .
Hesitating:
And that he . . .
Under the circumstances . . .
Be acquitted!
*During the 'prosecutor's' speech, a silent battle is taking place
between Begbick and the Accused. By raising his finger, the
Accused has indicated the amount of the bribe he is prepared to
pay. In the same manner, Begbick raises her demands higher and
higher. The pause at the end of Moses's speech marks the point
when the Accused has raised his offer for the last time.*

BEGBICK: Has the defence any point to raise?

FATTY: Who's the injured party here?

Silence.

BEGBICK: Since no injured party comes forward . . .

MEN *spectators*: Since dead men tell no tales . . .

BEGBICK: We by law have no course but acquitting him.

The Accused goes to join the spectators.

MOSES *reading*:

Second, the case of Jimmy Gallagher
For seduction, homicide, subversion and fraud.
Jim, handcuffed, is brought in by Bill.

JIM *before he takes his place on the prisoner's bench*:
  Billy, let me have a hundred dollars.
  It may help to make the court more friendly.

BILL:
  Jim, we're close as friends, you know:
  But with money, it's another matter.

JIM:
  Bill, you can't have forgotten
  About our time up in Alaska:
  Those seven winters of bitter weather
  When we felled timber, we two together.
  Please give me the dough.

BILL:
  I have never forgotten
  About our time up in Alaska:
  Those seven winters of bitter weather
  When we felled timber, we two together,
  And how hard we worked
  To make any money.
  That's why I simply can't
  Give you the money.

MOSES:
  The accused ordered rounds of whisky two times
  And broke a bar-rail, and did not pay.
  Never yet
  Has there been a crime so fraught
  With brutal baseness.
  Jimmy Gallagher, you've outraged
  Every decent feeling known.
  Yea, the naked soul of sorely wounded Righteousness
  Cries out for its retribution.
  I therefore must now as prosecutor move
  That we let the Law take its course unhindered.

*During the prosecutor's speech, Jim does not respond to Begbick's
finger-play. Begbick, Fatty and Moses exchange significant glances.*

BEGBICK:

Now we'll proceed to itemise the varied crimes
Charged to you, Jimmy Gallagher!
That, barely off the boat, you did with forethought
Seduce here a girl, by name Jenny Jones
And made her do what you would
By means of your money.

FATTY: Who's the injured party here?

JENNY *coming forward*: Me. I am.

A murmur among the spectators.

BEGBICK:

That, while we waited the big typhoon
You did, in that hour of desperation
Persist in singing a cheerful song.

FATTY: Who's the injured party here?

MEN:

The injured party has not come forth.
Maybe there's no injured party here.
If there's no injured party at all
Then there might be some hope for you, Jimmy Gallagher!

MOSES *breaking in*:

But that very night the man
Before you now behaved worse
Than a typhoon ever could
Subverting all our city meant
By destroying concord and peace here!

MEN: Three cheers for Jimmy!

BILL *standing up among the spectators*:

But this untutored lumberjack from Alaska
Had a vision of happiness that very night
And gave the laws of life to Mahagonny.

Remember, they came from Jimmy.

MEN:
You must bring in acquittal then for Jimmy Gallagher
The lumberjack from Alaska!

BILL:
Jim, I'm glad to do this for you
For I think of old Alaska
Those seven winters of bitter weather
When we felled timber, we two together.

JIM:
Bill, what you've done here to help me
Takes me back once more to Alaska
To seven winters of bitter weather
When we felled timber, we two together.

MOSES *pounding the table*:
And remember the boxing-match
When your dear 'untutored lumberjack from Alaska' –
To win mere money his motive –
Drove his best friend to sudden and certain death.

BILL *jumping up*:
Yes, but who, august tribunal
Who's the party whose punch really killed him?

BEGBICK: Well then, who did kill the so-called Alaskawolf
Joe?

MOSES *after a pause*: That, your honour, is unknown to this
court.

BILL:
Of all those hanging around the ring that night
Not one was risking a bet
On a man who might give his life there
But the man who stands before you risking his!

MEN *alternately*:
The verdict must be guilty then for Jimmy Gallagher!

You must bring in acquittal then for Jimmy Gallagher!
Jimmy Gallagher, the lumberjack from Alaska!
Applause and hissing.

MOSES:

But now the crown of our charges comes:
Yourself, you ordered two rounds of whisky
And destroyed one bar-rail just to amuse yourself –
Then tell me why, yes, why, Jimmy Gallagher
You have failed to pay for consuming them.

JIM: Because I am broke.

MEN:

The man is broke.
He consumes what he can't pay for.
Down, down with Jimmy Gallagher!
Take him away!

BEGBICK, FATTY AND MOSES: Who claim to be injured
parties here?
Begbick, Fatty and Moses rise.

MEN:

Three injured parties have shown themselves.
They are the true injured parties then.

FATTY: Your verdict, august tribunal!

BEGBICK: In view of the unpropitious economic situation
the tribunal will make itself allowances for mitigating circumstances. Jimmy Gallagher, you are sentenced . . .

MOSES: For conniving at the murder of a friend . . .

BEGBICK: To three days arrest.

MOSES: For destroying the concord and peace here . . .

BEGBICK: A year's loss of civil rights.

MOSES: For the seduction of a girl by name of Jenny . . .

BEGBICK: To four years in prison.

MOSES: And for singing forbidden songs during the big
typhoon . . .

BEGBICK:
  To ten years hard labour.
  But for my two rounds of whisky unpaid for
  And my one bar-rail as well unpaid for
  You by law must be sentenced to death in the electric chair.

BEGBICK, FATTY AND MOSES:
  For the penniless man
  Is the worst kind of criminal
  Beyond both pity and pardon.
  Wild applause.

19

Execution of Jimmy Gallagher. Many of you, perhaps, will be shocked at what you are about to see. But, Ladies and Gentlemen, ask yourselves this question: 'Would *I* have paid Jimmy Gallagher's debts?' Would you? Are you sure?

On the backcloth is projected a general view of Mahagonny bathed in a peaceful light. Many people are standing about in groups. On the right, an electric chair is being erected. Jim enters accompanied by Moses, Jenny and Bill. The Men remove their hats.

MOSES:
  Good day!
  Didn't you hear me? I said Good day.

JIM *laconically*:
  Hi.

MOSES:

If you've any worldly business to wind up, you'd better do
it now
For the gentlemen who are anxious to witness your
departure
Have no interest in your private affairs.

JIM:

Darling Jenny
My time has come.
The days I have spent with you
Have been happy days
And happy too
Is the ending.

JENNY:

Darling Jimmy
I also have had my golden summertime
With you
And I dread what
Will become of me now.

JIM:

Jenny dear
My sort are not so hard to find.

JENNY:

That isn't true.
I know what is gone is gone forever.

JIM:

Why, you're wearing a white dress
Just like a widow.

JENNY:

Yes. Your widow is what I am
Jimmy, and I shan't forget you
When I'm just one
Of the girls again.

JIM:

Kiss me, Jenny.

JENNY:

Kiss me, Jimmy.

JIM:

Don't be sore at me.

JENNY:

Why should I be?

JIM:

Kiss me, Jenny.

JENNY:

Kiss me, Jimmy.

JIMMY:

And now I leave you, my dear
To my best and last friend, Billy
Who's the only one left
Of the four men who came
From the woods of cold Alaska.

BILL *taking Jenny in his arms*:

So long, Jim.

JIM:

So long, Bill.
They turn towards the place of execution.

A GROUP OF MEN *tell one another as they pass by*:

One means to eat all you are able;
Two, to change your loves about;
Three means the ring and gaming table;
Four, to drink until you pass out.
Jim stops and watches them.

MOSES:

Have you anything more to say?

JIM: So you really mean to execute me?

BEGBICK: Why not? It's customary.

JIM: You don't seem to know that there's a God.

BEGBICK: A what?

JIM: A God.

BEGBICK: Oh, *Him*! Don't be silly. Didn't you ever see the play: *God Comes to Mahagonny*? We'll put it on now for you, if you like; and you shall have the best seat in the house. Just sit yourself in this chair.

Four men and Jenny Jones appear before Jimmy Gallagher and act the play of God in Mahagonny.

THE FOUR MEN:

One morning when the sky was grey
During the whisky
God came to Mahagonny:
During the whisky
We recognised God in Mahagonny.

Moses, who plays the role of God, detaches himself from the others, steps forward and covers his face with his hat.

MOSES:

Insatiable sponges
Lapping up my harvest year by year!
Little have you reckoned with your Maker!
Are you ready now when I appear?

JENNY:

Saw what they were, the people of Mahagonny:
Yes, answered the people of Mahagonny.

THE FOUR:

One morning when the sky was grey
During the whisky
God came to Mahagonny:
During the whisky
We recognised God in Mahagonny.

MOSES:

Did you laugh on Friday evening?

I saw Mary Weeman swimming by
Like a salted cod-fish in the salt sea
Mary never will again be dry.

JENNY:

Saw what they were, the people of Mahagonny:
Yes, answered the people of Mahagonny.

THE FOUR *behaving as though they hadn't heard anything*:

One morning when the sky was grey
During the whisky
God came to Mahagonny:
During the whisky
We recognised God in Mahagonny.

MOSES:

Whose is this ammunition?
Shot her, did you, shot my deaconess?
Are my thrones for brutes of your condition?
Is it drunken loafers I must bless?

JENNY:

Saw what they were, the people of Mahagonny:
Yes, answered the people of Mahagonny.

THE FOUR:

One morning when the sky was grey
During the whisky
God came to Mahagonny:
During the whisky
We recognised God in Mahagonny.

MOSES:

Down with all into hell-fire
Stuff your Henry Clays into your pack
Off with all of you to Hell, you scoundrels
Wriggle in the Devil's crowded sack!

JENNY:

Saw what they were, the people of Mahagonny:

No, answered the people of Mahagonny.

THE FOUR:

One morning when the sky was grey
During the whisky
You came to Mahagonny
During the whisky
Got going in Mahagonny.

But we won't budge a foot now!
We'll go on strike. We will never
Let you drag us off to Hell forever
For we *are* in Hell and always have been.

JENNY *through a megaphone*:

Saw God, they did, the people of Mahagonny:
No, answered the people of Mahagonny.

JIM:

Now I see it. When I came to this city, hoping that my money would buy me joy, my doom was already sealed. Here I sit now and have had just nothing. I was the one who said 'Everyone must carve himself a slice of meat, using any available knife'. But the meat had gone bad. The joy I bought was no joy; the freedom they sold me was no freedom. I ate and remained unsatisfied; I drank and became all the thirstier. Give me a glass of water.

MOSES *putting the helmet over his head*:

Ready!

20

And amid increasing confusion, inflation and universal mutual hostility those who had not yet been killed demonstrated for their ideals during the last weeks of Suckerville – having learnt nothing

Mahagonny is seen in flames on the screens in the background. Then groups of demonstrators begin appearing; they interweave and confront one another, continuing right up to the end.

First group. Begbick, Fatty the Bookie, Trinity Moses and supporters. The inscriptions on the first group's signs read:
  'FOR THE INFLATION'
  'FOR THE BATTLE OF ALL AGAINST ALL'
  'FOR THE CHAOTIC STATE OF OUR CITIES'
  'FOR THE PROLONGATION OF THE GOLDEN AGE'
FIRST GROUP:
  For this splendid Mahagonny
  Has it all, if you have the money.
  Then all is available
  Because all is for sale
  And there is nothing that one cannot buy.
  The inscriptions on the second group's signs read:
  'FOR PROPERTY'
  'FOR THE EXPROPRIATION OF OTHERS'
  'FOR THE JUST DIVISION OF SPIRITUAL GOODS'
  'FOR THE UNJUST DIVISION OF TEMPORAL GOODS'
  'FOR LOVE'
  'FOR THE BUYING AND SELLING OF LOVE'

'FOR THE NATURAL DISORDER OF THINGS'
'FOR THE PROLONGATION OF THE GOLDEN AGE'

SECOND GROUP:

We need no raging hurricane
We need no bolt from the blue:
There's no havoc they might have done
That we cannot better do.

The inscriptions on the third group's signs read:

'FOR FREEDOM FOR THE RICH'
'FOR VALOUR AGAINST THE DEFENCELESS'
'FOR HONOUR AMONG MURDERERS'
'FOR GREATNESS OF SQUALOR'
'FOR IMMORTALITY OF UNDERHANDEDNESS'
'FOR THE CONTINUATION OF THE GOLDEN AGE'

THIRD GROUP:

As you make your bed so you lie on it
The bed can be old or brand-new:
So if someone must kick, that is my part
And another get kicked, that part's for you.

FIRST GROUP *returning with its signs*:

Why, though, did we need a Mahagonny?
Because this world is a foul one
With neither charity
Nor peace nor concord
Because there's nothing
To build any trust upon.

FOURTH GROUP *of girls bearing Jim Gallagher's watch, revolver
and cheque book on a linen cushion, also his shirt on a pole*:

Oh, Moon of Alabama
We now must say good-bye.
We've lost our good old mama
And must have dollars
Oh, you know why.

Fifth group carrying Jim Gallagher's body. Immediately following
them a sign with the inscription:
'FOR JUSTICE'

FIFTH GROUP:

You can bring vinegar – to him
You can wipe his forehead – for him
You can find surgical forceps
You can pull the tongue from his gullet
Can't do anything to help a dead man.

Sixth group with a small sign:
'FOR BRUTE STUPIDITY'

SIXTH GROUP:

You can talk good sense – to him
You can bawl oaths – at him
You can just leave him lying
You can take care – of him
Can't give orders, can't lay down any law to a dead man.
You can put coins in his hand – for him
You can dig a hole – by him
You can stuff that hole – with him
You can heap a shovelful – on him
Can't do anything to help a dead man.

Seventh group with an enormous placard:
'FOR THE CONTINUATION OF THE GOLDEN AGE'

SEVENTH GROUP:

You can talk about the glory of his heyday
You can also forget his old days completely
Can't do anything to help a dead man.

Unending groups in constant motion.

ALL GROUPS:

Can't help him or you or me or no one.

The Seven Deadly Sins of the Petty Bourgeoisie

Ballet

Collaborator: K. WEILL

Translators: W. H. AUDEN and CHESTER KALLMAN

The Seven Deadly Sins of the Petty Bourgeoisie

SLOTH
  in doing a wrong
PRIDE
  in one's best characteristic (Incorruptibility)
WRATH
  at mean behaviour
GLUTTONY
  (Satedness, Self-devouring)
LUST
  (Selfless love)
AVARICE
  in pillage and deception
ENVY
  of the fortunate

This ballet is meant to represent the journey of two sisters from the southern states who hope to get enough money to buy a small house for themselves and their family. Both are called Annie. One of the two Annie is the manager, the other the artiste; one (Annie I) is the saleslady, the other (Annie II) the article sold. On the stage stands a small board showing the course of their travels through seven cities; Annie I stands before it with a small pointer. Likewise on the stage is the continually fluctuating market on which Annie I launches her sister. At the end of each scene showing how the seven deadly sins can be avoided Annie II returns to Annie I, with their family on stage and the little house which they have acquired by avoiding the seven deadly sins in the background.

Prologue

ANNIE I:
So my sister and I left Louisiana
Where the moon on the Mississippi is a-shining ever
Like you've heard about in the songs of Dixie.
We look forward to our home-coming –
And the sooner the better.

ANNIE II:
And the sooner the better.

ANNIE I:
It's a month already since we started
For the great big cities where you go to make money.
In seven years our fortune will be made
And then we can go back.

ANNIE II:
In six would be nicer.

ANNIE I:

  Our mum and dad and both our brothers wait in old
      Louisiana
  And we'll send them all our money as we make it
  For all the money's got to go to build a little home
  Down by the Mississippi in Louisiana.
  Right, Annie?

ANNIE II:

  Right, Annie.

ANNIE I:

  She's the one with the looks, I'm realistic;
  She's just a little mad, my head is on straight.
  You may think that you can see two people
  But in fact you see only one
  And both of us are Annie:
  Together we've but a single past, a single future
  And one heart and savings-account;
  And we only do what is best for each other.
  Right, Annie?

ANNIE II:

  Right, Annie.

I

Sloth

This is the first city on their journey, and the sisters get their first money by a trick. As they stroll through the city park they are on the lookout for married couples. Annie II hurls herself on a man as if she knew him; she flings her arms round him, reproaches him etc., in short reduces him to embarrassment while Annie I tries to restrain her. While Annie I is extracting money from the man for having got rid of

*her sister, Annie II suddenly falls on the wife and threatens her with
her parasol. They swiftly perform this trick a number of times. After
that however Annie I tries to blackmail a man she has enticed away
from his wife, on the assumption that her sister will meanwhile have
importuned the wife. She is appalled to see that her sister is sitting
dozing on a bench instead of getting on with the job. She is forced to
wake her up and set her to work.*

FAMILY:

Will she now? . . . will our Annie pull herself together?
  Lazy Bones are for the Devil's stock-pot –
For she was always quite a one for an arm-chair;
  Lazy Bones are for the Devil's stock-pot –
Unless you came and hauled her off the mattress
  Lazy Bones are for the Devil's stock-pot –
The lazy slug would lie abed all morning.
  Lazy Bones are for the Devil's stock-pot –
Otherwise, Annie was, we must admit, a most respectful
    child,
  Lazy Bones are for the Devil's stock-pot –
Did what she was told and showed affection for her
    parents.
  Lazy Bones are for the Devil's stock-pot –
This is what we told her when she left home:
  Lazy Bones are for the Devil's stock-pot –
'Think of us, and mind you keep your nose down to the
    grind-stone.'

  O Lord, look down upon our daughter
  Show her the way that leads the Good to Thy reward
In all her doings prevent her and comfort her
  Incline her heart to observe all Thy commandments
  That her works on earth may prosper.

2

Pride

A dirty little cabaret. Annie II enters to the applause of 4-5 customers whose frightful appearance greatly alarms her. Though poorly clad she dances in a most unusual way, puts her soul into it and is badly received. The customers are infinitely bored; they yawn like sharks (their masks portraying horrible teeth in preternaturally large mouths), hurl things on to the stage and manage to bring the one lamp crashing down. Annie II goes on dancing, utterly wrapped up in her art until removed from the stage by the proprietor. He sends on another dancer, a fat old frump who shows Annie how to set about winning applause in his establishment. The old frump dances in a vulgar sexy way and is vastly applauded. Annie refuses to dance like that. But Annie I, who has been standing beside the stage where she was the only one to applaud her sister and wept to see her lack of success, now gets her to dance in the required manner. As her skirt is too long, Annie I rips it off and sends her back on stage to be shown how to dance by the frump, pulling her skirts up higher and higher to the applause of the audience. And it is she who leads her sister back to the small board to be comforted.

ANNIE I:
  So we
  Saved up
  Bought ourselves an outfit:
  Nighties
  Nylons
  Beautiful dresses:
  Soon we
  Found a

Job that was going
A job as dancer in a cabaret
A job in Memphis, the second big town we came to
Oh how hard it was for Annie!
Beautiful clothes can make a good girl particular –
When the drinking tigress meets herself in the pool
She's apt to become a menace.
She began talking about art, of all things
About the Art, if you please, of Cabaret
In Memphis, the second big town we came to.

It wasn't art that sort of people came for
That sort of people came for something else;
And when a man has paid for his evening
He expects a good show in return.
So if you cover up your bosom and thighs like you had a
    rash
Don't be surprised to see them yawning.

So I told my art-loving sister Annie:
'Leave your pride to those who can well afford it.
Do what you are asked to do and not what you want
For that isn't what is wanted.'
Oh but
I had
Trouble, I can tell you
With her
Fancy
Pig-headed notions.
Many
Nights I
Sat by her bedside
Holding her hand and saying this:

'Think of our home in Louisiana.'

FAMILY:

O Lord, look down upon our daughter
Show her the way that leads the Good to Thy reward.
Who fights the Good Fight and all Self subdues
Wins the Palm, gains the Crown.

We're at a standstill! What she's been sending
It's not any money a man can build a home with.
She's as giddy as a cyclone!
All the profits go for her pleasure!
And we're at a standstill, for what she's been sending
Is not any money a man can build a home with.
Won't she settle down to business?
Won't she ever learn to save something?
For what the featherbrain is sending
Is not any kind of money
A man can build a little home with.

3

Wrath

A film is being made in which Annie is an extra. The star, a Douglas Fairbanks type, rides his horse over a basket of flowers. The horse is clumsy, so he beats it. It falls and is unable to get up despite the blanket they put beneath it and the sugar they put before it. So he beats it again. But at that point the little extra steps forward, takes the whip from his hand and, in her wrath, beats him instead. She is promptly dismissed. However, her sister rounds on her and per-

suades her to come back, go on bended knee to the star and kiss his
hand; upon which he once again recommends her to the director.

ANNIE I:

We're making progress. We have come to Los Angeles
And every door is open here to welcome extras.
We only need a bit of practice avoiding possible faux pas
And what can stop us going straight to the top then?

FAMILY:

O Lord, look down upon our daughter
Show her the way that leads the Good to Thy reward.

ANNIE I:

If you take offence at Injustice
Mister Big will show he's offended;
If a curse or a blow can enrage you so
Your usefulness here is ended.

Then mind what the Good Book tells us
When it says: 'Resist not Evil.'
Unforgiving Anger
Is from the Devil.

It took time to teach my sister wrath wouldn't do
In Los Angeles the third big town we came to
Where her open disapproval of injustice
Was so widely disapproved.
I forever told her: 'Practise self-control, Annie
For you know how much it costs you if you don't.'
And she saw my point and answered:

ANNIE II:

Yes I know, Annie.

4
Gluttony

Annie has herself become a star. Having signed a contract forbidding her to put on weight, she must not eat. One day she steals an apple and furtively eats it; and when she is weighed and found to weigh one gramme more, the impresario tears his hair out. From then on her eating is supervised by her sister. Two flunkeys with revolvers serve her food, and all she is allowed to take from the dish is a little miniature bottle.

FAMILY:

We've gotten word from Philadelphia:
Annie's doing well, she's making money.
Her contract has been signed to do a solo turn.
It forbids her ever eating when or what she likes to eat.
Those are hard terms for little Annie:
Who has always been very greedy.
Oh if only she doesn't break her contract –
There's no market for hippos in Philadelphia.
Every single day they weigh her.
Gaining half an ounce means trouble.
They have principles to stand by:
It's a hundred-and-eighteen that you were signed for –
Only for the weight agreed we pay!
Gaining half an ounce means trouble
More than that would mean disaster!

But our Annie isn't all that stupid
And she knows a contract is a contract
So she'll reason: After all

You still can eat like little Annie
In Louisiana –
Crabmeat! Porkchops! Sweet-corn! Chicken!
And those golden biscuits spread with honey!
Spare your home in old Louisiana!
Think! – It's growing! More and more it needs you!
Therefore curb your craving! Gluttons will be punished!

5
Lust

Annie now has an admirer who is extremely rich, loves her and brings her jewels and clothes; likewise a lover whom she in turn loves and who takes the jewels off her. Annie I reproaches her and persuades her to leave Fernando and be faithful to Edward. But one day Annie II passes a café where Annie I is sitting with Fernando, who is paying court to her (though to no effect). Thereupon Annie II assaults Annie I and they roll about in the street wrestling under the eyes of Fernando and his friends, together with a horde of street children and bystanders. The children point out her valuable bottom, and Edward runs away in horror. Then Annie I reproaches her sister and, after a touching parting from Fernando, sends her back to Edward.

ANNIE I:
  Then we met a wealthy man in Boston
  And he paid her a lot because he loved her.
  But I had to keep a watch on Annie
  Who was too loving, and she loved another;
  And she paid him a lot
  Because she loved him.

So I said: 'Cheat the man who protects you
And you've lost half your value then:
He may pay once although he suspects you
But he won't pay time and time again.

You can have your fun with money
When you've no provider you must face;
But for girls like us, it's not funny
If we ever even once forget our place.'

'Don't try to sit between two stools,' I told her.
Then I went to visit her friend
And said: 'If you're kind, you won't hold her,
For this love will be your sweetheart's bitter end.'

Girls can have their fun with money
When the money is their own to give;
But for girls like us, it's not funny
If we even once forget the way we live.'

Then I'd meet him as bad luck would have it.
There was nothing going on. Naturally!
Until Annie found out and, worse luck
Blamed the whole affair on me.

FAMILY:
O Lord, look down upon our daughter
Show her the way that leads the Good to Thy reward
Incline her heart to observe all Thy commandments
That her works on earth may prosper.

ANNIE I:
Now she shows off her little round white fanny
Worth twice a little Texas Motel
And for nothing the poolroom can stare at Annie

As though she'd nothing to sell.
That's why most girls don't get rich, for
They go wrong when they forget their place:
You're not free to buy what you itch for
When you've got a good provider you must face.

FAMILY:
Who fights the Good Fight and all Self subdues
Will gain her renown.

ANNIE I:
It wasn't easy putting *that* in order:
Saying good-bye to young Fernando
Then back to Edward to apologise
Then the endless nights I heard my sister
Sobbing like a baby and repeating;

ANNIE II:
It's right like this, Annie, but so hard!

6
Avarice

Shortly afterwards Edward shoots himself, having been ruined by Annie. Then the newspapers print flattering reports about her, with the effect that the readers doff their hats to her respectfully and immediately follow her, newspaper in hand, in the hope of being ruined too. Soon after that another young man flings himself out of a window after Annie has left him penniless; then her sister intervenes and saves yet another one from hanging himself, by taking his money back from Annie II and returning it to him. She does this because people are starting to shun her sister, who has got a bad name on account of her avarice.

FAMILY:
    Annie, so the paper says
    Is now set up in Baltimore:
    Lots of folk seem to be
    Shooting themselves for her.
    She must be doing all right
    And raking it in,
    To get in the news like that!
    Well, so far, so good; to be talked about helps
    A young girl up the ladder.
    Let her beware of overdoing it!
    Folk shy away from a girl
    Who's said to be mean.

    Folk give a wide wide berth
    To those who grab all they can get
    Point unfriendly fingers at
    One whose greed goes beyond all bounds.
    In the measure you give
    You will surely be given
    And as you do, so
    Will you be done by:
    Fair is fair.
    All must keep this law.

    We sincerely hope our smart little Annie
    Also has common sense
    And will let them keep a shirt or two
    When she lets them go for good.

    Shameless hoarders earn themselves a bad name.

7
Envy

Once again we see Annie traversing the big city and glimpsing other Annies as she goes – all the other dancers being masked to look like Annie – who indulge in idleness etc. etc., thereby committing with impunity all those deadly sins that have been forbidden her. A ballet represents the theme THE LAST SHALL BE FIRST *thus: As the other Annies proudly walk around in the light, Annie II laboriously drags herself in, bent double. But then her apotheosis begins and she walks with increasing pride, finally triumphing as the other Annies crumple, abashed, and are forced to make way for her.*

ANNIE:

And the last big town we came to was San Francisco.
Life, there, was fine, only Annie felt so tired
And grew envious of others:
Of those who pass the time at their ease and in comfort
Those too proud to be bought –
Of those whose wrath is kindled by injustice
Those who act upon their impulses happily
Lovers true to their loved ones
And those who take what they need without shame.
Whereupon I told my poor tired sister
When I saw how much she envied them:

'Sister, from birth we may write our own story
And anything we choose we are permitted to do
But the proud and insolent who strut in their glory –
Little they guess
Little they guess
Little they guess the fate they're swaggering to.

'Sister, be strong! You must learn to say No to
The joys of this world, for this world is a snare;
Only the fools in this world will let go, who
Don't care a damn
Don't care a damn –
Don't-care-a-damn will be made to care.

'Don't let the flesh and its longings get you.
Remember the price that a lover must pay
And say to yourself when temptations beset you –
What is the use?
What is the use?
Beauty will perish and youth pass away.

'Sister, you know, when our life here is over
Those who were good go to bliss unalloyed
Those who were bad are rejected forever
Gnashing their teeth
Gnashing their teeth
Gnashing their teeth in a gibbering void!

FAMILY:
Who fights the Good Fight and all Self subdues
Wins the Palm, gains the Crown.

Epilogue

ANNIE I:
Now we're coming back to you, Louisiana
Where the moon on the Mississippi is a-shining ever.
Seven years we're been away in the big towns
Where one goes to make money;
And now our fortune's made, and now you're there
Little home in old Louisiana.
We're coming back to you
Out little home down by
The Mississippi in
Louisiana. . . .
Right, Annie.
ANNIE II:
Right, Annie.

Notes and Variants

MAN EQUALS MAN

Texts by Brecht

1

Hey, Tom, have you joined up too, joined up too?
'Cos I've joined up just like you, just like you.
And when I see you marching there
I know I'm back on the old barracks square
Have you ever seen me in your life?
'Cos I've never seen you in my life.
  It ain't the plan
  For man equals man
  Since time began.
  Tommy boy, let me tell you, it really ain't the plan
  For man is man!
  There's no other plan.
  The red sun of Kilkoa shines
  Upon our regimental lines
  Where seven thousand men can die
  And not a soul will bat an eye
  'Cos all the lot are better gone
  So who cares where Kilkoa's red sun shone?

2

Hey, Tom, was there rice in your Irish stew?
'Cos I had rice in my Irish stew
And when I found they'd left out the meat
The army didn't seem such a treat.
Hey, Tom, has it made you throw up yet?
'Cos I've not stopped throwing up as yet.
  It ain't the plan
  For man equals man

Since time began.
Tommy boy, let me tell you, it really ain't the plan
For man is man!
There's no other plan.
The red sun of Kilkoa shines
Upon our regimental lines
Where seven thousand men can die
And not a soul will bat an eye
'Cos all the lot are better gone
So who cares where Kilkoa's red sun shone?

3

Hey, Tom, did you see Jenny Smith last night?
'Cos me I saw Jenny Smith last night.
And when I look at that old bag
The army don't seem half such a drag.
Hey, Tom, have you also slept with her?
'Cos you know I've also slept with her.
　It ain't the plan
　For man equals man
　Since time began.
　Tommy boy, let me tell you, it really ain't the plan
　For man is man!
　There's no other plan.
　The red sun of Kilkoa shines
　Upon our regimental lines
　Where seven thousand men can die
　And not a soul will bat an eye
　'Cos all the lot are better gone
　So who cares where Kilkoa's red sun shone?

4

Hey, Tom, have you got your kit packed up?
'Cos I have got my kit packed up.
And when I see you with your kit
I feel the army's fighting fit.
But did you have bugger all to pack yours with?
'Cos I find I've bugger all to pack mine with.
　It ain't the plan
　For man equals man

Since time began.
Tommy boy, let me tell you, it really ain't the plan
For man is man!
There's no other plan.
The red sun of Kilkoa shines
Upon our regimental lines
Where seven thousand men can die
And not a soul will bat an eye
'Cos all the lot are better gone
So who cares where Kilkoa's red sun shone?

5

Hey, Tom, are you quite ready to move off?
'Cos me I'm quite ready to move off.
And when I see you march I guess
I'll march wherever the army says.
Have you got a clue where we're marching to?
'Cos I've not got a clue where we're marching to.
  It ain't the plan
  For man equals man
  Since time began.
  Tommy boy, let me tell you, it really ain't the plan
  For man is man!
  There's no other plan.
  The red sun of Kilkoa shines
  Upon our regimental lines
  Where seven thousand men can die
  And not a soul will bat an eye
  'Cos all the lot are better gone
  So who cares where Kilkoa's red shone?

['Der Mann-ist-Mann-Song,' from the 1927 edition of the play,
republished in GW *Gedichte*, pp. 138 ff. The former edition gives
Brecht's own tune, subsequently arranged by Paul Dessau.]

PRESS RELEASE

Disastrous prank by three privates of the Worchester Regiment
stationed at Kankerdan, East India/Prank? Or crime?/J. Galgei,
docker, takes himself for a soldier called Jerome Jip.

Saipong. All Hindustan is talking about the incredible case of J. Galgei,* a porter at the docks. Four private soldiers from Kankerdan, on detachment to Saipong, are alleged to have committed a hitherto baffling crime *in order to obtain whisky* (!!!), and to have been forced to abandon one of their number in the process. Realising that the absence of the fourth man might have betrayed the crime in question they camouflaged it by exploiting the person of the docker J. Galgei. Moved in the first place by mere sympathy, the latter was twice persuaded to stand in at roll calls for the missing man, one Jerome Jip. However when he cited family reasons and refused to oblige them for an additional two days till the unit moved off they cast him as the leading player in *a comedy worthy of the silver screen.* Along with a canteen proprietress of most dubious character they conspired to give him an alleged British army elephant free gratis and for nothing to sell as he might wish. Due to the unbridled consumption of whisky then prevalent Galgei failed to detect the true character of this dangerous gift: a highly life-like elephant constructed of nothing but some tarpaulins and his would-be benefactors the three privates. They thereupon arrested him for this 'theft' at the 'scene of the crime', and summarily shot him beneath the three sycamore trees of Saipong. They then revived this helplessly befuddled accomplice, who had fainted away well before his (obviously) faked execution, and told him he was to deliver a funeral oration on a certain Galgei who had just been shot. Now highly confused, he complied with all their demands and offered virtually no resistance. The following day too inspired peculiar misgivings in the unfortunate docker, who by now had become unsure of his own personality. Using an army paybook the soldiers brought their cruel game to its climax. Galgei's attitude to his wife, who had managed to track him down in his military guise, showed that at this point he was already uncertain of his own identity. As soon as the 'fun-loving' soldiers started making difficulties for him even with regard to his use of the name Jip, he so vehemently annexed that name that even the reappearance of the real Jip could not prise him away from it. Together with the simultaneous case of Sergeant P., who was so infuriated by the loss of self-control due to his unrestrained sexual urges as to castrate

---

* This was at a time when the three-day concentration of the Afghan Division provoked an enormous mêlée of soldiers and supply racketeers in Saipong, to say nothing of the less reputable camp followers associated with army units on the move.

himself with his own hand, this entire episode shows how thin the
~~veneer~~ of individuality has become in our time.

['Für Zeitungen,' from GW *Schriften zum Theater*, pp. 973 f. Pre-
faced to the 1925 typescript of the play.]

EPIC SEQUENCE OF EVENTS

The transformation of a living person in the Kilkoa military cantonment in the year nineteen hundred and twenty-five.

1

then they all joined together to make a false elephant and led the
man galy gay unto it and bade him sell it but the sergeant came as
he was holding it by a rope and they were afraid saying: what will
he do? for they could not stay with him because of the sergeant and
they observed him over a wall when he was alone to see if he
would examine the elephant and notice that it was unreal however
they saw that the man never looked at it and from thenceforward
they knew that there was one who believed what was good for
him and would sooner know nothing therefore he ignored the
elephant not seeing that it was unreal for he wished to sell it and
the woman that was with him took the sergeant away

2

so the man sold the elephant that was not his and was unreal to
boot but thereupon one of them approached him laid his hand on
his shoulder and spake to him: what art thou doing? and because
he could not justify himself they brought suit against him but they
condemned him to death then he denied that he was the criminal
galy gay but they acted as if they believed him not and did shoot
deceivingly at him from seven riflebarrels and he fainted and fell

3

however when he awakened they put a box before him telling him
that the man galy gay who had been shot lay within it thereupon
his reason became utterly confused and he began to think that he
was not galy gay who had been shot and lay within the box nor
did he wish to be wherefore he stood up and spake about galy gay

as though he were a stranger that they might believe that he was not he for he feared to die and they buried the box which was empty and he delivered the funeral speech.

so they took him away with them that night

   ['Epischer Verlauf.' Fragment from BBA 348/68.]

Annex

a man was travelling in a train from kilkoa to tibet and they laid a woman beside him that he might sleep with her and ask no questions for they had told him that he was one of their men and when he woke he found the woman beside him but he knew her not then they said to him: who is the woman with whom thou hast slept? and he did not know for he had not slept with the woman but did not know it when they saw that he knew her not they mocked him saying perchance thou knowest not thyself then he said i know myself but he lied they however tested him in all ways and he was downcast and sat apart and knew not who he was but then he heard a voice behind the partition and a man began to lament and say what a disgrace has overtaken me where is my name that once was great beyond the oceans where is the yesterday that has vanished even my raiment is gone that i wore

   [Untitled. BBA 150/151.]

TWO PARAGRAPHS

Execution

Galy Gay is led to the place of execution, but since he is being 'inconspicuously' led by Jesse and Polly – 'the disgrace for the regiment is too great; nothing of this must get out' – at first he is treated as a hero ('It's Jeraiah! Last-man-last-round Jip, the hero of Cochin Kula'). They all fête him; somebody asks him for a cigarette, hoping for reflected glory ('Happy to make your acquaintance. Wait till I tell them back home'). Then Uriah yells 'It's a mistake!' and they all learn that he is a deserter. Throw things at him, spit at him.

Recruitment

Camp whores are sent ahead to admire his uniform. Two quarrel over him. He could sleep with three girls if it weren't for the discovery of some small outward lapse, an undone button or a missing button or a missing shoulder-strap, which leads to the suspicion that he is a swindler.

['Die Erschiessung' and 'Die Werbung', from BBA 1080/75.]

INTRODUCTORY SPEECH (FOR THE RADIO)

Look: our plays embrace part of the new things that came into the world long before the world war. This means at the same time that they no longer embrace a large part of the old things to which we are accustomed. Why don't they now embrace these old things which *were* once recognised and proper? I think I can tell you exactly. They no longer embrace these old things because the people to whom these things were important are today on the decline. But whenever a broad stratum of humanity is declining its vital utterances get weaker and weaker, its imagination becomes crippled, its appetites dwindle, its entire history has nothing more of note to offer, not even to itself. What a declining stratum like this does can no longer lead to any conclusions about men's doings. In the case of the arts this means that such people can no longer create or absorb art of any sort.

This stratum of humanity had its great period. It created monuments that have remained, but even these remaining monuments can no longer arouse enthusiasm. The great buildings of the city of New York and the great discoveries of electricity are not of themselves enough to swell mankind's sense of triumph. What matters most is that a *new human type* should now be evolving, at this very moment, and that the entire interest of the world should be concentrated on his development. The guns that are to hand and the guns that are still being manufactured are turned for him or against him. The houses that exist and are being built are built to oppress him or to shelter him. All live works created or applied in our time set out to discourage him or to put courage in him. And any work that has nothing to do with him is not alive and has nothing to do with anything. This new human type will not be as the old type imagines. It is my belief that he will not let himself be changed by machines but will himself change the machine; and whatever he looks like he will above all look human.

I would now like to turn briefly to the comedy *Mann ist Mann* and explain why this introduction about the new human type was necessary. Of course not all these problems are going to arise and be solved in this particular play. They will be solved somewhere quite different. But it struck me that all sorts of things in *Mann ist Mann* will probably seem odd to you at first – especially what the central figure, the porter Galy Gay, does or does not do – and if so it's better that you shouldn't think you are listening to an old acquaintance talking or to yourself, as has hitherto nearly always been the rule in the theatre, but to a new sort of type, possibly an ancestor of just that new human type I spoke of. It may be interesting for you to look straight at him from this point of view, so as to find out his attitude to things as precisely as possible. You will see that among other things he is a great liar and an incorrigible optimist; he can fit in with anything, almost without difficulty. He seems to be used to putting up with a great deal. It is in fact very seldom that he can allow himself an opinion of his own. For instance when (as you will hear) he is offered an utterly spurious elephant which he can resell, he will take care not to voice any opinion of it once he hears a possible purchaser is there. I imagine also that you are used to treating a man as a weakling if he can't say no, but this Galy Gay is by no means a weakling; on the contrary he is the strongest of all. That is to say he becomes the strongest once he has ceased to be a private person; he only becomes strong in the mass. And if the play finishes up with him conquering an entire fortress this is only because in doing so he is apparently carrying out the determined wish of a great mass of people who want to get through the narrow pass that the fortress guards. No doubt you will go on to say that it's a pity that a man should be tricked like this and simply forced to surrender his precious ego, all he possesses (as it were); but it isn't. It's a jolly business. For this Galy Gay comes to no harm; he wins. And a man who adopts such an attitude is bound to win. But possibly you will come to quite a different conclusion. To which I am the last person to object.

['Vorrede zu *Mann ist Mann*' from *Die Szene*, Berlin, April 1927, reprinted in GW *Schiften zum Theater*, pp. 976 ff. This was an introductory talk to the broadcast of the play by Berlin Radio on March 27, 1927. It also appears in a shortened and adapted form as a statement by Brecht in the opening programme of Piscator's 1927–28 season. Part of another 'introductory speech' is included in GW *Schriften zum Theater* as well, but discusses the theatre in general rather than this particular play.]

DIALOGUE ABOUT BERT BRECHT'S PLAY *Man equals Man*

– Where have you been to put you in such a bad mood and so foul a temper?

– I've been to Bert Brecht's play Man equals Man and it's a bad play let me tell you and a waste of an evening.

– What makes you say that?

– Because it is a play that deals with ugly things such as are remote from me and the men in it are badly dressed and caked with the filth of their debased life such as is remote from me. And the plays I like are those in which moving or delightful things happen and clean well-dressed people perform.

– What's the good of being surrounded by moving or delightful things and clean well-dressed people if a red-hot lump of iron hits you and blots you out of life and the world?

– It is a play whose wit fails to make me laugh and its serious side to make me weep. And the plays I like are those in which the wit sparkles like fireworks or some sad occurrence moves my heart to compassion. For life is difficult and for a brief while I would fain be relieved of its burden.

– What's the good of enjoying wit like fireworks or having your heart moved at some sad occurrence if a red-hot lump of iron hits you and blots you out of life and the world?

– The plays I like are those that speak of the delights of Nature, of the freshness of springtime and the rushing of the wind through the trees in summer, of the pale sky in April and the last blossoms in autumn.

– What's the good of the freshness of springtime and the rushing of the wind through the trees in summer, of the pale sky in April and the last blossoms in autumn, if a red-hot lump of iron hits you and blots you out of life and the world?

– I take pleasure in beautiful women and I love the desire that comes from the sight of them as they laugh and move in plays and seduce men and are taken by them. For then I feel that I am a man and mighty in sex.

– What's the good of feeling desire at the sight of beautiful women as they laugh and seduce men and are taken by them and feeling that you are a man and mighty in sex if a red-hot lump of iron hits you and blots you out of life and the world?
– But I loathe whatever is degrading and disparaging and I feel myself raised to a higher plane by the nobility immanent in the plays of the great masters; I love whatever is lofty and improving, such as makes me sense the might of a God and the existence of a just Power.
– What's the good of being raised to a higher plane by nobility and feeling the might of a God and the existence of a just Power if a red-hot lump of iron hits you and blots you out of life and the world?
– Why do you have to go on repeating the same words in answer to all I've been saying about the beautiful and elevating things in the plays of the great masters?
– Because you too can get caught up like that man in Bert Brecht's play so as to blot out your name and your self and your home and your wife and your memory, your laughter and your passion, your desire for women and your elevation to God; because you too can be lined up like that man in a formation one hundred thousand strong, between man and man, dinner pail and dinner pail, just as millions of men have been lined up in the past and millions of men will be lined up in the future; because like that man you too can be hit by a red-hot lump of iron and blotted out of life and the world!!!
– *shouting*: Oh now I realise that it's a good play and its moral one to be taken to heart.

['Dialog zu Bert Brechts "Mann ist Mann"' from GW *Schriften zum Theater* p. 978. Date uncertain, but probably pre-1930.]

NOTES TO THE 1937 EDITION

1. About the direction

The comedy *Man equals Man* being a play of the parable type, unusual methods were adopted for its Berlin production. Stilts and wire clothes-hangers were used to turn the soldiers and their sergeant into exceptionally large and broad monsters. At the very end the porter Galy Gay was transformed into a monster of the same sort.

The four transformations were clearly distinguished from one another (transformation of Jeraiah Jip into a god; transformation of Sergeant Fairchild into a civilian; transformation of the canteen into an empty space; transformation of the porter Galy Gay into a soldier).

The components making up the set were like so many props. During Galy Gay's transformation two screens in the background – canvas stretched across large iron frames – showed pictures of Galy Gay before and after he had been transformed. Galy Gay was lying before the latter when he woke up again after being shot. The numbers of the separate stages in the transformation process were given by projections. The set was constructed in such a way that its appearance could be entirely changed by the removal of just a few of its components.

The 'Song of the Flow of Things' recited by the canteen pro- prietress during this transformation was accompanied by three kinds of activity. First, gathering the awnings: the canteen pro- prietress took a stick with an iron hook fixed to its end and gathered the two awnings together as she walked along the front of the stage reciting, her face turned towards the audience. Secondly, washing the awnings: she knelt in front of an opening in the stage and dipped the soiled pieces of linen into it, swirled them round as if in water and lifted out clean ones. Thirdly, folding the awnings: the canteen proprietress and the soldier Uriah Shelley held the awnings so they hung vertically right across the diagonal of the whole stage, and folded them together.

Sergeant Fairchild's transformation into a civilian (no. IVa [of scene 9]) was clearly marked off as an insertion by the half-curtain closing before and after it. The stage manager stepped forward with the script and read interpolated titles all through this process. At the start: 'Presenting an insertion: Pride and demolition of a great personality.' After the sentence 'Yes, because that is a civi- lian coming' [p. 55]: 'During the mobilisation Sergeant Fairchild visits the Widow Begbick on a personal matter.' After the sen- tence 'Stop you gob, civvy!': 'Nor did he learn from bitter experi- ence. Clad as a civilian he staked his great military reputation to impress the widow.' After the sentence 'You really should, for my sake': 'In order to win the widow, he heedlessly demonstrated his skill as a shot.' After the sentence 'Eight women out of every nine would find this gory man divine': 'A famous episode was deprived of its shock effect.' After '. . . that for military reasons this canteen must be packed up': 'Though formally reminded of his duties, the sergeant insisted on having his will.' After '. . . or he'll demoralise the company': 'And so his inexplicable insistence on his private affairs caused him to forfeit his great name, the result of years of service.'

2. The Question of Criteria for Judging Acting

People interested in the ostensibly epic production of the play *Mann ist Mann* at the Staatsheater were of two opinions about the actor Lorre's performance in the leading part. Some thought his way of acting was perfectly right from the new point of view, exemplary even; others quite rejected it. I myself belong to the first group. Let me put the question in its proper perspective by saying that I saw all the rehearsals and that it was not at all due to shortcomings in the actor's equipment that his performance so disappointed some of the spectators; those on the night who felt him to be lacking in 'carrying-power' or 'the gift of making his meaning clear' could have satisfied themselves about his gifts in this direction at the early rehearsals. If these hitherto accepted hallmarks of great acting faded away at the performance (only to be replaced, in my view, by other hallmarks, of a new style of acting) this was the result aimed at by the rehearsals and is accordingly the only issue for judgement: the one point where opinions can differ.

Here is a specific question: How far can a complete change in the theatre's functions dislodge certain generally accepted criteria from their present domination of our judgement of the actor? We can simplify it by confining ourselves to two of the main objections to the actor Lorre mentioned above: his habit of not speaking his meaning clearly, and the suggestion that he acted nothing but episodes.

Presumably the objection to his way of speaking applied less in the first part of the play than in the second, with its long speeches. The speeches in question are his protest against the announcement of the verdict, his pleas before the wall when he is about to be shot, and the monologue on identity which he delivers over the coffin before its burial. In the first part it was not so obvious that his manner of speaking had been split up according to gests, but in these long summings-up the identical manner seemed monotonous and to hamper the sense. It hardly mattered in the first part that people couldn't at once recognise (feel the force of) its quality of bringing out the gest, but in the second the same failure of recognition completely destroyed the effect. For over and above the meaning of the individual sentences a quite specific basic gest was being brought out here which admittedly depended on knowing what the individual sentences meant but at the same time used this meaning only as a means to an end. The speeches' content was made up of contradictions, and the actor had not to make the spectator identify himself with individual sentences and so get caught up in contradictions, but to keep him out of them. Taken as a whole it had to be the most objective possible exposition of a contradictory internal process. Certain particularly significant sentences were therefore 'highlighted', i.e. loudly declaimed, and their selection amounted to an intellectual achievement (though of course the same could also be the result of an artistic process). This was the case with the sentences 'I insist you put a stop to it!' and 'It *was* raining yesterday evening!' By these means the sentences (sayings) were not brought home to the spectator but withdrawn from him; he was not led but left to make his own discoveries. The 'objections to the verdict' were split into separate lines by caesuras as in a poem, so as to bring out their character of adducing one argument after another; at the same time the fact that the individual arguments never followed logically on one another had to be appreciated and even applied. The impression intended was of a man simply reading a case for the defence prepared at some quite different period, without understanding what it meant as he did so. And this was indeed the impression left on any of the audience who knew how to make such observations. At first sight, admittedly, it was possible to overlook the truly magnificent way in which the actor Lorre delivered his inventory. This may seem peculiar. For generally and quite rightly the art of not being overlooked is treated as vital; and here are we, suggesting that something is magnificent which needs to be hunted for and found. All the same, the epic theatre has profound reasons for insisting on such a reversal of criteria. Part of the social transformation of the theatre is that the spectator should not be worked on in the usual way. The theatre is no longer the place where his interest is aroused but where he brings it to be satisfied. (Thus our ideas of tempo have to be revised for the epic theatre. Mental processes, e.g., demand quite a different tempo from emotional ones, and cannot necessarily stand the same speeding-up.)

We made a short film of the performance, concentrating on the

principal nodal points of the action and cutting it so as to bring
out the gests in a very abbreviated way, and this most interesting
experiment shows surprisingly well how exactly Lorre manages in
these long speeches to mime the basic meaning underlying every
(silent) sentence. As for the other objection, it may be that the epic
theatre, with its wholly different attitude to the individual, will
simply do away with the notion of the actor who 'carries the play';
for the play is no longer 'carried' by him in the old sense. A certain
capacity for coherent and unhurried development of a leading part,
such as distinguished the old kind of actor, now no longer matters
so much. Against that, the epic actor may possibly need an even
greater range than the old stars did, for he has to be able to show
his character's coherence despite, or rather by means of, interrup-
tions and jumps. Since everything depends on the development,
on the flow, the various phases must be able to be clearly seen, and
therefore separated; and yet this must not be achieved mechanic-
ally. It is a matter of establishing quite new rules for the art of
acting (playing against the flow, letting one's characteristics be
defined by one's fellow-actors, etc.). The fact that at one point
Lorre whitens his face (instead of allowing his acting to become
more and more influenced by fear of death 'from within himself')
may at first sight seem to stamp him as an episodic actor, but it is
really something quite different. To begin with, he is helping the
playwright to make a point, though there is more to it than that
of course. The character's development has been very carefully
divided into four phases, for which four masks are employed – the
packer's face, up to the trial; the 'natural' face, up to his awakening
after being shot; the 'blank page', up to his reassembly after the
funeral speech; finally the soldier's face. To give some idea of our
way of working: opinions differed as to which phase, second or
third, called for the face to be whitened. After long consideration
Lorre plumped for the third, as being characterised, to his mind,
by 'the biggest decision and the biggest strain'. Between fear of
death and fear of life he chose to treat the latter as the more profound.

The epic actor's efforts to make particular incidents between
human beings seem striking (to use human beings as a setting),
may also cause him to be misrepresented as a short-range episodist
by anybody who fails to allow for his way of knotting all the
separate incidents together and absorbing them in the broad flow
of his performance. As against the dramatic actor, who has his

character established from the first and simply exposes it to the inclemencies of the world and the tragedy, the epic actor lets his character grow before the spectator's eyes out of the way in which he behaves. 'This way of joining up', 'this way of selling an elephant', 'this way of conducting the case', do not altogether add up to a single unchangeable character but to one which changes all the time and becomes more and more clearly defined in course of 'this way of changing'. This hardly strikes the spectator who is used to something else. How many spectators can so far discard the need for tension as to see how, with this new sort of actor, the same gesture is used to summon him to the wall to change his clothes as is subsequently used to summon him there in order to be shot, and realise that the situation is similar but the behaviour different? An attitude is here required of the spectator which roughly corresponds to the reader's habit of turning back in order to check a point. Completely different economies are needed by the epic actor and the dramatic. (The actor Chaplin, incidentally, would in many ways come closer to the epic than to the dramatic theatre's requirements.)

It is possible that the epic theatre may need a larger investment than the ordinary theatre in order to become fully effective; this is a problem that needs attention. Perhaps the incidents portrayed by the epic actor need to be familiar ones, in which case historical incidents would be the most immediately suitable. Perhaps it may even be an advantage if an actor can be compared with other actors in the same part. If all this and a good deal more is needed to make the epic theatre effective, then it will have to be organised.

3. Making the play concrete

The parable *Man equals Man* can be made concrete without much difficulty. The transformation of the petty-bourgeois Galy Gay into a 'human fighting-machine' can take place in Germany instead of India. The army's concentration at Kilkoa can be made into the Nazi party rally at Nuremberg. The elephant Billy Humph can be replaced by a stolen motor-car now the property of the SA. The break-in can be located in a Jewish junk dealer's shop in lieu of Mr Wang's temple. The shopkeeper then engages Jip to be his Aryan partner. The ban on damaging Jewish shops could then be explained by the presence of English journalists.

[From Brecht *Gesammelte Werke*, London 1937, vol 1, pp. 220–
224. Of the three sections, 1 refers to the 1931 production; 2
reprints Brecht's letter to the *Berliner Börsen-Courier* of 8 March
of that year; while 3 dates from 1936. The SA or Storm Detach-
ments were Hitler's brownshirts. The term 'Aryan' was used by
the Nazis to denote non-Jewish.]

ON LOOKING THROUGH MY FIRST PLAYS (v)

I turned to the comedy *Man equals Man* with particular appre-
hension. Here again I had a socially negative hero who was by
no means unsympathetically treated. The play's theme is the
false, bad collectivity (the 'gang') and its powers of attraction,
the same collectivity that Hitler and his backers were even then
in the process of recruiting by an exploitation of the petty-
bourgeoisie's vague longing for the historically timely, genuinely
social collectivity of the workers. Before me were two versions,
the one performed at the Berlin Volksbühne in 1928 and the other
at the Berlin Staatstheater in 1931. I decided to restore the earlier
version, where Galy Gay captures the mountain fortress of Sir
El-Djowr. In 1931 I had allowed the play to end with the great
dismantling operation, having been unable to see any way of
giving a negative character to the hero's growth within the
collectivity. I decided instead to leave that growth undescribed.

But this growth into crime can certainly be shown, if only the
performance is sufficiently alienating. I tried to further this by one
or two insertions in the last scene.

[From 'Bei Durchsicht meiner ersten Stücke.' GW *Schriften
zum Theater*, p. 951. Written in March 1954 and originally forming part of the introduction of *Stücke I* and *II*.]

Editorial Notes

1. EVOLUTION OF THE PLAY

The name Galy Gay and the basic idea of one man being forced to assume the personality of another both derive from the *Galgei* project which Brecht appears to have conceived as early as 1918 and begun developing in spring or early summer of 1920. 'In the year of Our Lord . . .', says a diary note of 6 July 1920,

> citizen Joseph Galgei fell into the hands of bad men who maltreated him, took away his name and left him lying skinless. Everyone should look to his own skin.

It was to be 'just the story of a man whom they break (they have to) and the sole problem is how long can he stand it . . . They lop off his feet, chuck away his arms, bore a hole in his head till the whole starry heaven is shining into it: is he still Galgei? It's a sex murder story.'

This play was to have been set in Augsburg, and its theme was how 'Galgei replaces Pick the butter merchant for a single evening'. An early scheme specifies eight scenes, thus:

1. In the countryside. Pick's death.
2. The Plärrer [i.e. the Augsburg fair]. Galgei's abduction.
3. The Shindy Club. Dagrobu [?meaning]. Pick's funeral. Galgei.
4. Ma Col's bedroom. Galgei half saved. The big row.
5. River. Murder of Galgei. His rescue.
6. Next morning at the club.
7. Galgei's house. Galgei's burial.
8. In the countryside. Pick's resurrection.

A fragmentary text of the first three scenes shows Pick going off in dudgeon; a splash is then heard. Scene 2 is described as '*Big swing-boats. Evening. Violet sky*' and opens with the news of Pick's death:

> MATTHI: Who is going to pay Pick's taxes and emit Pick's farts?

Galgei, a fat man, is on the swings; by profession he is a carpenter. A bystander describes him:

> He is a most respectable man. Lives quietly and modestly with his wife. He's behaving very childishly today. It's the music. He's such a reliable worker.

Scene 3 at the Shindy Club's subterranean bar is subdivided into episodes. Ma Col (a proto-Begbick) is behind the bar polishing glasses. Enter Galgei with Ligarch, the club president, who was on the swings with him. Shaking hands, he says 'I must remain what I am. But I'm in top form tonight . . .', and there it breaks off. However, a slightly more detailed scheme than the first one takes it on:

> Galgei gatecrashes the Shindy Club. 1. He wants to ingratiate himself. 2. He takes part in the business. 3. He hasn't got a woman. 4. He takes the butter business over.

– while the remaining scenes are developed in a slightly different order thus:

> 4. Bedroom, white calico. Love.
>   *The screws are tightened.* Galgei is caught.
>   i. He falls in love with Ma Col.
>   ii. He gets money. Hunger.
>   iii. He falls out with Matthi.
>   iv. He goes to the butter business.
> 5. Bar. Brown. Beasts of prey. Schnaps.
>   *He is transformed.* The big row in the club. Galgei feels that he is Pick.
>   i. He fights for Ma Col.
>   ii. He stands up for Salvarsan.
>   iii. He abandons Lukas.
> 6. River meadows, green weeds, fat bodies.
>   *He turns nasty.*
>   i. He murders Matti.
>   ii. He is overcome by doubt.

7. Bar,
   i. He wakes up.
   ii. He consoles Ma Col until he is at home.

A further sketch for scene 8 describes the setting as 'River. Dawn light. Distant sound of bells.' and has Ligarch saying to Galgei 'Come. Today God is in Chicago. The sky is displaying the *cruel* constellations.'

Like Shlink in *In the Jungle*, a play which Brecht was only to start planning a year or more later, Galgei was supposed to lose his skin. He was fat and passive, so a note of May 1921 suggests, with

> a red wrinkled skin, particularly on his neck, close-cropped hair, watery eyes and thick soles. He seethes inwardly and cannot express himself. But everything derives from the fact that people look towards him.

This 'lump of flesh' was to be like a jellyfish, an amorphous life-force flowing to fill whatever empty shape was offered it. It was like 'a donkey living who is prepared to live on like a pig. The question: Is he then living?

> Answer: He is lived.

'What I'm not sure of,' reflected Brecht, 'is whether it is at all possible to convey the monstrous mixture of comedy and tragedy in Galgei, which lies in the fact of exposing a man who can be so manipulated and yet remain alive.'

From then on the project seems to have stagnated, only to be revived in the summer of 1924 when Brecht was about to leave Bavaria for Berlin. The Augsburg context was now discarded, to be replaced by an Anglo-Indian setting derived from Brecht's interest in Kipling and first foreshadowed in a story and poem about 'Larrys Mama', the 'mummy' in question being the British (or Indian) army. The first version of the new scheme specifies no less than fifteen scenes as follows:

1. galgei goes to buy a fish. 2. Soldiers lose fourth man. 3. buy galgei. 4. have to do without fourth man. 5. galgei plays jip. 6. jip's betrayal. 7. billiards. 8. elephant scene. 9. flight. 10.

execution. 11. departure. 12. train on the move. 13. jip. 14. mime, niggerdance, boxing match. 15. general clean-up.

– also mentioning 'Blody Five', a 'Saipong Song' and such key phrases as 'the gentleman who wishes not to be named', '1 = o' [einer ist keiner] and 'there must be two souls in you', the old Faustian principle. Starting on his own, then later with Elisabeth Hauptmann's help. Brecht completed this to make the first full version of the play, an extremely long text which included the whole of *The Elephant Calf*, more or less as we now have it, as the penultimate scene. The characters at first included besides Galgei: John Cakewater (or Cake), Jesse Baker (or Bak), Uria Heep (presumably after Dickens) and Jerome Jip as the four soldiers, and Leokadja Snize as the canteen lady, with a daughter called Hiobya. In the course of the writing, however, these names gave way respectively to Galy Gay, Jesse Cakewater, Polly Baker, Uria Shelley, Jeraiah Jip, and Leokadja and Hiobya Begbick. The sergeant remained Blody Five throughout. Saipong, the original setting, became Kilkoa, and at some point in 1925 Brecht decided that the play's title would be *Galy Gay or Man = Man*.

Bound in with the script of this version is a good deal of miscellaneous material, which sets the tone thus:

> the three knockabouts
> the worst blokes in the indian army
> the golden scum
> knife between the teeth gents
> you people stand in the corner when he comes in and smile
>   horribly (this happens)

A discarded episode between Bak and Galgei goes:

> bak: some people live like in a marriage ad to put it scientifically
>   their excrement is odourless but there are those who look life
>   straight in the eye i don't know if you've ever felt the carnal
>   pepper in you i'm talking about unchastity
> galgei: i know what you mean
> bak: have you ever handled a woman with paprika i'll never
>   forget how a woman once bit me on the tit because i didn't
>   beat her quite long enough
> galgei: she liked your beating her did she

bak: that's not so uncommon but don't put on an act with me i bet you're just as ready to give your flesh its head in that sort of situation don't tell me a man with a face like yours isn't sensitive to the impressions one can pick up in gents' urinals say

galgei: i must tell you that in the circumstances i find it difficult to put up with your remarks

bak: take a good look at your innermost self do you feel any impulse say to hit me in the face?

galgei: just a fleeting one

bak: look the other way i get too excited when you look at me excuse me

on another occasion someone describes a peculiarly bloody battle scene their hair stands on end as they sing like drunks he quivers like a rabbit

the scum is bawling

every spring blood has to flow

jabyourknifeintohimjackhiphiphurrah

It ends with two significant phrases: 'they bank on him entirely, will go to the stake for him' and 'he is ready to become a murderer, saint, merchant'. A third – 'He cannot say no' – comes in a slightly later scheme. There is also an unrealised idea for 'Galgay [*sic*] choruses':

> All those who do far too much
> Have no time for sleeping
> Have no longer a cold hand
> For their best crimes
> Whatever happens
> Under the sun and under the moon
> Is as good as if
> Sun and moon were thoroughly used to it
> You'll see three soldiers in Kilkoa
> Commit an offence
> And when night came with its dangers
> You saw them go to bed

But there are other criminals who
Bear Cain's mark on their brows
Before nightfall
Seated at the bicycle races
But these go to bed
So do not lose heart
For the moon goes on shining
While they are provisionally asleep
And next day they'll step with old
Feet into new water
For they are not always present
But leave the wind blowing through the bushes for one night
And the moon shining for one night
And next day look out on
Changed world

The first published version is dated 1926 and bears the final title *Mann ist Mann*. It represents a reduced and somewhat subdued revision of its 1924/5 predecessor, with the penultimate scene now separated as an appendix under the title *The Elephant Calf or The Provability of Any Conceivable Assertion*; the direction saying that it should be performed in the foyer only came later. This text, which doubtless bears a close relationship to that of the play's premières the same year, has been translated in full by Eric Bentley in the Grove Press *Seven Plays by Bertolt Brecht* (1961 – to be distinguished from later Grove Press editions where the play has been adapted). The original Ullstein (Propyläen) edition also gives melody and piano accompaniment for the 'Man equals Man Song' which seems to have developed out of the Saipong Song mentioned earlier. An amended version of this text was used for Erich Engel's 1928 production at the Volksbühne, after which Arkadia (another offshoot of the Ullstein publishing empire) issued a duplicated stage script. This in turn formed the basis of Brecht's own production with Peter Lorre at the Staatstheater in 1931. The major changes made up to this point included the cutting of Begbick's three daughters Hiobya, Bessie and Ann, who are described in the 1926 version as 'half-castes who form a jazz band', and an extensive reshuffling of lines between the three soldiers. Our scenes 4 and 5 were run into one and scenes 6 and 7 were cut, while in our long scene 9 the soldiers were to sing the Mandalay Song (as in *Happy End*) and the Cannon Song (as in the *Threepenny Opera*) finishing up with the

Man equals Man Song and a very short final scene. For Brecht's production however Begbick's Interlude speech was shifted to form a prologue, its place being taken by Jesse's speech 'I tell you, Widow Begbick' on p. 41, which was to be delivered 'before the portrait of Galy Gay as a porter'. Blody Five was changed to *Blutiger Fünfer* (Bloody Fiver) throughout; it will be seen how as a character he diminishes. Both the Man equals Man Song and the Song of Widow Begbick's Drinking Car were thrown out, but a new Song of the Flow of Things (stylistically very close to the 'Reader for Those who Live in Cities' poems) was brought in instead of the interpolated songs in scene 9. The play ended with the soldiers entraining as at the end of that scene. The programme described it as a 'parable'.

This in turn formed the basis for the second published version, that of the Malik collected edition in 1938. Its text is the same as ours up to the end of Galy Gay's long verse speech in scene 9 (v), after which a slight shuffling of the dialogue, followed by a final brief speech from Galy Gay, allowed the play to end with that scene. In 1954, however, 'on looking through his first plays' for Suhrkamp's new collected edition, Brecht decided to bring back scenes 10 and 11 from the 1926 version, modifying them slightly so as to include the final brief speech of 1938, which now occurs on p. 76. The result was the text which we now have. But of course Brecht never saw it staged in this form, and no doubt he would have modified it yet again. For of all his plays there was scarcely one that he found so difficult to let alone. All in all, he once wrote, 'from what I learnt from the audiences that saw it, I rewrote *Man equals Man* ten times'. Looking at the material in the Brecht Archive one soon loses count. But it is easy to believe that he spoke the truth.

2. NOTES ON INDIVIDUAL SCENES

Scene numbers and titles are given as in our version of the play. Numbers in square brackets refer to those in whichever text is under discussion.

1. Kilkoa

The 1924/5 text describes the setting simply as *'road'*. Otherwise this scene has remained unchanged apart from the wife's final line:

Please don't wander around. I am going to bolt myself into
the kitchen so you needn't be worried on account of all those
idle soldiers.

This survived till 1931 and was then cut.

2. Street outside the Pagoda of the Yellow God

The 1924/5 text has a version of his scene which finishes after 'I'm
hanging by the hair' (p. 7) and appears to have been added after
the writing of the following scene. In it Uria refers to the army
as 'Mummy':

> the army whom we call mummy and who sends her sons to
> such towns half way across india pays them two and a half
> bottles of whisky per head.

JESSE: nothing's stronger than mummy.

The opening stage direction specifies 'four soldiers and a machine-gun
marching to their camp on whisky'. The 1926 published version has
them also singing the Man equals Man Song, but in both texts the
talk throughout is of whisky rather than beer. The 1926 version
differs also from our text in (a) its omission of all Jesse's opening
speech after 'Kilkoa!' (p. 4): instead he continues with the words
now given to Polly ('Just as the powerful tanks' etc.); (b) the
wording of the first attempt to break into the temple; and (c) its
omission of the paybook episode (pp. 5–6).

[2, amended to 3. in the huts, evening. cake, bak, heep, hiobja sneeze.]

This is in the 1924/5 version only and was later absorbed in our
scenes 3 and 4. There are two alternatives for this short scene, the
second of which is marked 'Written by Hesse Burri to dictation'
(i.e. presumably Brecht's). In the first Hiobja, who is also known
as Hipsi, talks to the three soldiers as the 'wanted' notice is being
put up, and calls Blody 5 'the devil of saipong'. His voice is then
heard bawling out the men:

> call those trousers? what? i'll have you scrubbing the shit-
> house with a toothbrush till your hair turns white, you
> swine!

Rations are doled out and Jip's portion falls on the floor as there is no one to take it. Blody asks 'where is your fourth man?' as at the top of p. 9. The three then agree that they must find him before nightfall, and the text breaks off. A page of notes follows with phrases like 'the hell of kilkoa', 'begbick and bloodsucker', 'two cents a chair', 'one full whisky', 'our skins are at stake' and 'the fragile rocking-chair', then a fresh start with

> canteen. evening. hiobja begbick, soldiers

The soldiers sing 'In Widow Begbick's Splendid Drinking Truck', and one Jack Townley (see the end of the *Elephant Calf*) complains about the prices and says:

> i jack townley who unlike you footsloggers and gun-tuggers know such a metropolis as cairo like the back of my hand can only tell you i must have been in some 1500 gin- rum- and alebars there with say between two and five ladies on each storey but so sinful an establishment as this is more than jack ever . . .

Enter then the three, who are asked by the others about their missing fourth man. They buy drinks all round and are charged two cents per chair, one of which breaks. The 'Wanted' notice goes up and the sergeant's voice is heard cursing the men and announcing the Afghan campaign:

> i knew we'd be getting the scum of every regiment but now i come to look at you it's far worse than i thought it's my considered opinion that you're the most plague-ridden bunch of throwouts that ever wore its boots out in the queen's service today i observed some individuals among the huts laughing in such a carefree way that it chilled me to the marrow i know who they are and let me tell you there will be one or two hairs in *their* christmas pudding

The rations are doled out; the sergeant asks about the missing fourth man, and the scene breaks off, all much as before.

3. Country Road between Kilkoa and the Camp

In the 1924/5 text this is marked 'brecht first version' and described as 'deserted road. galgei carries leokadja begbick's cucumber basket for her'. It starts with the entrance of Begbick and Galy Gay, much as on our p. 9, and has two alternative endings of which the second is close to our version. The 1926 added the beginning of the scene somewhat as we now have it, taken from the abandoned canteen scene above. The rest of the scene was slightly revised and extended, leaving only a few lines to be added in the 1938 version to arrive at the present text.

4. Canteen of the Widow Leokadia Begbick

The 1924/5 scene 4 is set *in the cantonment. night. leokadja. hiobja. roll-call off.* The three soldiers are worried as now that if it rains Jip's palanquin will be taken indoors, so they go off with Begbick's scissors, leaving her and Galy Gay to discuss whether he was or was not the man who carried her cucumber. They make no serious approach as yet to Galy Gay.

The 1926 version starts as now, with material from the second part of the abandoned scene above. The opening song is accompanied by Begbick's three half-caste daughters, after which the dialogue (p. 14) is allocated rather differently from now, so that it is the soldiers who inquire about the missing man and say that the sergeant is 'not nice', while it is Hiobja ('thou flower on the dusty path of the soldiery', as her mother calls her) who describes the sergeant's habits:

> They call him Blody Five, the Tiger of Kilkoa. His hallmark is The Human Typhoon. His warcry on seeing a man ripe for the Johnny-are-you-dry wall is 'Pack your suitcase, Johnny.' He's got an unnatural sense of smell, he smells out crime. And each time he smells one he sings out 'Pack your suitcase, Johnny.'

– a reference, surely, to the line 'Johnny Bowlegs, pack your kit and trek' in Kipling's 'Song of the Banjo', which in turn derived from the South African song 'Pack your kit and trek, Ferrera'. The phrase recurs throughout this version of the play.

The appeal to Galy Gay which follows (p. 15) is much as now except that it is all given to Polly and Galy Gay's speech on entering is omitted. The other soldiers do not exit, but remain to comment; Galy Gay is not undressed; and the bargaining over the uniform is somewhat shorter. Begbick's account of the effect of rain on the sergeant is the same as now from 'Not a bit of it' (p. 18) to 'as a kitten', but goes on to end

> For when it rains Blody Five turns into Blody Gent and for three days the bloody gent only bothers about girls.

On Galy Gay's departure after the announcement of the roll-call there is no further bargaining (down to p. 19), nor are Polly's speech to Begbick and her seductive preparations included. Instead she tells Hiobja to put the tarpaulin over the waggon, after which Blody enters *'appallingly transformed'* and listens to the roll-call outside:

> BLODY: You're laughing. But let me tell you I'd like to see this all go up in flames, this Sodom with its bar and its rocking chair, and you who are a one-woman Gomorrah. Don't cast such devouring glances at me, you whitewashed Babylon.
> LEOKADJA: You know, Charlie, a woman likes to see a man being so passionate.

There is no verse speech by Begbick, and Blody goes on with his next speech as now, down to 'one means business' (p. 20), after which the voice off summons the MG section, so that there is no reference to Blody dressing in a bowler hat. The remainder is much as now, except that there is no verse speech by Galy Gay and no song by Begbick at the end, nor does Uriah provide beer and cigars. The song comes in the 1931 stage version, where it is sung through a megaphone. In 1926 Polly says 'Drink a few cocktails and put them down to us', which Galy Gay then proceeds to do. The scene ends with his denying having carried Begbick's basket, and Begbick saying 'It's begun to rain'.

5. Interior of the Pagoda of the Yellow God [misnumbered 6 in the 1926 edition which specifies that the sacristan is Chinese. Cut in the Arkadia scripts of 1929–30.]

The 1924/5 version is close to our text, except that after 'seem to slumber very well' (p. 24) Uriah goes on to say:

> i am sure you would be ashamed to tell a lie and here are 3 revolvers what's more made by everett & co each containing 6 bullets i am sure you would not wish to contain 6 bullets as you are not a revolver

– whereupon the sacristan aims a rifle at him. Wang shouts 'fire!' and the sacristan runs away.

The rest of the scene, with the drawing of the four men, is virtually as now. In the Arkadia scripts this is the only part to be retained; it is taken into the canteen scene when Wang enters to order drink.

6. The canteen [7 in the 1926 edition. Cut in the Arkadia scripts, but restored in modified form for the 1931 production.

This scene remained unchanged since 1926 and would be almost the same in the 1924/5 version too but for the omission of Jesse's and Polly's concluding remarks. It concludes with Baker saying after 'a mere thread' (p. 26):

> I shan't say anything more to him tonight.
> *Galgay yawns in his sleep and makes himself comfortable.*

7. Interior of the Pagoda of the Yellow God [8 in the 1926 edition. Cut in the Arkadia scripts].

In the 1924/5 version this comes after the next canteen scene, but it is almost word for word as now apart from the substitution of beer for the original whisky. The 1926 text is even closer.

The 1931 text simply showed Jip outside the pagoda surrounded by beer bottles and a large plate of meat, and had him deliver a verse speech paraphrasing his concluding speech here:

> What am I, Jeraiah Jip from Tipperary, to do
> When I'm told our entire army
> Twelve railway trains and four elephant parks
> Moved over the Punjab Mountains during the past month?
> Here however I can eat meat and drink beer
> My ten bottles a day, and in return have only to
> Look after the temple that there are no further incidents
> And get my food and get my beer and get my
> Orderly existence. True
> I ought to go and help them
> In their life's worst quandary, since I after all
> Am their fourth man. But why
> Does meat taste so good and
> Is beer so essential? True, Jesse will say 'Jip's sure to come.'
> Once he's sober Jip will come.

But this beefsteak suits me, good meat.
Uriah may not wait quite so patiently since
Uriah is a bad man.
Jesse and Polly will say 'Jip's sure to come.' But
Must a man abandon meat like this?
Can he go away? If he's hungry?
No, no. He mustn't if he cannot.

8. *The canteen.*

The 1924/5 version, like the 1926 published text, has Galy Gay
half asleep while the three soldiers play billiards. The scene follows
on scene 6 and starts with Polly's comment 'He must be frozen
stiff' (p. 30), then they wake Galy Gay up and continue approximately with the dialogue from 'Dear Sir' (p. 31) to where Galy
Gay wants to leave (p. 32), Uriah's speech about the joys of army
life being marked by Brecht 'written by Hesse Burri in Augsburg'.
Next it appears that Galy Gay wants to rejoin his wife:

CAKE: of course he needs a woman the fellow's like an elephant
URIAH: he can get one with his next week's pay
BAK: i'll go with him myself and select one so he doesn't go
sick
CAKE: meantime he can do it with begbick

Enter Blody 5, who brings in the wife (p. 35), after which the
dialogue is roughly as now up to the wife's exit (p. 37), after
which the soldiers congratulate themselves:

URIAH: it's an honour for us to have a man like you in the unit.
GALY GAY: the honour's mine you people are so much sharper
if i wasn't so uneducated i would never have become a porter
that woman's a bit stupid and she's even more uneducated
than me almost crude in some respects
POLLY: is she at all faithful to you?
GALY GAY: yes because i've got the money

Then they give him chewing gum:

GALY GAY: this is the first time for me but i think it tastes nasty
POLLY: that's just at first once you've got its inmost taste on
your lips you'll find your tongue can't do without this sport
any more than a boxer his punchball

As he polishes off his gum Polly tells him 'your way of spitting out your gum is exactly like jip's except that it went to the left'. The riddle (p. 34) appears to follow, though it is even more idiotic than now, being concerned with how many peas go in a pot. Then comes Wang's entry (p. 30) to buy drink. 'I don't serve niggers or yellow men,' says Begbick as he orders 'seven bottles of good Old Tom Whisky for a white man'; and the scene ends with Uriah saying 'Jip won't be back now.'

[Scene: Bungalow/Late Afternoon]

The 1924/5 version therefore omits the reflections on 'personalities' (p. 31) and all the preliminaries to the elephant deal. However, they come into the outline sketch of a separate scene which follows the pagoda scene (our scene 7 above), in which *'the three are packing their mg in grease galy gay is asleep on his chair.* This contains a first version of Uriah's speech about multiple opinions (p. 31), also an attack on 'personalities'; then when Galy Gay wakes up the soldiers pretend to be the voice of Buddha addressing him. Half awake, he knocks one of them flat and Blody 5 comes to see what the noise is about:

> URIAH: sorry sergeant we were just having a little game of
>   golf

Bak (i.e. Polly) thereupon congratulates Galy Gay on his 'phenomenal right hook' and reckons that he would make mincemeat of a 'company of shiks' (i.e., presumably, Sikhs). He is applauded by 'eleven soldiers of the worchester regiment stationed at kilkoa', with whom he then drinks toasts to the Queen, the Regiment and others. Once they have left he tries to go as on p. 32 and the text continues much as now up to Polly's inquiry about the elephant on p. 34, after which the episode concludes with a few changes.

In the 1926 published script all these elements are brought together to make scene 8 virtually as we have it. Wang orders 'seven bottles of good old Victoria Whisky'; Uriah's order and his remark about 'taking beer on board' are not included, nor is Polly's second speech about the peculiar attractions of military life in wartime (p. 32). The passage from Galy Gay's 'But I fancy I'm the right man' (p. 34) to 'you can rob a bank', with its portrayal of him as a wrestler, is not included, so that Blody Five

appears almost at once after the riddle. Nor is Galy Gay's important remark about his wife's origin in a 'province where nearly
everyone is friendly', a phrase presumably added in the 1950s,
since it is not in the 1938 edition either. The 1926 scene ended
without the Alabama lines but with Blody Five reappearing to
shout 'The army's moving off to Tibet!' After which

> *Exit, whistling 'Johnny'. Galy Gay picks up his clothes and tries to
> sneak away quietly. The three catch him and fling him into a chair.*

The duplicated Arkadia script (1930 version) greatly economised
by eliminating the second and third pagoda scenes (our scenes 5
and 7) and rolling scenes 4, 6 and 8 into one single canteen scene.
It makes various cuts and changes: thus in scene 4 Blody 5 makes
a pass at Hiobja, while at its end Galy Gay is seated in a rocking
chair, denying that he carried Begbick's basket. Then Wang
enters to order drinks as in scene 8 and does his demonstration
with the drawing (our scene 5) in order to prove that his white
servant cannot be the missing man. The soldiers have decided
that they must get Galy Gay to go with them, when Blody re-
enters:

LEOKADJA: Cocktail or Ale?
BLODY: Ale!

When Blody says he needs a woman Begbick calls 'Hiobja!', and he
starts telling her about his pornographic pictures, much as in the
1924/5 version of scene 9. Begbick accuses him of abusing his
uniform, saying that he should wear rubber shoes and a dinner
jacket, after which the text is roughly as ours from Polly's 'But
how do we manage it . . . ?' (p. 30) to Galy Gay's 'I'm the right
man for any bit of business' (p. 34). Blody's reappearance and the
rest of the scene are approximately as in the 1926 version.

All this was altered in the 1931 production, where the latter
part of scene 4 was much changed, with Galy Gay falling asleep
after his denials and Begbick singing her verse offstage through
a megaphone. A version of scene 6 followed under the title of
Return of the three soldiers the same night, after which the half-curtain
was closed for Jip's verse monologue outside the pagoda (given
above). It reopened on a version of scene 8 taken largely from the
Arkadia script.

Interlude

This is not in the 1924/5 version. In the 1926 text it was to be
spoken by Begbick 'alongside a portrait of Mr Bertolt Brecht'.
This was replaced in the Arkadia script by a 'portrait of Galy Gay
as a porter'. In 1931 the portrait remained but the speech was
shifted to make a prologue, being replaced by Jesse's long prose
speech from pp. 41–2. In the 1938 Malik edition, as now, there
was no mention of any portrait.

9. The canteen [10 in the 1926 version]

The 1926 text was very different from now, and a good deal
longer. The setting to start with was '*canteen made of hollow bamboos
and grass matting,*' which Leokadja and Hiobja are busy dismantling.
Galy Gay arrives all agog as Uriah and Polly are wondering what
form their business deal should take; asking Leokadja to lend them
her elephant's head they develop their plot from that. Enter
Blody 5 to show Hiobja his pictures:

BLODY: hiobja i have a definite feeling that my sentiments for
you have almost reached their peak scientifically speaking it's
nothing for a girl to visit a man's room if he asks her only a
swine would gossip about that my photographs are notable
sights i have items you won't find in the british museum when
you see them you may think them slightly too free but
against that once you've seen them you never forget them
HIOBJA: if they're truly scientific yes i'd like to see them but
not in your room for a girl is a poor weak thing

Galy Gay takes a drink ('so that's gin it really does taste like a
small fire') and the three soldiers assemble their elephant:

KAKE: this tarpaulin makes so many folds in his belly that even
leokadja begbick is blushing

Then Polly complains that he must work the tail by hand:

KAKE: polly when you look out of the back it isn't decent
URIAH: the front and back legs must be coordinated somehow
or it'll look bad

Meanwhile Hiobja is showing Blody's pictures to the troops. There is a poker game with Leokadja, Hiobja and Blody, who announces:

> better for them to be tied with a triple rope and dumped in an anthill than to be drunk this a.m. when we move off not even a sergeant could expect mercy in such an eventuality

> GALY GAY: that's order for you no matter whether it's a sergeant or an ordinary man he gets shoved in the hole

Among various disconnected snatches of dialogue here there is a Schweik-like reminiscence for Galy Gay:

> i had a friend a porter who in turn had a big red beard he could carry a hundredweight on his bare chest drank a pond dry daily and bashed the empire middleweight champion's eye flat for him this fellow had his beard removed one night because he'd seen a photo of the prince of wales and from then on he would run away from a chicken and couldn't lift more than 60 lb he was so scared of ghosts at night that he married a widow fancy that

Meantime Leokadja attacks Blody and tells him he would look better in civilian clothes. Then the artificial elephant is ready.

At this stage there appears to be no formal subdivision of the scene into separate 'numbers', nor is there an interspersed song. Galy Gay flings himself into the deal with 'One more swig' as in our text, while Uriah introduces Billy Humph as now. Galy Gay is by no means shocked at the latter's appearance:

> right billy you and i are going to get on splendidly as long as you're with me you can behave just like at home

Inside Billy, Bak (i.e. Polly) exclaims 'himmel arsch und wolken-bruch', prompting Galy Gay to ask 'did you say something billy'. Since Billy is 'a little souvenir of my grandfather' Galy Gay much regrets having to auction him:

> for instance i ride billy humph myself round the fortifications whenever i feel like it i may add i nurtured him at my bosom he was breastfed like you and me so everybody sing when he

comes up for auction since this is a moment i shall always
remember for after it's over my heart may well break
all sing 'it's a long way to tipperary' including billy

The auction follows, much as in our sub-scene II, though with
some additions, for instance:

SOLDIERS: billy what do you think of women?
BILLY *shits*
URIAH: that isn't nice of you billy you have a dirty mind

Galy Gay calls for bids, but is arrested. Blody Five enters in civilian
garb and Galy Gay chases the elephant out, shouting 'stop thief,
stop thief!'.

The next instalment, marked by Brecht '*blody's k.o.*', corresponds
to our sub-scene IVa. Blody invites Hiobja to 'a few cocktails' and
reads the newspaper, making a hole in it to spy on the soldiers,
who are drinking cocktails too. Uriah pops the bowler hat on him
and asks 'where did you get this personality from, mister?'. But
Leokadja sings his praises:

eleven days after the battle of lake tchad river (mind how you
dismantle the bamboos up there) 50 blokes from the 42nd
who'd seen the devil face to face sneaked into a bungalow
drank paraffin and shot crazily at everyone who passed by
then a man arrived riding an elephant and addressed them
for five minutes on his own and decided they ought to be
shot after which 50 men came out and let themselves be mown
down in a heap like young sick lamas the name of this man
was blody five the batik man

They invite him to show his skill with a revolver, as on p. 55, but
using a cigar instead of an egg; then after he misses it the text
goes on (as also in 1926) with Blody cursing them as 'piss con-
tainers' and telling them how he won the name Blody Five by
shooting five 'Shiks' at the battle of 'Dschadseefluss', literally
Lake Chad River. In both versions the soldiers then comment on
his military virtues: 'and at the same time you're such a nice person. Kindly too, come to think of it'. In the 1924/5 text they then
have a sack race with him, after which he takes Hiobja on his
knee, is photographed by flashlight, and has to pay up.

The next sub-scene, marked by Brecht 'hongkong', has the three
soldiers entering with Galy Gay and telling him that 'four hundred
shiks, an entire battalion, are looking for you'. So they take the
billiard table and use it as a boat in which to escape to Hongkong.
They sing 'Nearer, my God, to Thee', as on the doomed *Titanic*,
while Uriah cites a line from Brecht's early poem 'Tahiti' (which
was also to be incorporated in a similar episode in *Mahagonny* scene
16). What looks like another version has Heep (i.e. Uriah) saying:

> raise your eyes jerome jip d'you see the widows on the shores
> of bombay see them waving their petticoats they're crying
> their eyes out and on sumatra your orphans will soon be
> oppressed by usurers

KAKE: it's just grey fields on the coastline and the wind whip-
ping them   set the topsail there's going to be a storm tonight

BAK: hold tight jenny this gunboat is rocking dreadfully

KAKE: it's the atlantic rollers continually heaving up and down

GALGEI: hey you must go faster

HEEP: can you see a sail on the horizon behind us?

KAKE: no not yet

GALGIE: is it dangerous here   where have we got to?

KAKE: seven degrees east of ssw

BAK: if night doesn't fall too soon we can still make gibraltar

HEEP: the best thing would be to sing stormy the night to keep
up our spirits have you any biscuits left?

KAKE: stormy the night is a fine thing when your spirits are
getting low

GALY GAY [sic]: anyway let's just sing through it
they sing tho seemannslos [asleep on the deep]

HEEP: now pipe down and best pray by yourselves for i think
that's the island of tahiti the most charming island of them
all where as many ships have gone aground as there are fish
in the arctic sea

BAK: take off your hat you lout

HEEP: hear the wind whistling in the rigging?

GALY GAY: go quicker and go carefully for i tell you the wind's
rising hour by hour

KAKE: yes and now we must strike the foresail who knows
what will become of us if the storm goes on getting so much
worse?

A *'flight to hongkong'* sub-scene follows, starting with a soldier asking the four 'Who are you?'

BAK: oh just tourists

SOLDIER: we know them and where's your luggage?

BAK: yes galgay where's the luggage?

URIAH: bak's got a straw hat

SOLDIER: which of you is galgay?

URIAH: oh nobody

SOLDIER: someone just mentioned the name galgay

URIAH: really did you hear that name?

SOLDIER: you know perfectly well it's the name of a notorious criminal

URIAH: anyhow my name isn't galgay and i wouldn't wish it to be

SOLDIER: is your name galgay?

GALGAY: me? certainly not

BAK: ah?

SOLDIER: did you say something?

BAK: not a word sir

SOLDIER: what's your name supposed to be sir?

GALGAY: jip jerome jip

SOLDIER: what are you?

GALGAY: porter sir

SOLDIER: what?

GALGAY: soldier i mean a thousand apologies

SOLDIER: no nonsense from you now that stolen elephant is written all over your face

KAKE: sir i object to your way of addressing our friend jerome jip i can answer for him personally

GALGAY: there you are

KAKE: indeed yes let us through this is our jip and these are my fists

SOLDIER: all right so long as you answer for him very well

BAK: that went off all right d'you want to look round hong-kong galgei?

GALGAY: kindly don't call me galgei they seem to know everything in this place and i don't want to look at hongkong but to hide

BAK: all right then wait on the pier a moment till we've gone

GALGAY: no no don't leave now it's terribly risky

URIAH: yes but we must get our paybooks stamped you'll have to wait here

GALGAY: i'll have to come along

BAK: out of the question it'd look as if you were scared just wait here a moment and keep an eye on my straw hat

GALGAY: where is it?

BAK: if you hold out you'll be allowed to see it   goodbye

SOLDIER: got your paybook on you?

GALGAY: yes here sir

an elephant appears at the back   galgay sees him

GALGAY: would you come over here sir i've got my paybook

SOLDIER: where are you off to   stay where you are

GALGAY: you can see my paybook very well over here sir

SOLDIER: you   what's that?

GALGAY: for god's sake what do you mean sir?

SOLDIER: don't tell me there's anything wrong with your eyesight just look where i'm pointing

GALGAY: an elephant

SOLDIER: emphatically an elephant   very quick of you to spot it and who would you say that elephant belonged to eh?

Galy Gay wakes up and asks 'is this hongkong?', to be told by a soldier that it certainly isn't: it is Saipong. Then Blody Five appears and the episode ends with Galy Gay's protests as the soldiers threaten that he will be shot 'under the three ash trees of saipong'. 'oh uriah, ka, bak', he cries, 'help me!'

The *'trial'* sub-scene [numbered 5 by Brecht] corresponds to our III and is close to it as far as 'Yes, at Kankerdan I was with you' on p. 50, after which it goes on as in the 1926 version to where Galy Gay appeals to Uriah. Uriah then *'turns away'*, and as Galy Gay is marched off to be shot he sees Bak (ie. Polly) dressed as himself and exclaims 'there he is.'

GALY GAY: he was standing there all the time and i didn't see him

In the *'execution'* sub-scene they march Galy Gay off and on again to the sound of a drum, much as in the 1926 IV, which this resembles down to where Galy Gay is blindfolded. 'this galy gay in him has got to be shot', says Uriah. Bak bursts out laughing, but they shoot and he falls. Then Leokadja: 'what a noise you are making really you're pushing him too far   now he really believes he is dead he's just lying there but finish dismantling my walls first it's two a.m.' In a fragmentary passage she goes on:

> without generals my sweet child you can make a war but without the widow begbick my dear boy you would just burst into tears as soon as things got hot and where there's a bar there'll be a urinal too that'll probably apply as long as the world lasts

SOLDIERS: widow begbick you can count on our acting accordingly
BEGBICK: ah yes it's a pleasant life i shan't be coming back here there are all kinds of places for widow begbick and as long as the army eats and drinks widow begbick won't grow old today was a fine day so tomorrow we'll be travelling north in those rumbling trains i've always been fond of cigars and words like afghanistan

The last sub-scene in the 1924/5 version is marked '6. *breaking camp*'. As in the 1926 version it starts with the soldiers carrying in the box – Begbick's piano apparently in this case – and singing Chopin's Funeral March to the words 'Never again will the whisky pass his lips' (twice). After Galy Gay has been told that he is to deliver the funeral oration (p. 59) there are snatches of our present text, followed by the greater part of the oration ('Therefore raise up Widow Begbick's crate' etc. p. 63), then some dialogue where, as in the 1926 version, the soldiers fit him out with equipment, finishing up with the Anglo-German cry 'drei cheers für unsere cäpten'. Elements of Galy Gay's verse speech (p. 60) are appended.

In 1926 all this scene 9 material was pulled pretty well into its present shape. The scene was divided into six music-hall 'numbers', most of them followed by a verse of the Man equals Man song and formally introduced by Uriah who blows a whistle and announces the titles. Only IVa [5], the episode with Blody Five, is termed a 'subsidiary number'. The introductory section differs both from the 1924/5 version and from our present text, but includes parts of the latter, notably the concept of 'the man whose name must not be mentioned'. Blody is not on till [2], the auction episode, though his voice off is audible in [1] saying 'Johnny, pack your kit'; the display of dirty photographs, much shortened, takes place in [5]. In [1], which is close to our version, Galy Gay is disturbed by the elephant's ramshackle appearance, only cheering up in [2] when it becomes clear that Begbick will none the less buy it ('Elephant equals elephant, particularly when he is being bought'). After Galy Gay has been put in chains (p. 46) [2] continues with a dialogue between Leokadja and Blody, who desires her daughters but is at this point told to present himself in a dinner jacket and bowler hat. After that Blody's 'subsidiary number', deprived of the flashlight photo episode and all the passages of the 1924/5 version already cited, was shifted to follow the trial and execution, while the two Hongkong sub-scenes were cut.

[3], the Trial, is close to our text as far as 'at Kankerdan I was with you' (p. 50), but continues with Uriah's announcement of the verdict which is now in our IV (p. 51) as far as 'when a man is being slaughtered?' (p. 52), followed by a verse of the song. [4], the Execution, then follows on from there, starting with Begbick's next speech, and is virtually the same as our IV till Uriah's 'so that he can hear he's dead' on p. 54. This is where Blody enters in a dinner jacket and has his bowler hat rammed down by Uriah with the cry 'Stop your gob, civvy!'; verse 4 of the song follows. [5] then corresponds to our IVa, and starts with the dirty photographs, continuing with Uriah's 'Come on, Fairchild old boy!' (p. 55) and the shooting demonstration, done this time with eggs. The story about the five Shiks (or Hindus) follows (cf. p. 56) leading straight into the Soldier's entrance as at the end of our version (p. 57). After this Blody wants to dance and calls for Hiobja, then makes do with her mother, saying 'Dame equals dame'.

[6], corresponding to our V, is announced by Uriah as on p. 57. The box this time is Begbick's nickelodeon; the Chopin march is sung as before; then comes an approximate version of our text as far as the long verse speech, with Begbick's speech about the move ('This army', p. 62) brought forward to where the trains now whistle (p. 60). The verse speech itself is shorter than now, but the rest of the sub-scene is much the same, with the addition at the end of the loading of the bundled-up Human Typhoon and the singing of the last verse of the song.

In the Arkadia script of 1930 there was no Man equals Man song, and the 'numbers' were announced by projections. Blody's entry in civilian clothes, seeking Hiobja, took place at the beginning of 1, which had the soldiers singing 'Widow Begbick's House in Mandalay' with the refrain 'Quick, Blody, hey' etc. He did not appear in 2, which ended with Galy Gay in chains and the

singing of the Cannon Song. 3 was slightly shortened and 4 only
began with the soldiers' complaints about the bad light (p. 53),
then continued roughly as now to its ending. Next Blody appeared
and the projector started showing the time, starting with 2
o'clock. There was no 'number' corresponding to our IVa. At
2.00 the soldiers decide to feed Galy Gay, and Begbick tells them
to take the nickelodeon case and chalk his name on it, with a cross
against it. At 2.01 he eats and the soldiers bring in the case, singing
the Chopin march. At 2.03 Galy Gay starts practising his military
movements (p. 59) and Begbick offers him castor oil. At 2.05 the
trains start whistling and Begbick makes her speech about the
move. Galy Gay washes as instructed by her (p. 62) and asks how
many are going to Tibet (as in scene II of the 1926 version or our
scene 10, p. 70) and so on to 'Women the same' (p. 70).

> GALY GAY: You know, Widow Begbick, one equals no one. So
> let me tell you there's not all that much difference between yes
> and no, and so I'm going to get rid of what I didn't like about
> myself, and be pleasant.

At 2.07 the waggons roll in with Begbick's Ale-Waggon hitched
up to them, and the troops entrain. A projection says 'Funeral
obsequies and graveside address for Galy Gay, last of the personalities, in the year 1928' and leads into the oration and the
ensuing dialogue down to 'three cheers'. At 2.10 Polly delivers a
harangue, ending up with an NCO-like 'one-two-three-four'
repeated four times; then

> one-two-three . . .

> GALY GAY: Four! *Steps into the gap and marches radiantly behind
> the other three into the waggon, singing the Man equals Man song.
> The waggon rolls off.*

A projection then announces the title of our scene 11 and goes on:
'The shower capture it [i.e. the fortress] on behalf of Royal Shell.
Private Jeraiah Jip is among them. You have seen how he can be
used for any desired purpose. In our day he is used to make war.'
A brief ending to the play follows.

For the 1931 production, Begbick's poem of the Flow of Things
was included. The scene [9] began with a Voice as now; then
the start followed, finishing with Galy Gay's 'I might have one

for you' (p. 41) which led straight into 1. This was shortened, with a new bridge into 2, which added a new ending to the Arkadia version. 3 followed this version as far as Galy Gay's 'I think you're mistaking me' (p. 49), after which new material led into the next instalment of the song. In 4 there was a cut of about a page; in 4a of about a page and a half. 5 followed the Arkadia version as far as 'Women the same', then came 'Get entrained!' (p. 62) and the funeral oration, leading to the following ending of the play (which is also that of the 1938 Malik edition):

GALY GAY: Well, why haven't I got all my kit? (p. 63 bottom)
POLLY: A full set of uniform for our fourth man!
The soldiers bring in the things and make a ring round Galy Gay so as to hide him from the audience. Meanwhile the band plays the war march and Begbick comes to the centre of the stage and speaks.
BEGBICK: The army is on the move to the northern frontier. The fire-belching cannon of the northern battlefields are waiting for them. The army is athirst to restore order in the populous cities of the north.
The ring of soldiers opens. Galy Gay, Uriah, Jesse and Polly line up, with Galy Gay in the middle bristling with assorted weapons. They mark time to the music.
GALY GAY *loudly*: Who is the enemy?
URIAH *loudly*: Up to now we have not been told which country we are invading.
POLLY *loudly*: But it looks more and more like Tibet.
JESSE *loudly*: But we have been told that it is a pure war of defence.

Then Galy Gay speaks the concluding verses on p. 76, after which Begbick comes downstage and says 'Quod erat demonstrandum'. With the exception of this ending the Malik text of the scene is almost exactly the same as ours.

10. In the Moving Train [11 in 1926 version].

Like our scene 11 this was omitted from the Arkadia scripts, the 1931 production and the 1938 Malik edition, all of which ended with scene 9. In the 1950s Brecht restored it, using the 1926 text with small modifications of which the most significant was the insertion of the passage from 'Now you' to 'used to say' in Galy

Gay's speech on the Tibetan War (p. 66), with its indication that they are about to invade his wife's home.

The 1924/5 script contains two versions of the scene. In the first, which Brecht labelled 'old waggon scene' the setting is as now, but it opens with the three developing a photograph (presumably that of Blody and Hiobja). The dialogue approximates to ours as far as Galy Gay's 'If this train doesn't stop' (p. 65) after which Blody wakes up, sees the three defaulters and tells them to arouse Galy Gay:

> he's got too good a conscience hey wake that man up i want to get a bit better acquainted with him man to man

He tells the three to hand over their revolvers, but is scared off when Uriah dons his (Blody's) bowler hat. Galy Gay then asks what has been going on, to which Kake (Jesse) replies:

> yesterday you got mixed up in some affair of a porter trying to sell an army elephant and being shot for it then you were taken ill and didn't want to be who you were
> GALY GAY: who was i then?
> KAKE: you're no better i see you were private jip but for quite a time you didn't know it and kept talking about a grass hut and a wife and stuff like that and you'd entirely forgotten all about being a soldier

They continue to confuse him about his identity, talking about his paybook and its description of him, the tattooing on his arms etc. Polly puts his head out of the window and is guillotined, then he does the same to Galy Gay and suggests that they all sing 'the bilbao men's song', whose text however is not given. The soldiers go off to play cards, and Galy Gay asks 'What is it that's shaking so?' (p. 64), after which the scene continues very roughly as now, but omitting the whole Fairchild episode and ending slightly differently, with the troops all singing 'Tipperary'.

The second version is headed '2 Waggon-scene' and is close to our text as far as Galy Gay's speech on the Tibetan War. Then Blody Five appears with a long monologue version of the self-castration episode (pp. 69-70), after which the rest is much as above.

[*Outside the Camp Signs of an Army on the Move*]

In this discarded scene from the 1924/5 script Jip appears to the tune of 'Tipperary' in search of the other three.

> BEGBICK: you're in luck they've announced a big theatre per-
> formance for this evening to fish people's money out of their
> pockets one of them is actually going to act an elephant calf
> which is a piece of pure malice on their part as he's already
> been brought to his senses once by the sale of a phoney ele-
> phant the man's called jerome jip you probably know him
> *jip hurries on*

When Blody appears, full of threats, Begbick roars with laughter and pushes her cart past him. Fragments then suggest that prior to the writing of the second waggon scene (above) this was to have been the self-castration scene. In one Blody delivers his monologue carrying '*a lamp a length of catgut and a breadknife*'; another gives a shorter version as follows:

> BLODY: there's nothing can be done to stop this sensuality
> which simply prevents you doing your duty the enemy is in
> your own house but the army which has so far earned noth-
> ing but glory cannot have its best men attacked by rot but
> even if there is no way of making your conduct sheet white
> once more at least a terrible example should be instituted
>
> since a strong unchastity originating in the womb
> hung my breadbasket ever higher and failed to
> respond to hard beds and unseasoned fare
> but often and repeatedly dragged me down among the animals
> i shall utterly etch away this excess and herewith
> shoot off my cock
> *goes into the undergrowth*

[*Theatre a Plank Stage beneath a Few Rubber Trees with Chairs Facing*]

This scene, only found in the 1924/5 script, is the performance subsequently detached to form the *Elephant Calf*. As far as the Sorrowing Mother's Speech (p. 85) the text is almost word for word as now, except that it is Bobby Pall, not Jackie. Then Bak [Polly] says:

you may even be able to move them to tears it's the most moving bit if this goes over well perhaps i'll stay in the theatre for life *curtain rises* the elephant calf has had to leave because it feels unwell after those great proofs the criminal will be even deeper in the toils so tell me o elephant calf's mother something about thy son come deliver the sorrowing mother's speech

– which is differently worded. Then after the soldiers applaud and Uriah has told 'Jip' to 'Get on stage!' (p. 86):

galy gay trots along the footlights eyes the three and hums it's a long way as the soldiers cheer

URIAH: oh for christ sake drop that nonsense
BAK: he's waking up he's breaking through this damned notion of acting a singing elephant

Then Polly makes his speech (p. 86) asking if he thinks 'that this is thy mother?'

GALY GAY: it's a long way *cheers*
URIAH: you've misappropriated army funds
BAK: that's the disease you suffer from *aloud* the elephant calf has been overcome by the confusions of a guilty conscience
GALY GAY: get on with the play bak

The ending, after the Soldiers' 'It's a damned unfair business' (p. 86), is almost exactly as in our text except that the final song is omitted and two further pages are included after 'every decent human instinct' (p. 90). The closing stage direction adds '*to the singing of yes we have no bananas*'.

11. Deep in Remote Tibet Lies the Mountain Fortress of Sir El-Djowr [misnumbered 10 in the 1926 edition, which adds the direction '*Columns of troops are marching along singing the Man equals Man song*'.]

Like scene 10, this was omitted after the 1926 edition and re-introduced by Brecht in the 1950s. He then replaced the MG by a 'Kanone', cut Blody Five's entry (with his old catchphrase 'Johnny, pack your kit') and substituted Galy Gay's speech starting

'And I want to have first shot' (p. 72). After Galy Gay's call through the megaphone, too, the ending was different; the reference to the 'friendly people' from Sikkim once again dates from the 1950s. The verse comes from the conclusion of the Malik version of 1938, the final roll-call from that of 1926, which however ended with four marching off to the Man equals Man song and Polly calling back to the audience 'He'll be the death of us all yet'.

In the 1924/5 script there were several versions of this scene. One is virtually as in the 1926 edition. Another, called 'new last scene' is set in '*a dugout in tibet during an artillery bombardment*'. Enter the three soldiers asking if they can 'play a spot of pokker here?' [*sic*]. Blody, now quite subdued, is there and when Galy Gay enters they all stand up. He complains about the noise:

> if all this warfare doesn't stop soon i'm going to smash the place up *explosion* pokker demands total concentration above all how is one to bring off a decent royal flush with a din like this going on stop chewing your moustache sergeant

BLODY: i'm very sorry i'm afraid i forgot

In what seems the earliest version, marked by Elisabeth Hauptmann 'Summer 1925, Augsburg', the setting is '*canteen packing up towards morning signs of an impending move*', with Blody making all the troops except the machine-gunners do knees-bend. Jip arrives and is greeted, and a version of the first two-thirds of the present scene follows, as far as his exit (p. 74). Then there is a fragmentary '*long thin subdued conversation in the cool half-light*' between Galy Gay and Begbick, who thinks of selling her canteen and coming to Tibet with him. There is a long discussion with Hiobja, then Blody summons Galy Gay and the scene breaks off.

The version marked 'second ending' starts with Jip arriving as in the discarded 'outside the camp' scene above. The three enter, and Blody hobbles out of the undergrowth to introduce the real Jip, who is promptly knocked down by a hook to the chin from Galy Gay. Then comes '*Widow Begbick's canteen in the grey half-light. Noises outside of packing up and moving off.*' Confronting his friends much as on pp. 71–73, Jip curses them and is given Galy Gay's old paybook. Then Blody appears and marches the three off to the 'Johnny-wet-his-pants-wall', where they are shoved into an anthill.

Left alone with Begbick, Galy Gay orders 'a few cocktails and a cigar', and her approach to him (p. 74) follows. They are thinking of going to Tibet together as business partners; however, Blody summons him. Hiobja tells him she knows something discreditable about Blody, which makes Galy Gay slap Begbick's bottom and say they will get to Tibet all right. Blody then appears '*laughing horribly*' and asks Galy Gay who he is:

GALY GAY: A man. Named Jeraiah Jip. And Man equals Man, my lad. But not a man equals not a man.

With that he gives Blody a stare, opens the window and asks the world what makes Lionel Fairchild, a sergeant in the Indian Army, speak so softly and prance like a stilt-walker.

> Suppose that in a rice-field near the Tibetan frontier, unobserved by other men but observed by a young girl, a man tears out his legendary sensuality by the roots with the aid of a penknife. Suppose he bellows like a donkey bellowing. Sergeant Blody Five, Human Typhoon, what's it like when you bellow?
>
> SOLDIERS *laugh louder*: Go on, Typhoon, bellow!
> BLODY FIVE *bellows*: Man equals Man. But Blody Five equals Blody – *his voice goes into a shrill falsetto* – Five.
> SOLDIERS *roaring with laughter*: He's chopped off his manhood! He's castrated himself!
> *Galy Gay bares his teeth in a smile and sits down. The laughter spreads backward until it is as though the whole Indian Army were laughing. Exit Blody Five, swept away by the laughter. A soldier in the window points at him.*
> SOLDIER: That was the Human Typhoon. And here – *indicating Galy Gay* – sits Jeraiah Jip who blasted him into Abraham's bosom as you might say. He'll be the death of us all yet.
> *Dance. Military music. It's a long way to Tipperary.*

THE THREEPENNY OPERA

Texts by Brecht

ADDITIONAL SONGS FROM 'THE BRUISE'

Second Part

After Mr Peachum and his friend Macheath have left, Mr Brown sings these stanzas to the 'Mac the Knife' tune:

> Oh, they're such delightful people
> As long as no one interferes
> While they battle for the loot which
> Doesn't happen to be theirs.

> When the poor man's lamb gets butchered
> If two butchers are involved
> Then the fight between those butchers
> By the police must be resolved.

Third Part

As they drive up in four or five automobiles the gang sing:

SONG TO INAUGURATE THE NATIONAL DEPOSIT BANK

> Don't you think a bank's foundation
> Gives good cause for jubilation?
> Those who hadn't a rich mother
> Must raise cash somehow or other.
> To that end stocks serve much better
> Than your swordstick or biretta
> But what lands you in the cart
> Is getting capital to start.
> If you've got none, why reveal it?
> All you need to do is steal it.
> Don't all banks get started thanks to
> Doing as the other banks do?
> How did all that money come there? –
> They'll have taken it from somewhere.

And Mr Macheath walks with a light step in the direction of the West India Dock . . . humming a few new verses to an instantly obsolete ballad:

How's mankind to get some money?
In his office, cold like snow
Sits the banker Mac the Knife, but he
Isn't asked, and ought to know.

In Hyde Park behold a ruined
Man reclining in the sun
(While down Piccadilly, hat and cane, just think about it)
Strolls the banker Mac the Knife, and
God alone knows what he's done.

Fourth Part

CLOSING VERSES OF THE BALLAD

So we reach our happy ending.
Rich and poor can now embrace.
Once the cash is not a problem
Happy endings can take place.

Smith says Jones should be indicted
Since his business isn't straight.
Over luncheon, reunited
See them clear the poor man's plate.

Some in light and some in darkness
That's the kind of world we mean.
Those you see are in the light part.
Those in darkness don't get seen.

[From 'Die Beule' in Brecht; *Versuche*, re-edition 1959, pp. 229 ff., and GW *Texte für Film* pp. 329 ff. This was Brecht's proposed treatment for Pabst's *Threepenny Opera* film, for which see the introduction (p. xiii). In the Second Part the police also sing the 'Whitewash Song' subsequently used in the Berliner Ensemble production of *Arturo Ui*. Excepting the re-use of the Mac the Knife ballad, there were no settings to these songs by Weill. Three of them also occur in *The Threepenny Novel*.]

NEW CLOSING VERSES TO THE BALLAD OF MAC THE KNIFE

And the fish keep disappearing
And the Law's perturbed to hear
When at last the shark's arrested
That the shark has no idea.

And there's nothing he remembers
And there's nothing to be done
For a shark is not a shark if
Nobody can prove he's one.

THE NEW CANNON SONG

1

Fritz joined the Party and Karl the S.A.
And Albert was up for selection
Then they were told they must put all that away
And they drove off in every direction.
  Müller from Prussia
  Requires White Russia
  Paris will meet Schmidt's needs.
  Moving from place to place
  Avoiding face to face
  Contact with foreign forces
  Equipped with tanks or horses
  Why, Meier from Berlin is bound to
  End up in Leeds.

2

Müller found the desert too hot
And Schmidt didn't like the Atlantic.
Will they ever see home? That's the problem they've got
And it's making them perfectly frantic.
  To get from Russia
  Back home to Prussia
  From Tunis to Landshut:
  Moving from place to place
  Once they come face to face

With nasty foreign forces
Equipped with tanks or horses
Their leader gives no lead because he's
Gone off for good.

3

Müller was killed, and the Germans didn't win
And the rats ran around in the rubble.
All the same, in the ruins of Berlin
They're expecting a *third* lot of trouble.
    Cologne is dying
    Hamburg is crying
    And Dresden's past all hope.
    But once the U.S.A.
    Sees Russia's in its way
    With a bit of luck that ought to
    Set off a new bout of slaughter
    And Meier, back in uniform, might
    Get the whole globe!

BALLAD OF THE GOOD LIVING OF HITLER'S MINIONS

1

That drug-crazed Reich Marshal, who killed and jested
You saw half Europe scoured by him for plunder
Then watched him sweat at Nuremberg – and no wonder –
Outbulging those by whom he'd been arrested.
And when they asked him what he did it for
The man replied: for Germany alone.
So that can make a man weigh twenty stone?
Don't pull my leg; I've heard that one before.
No, what made him a Nazi was just this:
One must live well to know what living is.

2

Then Schacht, the Doctor who took out your money –
The sheer length of his neck still has me baffled –
As banker once he fed on milk and honey
As bankrupter he's sure to dodge the scaffold.
He knows he won't be tortured, anyway
But ask Schacht, now he's finally been floored

Just why he joined the others in their fraud
He'll say ambition made him go astray,
But we know what pushed him to the abyss:
One must live well to know what living is.

3

And Keitel, who left the Ukraine all smoking
And licked the Führer's boots clean with his spittle
Because he'd built the Wehrmacht up a little –
Ask that tank expert why, he'll think you're joking.
Sipping, he'll say: I followed Duty's call!
So Duty made his casualties so great?
No question of acquiring an estate:
That kind of thing we don't discuss at all.
We get one. 'How?' 's a question we dismiss.
One must live well to know what living is.

4

They all have great ideas in untold numbers
And lay claim to the loftiest of wishes
And none of them mentions the list of dishes
But each of them has demons plague his slumbers.
Each saw himself no doubt as Lohengrin
Or Parsifal; so how was he to fail?
Behind Moscow they sought the Holy Grail
And just Valhalla crumbled, not Berlin.
Their private problems all boiled down to this:
One must live well to know what living is.

NEW VERSION OF THE BALLAD IN WHICH MACHEATH BEGS FORGIVENESS

You fellow men who want to live, like us
Pray do not think you have to judge us harshly
And when you see us hoisted up and trussed
Don't laugh like fools behind your big moustaches.
Oh, you who've never crashed as we came crashing
Don't castigate our downfall like the courts:
Not all of us can discipline our thoughts –
Dear fellows, your extravagance needs slashing
Dear fellows, we've shown how a crash begins.
Pray then to God that he forgive our sins.

The rain washes away and purifies.
Let it wash down the flesh we catered for.
And we who saw so much, and wanted more –
The crows will come and peck away our eyes.
Perhaps ambition used too sharp a goad
It drove us to these heights from which we swing
Hacked at by greedy starlings on the wing
Like horses' droppings on a country road.
Oh, brothers, learn from us how it begins
I pray that you kindly forgive our sins.

The men who break into your houses
Because they have no place to sleep in
The gossipper, the man who grouses
And likes to curse instead of weeping;
The women stealing your bread ration
Could be your mothers for two pins.
They're acting in too mild a fashion –
I pray you to forgive their sins.

Show understanding for their trouble
But none for those who, from high places
Led you to war and worse disgraces
And made you sleep on bloodstained rubble.
They plunged you into bloody robbery
And now they beg you to forgive.
So choke their mouths with the poor débris
That's left of where you used to live!

And those who think the whole thing's over
Saying 'Let them expiate their sins'
Are asking for a great iron crowbar
To stave their ugly faces in.

NEW CHORALE

Don't punish small wrong-doings too much. Never
Will they withstand the frost, for they are cold.
Think of the darkness and the bitter weather
The cries of pain that echo round this world.

But tackle the big crooks now, all together
And chop them down before you're all too old:

Who caused the darkness and the bitter weather
And brought the pain that echoes round this world.

['Anhang' to *The Threepenny Opera*, in GW *Stücke* 2, pp. 491 ff.,
excluding the 'Neufassung der Ballade vom angenehmen
Leben', which differs only marginally from that in our text,
and the closing verses from the film version, which we have
given above (p. 304). The dates indicate that the first and
fourth of these songs were written in 1948, the other two in
1946].

ON *The Threepenny Opera*

Under the title *The Beggar's Opera*, *The Threepenny Opera* has been
performed for the past two hundred years in theatres throughout
England. It gives us an introduction to the life of London's
criminal districts, Soho and Whitechapel, which are still the refuge
of the poorest and least easily understood strata of English society
just as they were two centuries ago.

Mr Jonathan Peachum has an ingenious way of capitalising on
human misery by artificially equipping healthy individuals as
cripples and sending them out to beg, thereby earning his profits
from the compassion of the well-to-do. This activity in no sense
results from inborn wickedness. 'My position in the world is one
of self-defence' is Peachum's principle, and this stimulates him to
the greatest decisiveness in all his dealings. He has but one serious
adversary in the London criminal community, a gentlemanly
young man called Macheath, whom the girls find divine. Macheath
has abducted Peachum's daughter Polly and married her in highly
eccentric fashion in a stable. On learning of his daughter's marriage
– which offends him more on social grounds than on moral ones –
Peachum launches an all-out war against Macheath and his gang of
rogues; and it is the vicissitudes of this war that form the content
of *The Threepenny Opera*. However, it ends with Macheath being
saved literally from the gallows, and a grand, if somewhat paro-
distic operatic finale satisfactorily rounds it all off.

The Beggar's Opera was first performed in 1728 at the Lincoln's
Inn Theatre. Contrary to what a number of German translators
have supposed, its title does not signify an opera featuring beggars
but 'the beggar's opera', in other words an opera for beggars.
Written in response to a suggestion by the great Jonathan Swift,

The Beggar's Opera was a parody of Handel, and it is said to have had a splendid result in that Handel's theatre became ruined. Since there is nowadays no target for parody on the scale of Handel's theatre all attempt at parody has been abandoned: the musical score is entirely modern. We still, however, have the same *sociological* situation. Just like two hundred years ago we have a social order in which virtually all levels, albeit in a wide variety of ways, pay respect to moral principles not by leading a moral life but by living off morality. Where its form is concerned, the *Threepenny Opera* represents a basic type of opera. It contains elements of opera and elements of the drama.

['Über die Dreigroschenoper – 1' from GW *Schriften zum Theater* p. 987. Dated 9 January 1929, when it appeared as an article in the *Augsburger Neueste Nachrichten* to introduce the production in Brecht's home town.]

NOTES TO *The Threepenny Opera*

The Reading of Plays

There is no reason why John Gay's motto for his *Beggar's Opera* – nos haec novimus esse nihil – should be changed for *The Threepenny Opera*. Its publication represents little more than the promptbook of a play wholly surrendered to theatres, and thus is directed at the expert rather than at the consumer. This doesn't mean that the conversion of the maximum number of readers or spectators into experts is not thoroughly desirable; indeed it is under way.

The Threepenny Opera is concerned with bourgeois conceptions not only as content, by representing them, but also through the manner in which it does so. It is a kind of report on life as any member of the audience would like to see it. Since at the same time, however, he sees a good deal that he has no wish to see; since therefore he sees his wishes not merely fulfilled but also criticised (sees himself not as the subject but as the object), he is theoretically in a position to appoint a new function for the theatre. But the theatre itself resists any alteration of its function, and so it seems desirable that the spectator should read plays whose aim is not merely to be performed in the theatre but to change it: out of mistrust of the theatre. Today we see the theatre being given absolute priority over the actual plays. The theatre apparatus's priority is a priority of means of production. This apparatus resists all conversion to other purposes, by taking any play which it encounters and immediately changing it so that it no longer represents a foreign body within the apparatus – except at those points where it neutralises itself. The necessity to stage the new drama correctly – which matters more for the theatre's sake than for the drama's – is modified by the fact that the theatre can stage anything: it theatres it all down. Of course this priority has economic reasons.

The Principal Characters

The character of JONATHAN PEACHUM is not to be resumed in the stereotyped formula 'miser'. He has no regard for money. Mistrusting as he does anything that might inspire hope, he sees money as just one more wholly ineffective weapon of defence. Certainly he is a rascal, a theatrical rascal of the old school. His crime lies in his conception of the world. Though it is a conception worthy in its ghastliness of standing alongside the achievements of any of the other great criminals, in making a commodity of human misery he is merely following the trend of the times. To give a practical example, when Peachum takes Filch's money in scene 1 he does not think of locking it in a cashbox but merely shoves it in his pocket: neither this nor any other money is going to save him. It is pure conscientiousness on his part, and a proof of his general despondency, if he does not just throw it away: he cannot throw away the least trifle. His attitude to a million shillings would be exactly the same. In his view neither his money (or all the money in the world) nor his head (or all the heads in the world) will see him through. And this is the reason why he never works but just wanders round his shop with his hat on his head and his hands in his pockets, checking that nothing is going astray. No truly worried man ever works. It is not meanness on his part if he has his Bible chained to his desk because he is scared someone might steal it. He never looks at his son-in-law before he has got him on the gallows, since no conceivable personal values of any kind could influence him to adopt a different approach to a man who deprives him of his daughter. Mac the Knife's other crimes only concern him in so far as they provide a means of getting rid of him. As for Peachum's daughter, she is like the Bible, just a potential aid. This is not so much repellent as disturbing, once you consider what depths of desperation are implied when nothing in the world is of any use except that minute portion which could help to save a drowning man.

The actress playing POLLY PEACHUM should study the foregoing description of Mr Peachum. She is his daughter.

The bandit MACHEATH must be played as a bourgeois phenomenon. The bourgeoisie's fascination with bandits rests on a misconception: that a bandit is not a bourgeois. This misconception is
the child of another misconception: that a bourgeois is not a
bandit. Does this mean that they are identical? No: occasionally a
bandit is not a coward. The qualification 'peaceable' normally
attributed to the bourgeois by our theatre is here achieved by Macheath's dislike, as a good businessman, of the shedding of blood
except where strictly necessary – for the sake of the business. This
reduction of bloodshed to a minimum, this economising, is a
business principle; at a pinch Mr Macheath can wield an exceptionally agile blade. He is aware what is due to his legend: a certain
romantic aura can further the economies in question if enough care
is taken to spread it around. He is punctilious in ensuring that all
hazardous, or at any rate bloodcurdling actions by his subordinates get ascribed to himself, and is just as reluctant as any professor
to see his assistants put their name to a job. He impresses women
less as a handsome man than as a well situated one. There are
English drawings of *The Beggar's Opera* which show a short, stocky
man of about forty with a head like a radish, a bit bald but not
lacking dignity. He is emphatically staid, is without the least sense
of humour, while his solid qualities can be gauged from the fact
that he thinks more of exploiting his employees than of robbing
strangers. With the forces of law and order he is on good terms;
his common sense tells him that his own security is closely bound
up with that of society. To Mr Macheath the kind of affront to
public order with which Peachum menaces the police would be
profoundly disturbing. Certainly his relations with the ladies of
Turnbridge strike him as demanding justification, but this justification is adequately provided by the special nature of his business.
Occasionally he has made use of their purely business relationship
to cheer himself up, as any bachelor is entitled to do in moderation;
but what he appreciates about this more private aspect is the fact
that his regular and pedantically punctual visits to a certain Turnbridge coffee-house are *habits*, whose cultivation and proliferation
is perhaps the main objective of his correspondingly bourgeois life.

In any case the actor playing Macheath must definitely not base
his interpretation of the part on this frequenting of a disorderly
house. It is one of the not uncommon but none the less incomprehensible instances of bourgeois demonism.

As for Macheath's true sexual needs, he naturally would rather
satisfy them where he can get certain domestic comforts thrown in,

in other words with women who are not entirely without means. He sees his marriage as an insurance for his business. However slight his regard for it, his profession necessitates a temporary absence from the capital, and his subordinates are highly unreliable. When he pictures his future he never for one moment sees himself on the gallows, just quietly fishing the stream on a property of his own.

BROWN the police commissioner is a very modern phenomenon. He is a twofold personality: his private and official natures differ completely. He lives not in spite of this fission but through it. And along with him the whole of society is living through its fission. As a private individual he would never dream of lending himself to what he considers his duty as an official. As a private individual he would not (and must not) hurt a fly. . . . In short, his affection for Macheath is entirely genuine; the fact that it brings certain business advantages does not render it suspect; too bad that life is always throwing mud at everything. . . .

Hints for actors

As for the communication of this material, the spectator must not be made to adopt the empathetic approach. There must be a process of exchange between spectator and actor, with the latter at bottom addressing himself directly to the spectator despite all the strangeness and detachment. The actor then has to tell the spectator more about his character 'than lies in the part'. He must naturally adopt the attitude which allows the episode to develop easily. At the same time he must also set up relationships with episodes other than those of the story, not just be the story's servant. In a love scene with Macheath, for instance, Polly is not only Macheath's beloved but also Peachum's daughter. Her relations with the spectator must embrace her criticisms of the accepted notions concerning bandits' women and shopkeepers' daughters.

1.* [p. 103] The actors should refrain from depicting these bandits as a collection of those depressing individuals with red neckerchiefs who frequent places of entertainment and with whom no decent person would drink a glass of beer. They are naturally sedate persons, some of them portly and all without exception good mixers when off duty.

2. [p. 103] This is where the actors can demonstrate the practical

---

* These figures refer to numbered passages in our text.

use of bourgeois virtues and the close relationship between dishonesty and sentiment.

3. [p. 104] It must be made clear how violently energetic a man needs to be if he is to create a situation in which a worthier attitude (that of a bridegroom) is possible.

4. [p. 107] What has to be shown here is the displaying of the bride, her fleshliness, at the moment of its final apportionment. At the very instant when supply must cease, demand has once again to be stimulated to its peak. The bride is desired all round; the bridegroom then sets the pace. It is, in other words, a thoroughly theatrical event. At the same time it has to be shown that the bride is hardly eating. How often one sees the daintiest creatures wolfing down entire chickens and fishes! Not so brides.

5. [p. 119] In showing such matters as Peachum's business the actors do not need to bother too much about the normal *development of the plot*. It is, however, important that they should present a development rather than an ambience. The actor playing one of the beggars should aim to show the selection of an appropriately effective wooden leg (trying on one, laying it aside, trying another, then going back to the first) in such a way that people decide to see the play a second time at the right moment to catch this turn; nor is there anything to prevent the theatre featuring it on the screens in the background.

6. [p. 127] It is absolutely essential that the spectator should see Miss Polly Peachum as a virtuous and agreeable girl. Having given evidence of her uncalculating love in the second scene, she now demonstrates that practical-mindedness which saves it from being mere ordinary frivolity.

7. [p. 131] These ladies are in undisturbed possession of their means of production. Just for this reason they must give no impression that they are free. Democracy for them does not represent the same freedom as it does for those whose means of production can be taken away from them.

8. [p. 134] This is where those Macheaths who seem least inhibited from portraying his death agony commonly baulk at singing the third verse. They would obviously not reject the sexual theme if a tragedy had been made of it. But in our day and age sexual themes undoubtedly belong in the realm of comedy; for sex life and social life conflict, and the resulting contradiction is comic because it can only be resolved historically, i.e. under a different social order. So the actor must be able to put across a ballad like this in a comic way. It is very important how sexual life is represented on stage, if

only becuase a certain primitive materialism always enters into it.
The artificiality and transitoriness of all social superstructures
becomes visible.

9. [p. 137] Like other ballades in *The Threepenny Opera* this one
contains a few lines from François Villon in the German version by
K. L. Ammer. The actor will find that it pays to read Ammer's
translation, as it shows the differences between a ballade to be sung
and a ballade to be read.

10. [p. 156] This scene is an optional one designed for those Pollys
who have a gift for comedy.

11. [p. 160] As he paces round his cell the actor playing Macheath
can at this point recapitulate all the ways of walking which he has
so far shown the audience. The seducer's insolent way, the hunted
man's nervous way, the arrogant way, the experienced way and
so on. In the course of this brief stroll he can once again show
every attitude adopted by Macheath in the course of these few
days.

12. [p. 161] This is where the actor of the epic theatre is careful not
to let his efforts to stress Macheath's fear of death and make it
dominate the whole message of the Act, lead him to throw away
the depiction of *true* friendship which follows. (True friendship is
only true if it is kept within limits. The moral victory scored by
Macheath's two truest friends is barely diminished by these two
gentlemen's subsequent moral defeat, when they are not quick
enough to hand over their means of existence in order to save their
friend).

13. [p. 163] Perhaps the actor can find some way of showing the
following: Macheath quite rightly feels that in his case there has
been a gruesome miscarriage of justice. And true enough, if justice
were to lead to the victimisation of any more bandits than it does
at present it would lose what little reputation it has.

About the singing of the songs

When an actor sings he undergoes a change of function. Nothing
is more revolting than when the actor pretends not to notice that
he has left the level of plain speech and started to sing. The three
levels – plain speech, heightened speech and singing – must always
remain distinct, and in no case should heightened speech represent
an intensification of plain speech, or singing of heightened speech.
In no case therefore should singing take place where words are
prevented by excess of feeling. The actor must not only sing but

show a man singing. His aim is not so much to bring out the emotional content of his song (has one the right to offer others a dish that one has already eaten oneself ?) but to show gestures that are so to speak the habits and usage of the body. To this end he would be best advised not to use the actual words of the text when rehearsing, but common everyday phrases which express the same thing in the crude language of ordinary life. As for the melody, he must not follow it blindly: there is a kind of speaking-against-the-music which can have strong effects, the results of a stubborn, incorruptible sobriety which is independent of music and rhythm. If he drops into the melody it must be an event; the actor can emphasise it by plainly showing the pleasure which the melody gives him. It helps the actor if the musicians are visible during his performance and also if he is allowed to make visible preparation for it (by straightening a chair perhaps or making himself up, etc.). Particularly in the songs it is important that 'he who is showing should himself be shown'.

Why does the mounted messenger have to be mounted?

The Threepenny Opera provides a picture of bourgeois society, not just of 'elements of the Lumpenproletariat'. This society has in turn produced a bourgeois structure of the world, and thereby a specific view of the world without which it could scarcely hope to survive. There is no avoiding the sudden appearance of the Royal Mounted Messenger if the bourgeoisie is to see its own world depicted. Nor has Mr Peachum any other concern in exploiting society's bad conscience for gain. Workers in the theatre should reflect just why it is so particularly stupid to deprive the messenger of his *mount*, as nearly every modernistic director of the play has done. After all, if a judicial murder is to be shown, there is surely no better way of paying due tribute to the theatre's rôle in bourgeois society than to have the journalist who establishes the murdered man's innocence towed into court by a swan. Is it not a piece of self-evident tactlessness if people persuade the audience to laugh at itself by making something comic of the mounted messenger's sudden appearance? Depriving bourgeois literature of the sudden appearance of some form of mounted messenger would reduce it to a mere depiction of conditions. The mounted messenger guarantees you a truly undisturbed appreciation of even the most intolerable conditions, so it is a *sine qua non* for a literature whose *sine qua non* is that it leads nowhere.

It goes without saying that the third finale must be played with total seriousness and utter dignity

['Anmerkungen zur "Dreigroschenoper" ', from GW *Schriften zum Theater* p. 991 and *Stücke* p. 992, omitting paragraphs 2 ('Titles and screens') and 6 ('Why does Macheath have to be arrested twice over?'), which refer to Brecht's theatre as a whole rather than to this particular play. For these see *Brecht on Theatre*.]

Stage design for The Threepenny Opera

In *The Threepenny Opera* the more different the set's appearance as between acting and songs, the better its design. For the Berlin production (1928) a great fairground organ was placed at the back of the stage, with steps on which the jazz band was lodged, together with coloured lamps that lit up when the orchestra was playing. Right and left of the organ were two big screens for the projection of Neher's drawings, framed in red satin. Each time there was a song its title was projected on them in big letters, and lights were lowered from the grid. So as to achieve the right blend of patina and newness, shabbiness and opulence, the curtain was a small, none too clean piece of calico running on metal wires. For the Paris production (1937) opulence and patina took over. There was a real satin drapery with gold fringes, above and to the side of which were suspended big fairground lamps which were lit during the songs. The curtain had two figures of beggars painted on it, more than life size, who pointed to the title 'The Threepenny Opera'. Screens with further painted figures of beggars were placed downstage right and left.

Peachum's beggars' outfitting shop

Peachum's shop must be so equipped that the audience is able to grasp the nature of this curious concern. The Paris production had two shop windows in the background containing dummies in beggars' outfits. Inside the shop was a stand from which garments and special headgear were suspended, all marked with white labels and numbers. A small low rack contained a few worn-out shoes, numbered like the garments, of a kind only seen in museums under glass. The Kamerny Theatre in Moscow showed Mr Peachum's clients entering the dressing booths as normal human beings, then leaving them as horrible wrecks.

[‘Aufbau der “Dreigroschenoper”-Bühne’, from GW *Schriften
zum Theater* p. 1000. Dated c. 1937. Taïroff’s production at the
Kamerny Theatre in Moscow took place in 1930. The Paris
designer was Eugène Berman.]

Note by Kurt Weill

ABOUT *The Threepenny Opera* (A PUBLIC LETTER)

Thank you for your letter. I will be glad to say something about
the course on which Brecht and I have embarked with this work,
and which we mean to pursue further.

You speak of *The Threepenny Opera*’s sociological significance.
True enough, the success of our play has shown this new genre not
merely to have come at the right moment in terms of the artistic
situation but also, apparently, to have responded to a positive
longing on the public’s part to see a favourite form of theatre re-
vitalised. I doubt whether our form is going to replace operetta
[. . .]. What really matters to all of us is the establishment of a first
bridgehead in a consumer industry hitherto reserved for a very
different category of writer and musician. *The Threepenny Opera* is
putting us in touch with an audience which was previously ignor-
ant of us, or at least would never have believed us capable of interesting a circle of listeners so much wider than the normal
concert- and opera-going public.

Seen thus, *The Threepenny Opera* takes its place in a movement
which today embraces nearly all the younger musicians. The
abandonment of ‘art for art’s sake’, the reaction against individual-
ism in art, the ideas for film music, the link with the musical youth
movement and, connecting with these, the simplification of musical
means of expression – they are all stages along the same road.

Only opera remains stuck in its ‘splendid isolation’. Its audiences
continue to represent a distinct group of people seemingly outside
the ordinary theatrical audience. Even today new operas incorporate a dramaturgical approach, a use of language, a choice of
themes such as would be quite inconceivable in the modern
theatre. And one is always hearing ‘That’s all very well for the
theatre but it wouldn’t do in opera.’ Opera originated as an aristocratic branch of art, and everything labelled ‘operatic tradition’
goes to underline its basic social character. Nowadays, however,
there is no other artistic form whose attitude is so undisguisedly
social, the theatre in particular having switched conclusively to a

line that can better be termed socially formative. If the operatic framework cannot stand such a comparison with the theatre of the times [*Zeittheater*], then that framework had better be broken up.

Seen in this light, nearly all the worthwhile operatic experiments of recent years emerge as basically destructive in character. *The Threepenny Opera* made it possible to start rebuilding, since it allowed us to go back to scratch. What we were setting out to create was the earliest form of opera. Every musical work for the stage raises the question: what on earth can music, and particularly singing, be doing in the theatre? In our case the answer was of the most primitive possible kind. I had before me a realistic plot, and this forced me to make the music work against it if I was to prevent it from making a realistic impact. Accordingly the plot was either interrupted, making way for music, or else deliberately brought to a point where there was no alternative but to sing. Furthermore it was a play that allowed us for once to take 'opera' as subject-matter for an evening in the theatre. At the outset the audience was told 'Tonight you are going to see an opera for beggars. Because this opera was so opulently conceived as only a beggar's imagination could make it, it is called *The Threepenny Opera*.' And so even the finale to the third Act is in no sense a parody, rather an instance of the very idea of 'opera' being used to resolve a conflict, i.e. being given a function in establishing the plot, and consequently having to be presented in its purest and most authentic form.

This return to a primitive operatic form entailed a drastic simplification of musical language. It meant writing a kind of music that would be singable by actors, in other words by musical amateurs. But if at first this looked like being a handicap, in time it proved immensely enriching. Nothing but the introduction of approachable, catchy tunes made possible *The Threepenny Opera*'s real achievement: the creation of a new type of musical theatre.

['Über die Dreigroschenoper' from Kurt Weill: *Ausgewählte Schriften*, ed. David Drew, Suhrkamp, Frankfurt 1975, p. 54. Originally published in *Anbruch*, Vienna, January 1929, Jg. 11, Nr. 1, p. 24, where Weill was responding to a letter from the editors welcoming the success of a work which so accurately reflected contemporary social and artistic conditions, and asking for his theoretical views.]

Transcript

From a conversation between Brecht and Giorgio Strehler on 25 October 1955 with regard to the forthcoming Milan production. (Taken down by Hans-Joachim Bunge.)

Strehler had prepared twenty-seven precisely formulated questions for Brecht about the production of *The Threepenny Opera*. He began by asking its relation to the original *Beggar's Opera* and the extent of Elisabeth Hauptmann's and Kurt Weill's collaboration.

Brecht and Hauptmann told him that a play had been needed to open the Theater am Schiffbauerdamm under Fischer and Aufricht's direction on 28 August 1928. Brecht was engaged on *The Threepenny Opera*. It was based on a translation made by Elisabeth Hauptmann. The ensuing work with Weill and Elisabeth Hauptmann was a true collaboration and proceeded step by step. Erich Engel agreed to take over the direction. He had directed Brecht's early plays and Brecht had attended many of his rehearsals; he was the best man for an experiment like this. Perhaps the hardest thing was choosing the actors. Brecht went primarily for cabaret and revue performers, who had the advantage of being artistically interested and socially aggressive. During the summer Caspar Neher prepared his designs. According to Brecht the idea underlying *The Threepenny Opera* was: 'criminals are bourgeois: are bourgeois criminals?'.

Strehler asked whether there was any material about the first performance. He was convinced that 'Models' were useful and therefore needed it for his production. The sort of thing that would be of historical interest to him was to know the style of the production and the historical setting of the first performance. He asked if he was right in assuming that Brecht had shifted *The Threepenny Opera* to the Victorian era because of the latter's essentially bourgeois character, which meant that London rather than, say, Paris or Berlin provided the best setting. Brecht replied that from the outset he had wanted, primarily because of the shortage of time, to change the original as little as possible. Transporting it to Paris or some other city would have meant extensive changes in the portrayal of the setting, which in turn would have entailed much additional research. But even the best of principles couldn't be maintained indefinitely, and working on the play had led to the realisation that the original date could usefully be advanced a hundred years. A good deal was known about the Victorian age, which at the same time was remote enough to be judged with critical detachment, thus permitting the audience to pick out what was relevant to them. Set in that period the play would be more easily transported to Berlin than if set in that in which Gay had (of necessity) had to locate it.

Strehler observed that the music which Weill wrote in 1928 was of its own time and therefore evidently in deliberate contrast with the period of the play. Brecht said this was a gain for the theatre. The underlying thought was: beggars are poor people. They want to make a grand opera, but lack money and have to make do as best they can. How to show this? By a splendidly entertaining performance (which at the same time, of course, must lay bare the conditions prevailing at that period) and at the same time by making evident all that which failed to achieve the object intended, frequently indeed producing results actually opposed to it. For instance the beggar actors are quite unable to portray respectability (such as ought to be particularly easy in a Victorian setting), so that there are continual lapses, particularly in the songs. The grand manner at which they are aiming goes wrong, and suddenly it all turns into a dirty joke. This isn't what the beggar actors want, but the audience loves it and applauds, with the result that it all keeps slipping further into the gutter. They are alarmed by this, but all the same it works. Their plan to create a grand theatre proves impossible to realise. Because of their restricted means it only half comes off. (Here again the Victorian age gives the right picture.) In such a beggar's opera decency would be no inducement to the audience to stay in its seats; its preferences are accordingly respected. Only the finale has once again been carefully rehearsed, so that the level originally aimed at can at least be achieved here. Yet even this is a failure, for it succeeds only as parody. In short there is a perpetual effort to present something grandiose, but each time it is a fiasco. All the same a whole series of truths emerge.

Brecht gave an instance: unemployed actors trying to portray the Geneva conference. Unfortunately they have a quite wrong idea of it, and so with the best will in the world all their crocodile-like efforts to present Mr Dulles, for instance, as a Christian martyr are a failure, because they have no proper notion either of Mr Dulles or of a Christian martyr. Whatever they do is successful only in making people laugh. But to laugh is to criticise.

Strehler suggested that *The Beggar's Opera* was originally aristocratic in both form and content, a skit on Handel's operas for instance. Brecht had kept its form and its sense. All this was still valid in 1928. Capitalist society was still on its feet then, as was grand opera. Meantime there had been a war, but the problems had remained in many ways generally the same. Today however there were distinctions that must be made. Its relevance would still apply as forcefully in Italy and similar capitalist countries.

Brecht agreed. He thought the play ought to have the same power of attack in contemporary Italy as it had had at the time in Berlin.

Strehler asked how far was *The Threepenny Opera* an epic play and how epic ought the production to be.

Brecht emphasised that both considerations to a great extent applied. The socially critical stance must not be abandoned for a moment. The main prop here was the music, which kept on destroying the illusion; the latter, however, had first to be created, since an atmosphere could never be destroyed until it had been built up.

Strehler expressed regret that so many *Threepenny Opera* productions had been prettified. Not that its socially critical aspects could be entirely camouflaged, but it had remained a nice theatrical revolution which failed to get across the footlights, not unlike those lions that can be safely visited in zoos, where you are protected from attacks by iron bars. The average director made concessions to his audience, and it wasn't going to pay 2,000 lire to have filth thrown at it. The way *The Threepenny Opera* was normally performed, like an elegant Parisian opera, everybody found it 'nice'.

Brecht explained that when *The Threepenny Opera* was originally staged in Germany in 1928 it had a strong political and aesthetic impact. Among its successful results were:

1. The fact that young proletarians suddenly came to the theatre, in some cases for the first time, and then quite often came back.
2. The fact that the top stratum of the bourgeoisie was made to laugh at its own absurdity. Having once laughed at certain attitudes, it would never again be possible for these particular representatives of the bourgeoisie to adopt them.

The Threepenny Opera can still fulfil the same function in capitalist countries today so long as people understand how to provide entertainment and, at the same time, bite instead of mere cosy absurdity. The important point now being: look, beggars are being fitted out. Every beggar is a monstrosity. The audience must be appalled at its own complicity in such poverty and wretched-ness.

Strehler asked if Brecht could suggest any ways of ensuring that The Threepenny Opera should be as artistically effective and topically relevant in 1955 as in 1928. Brecht replied that he would heighten the crooks' make-up and render it more unpleasant. The romantic songs must be sung as beautifully as possible, but the falsity of this 'attempt at a romantic island where everything in the garden is lovely' needed to be strongly underlined.

Strehler was anxious to get material about the set, but what his Milan production most needed was some suggestions about costumes, since he felt that the 1928 costumes, which so far as he knew were based wholly on the Victorian era, would no longer be of use to him. Brecht corrected him, saying that far from being Victorian the 1928 costumes had been gathered from the costumiers and were a complete mixture. He would not think of abandoning the use of rhyme as in The Beggar's Opera, nor, with it, the 'jazzed up Victorianism' of the Berlin production. In the Moscow production Taïroff had entirely modernised the costumes so as to conjure up the (by Moscow standards) exotic appeal of Paris fashions.

Brecht said that Strehler had the right picture: up went the curtain on a brothel, but it was an utterly bourgeois brothel. In the brothel there were whores, but there was no mystique about them, they were utterly bourgeois whores. Everything is done to make things proper and lawful.

Strehler asked how far The Threepenny Opera was a satire on grand opera, to which Brecht replied: only in so far as grand opera still persists, but that this had never been so important in Germany as in Italy. The starting point must always be a poor theatre trying to do its best.

Strehler asked what did Brecht think about adaptation to bring it up to date. Brecht thought such a procedure acceptable. Strehler's question sprang from the fact that it would be impossible, for instance, to stage The Threepenny Opera in Naples using Kurt Weill's music. However, in Milan there were parallels with the reign of Umberto I which would be brought out. To this extent Milan was comparable with London, while the popular note struck by the music would have the same reception as in Berlin. The bourgeoisie was the same. But Strehler wondered if the need to Italianise the names might not eliminate the necessary critical detachment: for 'one must bare one's teeth for the truth'.

Brecht wondered if it might not be possible to set The Threepenny

Opera in the Italian quarter of New York around 1900 perhaps. The music would be right too. He had not gone into the question as yet but at the moment he thought it a possible transposition. The New York Italians had brought everything, including their emotions, from back home, but it had all got commercialised. There would be a brothel, but one like at home, to which they'd go because they felt it was 'like being back at mamma's'.

Strehler took this idea further and asked if it wouldn't mean adding a prologue. Here again Brecht agreed, in so far as some explanation would be needed. It would have to be established that the New York beggar actors were a group of Italians, that it was all like in Milan but a long way off. The first skyscrapers could have been built, but the group must be wretchedly poor. All they want to do is to stage something 'like back home'.

Strehler had a suggestion for the prologue. A film of Milan could be shown, leading the actors to want to perform something recalling that city, whereupon the curtain would rise and the play begin.

Another reservation of Strehler's concerned the Italian actor's penchant for improvisation. 'You send someone off to choose a costume and he comes back with fifty.' There was also the problem of 'the epic style of portrayal'. According to Strehler it is not easy for the Italian actor to play on more than one level at a time, i.e. roughly to the effect that 'I am acting a man trying to act this character.' He asked if it was at all possible to perform Brecht's plays – e.g. *The Mother*, which he described as the 'stronghold of the epic theatre' – except in an epic manner, and where if anywhere they could be performed if one had no actors or directors who had been trained for them. 'What is the result of acting them in the wrong way?' Brecht: 'They can certainly be performed, but what emerges is normal theatre, and three-quarters of the fun is lost.'

Strehler wanted some advice about what to do with actors who knew nothing about epic theatre. He asked if it was possible to perform a Brecht play given only *one* actor familiar with the epic theatre, and he inquired about methods for teaching the epic way of acting.

Brecht told Strehler not to worry and that our own acting too was only partly epic. It always worked best in comedies, since they anyway entail a measure of alienation. The epic style of portrayal was more easily achieved there, so that it was a good idea generally to stage plays more or less as comedies. He suggested using an aid which he had tried himself: having the actors intersperse what he called 'bridge verses', thus turning their speech into a report in indirect speech; i.e. interspersing the sentences with 'said he's. 'What's bad is that "epic" cannot be achieved without using the dialectic.'

Strehler said he was convinced that nowadays it was impossible to act either Shakespeare or the earlier tragedies without alienation if their performance was to be useful and entertaining.

Brecht once again suggested acting tragic scenes for their comic effect. What is most epic, he maintained, is always the run-throughs, and they should certainly be scheduled for the end of the rehearsals or better still conducted at regular intervals throughout the whole rehearsal period. 'The nearer the performance gets to being a run-through, the more epic it will be.' Strehler asked if his way of explaining epic portrayal to his actors was the right one, when he would cite the example of a director acting a scene, show-ing the actors in outline how to do something and all the time having his explanations ready even if he never voices them. Brecht approved of this and thought that the actors too could be put in the director's situation if one instituted run-throughs with minimal use of gesture, so that everyone simply noted how things should go.

Strehler feared that his *Threepenny Opera* production might turn out 'neither fish nor fowl'. His sense of responsibility had held him back from doing *Mother Courage*, since he was unable to find an epic actress to play the title part. This production of *The Threepenny Opera* too was something that he had been planning for years and always had to put off because of a shortage of suitable actors.

['Über eine Neuinszenierung der Dreigroschenoper', from *Bertolt Brechts Dreigroschenbuch* (Suhrkamp, Frankfurt 1960) pp. 130–134. Strehler's production for the Piccolo Teatro, Milan, in 1957 eventually transposed the play to an American setting around the time of the First World War, with the police as Keystone Kops and an early motor car on stage. Brecht and Elisabeth Hauptmann thought it excellent.

At the Geneva Conference of summer 1954 the Western powers, China and the Soviet Union agreed to create two Viet-nams, North and South. John Foster Dulles was then U.S. Secretary of State. King Umberto I's reign in Italy was from 1878 to 1900.]

Editorial Notes

Though there is little in the way of manuscript material or notes to show just how it evolved, *The Threepenny Opera* was clearly one of Brecht's more rapidly written works. Its producer Aufricht only took over the Theater am Schiffbauerdamm at the end of 1927, and it must have been in March or April 1928 that he and his dramaturg Heinrich Fischer went to Brecht in search of a play. What Brecht then offered them – apparently as his own work and under the title *Gesindel* or *Scum* – was a translation of *The Beggar's Opera* which Elisabeth Hauptmann had almost completed; he is said to have shown them the first two scenes. Nothing of this first script has come down to us, and there is no real evidence that Brecht himself had as yet taken any hand in it. The process of 'adaptation' credited to him by the original programme probably only started once the play itself and the principle of a collaboration with Weill had been accepted. Erich Engel, with whom Brecht had been working on the Berlin *Man equals Man*, was already earmarked as the play's director.

The next event seems to have been the production of a stage script which was duplicated by Brecht's and Hauptmann's agents, Felix Bloch Erben, and presumably represented the work done by the collaborators in the south of France that summer. Its title is given as 'The Beggar's Opera / Die Luden-Oper [The Ragamuffins' Opera] / translated by Elisabeth Hauptmann / German adaptation: Bert Brecht. Music: Kurt Weill'. Though its text is still a good way from the final version it already represents a considerable transformation of the original. Several subsequently discarded characters from Gay's original still remain (notably Mrs Coaxer and her girls), but Lockit has already been purged, together with all that part of the plot involving him, and replaced by the rather more up-to-date figure of Brown. Peachum's manipulation of the beggars is also new, as are the first stable and second gaol scenes. The main items retained from Gay in this script are, in our present

numbering, scenes 1, 3, 4, 5 (which is not yet a brothel but a room
in the hotel), 6, 8 and the principle of the artificial happy ending
There are no scene titles. However, Macheath's final speech before
his execution is already there, much as in our version, as are several
of the songs: Peachum's Morning Hymn (whose melody is in fact
a survivor from the original, being that of Gay's opening song),
Pirate Jenny, the Cannon Song, the Barbara Song, the Tango-
Ballade, the Jealousy Duet, Lucy's subsequently cut aria (in scene
8), the Call from the Grave and the Ballad in which Macheath Begs
All Men for Forgiveness; also the final chorus. Most of these are
not given in full, but only by their titles, and some may not yet
have been completed. There are also two of Gay's original songs,
as well as two translations from Kipling: 'The Ladies' and 'Mary,
Pity Women'. Neither the Gay nor the Kipling songs were, so far
as anybody knows, set by Weill, but the latter may explain why the
original programme spoke of 'interpolated songs . . . by Rudyard
Kipling'.

This script was altered and added to in the course of the rehearsals, when texts of several of the songs were stuck in and the
rest added. The piano score, which includes all the present songs
apart from the Ballad of Sexual Obsession, was published not long
after the première, the text in Brecht's *Versuche 3* only in 1931. This
1931 text has remained virtually unaltered, though Brecht appended a certain amount of alternative material later, and is to all
intents and purposes that used for our translation.

2. THE 1928 STAGE SCRIPT

ACT ONE

Scene 1

The dramatis personae originally included Gay's Mrs Coaxer and
Suky Tawdry; Jenny was Jenny Diver, as in Gay, which Brecht
later rendered 'Spelunken-Jenny' or literally 'Low Den Jenny',
perhaps on the assumption that 'Diver' meant a habituée of dives.
The script starts the play without any scene title and with the
following stage directions:

> *Mr Peachum's house. It is 7 am. Peachum is standing at a desk on which
> lie a ledger and a Bible. Round the walls are notices with such sayings as
> 'Give and it shall be given unto you', 'Close not thine ear to misery', 'You
> will benefit from the interests of a powerful organisation' and 'If you are
> satisfied tell the others, if you are dissatisfied tell me'.*

Peachum sings his Morning Hymn, then:

> So. Now, one glance at the Bible and then to work. Matthew
> 5. I'm always combing Matthew for something I can use. No
> good. I'll have to cut it out once and for all. Salt without an
> egg. Matthew 6: feeble, feeble. No personality there. Wait.
> Verse 25: Give and it shall be given unto you. Flat, but it's
> been used already. Proverbs is still the best, particularly
> chapter 6. All kinds of useful lessons, if a bit old-fashioned.
> Yes, a business man like me, Robert Jeremiah Peachum and
> Co., who's forced to live among thieves, whores and lawyers,
> cannot do without God. Or let's say, without God and ac-
> countancy. We must add to that application, seriousness,
> circumspection, genius and economy. Not to mention early
> rising and kindness and loyalty . . .

This leads to Filch's entrance, after which the dialogue continues
much as now up to the production of outfit C (p. 98). There is then
no showcase with wax dummies; instead Mrs Peachum '*drags out a
box full of indescribably ragged clothes*'. Instead of Peachum's
speech exhibiting the various outfits Filch is simply told to 'Take
off your clothes' etc. (p. 98), and these then become outfit A, the
young man who has seen better days.

Filch removes his socks under protest (p. 99), and then as Mrs
Peachum brings in the screen Peachum asks, much as in Gay's
scene 4:

> Did that fellow Macheath come round yesterday? The one
> who's always coming when I'm out?
> MRS PEACHUM: Certainly, Bobby dear. There's no finer gentle-
> man. If he comes from the Cuttlefish Bar at any reasonable
> hour we're going to a little hop with him – the Captain, Polly,
> Bob the Saw and me. Bobby, my Dear, is the Captain rich?

The dialogue remains close to Gay's (which we will make identifi-
able by its use of capital letters for nouns, as in German), down to
Mrs Peachum's statement of her concern about Polly (which comes
just before her first song in *The Beggar's Opera*). Then Filch appears
in his new begging outfit and asks for a few tips (p. 100).

> PEACHUM *inspects him, then to Mrs Peachum:* Half-wit? Yes,
> that'll be the best thing. *To Filch:* Nobody stupid can play the
> half-wit, you know. Come back this evening . . .

etc. (which is not in Gay). But after his 'Fifty per cent!' Peachum

says 'To come back to Polly . . .' and returns to a cross between
Gay's text and ours. Thus:

> A handsome Wench in our way of Business is as profitable as
> at the Bar of a *Temple* Coffee-House. You should try to in-
> fluence the girl in the right direction. In any thing but Mar-
> riage! After that, my Dear, how shall we be safe? You must
> imagine we can live on air. The way you chuck your daughter
> around anyone would think I'm a millionaire. The fellow
> would have us in his clutches in three shakes. In his clutches!
> Do you think your daughter can hold her tongue in bed any
> better than you? *Polly* is Tinder, and a Spark will at once set
> her on a Flame. Married! All she can think about is her own
> Pleasure, not her own Profit. Do you suppose we nurtured her
> at our breast . . .?

MRS PEACHUM: Our?

PEACHUM: All right, you nurtured her; but did you nurture her
so we should have no crust to eat in our old age? Married! I
expect my daughter to be to me as bread to the hungry – *He
leafs through the book.* – it even says so in the Bible somewhere.
Anyway marriage is disgusting. I'll teach her to get married.

MRS PEACHUM: Dear Bobby, you're just a barbarian. You're
being unfair to her. She is doing exactly what any decent girl
would do: a few Liberties for the Captain in the interest of the
business.

PEACHUM: But 'tis your Duty, my Dear, as her mother, to
explain to the girl what she owes to herself, or to us, which
amounts to the same thing. I'll go to her this moment and sift
her.

At this point, corresponding to the end of Gay's scene 4, Peachum
moves on to what became part of his long speech on p. 98, the
complaints of client no. 136, then goes out telling Mrs Peachum to
get on with ironing in the wax. Left alone, as in Gay's scene 5, she
says:

> God, was Bobby worked up! I can't say I blame him, though;
> I can't say I blame him.

Peachum returns, and the final exchanges are as in our text, less the
song.

Scene 2

Again there is no title (this applies throughout the stage script), but
the stage direction says '*Empty stable. 5 pm the next day. It is fairly*

dark. Enter Macheath with Matt of the Mint and Polly.' There is nothing in Gay corresponding to this scene.

The dialogue starts as in our text, roughly as far as Ned's 'Dear Polly' (p. 104), though without the lines in which Macheath shows his ignorance of Peachum. After Ned says this Mac, having knocked his hat off, '*shoves him against the wall, pushing his face with the flat of his hand – a favourite manoeuvre*'. Thence it continues as now down to Polly's inquiry 'Was the whole lot stolen? (p. 104).

MACHEATH: Stolen? Selected! Anybody can steal, and everybody does. But selecting the right items . . . That's where art comes in. What incompetence! [etc. as now, p. 105].

Thereafter the dialogue is much as now down to Jimmy's 'Hey, Captain, the cops!' (p. 108), though there is no mention of Jenny Diver by Jake (p. 107). Jimmy's exclamation this time heralds Brown's entrance, not that of the Rev. Kimball (who does not appear at all), and it turns out it is Brown's prospective son-in-law the Duke of Devonshire who is the stable's owner: 'Did it have to be Teddy's stable?' says Brown. 'At this of all times?' Mac welcomes him with 'Sit down, you old bugger and pitch into the egg mayonnaise' (cf. p. 113). He observes the origins of the plates and the eggs, then listens to the gang sing 'Bill Lawgen' (which is not from the original) and comments on the salmon:

Clark's, the fishmongers. Breaking and entering reported this morning. Tastes delicious.

This is where Polly performs 'Pirate Jenny', which provokes the same reactions as in our text, apart from its references to Rev. Kimball. After 'let's not have any more of it' (p. 112) Mac goes straight on with 'You have today in your midst . . .' (p. 113), the speech leading into the Cannon Song. Only the title of this is given, but its first version had already been written some years earlier and published in the *Devotions for the Home* under the title 'Song of the Three Soldiers'; it is sometimes, on no clear grounds, described as 'after Kipling'.

After the song the text is much as now down to Brown's 'There's nothing whatsoever on record against you at Scotland Yard' (p. 115), apart from the interpolation at the end of Macheath's long speech (p. 114) of 'Cheers, Brown! And now for some music! – at which '*Everything is cleared to one side. Three of the guests take it in turns to form a little jazz band.*' This prepares the way for the

dance which concludes the scene. During it Macheath stands in the
centre and says:

> My dear friends. Let us bring this day to a worthy conclusion
> by conducting ourselves as gentlemen.
> WALTER *dancing with Polly*: Oh, stuff this day.

After which 'The party continues in full swing. Once again we hear the
chorus "Bill Lawgen and Mary Syer"' – i.e. not the present Love
Duet.

Scene 3

This starts close to Gay's scene 6, with indications of some in-
timacy between Mrs Peachum and Filch:

> *Mr Peachum's office. Morning. Mrs Peachum. Filch.*
> MRS PEACHUM: Come hither, *Filch*. I am as fond of this Child,
> as though my Mind misgave me he were my own. Why are
> you so sad? Can your mamma not help?
> FILCH *tonelessly*: Oh dear, I can't regard you as my mamma,
> Mrs Peachum, even though I shouldn't say it.

He says how hard it is to beg, and regrets his choice of profession.
She wants him to find out about Macheath and Polly, who has now
been away from home for three days. Filch knows, but as in Gay
has promised not to tell:

> MRS PEACHUM: Right, Filch, you shall go with me into my own
> Room, Filch. You shall tell me the whole Story in comfort,
> Filchy, and I'll give thee a Glass of Cordial Médoc that I keep
> locked up in my bedside table for my own drinking. *Exeunt.*

Peachum enters with Polly, and Gay's scene 7 follows, including
Polly's song 'Virgins are like the fair Flower', whose text is translated in toto. Mrs Peachum then appears, but without her song
from the original, and goes straight into her opening speech of the
scene in our version. A shortened version of Gay's scene 8 dialogue
follows, down to where Peachum pinches Polly, asking 'Are you
really bound Wife to him, or are you only upon liking?'; he forbids
Macheath the house, and Polly (in lieu of 'Can Love be control'd
by Advice?') goes into the Barbara Song (which expands and up-
dates the same theme, and whose text is given in full). Mrs
Peachum's faint (p. 119) then follows much as in Gay, though now
she asks for the Cordial and doubts Polly's 'Readiness and Concern'.

Only one beggar then enters, who proves to be the disgruntled no. 136. 'First-class stains, Mr Twantry,' says Polly, handing over the criticised outfit. The problem now, as in Gay's scene 10, is: how is Polly to live. Peachum answers 'It's all perfectly simple' etc. as now (p. 120), and Polly's refusal to consider divorce follows. Then back, more or less, to Gay:

> PEACHUM: Yes, yes, yes. You're a silly little goose. But it's all so simple. You secure what he's got; I get him hanged at the next Sessions, and then at once you are made a charming Widow.
> POLLY: What, murder the Man I love! The Blood runs cold at my Heart with the very thought of it. But it would be murder!
> PEACHUM: Murder? Rubbish. Self-defence. It's all self-defence. My position in the world is one of self-defence.

– this last, crucial idea being new. Mrs Peachum then reminds Polly of her filial duties, as in Gay, and refers to 'Those cursed Play-Books she reads' before threatening to 'tan her behind' (p. 120). Peachum's last word is 'Polly, you will get a divorce!'

The rest of the scene is not in Gay. It strikes eleven, and a crowd of beggars streams in – 'The second shift,' says Peachum. They arrive decently dressed, but change into their begging outfits, stumps, bandages etc. This introduces the present dialogue from the speech of complaint half-way down p. 119 down to 'This one will do,' with the addition of a tirade by Peachum against his daughter. Mrs Peachum's speech 'Anyway, he's got several women' (p. 121) follows, after which the dialogue continues much as ours down to Polly's 'There's nothing on record against Mac at Scotland Yard' (p. 122):

> PEACHUM: Right. Then put on your hat, and we will go to Mr Brown. *To his wife:* And you'll go to Turnbridge. For the villainy of the world is great, and a man needs to run his legs off to keep them from being stolen from under him.
> POLLY: I, Papa, shall be delighted to shake hands with Mr Brown again.

But in lieu of the First Act finale, Polly then sings a translation of Gay's song against lawyers, 'A Fox may steal your Hens, Sir'.

ACT TWO

Scene 4 [1 in script]

This is set as '*Stable. Morning. Macheath. Enter Walter.*' The two men start with a version of the Peachum–Filch dialogue from Gay's Act 1, scene 2. Black Moll becomes 'Blattern-Molly' [Pockmarked Molly], who can be 'back on the beat tomorrow', says Macheath. Betty Sly is 'Betriebs-Betty' [Busy Betty]. Tom Gagg is unchanged. After Gay's line 'There is nothing to be got by the Death of Women, except our Wives' Walter (not Filch) is sent with a message to Newgate, having first been told to look through the storeroom to see if there are any decent clothes. Mrs Trapes needs them 'to clothe five young pigeons to work Kensington Street'. On his exit Polly enters as at the start of our scene, whose opening dialogue approximately follows, as far as the entry of the gang (p. 127). Once again, the listing of the gang members (p. 126) derives from Peachum's speech in Act 1 scene 3 of the original, and includes such figures as Harry Paddington, Slippery Sam ('Schleicher-Samuel') and Tom Tipple ('Tippel-Tom'). The poetic naming of 'Bob the Pickpocket alias Gorgon alias Bluff-Robert alias Carbuncle alias Robert the Saw' is mainly from Gay, but Brecht makes him the gang member Polly likes best. The speech about Jack Poole and banking is not in the script; the list simply ends, and Polly says her 'Why, Mac!' etc. as on p. 127, to introduce the gang's entry.

Their first exchanges are somewhat different, to where Mac tells them of his 'little trip' (p. 127). He and they then go into the storeroom while Polly delivers a monologue; there is no demonstration of her authority over the gang. They re-enter, and Mac resumes 'The rotten part of it is' etc. (p. 128) down to 'toffs are all drunk'. Robert follows with 'Ma'am, while your husband is away', etc.; Polly says 'goodbye, Mr Robert' and shakes hands; then they leave as on page 129. Her dialogue with Macheath follows as now, as far as 'Highgate Heath' (middle of page):

> POLLY: Then everything is all right. Goodbye, Mac.
> MAC: Goodbye, Polly. *He shuts the door behind here. Lighting a pipe:* Polly is most confoundedly bit. Now I must have Women. There is nothing unbends the Mind like them. Cocktails are not nearly such a help.

– the last sentence being Brecht's gloss on Gay's lines. He then opens the storeroom door and tells Walter to assemble the Drury

Lane ladies for him at 8 pm in Room 5 of the Cuttlefish Hotel (equivalent to the Tavern near Newgate of Gay's Act 2).

> MAC: Hurry! *Exit Walter.* This London owes me something for having fixed it up with a capital lot of women.

He speaks the final rhymed couplet, which our text gives to Polly, and there is no Interlude.

Scene 5 [2 in script]

> *Cuttlefish Hotel. 8 pm. Room 5. Mac and Walter.*
> MACHEATH *rings.*
> WALTER: Captain?
> MAC: How long am I to wait for the ladies?
> WALTER: They're bound to be here soon.

Macheath then sings 'The Ballad of the Ladies', translated from Kipling (and now included in GW *Gedichte* p. 1052). The bell rings again, and they troop in, the complete party from Gay's Act 2 scene 4: Mrs Coaxer, Dolly Trull, Mrs Vixen, Betty Doxy, Jenny Diver, Mrs Slammekin, Suky Tawdry and Molly Brazen, with Walter bringing up the rear. Macheath makes approximately the same speech of welcome as there, down to where the music strikes up 'the *French* Tune', i.e. the Cotillon. Molly: 'Ach, cash makes you randy' (a phrase of Brecht's which comes in others of his plays); then in lieu of the Cotillon the ladies *dance a little "Step"*', and Gay's dialogue follows, down to Mrs Vixen's 'to think too well of your friends'. Mac interrupts it with his 'Nice underwear you've got there, Vixen,' introducing our present dialogue down to Second Whore's 'I just don't wear any' (p. 133). Gay takes over again with the exchange between Mac and Jenny, which leads, however, not to her 'Before the Barn-Door crowing' song but to 'the brothel-ballade by François Villon', as yet without its text. The hand-reading episode follows as in our text from Dolly's first line down to Mac's 'Go on!' (p. 132), after which Jenny says she cannot do so, and then disarms him, aided as in Gay by Suky Tawdry. It is, however, Mrs, not Mr Peachum who enters with the constables, and she then makes very much the Peachum speech from Act 2 scene 5 of the original. Walter, who has been sitting reading, runs out like Jake in our text, and all exeunt '*most ceremoniously*'.

Scene 6 [3 in script]

This is described as 'Prison in Newgate. Brown sitting impatiently in a cell'. The scene begins as in our text, down to Brown's exit (p. 136). Gay's Act 2 scene 7 then follows, with Smith filling Lockit's rôle. Left alone, Macheath makes his speech 'That miserable Brown . . .' as in our text (p. 136), but instead of the exchange with Smith he then continues 'But the worst of it . . .' (p. 136) as far as 'into a tiger', after which he goes on much as in Gay's scene 8:

> I shall have a fine time on't betwixt this and my Execution. Here must I (all Day long) be confin'd to hear the Reproaches of a Wench who lays her Ruin at my Door – just when a prisoner has some right at least to peace and solitude. But here she comes: Lucy, and I cannot get from her. Wou'd I were deaf!

Lucy enters and upbraids Macheath, as in Gay's scene 9, whose dialogue is then approximately followed, omitting the three songs, down to the end of that scene: Lucy's cry 'Oh Mac, I only want to become an honest woman,' as in our text (p. 138). After that she 'sings the song "Maria, Fürsprecherin der Frauen"', i.e. Kipling's 'Mary, Pity Women', whose translation follows in full, and is also given in GW Gedichte p. 1055.

The next section is not in Gay: Lucy continues 'Oh, Macheath, I do hope you will lift my troubles from my shoulders.'

MAC: Of course. As I said: as soon as I'm master of my own decisions.
LUCY: But how are you going to get free? My father truly was your best friend, and even if you played a dirty trick on him over me he can't realise it. So what is he after you for?
MAC: Don't talk to me about your father.
LUCY: But I just don't understand what could have led him to put you in irons. There's some secret involving Peachum and his making such an awful threat that Daddy fainted on hearing it.
MAC: If that's so it's all up with me.
LUCY: No, no, you must become master of your decisions. My whole life depends on it. You must do all right, Mac. You'll end up all right, Mac.

Polly then appears as in Gay's Act 2 scene 13 (middle p. 138), his dialogue being followed approximately as far as the song 'How happy could I be with either?' Instead of this song, however, 'Polly and Lucy sing "Come on out, you Rose of Old Soho" ' (whose title only is given, and which could well relate also to the next song 'I am bubbled, I'm bubbled, O how I am troubled'). Then Gay's dialogue is resumed as far as Peachum's entrance at the end of the scene, but prolonging the Polly–Lucy dialogue as in our text from Lucy's 'What's that? What's that?' (p. 142) to Mac's 'Polly!'. Peachum's entrance is then replaced by that of Mrs Peachum, who drags Polly off much as he did in Gay's scene 14, after which scene 15 is followed for much of the exchanges between Macheath and Lucy, down to her 'It's wonderful the way you say that. Say it again' (p. 143). On his saying that she must help him she embroiders Gay's original thus:

> If only I knew what was the matter with my father. Anyway the constables are all drunk and it's the coronation tomorrow and my father sent someone out for fifteen bottles of gin and when he didn't come back at once his worries overcame him and he upped and drank a whole bottle of the housekeeper's scent. Now he's lying drunk as a lord beside his desk muttering 'Mackie!' If I can find the key shall I escape with you, darling?

They leave together as at the end of Gay's Act. Then a new concluding episode follows, starting with a 'gentle knock' and Brown's voice calling 'Mac!' (p. 143). Peachum appears much as in our text, though without his opening remarks to Smith, and our dialogue follows as far as his 'People are sure to say . . . that the police shouldn't have let him escape' (p. 144). He rounds off this speech with 'A pity: the coronation might have passed off without a single ugly incident.'

BROWN: What is that supposed to mean?
PEACHUM: That as it is the poorest of the poor won't let themselves be done out of attending the coronation tomorrow morning.
BROWN: What do you mean by the poorest of the poor?
PEACHUM: It is reasonable to assume that I mean beggars. You see, it is like this. These poorest of the poor – give and it shall be given unto you, and so on – have nothing in the world apart from celebrations. Well, there are various possibilities. Of course there has to be a criminal. What happens to him is less important. Either they want to see a murderer hanged or they want to see one crowned. All the rest is immaterial.

BROWN: Look here, Mr Peachum, what do you mean by a
murderer being crowned?

PEACHUM: Same as you do, Mr Brown.

BROWN: That's outrageous.

PEACHUM: Quite right, that's outrageous.

BROWN: You have given yourself away, Peachum. Hey,
Smith!

PEACHUM: Don't bring him into this. Or I'll be awkward.
There'll be a lot happening tomorrow morning. The papers
will report how in the morning fog an unusual number of poor
people of all kinds could be observed in the twisting alleys,
patriots all of them with joyous faces and little signs round
their necks: 'I gave my leg for the king', or 'My arm lies on
Clondermell Field', or 'Three cheers for the king; the Royal
Artillery made me deaf'. And all these patriots with just one
objective, the streets the coronation procession will take.
Drily: Of course any of these people would much prefer, just
supposing there could be an execution of a really well-known
and reasonably popular murderer around the same hour, to
attend that, as it is always more agreeable to see murderers
hanged than crowned. Your servant, Brown. *Exit.*

BROWN: Now only the mailed fist can help. Sergeants! Report
to me at the double!

There is no Second Act finale in the script.

ACT THREE

Scene 7 [1 in script]

The setting is *'Peachum's Beggars' Outfitting Shop. 5 am'*, and a
Salvation Army hymn is being played *off*. Beggars are dressing.
Great activity. Peachum is not on, so his opening remark (of our
text) occurs later. Otherwise the dialogue is close to ours as far as
Brown's entrance (p. 150), except that the Ballad of Sexual Ob-
session is not included, nor the dialogue following it down to Mrs
Peachum's appearance with the tray (p. 149). Instead there is an
exchange between a phony cripple and an authentic one. When
Brown enters he *'appears to have been transformed into a tiger'*,
and goes round *'spreading alarm like a great beast of prey'*. His big
opening speech starting 'Here we are. And now, Mr Beggar's
Friend' (p. 150) goes on:

> In the very earliest times – listen, now just you think about it –
> humanity understood the idea of friendship. Even the most
> bestial examples – look carefully – felt the urge to acquire a
> friend. And whatever they may have done in that grey pre-
> historic age they stood by their comrades. Thigh to thigh they
> sat in danger, arm in arm they went through this vale of tears,
> and whatever they grabbed they shared, man to man: think
> about it. And that is what I feel too, just as I've described
> it. I too, despite all weakness and temptation place a value on
> friendship, and I too . . .
>
> PEACHUM: Good morning, Brown, good morning.

The speech echoes Brecht's early 'Ballad of Friendship' (*Poems
1913–1956*, p. 52), and after it the dialogue remains close to ours
from Peachum's remark (p. 150) to his 'You see, Brown' (p. 151)
immediately before the music, though omitting the ten lines before
the drum-roll. Then he goes on to tell Brown that the beggars are
fakes, just a few young people dressing up to celebrate having a
king once more, and concludes 'I've nothing against it; it was quite
harmless.' When no sound follows he repeats this remark. Then '*a
kind of band is heard playing an excruciating "Step"* '.

> BROWN: What's that?
> PEACHUM: Dance music.
> *Beggars and whores 'steppen'* [*dance a 'step'*].
> PEACHUM: Take off those chains, Smith. Yes, this is how the
> poor enjoy themselves . . .

He goes up to Brown and says:

> As for you, Brown, your situation is no laughing matter. This
> is a little dance, but in Drury Lane it is bloody serious. You
> see, there are so many poor people. Thousands of them. When
> you see them standing outside the Abbey . . .

and so on, roughly as in our text from the foot of p. 152 to Brown's
exit a page later. Then the *Step* breaks off, the beggars gather
round Peachum, and he makes them a long speech saying how
much he has done for them. Pointing out how the rich cannot bear
seeing people collapse from hunger because they are frightened
that it might happen to them too – their one vulnerable point – he
concludes 'Tomorrow will show whether poverty can overcome
the crimes of those on top.' And '*the beggars feverishly start getting
ready*'. End of scene.

Scene 8 [2 in script]

This corresponds to our optional scene, and it derives from Gay's Act 3 scenes 7 to 10. It starts thus, with the 'Lucy's Aria' whose setting by Weill is given as an appendix to the miniature score of 1972.

> *Newgate. Lucy's bedroom above the cells. Lucy is drinking non-stop.*
>
> LUCY: Jealousy, Rage, Passion and Likewise Fear are tearing me to pieces, a prey to the raging tempest, tormented by worry! I have the Rats-bane ready. For the past day she has come here every hour wanting to speak with me. Oh, what a two-faced bitch! No doubt she wants to come and gloat at my desperation. O world! How evil the human race! But that lady doesn't know who she is dealing with. Drinking my gin is not going to help her have a high old time with her Mackie afterwards. She'll die thanks to my gin! It's here that I'd like to see her writhing! I rescue him from hanging, and is this creature to skim off the cream? Once that slut has drunk the poison, then let the world breathe freely!

Thereafter the dialogue generally follows Gay's (omitting his songs) down to Polly's 'I hear, my dear *Lucy*, our Husband is one of these.' Brecht then interpolates:

> LUCY: I'll never be anything but a common trollop of the lowest sort. And why? Because I fail to put everything on a business footing.
>
> POLLY: But my dear, that's a misfortune could occur to any woman.

They continue with the original dialogue, past Lucy's offer of the drink, as far as her 'unless 'tis in private' in Gay's scene 10. Then Polly excuses herself, saying she is hungry. The next passage is close to our text from Polly *'gaily'* (p. 158) to Lucy's 'They've caught him once more' just before the end of our scene, but with some small changes and one or two additions, of which the most notable is after 'Really, I don't deserve it' (p. 158):

> LUCY: It's so unfair that one must use such means to keep a man; but it's one's heart, Polly. But enough of that.
> *She takes the gin bottle and empties it, off.*
>
> POLLY: What are you doing?
>
> LUCY *with a peculiar manner*: Emptying it.
>
> POLLY: You really are a hypocritical strumpet. But I spotted that right away.

LUCY: Yes, Polly. On the edge of the precipice, that's where you were.

POLLY: Anyway it was very considerate of you. Here, have a sip of water. You must feel terrible. Why don't you come and see me. I truly am your friend.

LUCY: Polly, men aren't worth it . . .

There is then no change of scene, since the set is a split one, with the bedroom above and Macheath's cell below. A change of lighting introduces our

Scene 9 [still 2 in script]

The bells ring, Smith leads in Macheath, and the dialogue is much as in our text as far as Smith's exit shrugging his shoulders (p. 161). Macheath then 'sings the "Epistle to his Friends" by François Villon', in other words our 'Call from the Grave', whose text is given. After its second stanza Mrs Coaxer appears, and Macheath tries to borrow £600 from her. 'What! At five in the morning?' she asks. Mac: 'Five? *He bellows:* Five twenty-four!' Smith then puts his question about the meal. Macheath says there isn't going to be a mounted messenger arriving like in a play to shout 'Halt, in the King's Name!' then tells Smith: 'Asparagus!' Mrs Coaxer grumbles about her overheads, but eventually agrees that she might be able to manage £400.

Then the lights go up briefly in the bedroom again, showing Lucy prostrate, with Polly giving her cold compresses. Enter Mrs Peachum, with Filch in attendance carrying a cardboard box. 'Go outside, Filch; this is not for your eyes,' she says, and tells Polly to get changed. 'You must do like all widows. Buy mourning and cheer up.' The bedroom darkens and the light returns to the cell, where Smith makes his inquiry about the soap (shifted from p. 162). After saying 'This place is a shambles' he brings in the table as on page 163, followed by Brown's entrance. The dialogue is then close to ours up to the end of Macheath's verse (p. 164). More persons in mourning enter, including Peachum and five beggars on crutches, while Brown and Macheath prolong their haggling over the former's percentages. Then Macheath looks at his watch and says '5.48. I'm lost'.

MAC: Jack, lend me £200. I'm finished. I must have those £200 – for Polly, you know. 5.50. Here am I, talking . . .

BROWN *has come up to him:* But Mackie, you only have to . . . you only have to ask, you can right away . . . 500 right away

— I owe you so much . . . Do you imagine I've forgotten
Peshawar?

MAC *weakly:* 200, but right away. Right away, right away.

BROWN: And Saipong and Azerbaijan and Sire, how we stood
in the jungle together, shoulder to shoulder, and the Shiks
mutinied, and you said . . .

The bells of Westminster interrupt him. Macheath gets up.

MAC: Time is up. Jack, you're too emotional to rescue your
friend. And you don't even know it.

Smith then opens the door, and a group including eight whores
enters the cell.

*Walter, with a little money-bag, stands near Macheath. Mrs Coaxer too
has the money.*

SMITH: Got it?

Mac shakes his head.

Peachum then asks which is Macheath, as in our text (p. 165), which
thereafter is approximately followed down to (inclusive) Jenny's
'We Drury Lane girls . . .' (p. 166), but missing out the second half
of Peachum's long speech (from 'Mr Macheath, you once . . .' to
'no place at all') and Matt's ensuing remarks ('See here' etc.).
Brown too makes no more reference to Azerbaijan but simply says
farewell and leaves for the Coronation, gulping as he goes. Macheath's farewell speech follows, starting 'Farewell, Jackie. It was
all right in the end' and going on with his 'Ladies and gentlemen . . .' as now, down to 'So be it – I fall' (p. 166). As in Gay,
however, it is Jemmy Twitcher who has betrayed him, not Jenny.

The speech over, Macheath asks for the doors and windows all
to be opened, and *'Through the windows we see treetops crowded with
spectators'*. He then sings *'Ballad to his Friends by François Villon'*,
whose text, however, is not given. After the ensuing farewells to
Polly and Lucy, Macheath is led to the door, the whores sob, and
the procession forms behind him. Then:

*The actor playing Macheath hesitates, turns round suddenly and doubt-
fully addresses the wings, right.*

ACTOR PLAYING MACHEATH: Well, what happens now? Do I
go off or not? That's something I'll need to know on the night.

ACTOR PLAYING PEACHUM: I was telling the author only
yesterday that it's a lot of nonsense, it's a heavy tragedy, not a
decent musical.

ACTRESS PLAYING MRS PEACHUM: I can't stand this hanging
at the end.

WINGS RIGHT, THE AUTHOR'S VOICE: That's how the play was written, and that's how it stays.

MACHEATH: It stays that way, does it? Then act the lead yourself. Impertinence!

AUTHOR: It's the plain truth: the man's hanged, of course he has to be hanged. I'm not making any compromises. If that's how it is in real life, then that's how it is on the stage. Right?

MRS PEACHUM: Right.

PEACHUM: Doesn't understand the first thing about the theatre. Plain truth, indeed.

MACHEATH: Plain truth. That's a load of rubbish in the theatre. Plain truth is what happens when people run out of ideas. Do you suppose the audience here have paid eight marks to see plain truth? They paid their money *not* to see plain truth.

PEACHUM: Well then, the ending had better be changed. You can't have the play end like that. I'm speaking in the name of the whole company when I say the play can't be performed as it is.

AUTHOR: All right, then you gentlemen can clean up your own mess.

MACHEATH: So we shall.

PEACHUM: It'd be absurd if we couldn't find a first-rate dramatic ending to please all tastes.

MRS PEACHUM: Right, then let's go back ten [?] speeches.

– and they go back to Macheath's 'So be it, I fall' once more. Then after the farewells to Polly and Lucy:

POLLY *weeping on his neck:* I didn't get a proper wedding with bridesmaids, but I've got this.

LUCY: Even if I'm not your wife, Mac . . .

MAC: My dear Lucy, my dear Polly, however things may have been between us it's all over now. Come on, Smith.

At this juncture Brown arrives in a panting hurry and his gala uniform.

BROWN *breathlessly:* Stop! A message from the Queen! Stop!

Murmurs of 'Rhubarb' among the actors, with an occasional amazed 'From the Queen?'

Then Brown calls for 'Bells!' into the wings, and makes his speech as now (p. 168), adding at the end 'Where are the happy couples?'

MRS PEACHUM *nudges the others:* Happy couples!

Whores, bandits and beggars pair off with some hesitation, choosing their partners with care.

Peachum thumps Macheath on the back and says 'It's all right, old man!' Mrs Peachum speaks the last speech as now given to Peachum, and the final chorale is given in full. After it Mrs Peachum has the concluding line: 'And now. To Westminster!'

3. FROM THE STAGE SCRIPT TO THE PRESENT TEXT

The prompt book for the original production, which established the greater part of the final text, is essentially a copy of the stage script just discussed with new typescript passages interleaved, texts of songs, and many cuts. It is now in the East German Academy of Arts in Berlin. At the beginning there is a full text of the Mac the Knife ballad, only lacking its stage directions, while interleaved in the first Act are the 'No, they can't' song, the Love Duet, the Finale and two verses of the Ballad of Sexual Obsession. The version of Peachum's opening speech cited above is deleted and replaced by ours; the speech presenting the types of human misery also seems to have been added; and there is a fresh version of the ending of the scene, starting from Filch's protest at washing his feet (p. 99), virtually as now. In the stable scene the start is retyped and the 'Bill Lawgen and Mary Syer' song pencilled in; the rest emerges more or less in its final form, aside from the presentation of the nuptial bed, which is still missing. Scene 3 seems to have been completely revised twice, the first time remaining close to the stage script, the second resulting almost in the text as now, apart from the section on p. 122 where Peachum apostrophises Macheath (which is also lacking where recapitulated in scene 9).

In the second Act an amendment to the end of scene 4 made the gang go out shouting 'Three cheers for Polly!' who then went on to sing 'Nice while it lasted' and continued with her monologue as in the stage script. This was then changed to give the complete text as now spoken over the music, from 'It's been such a short time' on. The song, of course, is all that remains of the second of the Kipling ballads, whose refrain it is; it was omitted from the song texts as published by Universal-Edition in 1928. The 'Ballad of Sexual Obsession', which follows in our text, is inserted before the beginning of the scene, but was omitted from the production and from the piano score of 1928. Scene 5, the brothel, was revised as far as the Villon song (or 'Tango Ballade'), but the setting remained the Cuttlefish Hotel; thereafter there were cuts. In scene 6 the only important additions were the text of the Jealousy Duet and Peachum's Egyptian police chief speech (p. 144–5), replacing the speech cited above in answer to Brown's 'What do you mean?'.

The text of the second Act finale, too, was inserted just before the end of the scene.

In the third Act scene 7 was redesignated 'Peachum's Counting-House' and entirely revised; the additions included the 'Ballad of Insufficiency' (described as 'sung before the Sheriff of London') and the remaining verse of the 'Ballad of Sexual Obsession'. Brown's long speech about friendship was cut, also virtually everything following his exit. Though Lucy's Aria at the beginning of scene 8 was now cut out for good, the cut was not actually marked, perhaps because the whole of that scene was omitted from the production. Thereafter in the equivalent of our scene 9 Mrs Coaxer's appearance was cut, likewise most of the passage where Macheath tries to borrow money from Brown, down to Smith's opening of the door. What follows was retyped, again, however, omitting Peachum's apostrophising of Macheath (p. 165). Peachum's verse speech was interpolated and the Third Finale revised. The scene titles were separately listed, with instructions for their projection.

A later version of the Bloch stage script bore the title 'The Threepenny Opera (The "Beggar's Opera"). A play with music in a prologue and eight scenes from the English of John Gay', then gave the credits as before. The first published edition was number 3 of Brecht's *Versuche* series, which appeared in 1931 and described it as 'an experiment in epic theatre'. This contained the text as we now have it, as also did the collected Malik edition of 1938. After the Second World War, however, Brecht made certain revisions, notably for a production at the Munich Kammerspiele by Hans Schweikart in April 1949. For this he devised the amended song texts now given as an appendix to the play, and made some small changes in the first Act, eliminating for instance the entry of the five beggars in scene 3. He discarded these improvements in the 1950s when it was decided to include the play in volume 3 of the new collected edition, for which he went back to the *Versuche* text. The new songs, for instance, were not used in Strehler's Milan production of 1956, though this included a version of the final chorale which Brecht wrote for the occasion and whose German text has been lost. A rough rendering would be:

> Since poverty won't haunt this earth for ever
> Don't blame the poor man too much for his sins
> But fight instead against perverted justice
> And may it be the human race that wins.

THE RISE AND FALL OF
THE CITY OF MAHAGONNY

Text by Brecht

NOTES TO THE OPERA *The Rise and Fall of the City of Mahagonny*

OPERA –

Our existing opera is a culinary opera. It was a means of pleasure long before it turned into merchandise. It furthers pleasure even where it requires, or promotes, a certain degree of education, for the education in question is an education of taste. To every object it adopts a hedonistic approach. It 'experiences', and it ranks as an 'experience'.

Why is *Mahagonny* an opera? Because its basic attitude is that of an opera: that is to say culinary. Does *Mahagonny* adopt a hedonistic approach? It does. Is *Mahagonny* an experience? It is an experience. For – *Mahagonny* is a piece of fun.

The opera Mahagonny pays conscious tribute to the irrationality of the operatic form. The irrationality of opera lies in the fact that rational elements are employed, solid reality is aimed at, but at the same time it is all washed out by the music. A dying man is real. If at the same time he sings we are translated to the sphere of the irrational. (If the audience sang at the sight of him the case would be different.)

The more unclear and unreal the music can make the reality – though there is of course a third, highly complex and in itself quite real element which can have quite real effects but is utterly remote from the reality of which it treats – the more pleasurable the whole process becomes: the pleasure grows in proportion to the degree of unreality.

The concept of opera – far be it from us to profane it – leads in *Mahagonny*'s case to all the rest. The intention was that a certain unreality, irrationality and lack of seriousness should be introduced at the right moment, and wash itself out altogether.[1] The irrationality which enters thus only fits the point where it enters.

[1] These narrow limitations do not prevent the introduction of an element of

Such an approach is purely hedonistic.

As for the content of this opera, *its content is pleasure*. Fun, in other words, not only as form but as object. At least, enjoyment was meant to be the object of the inquiry even if the inquiry was intended to be an object of enjoyment. Enjoyment appears here in its current historical role: as merchandise.[2]

It is undeniable that this content is bound at present to have a provocative effect. In the thirteenth section, for instance, where the glutton stuffs himself to death, it is provocative because hunger is the rule. Although we never even hinted that others were going hungry while he stuffed, the effect was provocative. Not everyone who is in a position to stuff himself dies of it, yet many are dying of hunger because he dies from stuffing himself. His pleasure is provocative because it implies so much.[3] Opera as a means of pleasure is generally provocative in contexts like this today. Not of course so far as the handful of opera-goers are concerned. In its power to provoke we can see reality reintroduced. *Mahagonny* may not taste all that good; it may even (thanks to guilty conscience) make a point of not doing so; but it is culinary through and through.

Mahagonny is nothing more or less than an opera.

---

instruction and directness or the basing of the whole arrangement on gests. The eye that reduces everything to its gestic aspect is morality. I.e. the depiction of mores. But from a subjective point of view . . .

> Let's have another drink
> Then we won't go home tonight
> Then we'll have another drink
> Then we'll have a break.

The people who sing like this are subjective moralists. They are describing themselves.

[2] Romanticism likewise is merchandise. It figures only as content, not as form.

[3] 'A dignified gentleman with an empurpled face had fished out a bunch of keys and was making a piercing demonstration against the Epic Theatre. His wife stood by him in this decisive moment. She stuck two fingers in her mouth, screwed up her eyes and blew out her cheeks. Her whistle made more noise than the key of his cash-box.' (Alfred Polgar, describing the Leipzig première of *Mahagonny*.)

– WITH INNOVATIONS!

When the epic theatre's methods begin to penetrate the opera the first result is a radical *separation of the elements*. The great struggle for supremacy between words, music and production – which always brings up the question 'which is the pretext for what?': is the music the pretext for the events on the stage, or are these the pretext for the music? etc. – can simply be bypassed by radically separating the elements. So long as the expression 'Gesamt-kunstwerk' [or 'integrated work of art'] means that the integration is a macédoine, so long as the arts are supposed to be 'fused' together, the various elements will all be equally degraded and each will act as a mere 'feed' to the rest. The process of fusion extends to the spectator, who gets thrown into the melting pot too and becomes a passive (suffering) part of the total work of art. Witchcraft of this sort must of course be fought against. Whatever is intended to produce hypnosis, or is likely to induce improper intoxication, or creates fog, has got to be given up.

Words, music and setting must become more independent of one another.

(a) Music

For the music, the change of emphasis proved to be as follows:

Dramatic Opera	Epic Opera
The music dishes up	The music communicates
Music which heightens the text	Music which sets forth the text
Music which proclaims the text	Music which takes the text for granted
Music which illustrates	Which takes up a position
Music which depicts the psychological situation	Which gives the attitude

Music plays the chief part in our thesis.[4]

---

[4] The large number of craftsmen in the average opera orchestra allows of nothing but associative music (one flood of sound leading to another), and so the orchestral apparatus needs to be cut down to thirty specialists or less. The singer becomes a reporter, whose private feelings must remain a private affair.

(b) Text

We had to make something instructive and direct of our piece of
fun if it was not to be merely irrational. The form that suggested
itself was that of the moral tableau. The tableau is depicted by the
characters in the play. The text had to be neither moralising nor
sentimental, but to put morality and sentimentality on view. The
spoken word was no more important than the written word (of the
titles). Reading seems to encourage the audience to adopt the
most relaxed attitude towards the work.

(c) Image

Showing independent works of art as part of a theatrical performance is a new departure. Neher's projections adopt an attitude
towards the events on the stage; as when the real glutton sits in
front of the glutton whom Neher has drawn. Each scene repeats
in fluid form what is fixed in the image. These projections of
Neher's are quite as much an independent component of the opera
as are Weill's music and the text. They provide its visual aids.

Of course such innovations also demand a new attitude on the
part of the audiences who frequent opera houses.

[. . .]

Perhaps *Mahagonny* is as culinary as ever – just as culinary as
an opera ought to be – but one of its functions is to change
society; it brings the culinary principle under discussion, it
attacks the society that needs operas of such a sort; it still perches
happily on the old limb, perhaps, but at least it has started (out of
absent-mindedness or bad conscience) to saw it through. . . . And
here you have the effect of the innovations and the song they sing.

Real innovations attack the roots.

[From 'Anmerkungen zur Oper "Aufstieg und Fall der Stadt
Mahagonny"' in GW *Schriften zum Theater*, p. 1004, originally
published over the names of Brecht and (Peter) Suhrkamp in
Versuche 2, 1931. These notes, which are given complete in
Brecht on Theatre under the title 'The Modern Theatre is the

Epic Theatre', have here been shorn of those passages which are not primarily relevant to the present work. This has meant the omission of all section 1, the long table contrasting epic and dramatic theatre in section 3, all but the last two paragraphs of section 4 and the whole of section 5. The full essay is perhaps the most important pre-1933 statement of Brecht's ideas about the theatre in general.]

Notes by Weill and Neher

NOTES TO MY OPÉRA *Mahagonny*
by Kurt Weill

When Brecht and I first met in spring 1927 we were discussing the potentialities of opera, when the word 'Mahagonny' was mentioned and with it the notion of a 'paradise city'. The idea instantly seized me, and with a view to developing it and trying out the musical style I had in mind I set the five 'Mahagonny Songs' from Brecht's *Devotions for the Home*, combining them in a small-scale dramatic form to make a 'Songspiel' which was performed at Baden-Baden that summer. This Baden-Baden *Mahagonny* was thus nothing but a stylistic exercise for the opera proper, which had already been started and was taken up again as soon as the style had been tested. Brecht and I worked on its libretto for almost a year. The score was completed in November 1929.

The 'Song' form established in the Baden-Baden piece, and carried on in such subsequent works as *The Threepenny Opera*, the *Berlin Requiem* and *Happy End*, was of course inadequate for a full-length opera; it needed to be supplemented by other, larger-scale forms. None the less the simple ballad style had to be maintained.

The content of this opera is the history of a city: its foundation, its early crises, followed by the decisive turning-point in its evolution, its golden age and its decline. These constitute 'moral tableaux for the present day', projected on a large surface. It was a choice which allowed us to use the purest form of epic theatre, which is likewise the purest form of musical theatre. They make a sequence of twenty-one self-contained musical forms, each being a self-contained scene and each introduced by an inscription in narrative form. The music therefore no longer furthers the plot but only starts up once a situation has been arrived at. The libretto accordingly was arranged from the outset so as to represent a linear sequence of situations which add up to a dramatic form only in the course of their musically fixed dynamic succession.

['Anmerkungen zu meiner Oper "Mahagonny"', from Kurt Weill: *Ausgewählte Schriften*, ed. David Drew, Suhrkamp, Frankfurt 1975, p. 56. Reprinted from *Die Musik*, March 1930, Jg 22 Nr 6, p. 29.]

INTRODUCTION TO THE PROMPT-BOOK OF THE OPERA
Mahagonny
by Kurt Weill

The Threepenny Opera represented an attempt to revive the earliest form of musical theatre. The music in question does not further the plot; each entrance of the music, rather, amounts to an interruption of the plot. The epic form of theatre is a step-by-step juxtaposition of situations. This makes it the perfect form of musical theatre, since self-contained musical forms can only express situations, and the juxtaposition of situations according to musical criteria leads to that heightened form of musical theatre, an opera.

In *The Threepenny Opera* the plot had to be advanced in the intervals between the musical numbers. This led to something like a form of 'dialogue opera', a cross between opera and play.

With *The Rise and Fall of the City of Mahagonny* the material permits of *construction strictly according to the laws of music*. For the chronicle form here adopted is nothing but a 'juxtaposition of situations'. So each new situation in the history of the city of Mahagonny is introduced by an inscription which provides a bridge to the next scene in narrative form.

Two men and a woman, on the run from the constabulary, are stuck in a desolate area. They decide to found a city in which every man arriving from the gold coast can get his requirements satisfied. A 'paradise city' consequently springs up, whose in-habitants lead an idyllic life of contemplation. Sooner or later however the men from the gold coast become dissatisfied with it. Discontent sets in. Prices fall. During the night of the typhoon, while it is bearing down on the city, Jim Mahoney discovers the city's new law. It is 'Anything goes'. The typhoon veers away. Life goes on according to the new laws. The city blooms. People's requirements multiply – prices likewise. For anything goes: yes, but only so long as you can pay for it. Even Jim Mahoney gets condemned to death when he runs out of money. His execution sparks off a vast demonstration against the cost-of-living increases that herald the city's fall.

That is the story of the city of Mahagonny. It is conveyed in a loose form of juxtaposed 'twentieth-century moral tableaux'. It is a parable of modern life. The play's protagonist is the city. This springs from people's requirements, and it is these requirements that lead to its rise and fall. The individual phases of the city's history however are shown exclusively through their impact on people. For just as people's requirements influence the develop-ment of the city, so does the development of the city in turn influence people's attitudes. All the songs in this opera are accord-ingly expressions of the masses, even where it is a single repre-sentative of those masses that sings them. At the start the group of founders is set against the group of newcomers. At the end of Act 1 [i.e. after scene 11] the group supporting the new law is fighting the group of its opponents. The fate of the individual is only shown in passing, and then only when it stands for the fate of the city.

It would be wrong to look for any psychological or topical links except within the framework of this basic idea.

The name 'Mahagonny' signifies nothing except the notion of a city. Phonetic (sound) reasons determined its choice. The city's geographical location is not relevant.

It is not at all advisable to tilt the performance of this work in the direction of irony or the grotesque. The events are not sym-bolic but typical, and this entails the utmost economy of scenic means and individual expression on the part of the actors. The directing of the singers in their capacity as actors, the movements of the chorus, indeed the whole style of performance in this opera are all determined by the style of the music. This music is never in the least illustrative. It sets out to realise human attitudes in the various circumstances leading to the city's rise and fall. Human attitudes are already so embodied in the music that a simple, natural interpretation of the music will establish the right style for their portrayal. The actor accordingly can limit himself to the simplest and most natural gests.

In staging the opera it must always be borne in mind that one is dealing with *self-contained musical forms*. Hence it is important firmly to establish its purely musical development and to group the actors in such a way as to allow something close to a concert performance. Its style is neither naturalistic nor symbolic. It would be better described as 'real', since it shows life as represented in the sphere of art. Any exaggeration in the direction of emotion or ballet-like stylisation should be avoided.

Caspar Neher's projections are an essential part of the material going to make up the performance (and should accordingly be sent out to theatres along with the music). These projections make use of a painter's resources to provide an independent illustration of the events on stage. They supply visual aids to the history of the city, to be projected on a screen or between the individual scenes. The actor performs his scenes in front of the screen, and no more props are needed than are essential for him to clarify his performance. It is an opera that does not call for any use of complex stage machinery. The important thing is to have a few good projectors, together with an adroit arrangement of surfaces so that the pictures and still more the explanatory writing can be clearly understood from all parts of the house. The set needs to be so simple as to be equally well transferable from the theatre to any old platform. The solo scenes should be played as close to the audience as possible. It is therefore advisable not to sink the orchestra pit but to make it level with the stalls and build out a platform from the stage in such a way as to allow some scenes to be played in among the orchestra.

['Vorwort zum Regiebuch der Oper "Mahagonny"', from Kurt Weill: *Ausgewählte Schriften*, ed. David Drew, Suhrkamp, Frankfurt 1975, p. 57, reprinted from *Anbruch*, Vienna, Jan 1930, Jg 12 Nr 1, p. 5. Drew cites *Anbruch*'s accompanying

comment that Weill, Neher and Brecht were preparing a
prompt-book for supplying to any theatre staging the work
This however seems not to have got beyond note form, as
translated below, nor did Brecht in fact collaborate, his own
'Notes to the Opera' (p. 345 ff) being independently written later.
Weill wanted his Foreword to precede the notes that now
follow.]

SUGGESTIONS FOR THE STAGE REALISATION OF THE OPERA *The Rise and Fall of the City of Mahagonny* by Kurt Weill and Caspar Neher

General

The background is formed by a big wooden (or canvas) screen
which ideally should be capable of being pushed aside. Downstage
a half-curtain 2.50 metres high running on a wire. Built out into
the orchestra pit a semi-circular apron, size determined by the
size of the orchestra, edged by a line of small lamps that can come
into operation each time a scene is played on the apron. From its
middle a gangway leads up on to the main stage. To start with
it runs horizontally from the front of the apron, then it goes
slantwise across the footlights on to the stage.

With respect to set and costumes, it is important to avoid any
tendency to Wild West and Cowboy romanticism, as also any
stressing of a typically American ambience.

Act 1

No. 1. The dialogue between Fatty and Moses to be sluggish and
lazy and continually petering out.

No. 5. The side gangway is now a passenger gangway at the docks
in Mahagonny and bears a sign 'To the boats'. Downstage left
is a signpost not unlike a small gallows with a legible inscription
saying 'To Mahagonny'. On the same side there is a big blackboard which can be chalked on. At the top it says 'Prices in the
City of Mahagonny'.

The pictures of girls (p. 181) are rolled up like maps and
hung on a cord in front of the list of prices. They are drawn in

the Japanese manner. At the start of the scene the four men are
on the apron. The whole scene is played partly on the apron,
partly on the front part of the stage. [. . . At the end of the
scene] Jim holds Jenny back and remains with her on the apron
as the half-curtain closes behind them. [. . .]

No. 7. Half-curtain open. The lorry of scene 1 has been transformed into a kind of bar, inscribed 'The As-You-Like-It
Tavern'. As Begbick gets more and more worked up the two
men remain maliciously relaxed, which only adds to Begbick's
anger. Their interpolations are accompanied by broad grins.
[. . .]

No. 9. Half-curtain open. Again the As-You-Like-It Tavern.
Minor improvements and developments however show that a
certain amount of time has passed, during which the city has
expanded. [. . .] At the beginning of the row [*He jumps to his
feet*, p. 192], the male members of the chorus are relatively un-
involved. They merely express their resentment at having their
rest disturbed. The more the row gets under way, the more
scornful and threatening their attitude towards Jim . . . till they
become like a street riot. [. . .]

No. 10. All movement on stage is frozen. At figure 138 [of the
musical introduction] projection number 10 (people fleeing).
People fleeing rush across the front of the stage from left to
right, with hand carts, luggage, women, children, animals; a
wounded man is led past. . . . [Just before the entry of the
chorus] the whole ensemble moves down to the front of the
stage. [At its end] all disperse in different directions. A wind
gets up, driving scraps of paper, leaves etc. before it.

The whole representation of the typhoon must take place
without noises; there must be no storm or rain effects. When
the chorus crashes [on its dispersal] Jenny, Begbick, Jake, Bill
and Joe are left lying downstage motionless with their faces to
the ground.

No. 11. Posters are stuck up on the wall saying 'It is prohibited . . .'.

Act 2

[. . .]

No. 13. Between numbers 12 and 13, projections 12, 13 and 14 are shown one after the other in total silence. They show the transition from a simple gold-prospectors' town to a modern city. Over each of them stand the words 'Do it' in big letters. [. . .]

No. 15. At figure 63 [i.e. at the end of their duet, p. 210] Joe and Jim pose in an attitude of friendship and are photographed by a press photographer. At [the Referee's entry] the combatants are weighed on a big decimal machine, Moses first, then Joe. [. . .]

No. 17. By the footlights stands a lantern. Against it, on a little platform, Jim stands in a wooden box that covers him from his neck to his knees. He is being put on public view. At first one or two people pass by him on their own during the short musical interludes. After that he is entirely alone. It is night. No light other than the lantern. [. . .]

Act 3

No. 18. A stand has been put up, consisting of three parts: one upstage centre, with left and right adjoining sections running slantwise downstage. It is so constructed that each row of seats is about 50 cm higher than the one in front. Right at the top behind the seats there is beer on tap. A plain wooden table stands in the centre at the bottom.

Moses's speech for the prosecution ('Never yet', p. 222) is delivered like a universally familiar song which a tedious formality demands; nobody listens to it; instead they are all following the bribery negotiations, and Moses himself is only interested in squeezing all he can out of the accused. During the murder case the spectators read the paper, smoke, drink beer. It is only with the opening of the case against Jimmy Gallagher that they start to show some interest [. . .]

No. 19 [20 in piano score]. [Initial stage direction as in our text, except that instead of the electric chair there is a makeshift gallows. As Jim sings 'Dreams have all one ending' (see editorial notes)] enter right a number of men, who quickly pass by

with a preoccupied air and disappear into the doorway of the
As-You-Like-It Tavern (now the height of elegance, complete
with revolving door etc.). [. . .]

After the words 'Is nothing but the grave' the half-curtain
closes. Behind it Moses can be heard giving the order 'Ready!'
(p. 232). Lights throughout the theatre flicker and suddenly
go out. Then the small lamps along the apron light up. Begbick
gets up, goes to the blackboard, crosses out the words 'Sold
Out' and substitutes '100 dollars'. She has some fresh whisky
bottles under her arm. Jenny and Bill enter through the half-
curtain. Bill and the murder-case man each give her a hundred-
dollar bill and take a bottle of whisky. Throughout the next
scene Begbick sits under the blackboard, saying nothing, but
clasping her two hundred-dollar notes.

Ditto [21 in piano score]. The [four] men start singing the song
of God in Mahagonny. [. . .] Moses appears through the half-
curtain wearing a long black coat, with his hat right down over
his eyes. The men are amazed that God should actually appear.
At first their answers are highly disconcerted, till in the end they
rebel with 'For we *are* in Hell and always have been!' (p. 232).
At the ensuing *Furioso* they break up the blackboard and the
chairs. Arming themselves with chair legs, planks and revolvers
they rush off through the half-curtain on to the main stage.

Finale [i.e. our no. 20]. [Initial stage direction as in our text,
except:] Each of the groups consists of about five to seven
people. [. . .] At the last line the wooden screen parts in the
middle, revealing a great number of groups, who advance in
between the leading columns. [. . .] They all start moving forward as if the entire demonstration, spreading right across the
stage, were proposing to march into the auditorium. When they
are almost down to the footlights the main curtain cuts them off.

['Vorschläge zur szenischen Aufführung der Oper "Aufstieg
und Fall der Stadt Mahagonny"' in the Kurt Weill Archive.
Our translation is of extracts from a transcript kindly lent by
David Drew, shortened to eliminate points already in our text
or otherwise irrelevant. In the original the scene and page
references were all to the 1929 piano score; we have varied them
to refer to our text. The actual date of these 'Suggestions' is

November or December 1929, i.e. more than a year before the
Leipzig première. Drew suggests that too many of them were
then found to be unworkable for the collaborators to go ahead
with their planned publication.]

Editorial Notes

1. SONGS, SONGSPIEL, OPERA

Possibly the first of Brecht's writings about his mythical city was a fragmentary scene with two whores headed 'AUF NACH MAHA-GONNY', which seems to bear no relation at all to the subsequent opera. Already before leaving Bavaria however he had begun writing the 'Mahagonny Songs', of which three were included in his 1924 plan for his first collection of poems, the *Devotions for the Home*. There were four in all, each with a strongly American flavour (whisky, poker, Jack Dempsey, the moon of Alabama and so on), and in Berlin he added two more songs which his new collaborator Elisabeth Hauptmann actually wrote for him in English. These are almost the only tangible evidence of the kind of theme discussed by Brecht and Kurt Weill when they first met nearly three years later, shortly after the publication of the *Devotions*, which now included all six songs with Brecht's own tunes. What they at once envisaged, it seems, was a large-scale opera in which Mahagonny would emerge as a contemporary Sodom or Gomor-rah. But the immediate task which presented itself in May 1927 was the provision of a small-scale 'scenic cantata' for the forth-coming Baden-Baden music festival, and they decided to base this on the Mahagonny Songs. Weill accordingly set Songs 1 to 3 (omitting the still unpublished no. 4) and the two English-language parodies, while Brecht wrote a new poem to serve as a finale under the title 'Aber dieses ganze Mahagonny'. The six songs were then alternated with orchestral interludes on the following pattern: Mahagonny Song no. 1 / Little March / Alabama Song / Vivace / Mahagonny Song no. 2 / Vivace assai / Benares Song / Sostenuto (Choral) / Mahagonny Song no. 3 / Vivace assai / Finale 'Aber dieses ganze Mahagonny'. There was no dialogue, but the charac-ters were given suitably Anglo-Saxon names: Jessie, Bessie, Charlie, Billy, Bobby and Jimmy. This was the work performed on 17 July, after which it was shelved for the next thirty years.

A 'first sketch' for the opera, published in the magazine *Das Neue Forum in 1927/8*, would appear to list the texts for Caspar Neher's projected scene titles in the Songspiel, as the Baden-Baden version was termed. They run: '1. The great cities in our day are full of people who do not like it there. 2. So get away to Mahagonny, the gold town situated on the shores of consolation far from the rush of the world. 3. Here in Mahagonny life is lovely. 4. But even in Mahagonny there are moments of nausea, helplessness and despair. 5. The men of Mahagonny are heard replying to God's inquiries as to the cause of their sinful life. 6. Lovely Mahagonny crumbles to nothing before your eyes'. Although we have none of Brecht's characteristic notes and schemes other than this to show how the opera was planned, the basis of the work is fairly clear. On the one hand there were the songs taken over from the Songspiel version, together with part of Mahagonny Song no. 4 and seven other pre-existing poems, which the collaborators now cut, changed and threaded together to make the backbone of the opera. On the other there was this new framework with its apocalyptic message deriving apparently from Brecht's discarded plan for *The Flood* or *Collapse of the Paradise City Miami*, which originally had nothing directly to do with the Mahagonny myth. The result was the libretto script which is now in the archives of Universal-Edition, Weill's publishers. This antedates not only the version which Brecht published in the *Versuche* in 1931, which is the basis for the *Gesammelte Werke* text which we reproduce, but also the piano score of 1929. It is entitled simply *Mahagonny*, 'opera in 3 acts by Kurt Weill. Text by Bert Brecht'.

This script gives the characters as Widow Leokadja Begbick, Fatty der Prokurist, Trinity Moses (identified as a bass), Jimmy Mahoney, Fresserjack (or Guzzlerjack), Sparbüchsenbilly (Piggy-Bank Billy), Alaskawolfjoe and Jenny Smith. Of these only Jimmy and Billy are taken over from the Songspiel, though the name Jenny occurs in a rough draft of a 'Mahagoni' song in one of Brecht's notebooks of 1922–23. The piano score of 1929 amends Jimmy to Jim Mahoney (with the normal single 'n'), drops Jenny's surname and adds Tobby Higgins, noting that he can be doubled with Jack. Auden and Kallman in their translation improved on this by making Jenny's name Jones (presumably because Jack or Jake is also named Smith) and Jimmy's Gallagh (presumably because Māhŏněy with three syllables will not do for Anglo-Saxons, let alone Irishmen). Just about that time, however, Weill decided that 'the use of American names ... risks establishing a wholly false idea of Americanism, Wild West or suchlike', so that with Brecht's concurrence a note was added to the full score saying:

> In view of the fact that those amusements of man which can be had for money are always and everywhere the same, and since the amusement town of Mahagonny is thus international in the broadest sense, the names of the leading characters can be changed into the customary [i.e., local] forms at any given time. The following names are therefore recommended for German performances: Willy (for Fatty), Johann Ackermann (for Jim), Jakob Schmidt (for Jack O'Brien [actually the name of one of the world middleweight champions about whom Brecht wrote a poem in 1927]), Sparbüchsenheinrich (for Bill), Josef Lettner (for Joe).

These German names are to be found in *Versuche 2*, where the work is described as 'an attempt at epic opera, a depiction of mores'. However, Brecht now (see p. xxiv) made Ackermann Paul, not Johann, though he is always the latter in performance.

The various incorporated poems, including the Mahagonny songs, will be given in full in the volume of *Songs and Poems from Plays* currently being prepared. They are, in brief:

Alabama Song (scene 2)
On the cities (scene 3)
Mahagonny Song no. 4 (scene 3, refrain only)
Mahagonny Song no. 1 (scene 4)
The Johnny-doesn't-want-to-be-human Song (scene 8)
Against being deceived (scene 11 in our text, scene 20 in piano score)
Blasphemy (scene 11)
The Lovers (scene 14)
Mahagonny Song no. 2 (scene 16)
Tahiti (scene 16)
Jenny's Song (scene 16)
Benares Song (scene 19 of piano score, later cut)

Mahagonny Song no. 3 (scene 19)
Poem on a Dead Man (scene 20)

There was also a discarded 'Chewing-gum Song'. How all these were treated in order to work them into the opera will be discussed in the notes on individual scenes which follow.

These are based on a comparison of the typescript libretto (which bears no signs of correction or amendment by Brecht), the piano score (1929) and the final *Versuche* text of 1931, which has subsequently remained unchanged. Since Auden and Kallman's translation of the opera was made from the piano score, we quote variant passages from the latter in their version. It can be found in its original form in Brecht: *The Rise and Fall of the City of Mahagonny*, edited by A. R. Braunmuller and published by David R. Godine, Boston 1976.

2. THE OPERA: NOTES ON INDIVIDUAL SCENES
Scene 1

In the typescript and the piano score (and accordingly in the original Auden–Kallman version) the stage directions are as under. Note however that Auden–Kallman's 'screen' is a mistranslation of Brecht's *Gardine* or flimsy curtain hung from wires 'not more than 2½ metres' (i.e. about eight feet) above the stage.

> *The place of the conventional curtain is taken by a small white screen suspended on both sides on metal wires about a yard above the stage. On this screen appear all the projections of the scene titles. As the music begins, a warrant for the arrest of Ladybird Begbick, Trinity Moses and Henry Wilson alias Fatty The Bookie, appears on the screen. The charges are: Robbery with Violence, Forgery and Fraud. Under this is printed: All Three are Fugitives from Justice. Their photographs then appear. Then, moving across this projection in red letters the title of the first scene: The Founding of the City of Mahagonny, otherwise known as Suckerville.*
> *The screen divides in the centre and opens inwards. Projection No. 1. appears on the backcloth: a desert landscape. A large, battered truck rolls on to the stage; the motor splutters and dies; the truck stops. Trinity Moses climbs out of the driver's seat and peers under the hood; Fatty peers out from the back of the truck.*

The 'As-You-Like-It Tavern' (of A/K following the piano score) later became the 'Rich Man's Arms Hotel'. This solo by Begbick (starting on p. 174) was originally termed 'Aria' in the script. The ending of her immediately preceding speech (from 'This is the spot' to 'settled') was added by A/K and is not in the German texts, while 'Girls for the asking' is literally 'Girls and boys'.

Scene 2

According to the piano score this is to be played before the half-height curtain (A/K's 'screen'). It consists of the Alabama Song originally written in English by Elisabeth Hauptmann and provided with a rudimentary tune by Brecht. The piano score omits the second verse, which originally had 'girl' rather than 'boy' throughout but was changed on the script and on Weill's MS score. We have followed the later reading, which has been observed ever since, and disregarded A/K's amendment of 'pretty boy' to 'Mister Right' and of 'boys' in the penultimate line of this verse to 'misters'.

Scene 3

In the typescript there was to be an opening projection 'showing a view of the city of New York and also the photographs of a lot of men'. In the piano score the former was amended to literally 'a city of millions'. The initial four-line chorus was published as a poem in *Simplicissimus* for 6 September 1927 under the title 'On the Cities'; later Brecht wanted to take it into the *Devotions*. The duet by Fatty and Moses which follows, according to the Weill–Neher 'Suggestions', was to be sung into a microphone. With 'But once you puff' (p. 177) it takes up the refrain of Mahagonny Song no. 4.

Scene 4

Is again performed before the half-curtain, and consists of Mahagonny Song no. 1.

Scene 5

The script has Trinity Moses putting up pictures of nudes, not simply of 'girls' (p. 181). It calls Jenny's song 'Have you thought at all' (p. 182) her 'Arietta' and words it slightly differently; thus in the verse starting 'Jenny Jones from Oklahoma' the third line reads 'I have been in the cold cities'. Doubtless seeing some inconsistency with the earlier 'My home is Havana' A/K give the alternatives 'Jenny Jones. Havana, Cuba' and 'Jenny Jones. From Havana' – the latter as part of a spoken quatrain to run on:

I got here just about nine weeks ago.
I used to live in the big cities down there.
I do anything that's asked of me.

Also in the script the solo and chorus following straight on from there, starting 'I know you Jimmies, Jimmies, Jimmies from Alaska well' is separated off and headed 'Song', with the six girls joining in after 'what Mahagonny has to sell'. All this is given its present wording in the piano score, which has a different setting of the Arietta from that now used. Weill subsequently rewrote this song for Lotte Lenya to sing in the Berlin production of 1931.

Scene 6

Script and piano score specify that this is to be played before the half-curtain, on which is projected a plan of the city.

Scene 7

According to Drew the Tavern's name was changed to Hotel zum Reichen Mann (or The Rich Man's Arms) a few weeks before the Leipzig première.

The script divides Begbick's opening speech into verse lines and makes it end after 'I saw them there' with 'They're taking their money away with them!'. In her cantabile solo starting 'I too was once' (p. 187) instead of 'And it was love' the script has 'And it was the future'.

Scene 8

In script and piano score this starts with the same projection as scene 5. Jim's solo 'I think I will eat my old felt hat' (p. 189) is headed 'Song' on the script and derives from an earlier 'Johnny-willkeinmenschsein Song' which evidently antedates the naming of the characters. It is said by Werner Otto to derive from an unidentified record of a song in English. It had a melody by Brecht, a middle verse which went:

I think I had better get rid of my woman
I think she and I are through.
And why should a man be stuck with his woman
When he's stuck for money too?

– and a longer refrain, taking in all that follows the present second (Arkansas) verse from 'You've learned' right down to 'What is it man was born for?' In script, piano score and A/K version this follows each of the two verses.

Scene 9

The script introduces this scene by a title in 'giant flaming letters' saying 'SENSATION!' In our version A/K have added extensively to the inscriptions specified in the stage direction, and also signed each of them with Begbick's initials. Following the piano score they include a lot of repetition ('Hold me, hold me back! Hold me, hold me back! Hold me, hold me back' etc.) which the published texts dispense with and which we have accordingly cut. We have also followed Brecht in going straight into Jim's 'Deep in the woods' solo and omitting Jake's heartfelt 'This is the *real* immortal art!' which follows the introductory piano solo (derived from 'The Maiden's Prayer') in A/K and the piano score.

After 'The rivers jammed with floating ice' (p. 192) and Jim's three lines following, the script has a different version of the rest of the scene, as follows:

BEGBICK:
    If only those stupid idiots

Would stay put in Alaska
For all they want is to disturb
Our peace, our concord.

JENNY:

Jimmy, listen to me
And put your knife away

BEGBICK:

What is it you want?
Catch a fish and be happy
Smoke a cigar and forget
Your crappy Alaska.

THE GIRLS:

Put your knife back in your belt again!

CHORUS OF MEN:

Quiet! Quiet!

JAKE, JOE, BILL:

Jimmy, put your knife away!
Jimmy, be a gentleman!

JIM:

Hold me back
Or something nasty'll happen!

CHORUS *mocking*:

We know these Jimmies, Jimmies, Jimmies from Alaska well:
They have it worse in winter than the dead have.
But you get rich in hell. But you get rich in hell.

JIM *shouting*:

For there's no life here!

CHORUS *general tumult*:

Throw him out!

At this point the stage lights go out. Sudden deathly hush. On the background in big writing 'Hurricane over Florida!!' If possible to be followed by 160 feet of film with shots of typhoons.

SINGLE VOICES:

A hurricane!!
A typhoon!!!
A hurricane over Florida threatening Mahagonny!!!!!!

The darkness lightens somewhat.

CHORUS *bursting forth*:

No! Not utter destruction!

Our golden Joytown will be lost!
For the raging storm hangs over the mountains:
We shall die, drown in the waters of death.
O is there no wall to shelter us now?
O is there no cavern which will hide us?
Chorus rushes out. Begbick, Moses, Fatty and Jim remain.

MOSES:
Lock the doors!
Take the money to the cellar.

BEGBICK:
Oh, don't bother
It doesn't matter.
Jim laughs.

Scene 10

The script accordingly makes our scene 10 the concluding part of the previous scene. The piano score separates it off exactly as now, except that there is a note soon after the second projection, saying 'Thereafter typhoon scenes can be shown, using scenic or filmic means: storms, water, collapsing buildings, men and animals fleeing etc.'.

Scene 11 [10 in script]

Script locates this 'Inside the As-You-Like-It Tavern' as in scene 7. It omits Jenny's repeat of 'O moon of Alabama' (p. 195) which is now sung over the top of Jake's solo, give this solo to the trio Jake–Joe–Bill, and shortens it, omitting the last line. Then after Begbick's 'So you think I was wrong to forbid anything' (p. 200) Jim's answer (in verse) is:

Yes. Now I am cheerful
I would rather smash up your chairs
And your lamp
And your glasses must be destroyed.
He does so.
The hurricane will not pay you for them
But I will.

Here.
Take this.

Begbick's answer was then addressed to him only and to be sung on top of a repeat of 'We need no raging hurricane' etc. by the other three men. The script also provides a different ending to the scene after Jim's four lines starting 'You are free, I say, if you dare' (p. 201), cutting straight from 'If it's prohibited' to his repeat of 'As you make your bed' six lines later. There is then no chorus, and Jenny says:

> Be quiet, boys
> If they hear us we'll be lynched.

JIM: No, we're going to stop being quiet from now on.
He smashes the boards announcing prohibitions.

> *Lights dim down. Projection at the back: Mahagonny on the point of destruction, illuminated with blood-red rays. From the darkness we hear the chorus of Mahagonnyites, interrupted by the subversive songs of Jimmy and his friends: let each one do just what he likes, etc. The 'As you make your bed' song becomes increasingly dominant, and is eventually taken up by the entire chorus. The singing stops, the projection disappears, till all that can be seen in the background is a geographical sketch with an arrow slowly approaching Mahagonny, showing the hurricane's path.*

The piano score has the scene as now, except that it puts Jim's solo 'Dreams have all one ending' (p. 198) in the last scene but one, just before his execution. This was also followed by Auden/Kallman. The present placing of the song seems to have been decided without Weill's agreement.

This song comes from a poem of about 1920 which had been included in the *Devotions* under the title 'Against Deception' but was earlier called 'Lucifer's Evening Song'. Jim's other solo which succeeds this in our text ('If you see a thing', p. 199) forms part of the 'Reader for Those Who Live in Cities' cycle of 1926–27, and was published as such in 1960 under the title 'Blasphemy'.

Scene 12 [11 in script]

This opens the second Act of the opera (see script and piano score). In the script the stage directions begin as now, but the first place mentioned is not the seemingly fictitious Atsena but Miami. The Auden–Kallman version groups the three loudspeaker announcements thus:

> LOUDSPEAKER:
> The hurricane is now approaching Atsena at a speed of one hundred and twenty miles an hour. In Pensacola, eleven thousand are reported dead or missing.
> The hurricane has reached Atsena. Atsena totally destroyed.
> The hurricane is making straight for Mahagonny. It is now only three minutes away.

Then as our text, except that the word 'Loudspeaker' is omitted.

Scene 13 [12 in script]

The script puts the opening chorus as part of the preceding scene, but introduces it by the same projected titles as now. It is however not sung by the chorus proper but by the four friends, in front of the half-curtain. The piano score has it as now, but with the wording bowdlerised to read 'Zweitens kommt die Liebe dran', instead of 'Zweitens kommt der Liebesakt'. Auden/Kallman follow the former reading. The two musicians of Brecht's stage direction are there to play zither and bandoneon, a type of accordion, in the accompaniment to Jake's solo.

At the end of the scene the script makes the friends appear without Jake to sing the 'One means to eat' etc. refrain. From now on however the order of the lines rotates. Thus it is now love first, followed by ring, drink and 'Fourth means to eat all you are able'; then at the end of the next scene it is ring, drink, eating and love; then at the end of the boxing scene, when only Jim and Bill are left to sing it, drink, eating, love and ring, in that order; then finally when Jim is arrested at the end of the next scene it is back to normal, with the whole chorus singing 'Now you can eat all you are able' and so on.

Scene 14 [13 in script]

The script shows that this was originally to be considerably tighter and more realistic. Its opening stage direction is:

> *The word* LOVE *in huge letters on a background with, in front of it, right, the Mandlay* [sic] *Brothel with a queue of men lining up. The three friends join the queue. Erotic pictures are immediately shown on a canvas screen. Meanwhile Begbick's voice is heard off.*

Begbick's and the men's opening lines are as now, but the stage directions differ: the men '*murmur after her*' and instead of the room getting dark '*The men are getting impatient*' before their 'Get to it soon!' etc. From there on the rest of the scene is different. First Trinity Moses

> *steps out in front of the brothel.*
> We thank all you gents for the patience you've been showing.
> I'm told that another three gents can shortly go in.
> Experience will tell you: to savour love at its best
> Every client needs a moment to rest.

> *Moses ushers out three gentlemen and lets three in. The others go on waiting. The three who have been ushered out rejoin the queue. Further pictures are shown, and Begbick's voice is again heard.*

BEGBICK:
> Let the tips of your fingers
> Stroke the tips of her breasts
> And wait for the quivering of her flesh.

THE MEN *murmur after her*:

[the same words, then] '*the men become impatient*' once more and repeat their 'Mandelay' chorus. Moses '*reemerges from the brothel*' and again sings his four lines. Then

> *Moses ushers out the three gentlemen just admitted and lets in Jim, Bill and Joe, who have jostled their way to the front. The remainder are once again shown pictures.*

BEGBICK'S VOICE:
> Introducto pene frontem in fronte ponens requiescat.

THE MEN *in frantic impatience*:
> Mandalay won't glow forever below such a moon.
> Hurry, the juicy moon is green and slowly setting.
> *The three friends are ushered out and step in front of the half-curtain,*
> *which closes.*

They close the scene by singing the next round of the refrain.

This version of the scene, which omits the Crane Duet (p. 206), was originally set by Weill as shown in the revised 1969 edition of the piano score which David Drew has edited for Universal-Edition. In the script however there is also an alternative version marked 'for the libretto'. Here, and in the piano score followed by A/K, the opening stage direction has the Men 'leaning their backs against' the platform and 'sitting on a long bench'. The scene follows much as we have it, with the lights going up and down in the room until Jim and Jenny are discovered there and go into the Crane Duet. In the piano score of 1929 not only is the duet fully composed but everything before it (from the opening of the half-curtain at the start of the scene) is marked as an optional cut. Within this all Moses's lines, the script's stage directions showing the admission of three men at a time, and Begbick's remark in Latin have anyway been omitted, leaving purely orchestral passages where Moses had been meant to sing. Thereafter the refrain 'Get to it soon' lost its last three lines in the printed versions (though we retain A/K's rendering of them). Two other lines following Jenny's 'For nowhere' (p. 207) and translated by A/K

> So all true lovers are,
> True lovers are, true lovers are

were likewise cut.

The Duet is thought by Drew to derive from one of Brecht's love sonnets, in which case it could hardly be earlier than 1925; but no such poem is known. It was published as a poem in his *A Hundred Poems* (1951) under the title 'The Lovers'. Weill's setting dates from October 1929.

For the 1931 Berlin production the first part of the scene, in its bowdlerised version, was restored and the duet cut instead. At some later point Weill decided that the duet would go best in the last Act, but he never prescribed a place for it and there is no evidence that he discussed the problem with Brecht. The revised piano score of 1969 suggests putting it in scene 19 in lieu of the spoken dialogue from Jim's 'Why, you're wearing a white dress' (p. 228) to Jenny's 'Kiss me, Jimmy' (p. 229).

Scene *15* [14 in script]

Apart from the rotation of lines in the final refrain, and the effects of the musical setting, this scene has scarcely changed since the first script.

Scene *16* [15 in script]

In the script the stage direction omits all mention of playing billiards. Where our text has 'MEN' it has 'JIM AND THE MEN'; the piano score and A/K however have a quartet of JIM, BILL, FATTY and MOSES. Their song 'Mahagonny sure was swell' is Mahagonny Song no. 2, which the script gives them to sing as printed in the *Devotions*, but without verse 2 and its refrain. In the piano score and our text verse 2 and refrain follow verse 1, while the refrain of verse 3 ('Stay-at-homes do very well') concludes the scene. For the Leipzig production however there was a cut from the first 'But at least they saw the moon' (p. 213) as far as Begbick's 'Time to settle the bill, gentlemen' (p. 214), and this was accepted by the composer from then on.

Script and piano score (followed by Auden–Kallman) have Jim, '*dead-drunk*', bawling the song 'Pour cognac down the toilet and flush it' (p. 215) which uses verses 1, 3 and 2 (in that order) of the poem 'Tahiti' which Brecht wrote about 1921. In the Men's chorus that follows ('Death now is nigh!') and continues under the spoken exchange between Jenny, Jim and Bill, Auden and Kallman have written new text rather than repeat phrases as in Weill's setting; the whole chorus then reads:

Death now is nigh!
Now black as pitch the sky
The white-caps high.

The dark draws in
And heaven is heaven with menace
Black, black as sin!
Black, black as sin
Black, black as sin
The menace of darkness draws in!

'Stormy the night', of which one quatrain follows, was first
cited in *In the Jungle of Cities* (see *Collected Plays 1*, p. 451) and
comes from the nineteenth-century ballad 'Das Seemannslos'
('The Sailor's Lot'), which Brecht evidently knew from his childhood. In the contemporary English version by Arthur J. Lamb it
is known as 'Asleep on the Deep', and the corresponding quatrain
there reads

Stormy the night and the waves roll high
Bravely the ship doth ride.
Hark! while the light-house bell's solemn cry
Rings over the sullen tide.

Auden presumably did not know it, or it might well have been in
his anthology *The Poet's Tongue*. It was set to music by H. W. Petrie
in 1895.

In the script Jenny's solo 'Let me tell you' (p. 218) is headed
'Jenny's Song'. Besides some minor verbal differences it has a
third verse, which was apparently never set, but goes:

I can't go with you in future, Jimmy
Yes, Jimmy, it's sad for me.
You'll still be my favourite all right, but
You're a waste of my time, you see.
I must use the little time that's left me
Jimmy
Or I'll lose my grip on it.
You're only young once, and that's
Not enough.
I tell you, Jimmy
I am shit.

Oh, Jimmy, you know what my mother told me . . .

– and so on as we have it. Thereafter the scene ends almost immediately, thus:

BEGBICK:
   Again I say:
   Pay!
JIM *says nothing.*
BEGBICK:
   Then let the police take him away!

– followed by Moses's lines (p. 219) and then the refrain, this time by all the men, starting 'Now you can eat all you are able'. This was cut by Weill (see the 1969 revised piano score).

A version of Jenny's song, starting 'When I put on my wedding dress' is included in a fragmentary *Threepenny Opera* scene set in Polly's room. It has a melody in Brecht's notation.

Scene *17* [16 in script]

The script has Jim sitting shackled in a little cage, past which the chorus of the previous scene pass as they leave the stage. His solo is headed 'Jimmy's Aria'. In the piano score (followed by Auden/Kallman) he *'lies in the forest, one foot chained to a tree'*. For the Kassel production of 12 March 1930 the aria was shifted to the next scene, its place being taken by 'Dreams have all one ending' (now in our scene 11) from the penultimate scene. Weill found this made a more effective ending to the second Act, but for the Berlin production he reduced it to one verse only and reset it for chorus (or male chorus) leaving it in full in the penultimate scene.

Scene *18* [17 in script]

According to script and piano score this starts the third Act. The former specifies a projected title saying 'Like the rest of the world's law courts, that of Mahagonny sentences people if they are poor'. The first defendant then is Joe, who is charged in Moses's words

With premeditated murder of 5 men
Done to test a newly purchased revolver.

Accused, you have destroyed
5 human lives in full bloom.

Then 'Never yet' etc., as now. Jim's offence, however, is announced thus by Moses (p. 222):

Second, the case of Jim Mahoney
Indicted on account of
Three bottles of whisky and a bar-rail
He failed to pay for.

– 'bar-rail' being A/K's substitute for Brecht's word 'curtain-rod'.
In A/K (following the piano score) the courtroom is not specifically located in a tent, and the first defendant's name is given
(amended by them from Brecht's Tobby Higgins to Toby throughout).

After Bill's plea 'Of all those hanging around' etc. (p. 225) the
script has the Men saying nothing, merely applauding and hissing.
Moses, not Fatty, calls for 'Your verdict, august tribunal' (p. 226);
while Begbick gives Jim four years in prison (rather than the four
years' probation of the final text) for the seduction of an unnamed
girl. Auden/Kallman (following the piano score) omit Begbick's
sentence starting 'In view of' (p. 226) and add a stage direction at
this point saying *On the backcloth is projected the "Wanted"
poster that was seen at the opening of Act One*.

[Scene 19 in piano score only]

This was not in the script and was cut in the Leipzig production.
It consisted of the Benares Song, which Elisabeth Hauptmann
wrote in English in 1926, and which in Auden/Kallman's version
goes thus. The original text is given in brackets where altered by
them:

19

At this time a good many people in Mahagonny who wanted something different and
better began dreaming of the city of Benares.
But meanwhile Benares was visited by an
earthquake.

Jenny, Begbick, Fatty, Bill, Moses and Toby enter in front of the screen
[i.e. the half-curtain], *seat themselves on high bar-stools and drink*
ice-water: the Men read newspapers.

BEGBICK:
  There is no whiskey in this town   ['whisky' throughout]
JENNY:
  No bar that doesn't get us down.
                                [There is no bar to sit us down.]
FATTY, BILL AND MOSES:
  Oh!
BEGBICK *sentimentally*:
  Where is the telephone?
FATTY, BILL AND MOSES:
  Oh!
JENNY *urgently*:
  Is there no telephone?   [Is here no telephone?]
MOSES:
  O God, so help me, no.   [Oh Sir, God damn me, no.]
FATTY, TOBY AND BILL:
  Oh!
JENNY AND BEGBICK:
  Let's go, let's go   [Let's go to Benares]
  To Benares where the sun is shining.
                                [Where the sun is shining.]
  Let's go, let's go to Benares,   [Let's go to Benares]
  To Benares, Johnny, let us go.   [Johnny, let us go.]

BEGBICK:
    There is no money in this land,
JENNY:
    No boy that's glad to shake your hand.
                            [There is no boy to shake with hands.]
etc., to:
BILL AND MOSES:
    To Benares where the sun is shining.
BEGBICK·
    There is no prize here we can win,
                            [There is not much fun on this star.]
JENNY:
    No door that lets us out or in.
                            [There is no door that is ajar.]
FATTY, BILL AND MOSES:
    Oh!
BEGBICK *sentimentally*:
    Where is the telephone?
FATTY, BILL AND MOSES:
    Oh!
JENNY *urgently*:
    Is there no telephone?
MOSES:
    No, no, goddamit, no!   [As before, to end of refrain.]
FATTY, TOBY AND BILL:
    Oh!
    *They find out from the papers about the earthquake in Benares. They
    jump to their feet in horror.*
ALL SIX:
    Worst of all,   [Worst of all, Benares]
    Benares is now reported perished in an earthquake!
                [Is said to have been perished by an earthquake.]
    O my dear Benares,   [Oh my good Benares!]
    Now where shall we go?   [Oh where shall we go?]

Scene 19 [18 in the script, 20 in the piano score and A/K]

The script has the opening stage direction as now, except that
instead of an electric chair being made ready *'On the right stands a*

makeshift gallows'. The white dress (p. 228) was black. Jim's speech leaving Jenny to Bill (p. 229) had an extra line: 'For *he* can live without fun'. Moses called 'Ready!' before they turned *'towards the place of execution'* (p. 229), and then asked after the 'One means to eat' refrain:

Have you a last request?

JIM:
Yes.
I would like once again
To hear the girls sing
The song of the moon
Of Alabama.

The girls sing the Alabama Song as Jim mounts the gallows.

MOSES:
Have you anything else to say?

JIM:
Yes.
I would like
You all not to let my horrible death
Put you off living the way that suits you, carefree.
For I too
Am not sorry
That I did
What I wanted.
Listen to my advice.
He climbs on a bucket, and as they fasten the noose round his neck he sings

– all four verses of 'Dreams have all one ending' (as in our scene 11), after which Moses says 'Ready!' again, and there is a black-out. Then the half-curtain closes, and Jenny, Fatty, Moses and two unnamed Men come out and sing Mahagonny Song no. 3 (God in Mahagonny). It is arranged as in our text, except for the omission of verse 2 (Mary Weeman etc.), and in the script it concludes the scene.

In the piano score there is no repeat of the Alabama Song; so Jim's speech 'Yes. / I would like /' etc., now printed as prose,

follows directly after Moses's 'Have you a last request?'. Auden/
Kallman here substitute the following speech, based very loosely
on the *Versuche* text:

> JIM: Yes. At last I realize what a fool I've been. I came to this
> city believing there was no happiness which money could not
> procure. That belief has been my downfall. For now I am
> about to die without ever having found the happiness I
> looked for. The joy I bought was no joy; the freedom I was
> sold was no freedom. I ate and remained unsatisfied; I drank
> and became all the thirstier. I'm damned and so, probably, are
> most of you. Give me a glass of water.
> *Jim stands in front of the electric chair. During the following, he is
> being prepared for execution.*

– the following being his singing of 'Dreams have all one ending'.
After it the piano score (which A/K again abandon here) ends
quickly with:

> *Jim sits on the electric chair. They put the helmet over his head.*
> MOSES:
> Ready!
> *Black-out.*

'God in Mahagonny' then becomes the beginning of the following
scene, where it is sung before the half-curtain by Jenny, Fatty,
Bill, Moses and a fourth man.

Jim's final speech of remorse (p. 232), which Auden and Kallman
put in the place of the earlier 'Yes. / I would like /' etc., derives
from a letter from Weill to his publisher dated 25 March 1930 (i.e.
just after the Leipzig and Kassel performances) saying that some
such speech was needed 'for the understanding of the whole
thing'; it was wrong for Jim to remain unrepentant.

When or why Brecht decided to shift 'Dreams have all one
ending' back to scene 11 is unknown, though clearly it was before
Versuche 2 (1930) went to press. For the Kassel performance Weill
had moved it forward, but only to precede our scene 17 (q.v.),
while for the Berlin production he decided it was needed in its
original position.

The opening inscription is rather freely translated by A/K, who
omit the final phrase cited on p. xxxii.

Scene 20 [19 in script, 21 in piano score, 22 in A/K]

In the script this is preceded by a projected inscription saying

NEXT DAY THE WHOLE OF MAHAGONNY WAS ON FIRE. THE BURIAL
OF J. MAHONEY THE LUMBERJACK BECAME A TURNING-POINT IN
THE CITY'S HISTORY. DO NOT BE RESENTFUL BUT OBSERVE THIS
VAST DEMONSTRATION, WHICH IS BEING STAGED IN THE PUBLIC
INTEREST.

Then the half-curtain opens, showing the projection of Mahagonny in flames and the people of the city gathering upstage with
'*placards, signs and banners*'. The only words here are those of the
chorus 'Why, though, did we need a Mahagonny?' as at the end of
our scene 1, which is taken from the finale of the Songspiel. They
are followed by a stage direction saying:

*After the song the crowd starts moving in small groups, each carrying
its placards etc. and marching in a big semicircle from back left down
past the footlights to back right. The placards say roughly:*
  1. For the natural order of things
  2. For the natural disorder of things
  3. For the corruptibility of our courts
  4. For the incorruptibility of our courts
  5. For freedom for the rich
  6. For freedom for everybody
  7. For the unjust division of temporal goods
  8. For the just division of spiritual goods
  9. For the underhandedness of the human race
  10. (*A giant placard*) Against the human race
*In the middle of the procession comes a group carrying Jim's coffin. The
play ends with huge songs as the demonstrators continue their constant
marching.*

Curtain.

End of the opera.

In the piano score the '*stage darkens*' after the conclusion of 'God
in Mahagonny' (which, it will be remembered, opens the final

scene there), and is followed by a projection. This introduces a separate scene 22 in Auden/Kallman's version, which otherwise follows the piano score and goes thus:

22

In these days, because of the unheard-of rise in prices, gigantic riots broke out in Mahagonny, preluding the end of Suckerville. The rioters carried the body of Jimmy Gallagher in procession

The screen opens. On the backcloth one sees Mahagonny in flames. Begbick, Fatty and Moses stand downstage. After they sing, groups of Demonstrators enter in continual succession until the close.

BEGBICK, FATTY AND MOSES:
   Why, though, did we need a Mahagonny?
   Because this world is a foul one
   With neither charity
   Nor peace nor concord,
   Because there's nothing
   To build any trust upon.
GROUP OF MEN *enter bearing Jim's hat and cane on velvet cushions*:
   We need no raging hurricane,
   We need no bolt from the blue:
   There's no havoc which they might have done
   That we cannot better do.
A SECOND GROUP *enter with Jim's ring, revolver and cheque-book*:
   As you make your bed so you lie on it,
   The bed can be old or brand-new:
   So if someone must kick, that is my part,
   And another get kicked, that part's for you.
   As you make your bed so you lie on it
   And you buy the sheets for it too:

30 If someone must kick, that is my part,
And another get kicked, that's for you.

BEGBICK, FATTY AND MOSES:
Why, though, did we need a Mahagonny?
Because this world is a foul one
With neither charity
Nor peace nor concord,
Because there's nothing
To build any trust upon.

JENNY AND SOME GIRLS *enter carrying Jim's shirt*:
Oh, moon of Alabama
We now must say good-bye
We've lost our good old mama
And must have dollars, oh, you know why.
Oh, moon of Alabama
We now must say good-bye
We've lost our good old mama
And must have dollars, oh, you know why.
Bill enters at the head of another Group of Men.

BILL:
You can bring vinegar – to him
You can wipe his forehead – for him
You can find surgical forceps
You can pull the tongue from his gullet
Can't do anything to help a dead man.

BILL'S GROUP:
Can't do anything to help a dead man.
Various placards are displayed. They run more or less:
For the natural order of things
For the natural disorder of things
For the freedom of the rich
For the freedom of all
For the unjust division of temporal goods
For the just division of spiritual goods
For pure love
For brute stupidity
Can't do anything to help a dead man.
Moses enters at the head of a new group.
You can talk good sense – to him

You can bawl oaths – at him
You can just leave him lying
You can take care – of him
Can't give orders, can't lay down any law to a dead man.

MOSES'S AND BILL'S GROUPS:
Can't do anything to help a dead man
No one can do nothing for a dead man.

Begbick enters with a third group that is carrying Jim's body.

BEGBICK:
You can put coins in his hand – for him
You can dig a hole – by him
You can stuff that hole – with him
You can heap a shovelful – on him
Can't do anything to help a dead man.

BILL, MOSES AND THREE GROUPS OF MEN:
Can't do anything to help a dead man
Can't do anything to help a dead man.

Fatty enters with a fourth group. They carry an enormous placard: For the re-establishment of the golden age.

FATTY:
You can talk about the glory of his heyday
You can also forget his days completely
You can change his old shirt for a clean one
Can't do anything to help a dead man.

ALL:
No one can do nothing for a dead man
Can't help him or you or me or no one.

Curtain

This 'Poem on a Dead Man' also formed part of Weill's *Berliner Requiem*, written in the winter of 1928–29. In the version which Brecht had written some four and a half years earlier its fourth verse went

You can talk about the glory of his heyday
You can also forget his days completely
You can lead a better life, lead a worse one
Can't do anything to help a dead man.

– without the opera's final line.